practical evaluation

practical
evaluation

Michael Quinn Patton

SAGE PUBLICATIONS
The International Professional Publishers
Newbury Park   London   New Delhi

For information address:

SAGE Publications, Inc.
2455 Teller Road
Newbury Park, California 91320

SAGE Publications Ltd.
6 Bonhill Street
London EC2A 4PU
United Kingdom

SAGE Publications India Pvt. Ltd.
M-32 Market
Greater Kailash I
New Delhi 110 048 India

Printed in the United States of America

Library of Congress Cataloging in Publication Data

Patton, Michael Quinn.
   Practical evaluation.

   Bibliography: p.
   1. Evaluation research (Social action programs)
I. Title.
H62.P322   1982   001'.4'33   82-16786
ISBN 0-8039-1904-2
ISBN 0-8039-1905-4 (pbk.)

EIGHTH PRINTING, 1991

Contents

To J. Quinn Patton

He engrained in his son, from an early age,
the importance of grounding book learnin'
in practical experience, and did his best
to pass on his own finely honed
common sense.

To my first and most important teacher of
things practical. Thanks, Dad.

Preface

In 1915 Funk and Wagnalls published a set of ten self-improvement books in what they called their "Mental Efficiency Series":

Poise: How to Attain It

Character: How to Strengthen It

Timidity: How to Overcome It

Influence: How to Exert It

Common Sense: How to Exercise It

Opportunities: How to Make the Most of Them

Perseverance: How to Develop It

Speech: How to Use It Effectively

Personality: How to Build It

Practicality: How to Acquire It

Add to this list a methods book and one has a complete training course for evaluators. It is, I think, quite impressive that nearly 70 years ago Funk and Wagnalls anticipated so completely the personal development needs of evaluators. In this book I have humbly undertaken to supply the missing evaluation methods volume.

These eleven books (including the present addition to the series) can be read in any order. Thus, to benefit from this book, it is not necessary to have already attained poise, strengthened your character, overcome timidity, developed perseverance, acquired practicality, and built your personality; nor is it already necessary to know how to exert influence, exercise common sense, make the most of opportunities, and use speech effectively. You can put off the development of these traits another couple of days while you master the evaluation fundamentals in this book, keeping in mind as you read that, if you want to become a really effective evaluator, eventually you'll have to achieve poise, character, confidence, influence, common sense, opportunity maximization skills, perseverance, effective speech, personality (actually several of these are desirable), and practicality.

Lest some of you find this list slightly awesome, it is worth reflecting for a moment on some of the things that aren't included and won't be needed to attain "mental efficiency"—things like intelligence, good looks, a great body, and training in classical ballet. The mental efficiency list is really quite carefully constructed to include only attainable essentials. No self-respecting evaluator, for example, would ever go out in public without poise, character, and personality. But there is scant evidence from recent political history to suggest that intelligence is in any way a requisite for public service.

From the title of this book, *Practical Evaluation,* it is obvious that this volume follows naturally from R. Nicolle's mental efficiency contribution, *Practicality: How to Acquire It.* Nicolle explains that practicality consists of "judgment, attention, perception, patience, perseverance, will, decision, finesse, and foresight." It is acquired through the exercise of "good nature, insight, perspicacity, and by experience." Metaphorically, practicality is "an inexhaustible wonder-working currency accepted everywhere." (Leave home without your American Express card, but don't leave home without your practicality.)

> TRUE PRACTICALITY is the application of TACT to daily life. . . . Self-control and self-reliance are the beginnings of practical wisdom. True strength springs from the mastery of self which, with self-reliance, equips and sustains us for the trials that life compels us to endure. . . . He who would become a power in Practicality must first become master of himself.
>
> To become a Master of Practicality—study life, observe closely, keep an eye on detail, avoid waste, practise small economies, recognize the worth of trifles and utilize them to their full value—and reap the benefits it affords. To the practical man the great highroad of human welfare is reached by the by-path of steadfastness. Life promises much but gives little; work forces it to pay when Experience guides and Purpose is undeterred. But Life's current coin is struck in the mint of Experience with the one indelible word PRACTICALITY, and therefore, it is that inexhaustible wonder-working currency accepted everywhere [Nicolle, 1915: iii-v].

I must admit that I was initially hesitant to make explicit the connection between this present volume and the mental efficiency series, the latter being the nonfiction equivalent of the Horatio Alger classics (Horatio never having had the chance to rise from rags to riches as an evaluator because the evaluation profession didn't exist at that time). After all, with the sophisticated audiences in today's modern world, it's rather embarrassing to be associated with old-fashioned and simplistic virtues like character building, personality enhancement, self-reliance, steadfastness, perspicacity, and common sense. Psychology and the human potential movement have come a long way since 1915. Now we have more modern and sophisticated standards to guide us, traits like "pulling your own strings," "doing your own thing," "winning through intimidation," "being your own person," and the sensual man/woman. So much progress in such a short period of time!

The relevance of all this discussion of virtue to the field of evaluation is that evaluators have become concerned about what constitutes virtue in evaluation. In recent years, professional evaluation groups have been working to identify standards of excellence and guidelines for professional conduct. The concern has been less with the qualities to be exhibited by evaluators than with the qualities of "good" evaluations—but the two are likely to be related, "good" evaluations being done by "good" evaluators. The search for standards of excellence is made particularly difficult by our collective loss of faith in *absolute* truth: Having eaten the apple from the tree of knowledge, we have become aware that all things are *relative*. But perhaps that's why there was no profession of evaluation in 1915. Everyone knew, then, what was right and wrong, good and bad, so there was no need for evaluators to help figure out relative degrees of merit and worth.

This book takes seriously the notion that evaluation practice should be guided by attention to criteria of excellence. This book builds on the work of the Evaluation Standards Committee (1981), the Evaluation Network, the Evaluation Research Society, and the various disciplinary associations in their efforts to improve the quality of applied social science. In so doing, this book explores the practical implications of conducting evaluations that exhibit four fundamental criteria of excellence: utility, feasibility, propriety, and accuracy.

These criteria represent the considerable advancement that has been made in recent years in identifying meaningful professional standards of excellence for evaluation. The task now is to apply those ideals in a serious way to concrete evaluation practice. The challenge is to implement the ideals of evaluation—to make them practical. In that regard, Nicolle's definition of practicality is still relevant:

> Practicality is the sense of seeing things as they are and doing things as they ought to be done. Specifically, it is defined as the science of being skilled in the application of means to attain particular ends [1915: iii].

The ends to be attained in this case are evaluations that are useful, feasible, moral, and accurate. *Practical Evaluation* discusses the means to attain those ends.

* * *

In attaining the end of writing this book, I've had substantial assistance. In conducting evaluation workshops, doing consulting, teaching seminars, working with evaluation clients, and discussing evaluation experiences with colleagues, I've had the opportunity to learn about things practical from lots of different people. I am grateful to the hundreds of people with whom I have worked over the last several years who have contributed to my thinking and, therefore, to this book.

Kay Adams and Nick Smith reviewed first drafts of most chapters and provided important suggestions for revisions. Yvonna Lincoln did a thorough review of the entire manuscript, which led to a number of final deletions, additions, and revisions—all of which were made easier by her good humor and encouragement. These three highly professional evaluators helped me tremendously by sharing their keen sense of recent trends and important issues in evaluation.

Kathy Manger was a godsend. She wrote to me shortly after publication of *Creative Evaluation* (1981) with a list of typographical errors in that book. The errors had resulted from lost proofs and communication problems between Trinidad, where I was working at the University of the West Indies, and California during the final stages of publication. Sage Publications has since used Kathy's list to revise subsequent printings of *Creative Evaluation*. On this book, Kathy did editing and proofreading *prior* to publication. She has an eye for detail that, in my experience, is unmatched. In reading her margin comments, virtually on every page of the manuscript, I learned more about my writing patterns and ways of improving my writing than I'd learned since high school. She is a superb editor.

Finally, I want to thank the people who helped with typing, editing, layout and design: Janet Donicht, Chris Haupert, and Robert Maier in the United States; Colleen Johnson and Claudia Henderson in Trinidad. Colleen and Claudia were particularly helpful in their willingness to work during unpredictable hours as determined by the availability of Trinidad's unpredictable electrical supply.

—*Michael Quinn Patton*
St. Augustine,
Trinidad

PART I

The Practical Mandate

THE SNOW WHITE EVALUATION

From *Halcolm's Evaluation
Fairy Tales*

Not so long ago, in a faraway kingdom, there lived a Queen whose beauty was matched only by her vanity. She desired to be assured that her beauty was unparalleled. While she was constantly so assured by her loyal court subjects, she came to doubt their objectivity. She knew they feared the powerful spells she could cast when provoked by something that displeased her, like any suggestion that she might not be the fairest of the fair.

Having been well schooled in the lore of queens, she became obsessed with the desire to obtain one of those magic talking mirrors mentioned in ancient tales. Lacking a magic mirror, the Queen stood daily in front of her quite ordinary mirror, repeating hopefully:

*Mirror, mirror, on the wall,
Who's the fairest of them all?*

Her distress at receiving no answer grew until one day she shouted in rage:

*Stupid mirror on the wall,
Why in hell don't you answer my call?*

The silence that followed her outburst was short lived, for that quite ordinary mirror suddenly became quite extraordinary:

*Sorry, my Queen, for making you vexed,
But the question you pose is terribly complex.*

The Queen was startled, but not speechless. In a twinkling she had overcome all sense of shock, and with queenly cool she proceeded to pose yet again her burning question.

Mirror, mirror, tell me at last,
Am I the fairest that this world hast?

The Queen waited expectantly, but, alas, the magical mirror seemed once again to have lost its magic, or at least its voice. The Queen was becoming convinced that her obsession had made her hallucinatory, when finally the mirror spoke again, this time at length.

Sorry, my Queen, for this slight delay,
But I've been in search of a practical way
To approach your question with scientific care.
There are a few things of which to beware.

We'd have to observe all the women there are,
The ones who are near, the ones who are far.
Even in fairy tales the task is so great,
Our evaluation data would be soon out of date.
Two years in the making such research would be,
And then the results would be old, you see.
A judgment of beauty that's two years old
Might be thought invalid by those who behold
A Queen whose appearance must change over years,
Giving statisticians "maturation effects" fears.

Now instead of the universe, we might try a sample,
But the size of the sample would have to be ample,
And then there's the chance we'd miss the most pretty.
That design would leave doubts: a validity pity.

Nor is measurement easy in a case like this.
Judgments of beauty are like judgments of bliss.
What's beauty to the gander, may not be to the goose;
The definitions, I fear, are terribly loose.

Then, too, it would seem, the question needs rephrasing,
So that, scientifically speaking, it isn't so fazing.
It would help if you asked this magic mirror on the wall,
"Within how many standard deviations does my beauty fall?"

And then there's the problem of political propriety,
When studying beauty in today's society.
Some might raise objections reflecting the schism
Over whether beauty judgments constitute sexism.

So, you see, my Queen, the study can hardly be done.
But wait! Here's data from a new computer run:
Observations just made at your stepdaughter's college,
By fraternity boys with very personal knowledge,
Definitely show that of all girls in the dorm,
Your stepdaughter's beauty is way above the norm.
Compared to all girls we have on our file,
Your stepdaughter's in the 99th percentile.

The Queen was incensed that her stepdaughter, of whom she had long been jealous, should receive such a judgment, while she, the Queen, received no satisfaction from the mirror. Her rage renewed, she took hold of her jeweled hairbrush to smash the mirror. As she cocked her arm to deliver the fatal blow to scientific reflection, the mirror hastened to add a mitigating observation.

Your stepdaughter's ranking is from a small study,
The results of which are clearly quite muddy.
There's really no call for you to feel exasperation
Over some psych student's first draft dissertation.

As for yourself, Queen, I've searched far and wide,
There just is no research that yet can provide
The statistics on beauty, your question to answer.
The norms just aren't there. All the funds went to cancer.

But this current state of knowledge does permit one conclusion,
(For the absence of numbers need not result in confusion).
Based on available data as to who is now most fair,
Your Queenship's royal visage is simply beyond compare.

The Queen relented from her threatened blow. The mirror's snow white job proved to be quite effective. She immediately arranged for her stepdaughter to have a fatal accident while serving as a control subject in research on dwarfism. But seven dwarfs in the experiment rescued her from the machinations of the evil experimenter, an unscrupulous researcher living off fat royal grants, who, nevertheless, managed to always avoid having his proposals reviewed by the local committee for the protection of human subjects.

The Queen became a lavish supporter of social science research on new ways of studying beauty. While awaiting a methodological breakthrough, she purchased her own personal Apple IX computer and commissioned a software package that allowed her to use dummy data to run simulations showing that she was, indeed, the fairest of the fair.

When the breakthrough failed to come, and she had grown tired of alternately running simulated beauty studies and playing Kingdom Invaders on the castle computer, she cast a spell on the whole kingdom. This spell put everyone to sleep for a hundred years in the hope that, by then, somewhere in the rest of the world an evaluator would have developed new methods to deal with the practical problems so arduously detailed by the magical mirror. The spell is timed to wear off any year now. This book was written to warn evaluators worldwide that the Queen's rage will be turned on them if she awakens to find no progress in practical evaluation.

CHAPTER 1   *The Source of the Mandate to Be Practical*

> *A rational man acting in the real world may be defined as one who decides where he will strike the balance between what he desires and what can be done.*
>
> Walter Lippmann

There is a certain obvious quality to the assertion that evaluations—and evaluators—ought to be practical. One nods one's head in commonsensical agreement and says, "Okay, so now tell me something I don't know."

What may not be known is that one of the most common complaints about program evaluation proposals is that they're *not* practical. Program staff complain that the evaluation data collection takes too much time and involves too much money; the evaluation isn't feasible administratively. Program directors complain that evaluation designs can't reasonably be implemented because they require too many artificial controls on program operations—controls like not changing the program in any significant way during the evaluation (six months, one year, two years); controls like random selection and/or random assignment of clients to the program, or to treatment groups. Funders complain that evaluation proposals aren't feasible because they cost too much ("Do you really need that much data? Can't the sample size be smaller? Can't you shorten the interview?"). Program clients complain that evaluations aren't sensible because they're asked questions they don't understand and can't answer ("What do you mean, 'How effective is the program in accomplishing its goals on a ten-point scale?' What goals? What ten-point scale?"). Public officials and legislators complain that evaluation proposals are often impractical because they would require actions that are politically unacceptable ("No way are you using my county as a control group. If the people in the neighboring county get that program then you better be damn sure the people in my county get that program.").

This book attempts to address these kinds of complaints. After defining evaluation in the next section, this chapter will examine how the professional standards by which evaluations are judged have changed to focus greater attention on practical problems and feasible solutions to evaluation questions. The general concern about practicality will then be broken down into several concrete issues.

THE PROFESSIONAL PRACTICE OF EVALUATION

In the last fifteen years evaluation has emerged as a distinctive field of professional social science practice. The practice of evaluation involves the systematic collection of information about the activities, characteristics, and outcomes of programs, personnel, and products for use by specific people to reduce uncertainties, improve effectiveness, and make decisions with regard to what those programs, personnel, or products are doing and affecting. This definition of evaluation emphasizes (1) the systematic collection of information about (2) a broad range of topics (3) for use by specific people (4) for a variety of purposes. In this book I use "evaluation" as a general term that encompasses program evaluation, personnel evaluation, policy evaluation, product evaluation, and other evaluative processes. However, the central focus is on evaluation studies and consulting processes that aim to improve program effectiveness. Personnel evaluation aims to improve the effectiveness of programs by improving the effectiveness of people who have responsibilities for program activities and outcomes. Programs are the means of implementing plans and policies, and products are developed, tested, and evaluated to enhance the effectiveness of people and programs. While these linkages and distinctions are certainly more complex than I've drawn them here, the point of this simplification is to explain my generic use of the terms "evaluation research" and "program evaluation." The differences among various types of evaluation (program, personnel, product, and so on) need not concern us at this point since I am interested in a broad overview of evaluative research as a field of study and practice.

There are now standards for evaluation practice. These standards of conduct are guidelines specifying how evaluators should engage in the practice of their profession. The standards are meant to be broadly applicable to all evaluation situations indicating what constitutes excellence and minimally acceptable professional behavior. *These standards explicitly include the mandate to be practical.* Before actually examining the standards in some detail, it will be helpful to understand how, and from where, they emerged.

Before about 1975, the premises and standards of evaluation research could scarcely be differentiated from those of basic researchers in the traditional social and behavioral science disciplines. Technical quality and accuracy were the primary concerns of researchers. Methods decisions dominated the evaluation decision making process. Methodological rigor was the primary, often the only, criterion by which evaluations were judged. Methodological rigor meant experimental designs, quantitative data, and detailed statistical analysis. Validity, reliability, measurability, and generalizability were the dimensions that received the greatest attention in evaluation research proposals (see Bernstein and Freeman, 1975). In judging the quality of an evaluation one simply followed the methodological rules, norms, and trends of one's discipline.

Today, evaluation practice is not quite so simple. The specialization of evaluation research has become sufficiently differentiated from other social science activities and perspectives to constitute the emergence of a new field of practice founded on and characterized by a radical shift in outlook—a scientific revolution, paradigmatically speaking (Kuhn, 1970). Evaluators found that methodological rigor did not guarantee that findings would be used. Utilization of evaluations became a major concern (Patton, 1978). Moral and political issues received increasing attention in the evaluation decision making process. Questions about methodological appropriateness, situational sensitivity, evaluator responsibility, and abuses of evaluation research emerged. Adequate answers to these questions could not be found within any single disciplinary tradition. Thus, evaluators took up the task of developing their own set of standards to guide professional practice.

STANDARDS OF EXCELLENCE IN EVALUATION AND THEIR IMPLICATIONS

The most comprehensive effort at developing standards was hammered out over five years by a 17-member committee appointed by 12 professional organizations, with input from hundreds of practicing evaluation professionals. The standards published by the Joint Committee on Standards for Educational Evaluation (1981) dramatically reflect the ways in which the practice of evaluation has developed and changed during the last decade. Just prior to publication, Dan Stufflebeam, chair of the committee, summarized the committee's work as follows:

> The standards that will be published essentially call for evaluations that have four features. These are *utility, feasibility, propriety* and *accuracy*. And I think it is interesting that the Joint Committee decided on that particular order. Their rationale is that an evaluation should not be done at all if there is no prospect for its being useful to some audience. Second, it should not be done if it is not feasible to conduct it in political terms, or practicality terms, or cost effectiveness terms. Third, they do not think it should be done if we cannot demonstrate that it will be conducted fairly and ethically. Finally, if we can demonstrate that an evaluation will have utility, will be feasible and will be proper in its conduct then they said we could turn to the difficult matters of the technical adequacy of the evaluation, and they have included an extensive set of standards in this area [Stufflebeam, 1980: 90; emphasis in the original].

The articulation of new priorities in this statement of evaluation standards represents a cohesive ideology for evaluation practitioners and professionals. These changes in beliefs have profound implications for the practice of evaluation. In comparison to the traditional paradigms and practices of basic social and behavioral science research, *implementation of a utility-focused, feasibility-conscious, propriety-oriented, and accuracy-based approach to evaluation research will require situational responsiveness, methodological flexibility, multiple evaluator roles, political sophistication, and, probably, substantial doses of creativity.* In *Creative Evaluation* (Patton, 1981) I explored at length the creative imperative in the practice of evaluation, if one takes the new standards seriously. That book suggested ways of dealing creatively with the challenge of the new evaluation standards, particularly their implicit demand that evaluators be *truly* situationally responsive.

Situational evaluation means that evaluators have to be prepared to deal with a lot of different people and situations. Situational responsiveness is the challenge to which creative, yet practical, evaluation thinking is the response. Situational responsiveness is a challenge because the evidence from behavioral science is that in most areas of decision making and judgment, when faced with complex choices and multiple possibilities, we fall back on a set of deeply embedded rules and standard operating procedures that predetermine what we do, thereby effectively short circuiting situational adaptability. This may help explain why so many evaluators who have genuinely embraced the ideology of situational evaluation find that the approaches in which they are trained and with which they are most comfortable *just happen* to be particularly appropriate in each new evaluation they confront—time after time after time. In *Creative Evaluation* I reviewed the research findings from studies of human heuristics that support this claim that most of the time evaluators, and the decision makers with whom they work, are running—and thinking—according to preprogrammed tapes. It turns out that most of the time, in order to make even trivial decisions, we rely on routine heuristics, rules of thumb, standard operating procedures, standard tricks of the trade, and scientific paradigms. Such reliance blocks creativity and limits the capacity to see, and make, practical adaptations.

A major difficulty posed by the human reliance on paradigms and heuristics for problem solving and decision making is not just their existence, but our general lack of awareness of their existence. Autonomic thinking systems and conditioned reflexes are barriers to situational responsiveness. It is difficult to be attuned and responsive to the uniqueness of practical constraints in new situations when our programmed heuristics and paradigms are controlling the analytical process, screening unfamiliar data, anchoring the new situation within the narrow parameters of our past experiences, and making available to us primarily those definitions and approaches we've used most often in the past. Yet there is also evidence that, while it is neither easy nor usual, it is possible to become aware of our paradigms and heuristics, and in that awareness take control of our decision processes, thereby releasing our creative potential and enhancing our ability to be truly situationally responsive and adaptive. *Creative Evaluation* was aimed at increasing heuristic awareness and enhancing the potential for creative evaluation by enlarging the evaluator's repertoire of approaches to evaluation consulting, teaching, communicating, and thinking. *Practical Evaluation* is aimed at further enlarging that creative repertoire—at increasing the number of "holes" into which evaluators can retreat for reflection when they run into trouble, this last metaphor being a reference to the counsel of Plautus in the second century B.C.:

> *Consider the little mouse, how sagacious an animal it is, which never entrusts its life to one hole only.*

BASIC PREMISES

The techniques, ideas, and approaches presented in later chapters of this book are the operational manifestation of a particular approach to evaluation. In making explicit these premises I am attempting to construct a general framework that goes beyond the grab-bag approach of technique mongering that leaves one with a limited bag of tricks, but no real foundation on which to build new approaches to deal with new situations and unanticipated problems. Robert S. Lynd (1939: 183) has dramatically commented on the ultimate emptiness of technical work that is not grounded in a set of standards and basic premises:

> Research without an actively selective point of view becomes the ditty bag of an idiot, filled with bits of pebbles, straws, feathers, and other random hoardings.

This book is built on the same premises that undergirded *Creative Evaluation.* The difference is that this book focuses specifically on the feasibility dimension in the new standards, conducting evaluations that are practical. In *Utilization-Focused Evaluation* (Patton, 1978) I focused specifically on the utility criterion. The themes of these previous books recur in this volume inasmuch as all of my writings are an articulation of a general framework for evaluation practice. The premises of that framework are that:

- concern for how specific decision makers will use evaluative information should be the driving force in an evaluation, i.e., evaluation processes should be user and utilization focused;
- effective evaluators must also be effective trainers because every evaluation presents opportunities to train decision makers in evaluation processes and the uses of information;

- situational responsiveness is imperative for effective and moral evaluation practice;
- realizing the potential for creative evaluation requires, first, awareness of routine response patterns and blinders that limit situational insight, then a willingness to consciously move beyond limitations to risk new ways of doing things;
- effective evaluators must be prepared to play multiple roles, to be, alternatively, scientists, program consultants, group facilitators, keen observers, statisticians, project administrators, diplomats, politicians, writers, entertainers, and teachers, to name only a few common roles; and
- individual evaluator style is part of what makes each evaluation situation unique, so that effective evaluators are conscious of, deliberate about, and take responsibility for what they bring to, and how they affect, the evaluation decision making process, evaluation findings, and utilization of those findings.

This book examines the implications of these premises with special attention to the problem of designing and implementing practical evaluations. In so doing, frequent reference will be made to ways in which *the mandate to be practical is contained in and part of the creative imperative in utilization-focused evaluation.* Fulfilling the mandate to be practical may sound like a rather mundane, simplistic, and uncreative process. Quite the contrary; my own experiences suggest that finding feasible solutions to enormously complex problems is the epitome of the evaluation challenge, requiring hard work, flexibility, and all the pains and insights of creative problem solving grounded in evaluation fundamentals.

It's relatively easy to generate a great deal of information with sophisticated evaluations made possible by fairly ample resources. It's also relatively easy to design an extremely simple evaluation with very limited resources, one that generates a certain minimum amount of acceptable information. What is more difficult is to generate a great deal of really useful information with extremely scarce resources. The latter challenge seems also to be the most typical.

It's relatively easy for a group of researchers to work alone in making evaluation methods and analysis decisions. It's also relatively easy to accept at face value the initial requests of a decision maker and to simply carry out a technical contract. What is difficult is for the evaluation researcher to work actively—reactively—adaptively with a group of decision makers in a consultative fashion to design and implement an evaluation that is responsive, useful, accurate, understandable, and practical.

What I'm reacting to here, and perhaps anticipating, is an inference drawn by a colleague upon hearing the title of this book, in contrast to my previous book, *Creative Evaluation.* "I suppose," he said, "that practical evaluations are what you do when you can't come up with a creative evaluation." Quite the contrary; given the ever-present constraints of limited time, resources, and knowledge, practical evaluations that are really useful may be the most creative of all. Like the acrobat who makes the most daring trick look easy, the simple elegance of practical solutions often disguises the creative work, disciplined talent, and grounding in fundamentals contained therein.

BEING GROUNDED IN FUNDAMENTALS

While the mandate to be practical is contained in and part of the creative imperative in utilization-focused evaluation and the new standards, *the prerequisite for situational responsiveness is a firm grounding in fundamentals.* The primary purpose of this book is to provide grounding in evaluation fundamentals within the framework of the basic premises presented in the previous section.

Most of the chapters in this book summarize the content of a one-day workshop I've conducted for evaluators, program staff, and/or program directors. None of these workshops required that participants have prior experience with or knowledge about evaluation. Each workshop was devoted to basics. This doesn't mean that the workshops were not relevant to experienced practitioners. Experienced participants regularly reported that it was very helpful to go through a refresher workshop on fundamentals. What I'm referring to as evaluation fundamentals are such activities as writing proposals, identifying, organizing, and working with an evaluation task force, goals clarification, design alternatives, questionnaire construction, interviewing, managing information systems, data analysis, making recommendations, and fostering utilization of findings. None of these topics is covered thoroughly and comprehensively. Rather, what I've done is present the basic material I use in responding to the short-term training requests I receive most frequently. Other chapters represent my answers to the practical questions I'm asked most often, many of these questions coming in correspondence generated by one of my previous books.

To explain what I mean by being grounded in practical fundamentals, it may be helpful to consider some analogies and metaphors. William J. Gephart is an accomplished watercolor artist and an accomplished evaluator. He has written a provocative and insightful article on watercolor painting as a metaphor for evaluation. One of the themes that emerges most powerfully in that article is the importance of mastering the primary tools and basic techniques of one's craft. He describes the importance of selecting the right kind of paper, knowing how to dilute pigments with varying amounts of water, selecting the right brush, and properly wetting the paper.

> Watercolor can be applied to a paper when the paper is wet or dry. Most beginners assume that this is a dichotomy, that paper is wet or dry. But this is another of the peculiar characteristics of this medium that makes all but the very persistent give up early: paper can be bone dry, slightly damp, wet, running wet, or any stage in between. The importance of this concept is that the pigment does different things with differing wetnesses of the surface.

These thoughts preface one of the rules that must be known thoroughly if a person wants to enjoy a modicum of success as a watercolor painter. If you want sharp demarcation between two colors, the paper must be dry. If you want gradual diffusion of one color into another, the paper needs to be wet. That is immutable; if you want sharp change from one color to another, the paper *cannot* be wet. You have to wait until the surface where that abrupt change is to be is completely dry [Gephart, 1981: 256–257].

Gephart is here describing some of the fundamentals of watercolor painting. One has to return to these fundamentals over and over again to be a successful artist. The same is true of evaluation, a point he makes in comparing the two.

In both cases, a person can proceed without much knowledge of the basic principles and characteristics. People evaluate. Many times they do it without a fund of knowledge about the systematic evaluation process. People can paint with watercolors without knowledge of the medium. Most people who try to paint with watercolors without first developing that fund of knowledge do not do a painting that is worth saving. (There are few, very few, who are blessed with dumb luck.) In contrast, most of us who evaluate without a fund of knowledge about evaluative procedures and techniques are unaware of the subjective inaccuracies in our evaluation. If we want to be systematic, comprehensive, and consistent in the quality of our evaluations, we must master the meaning of and skill in using a sizable body of knowledge about the evaluation process itself and about its application [Gephart, 1981: 257].

Firm grounding in fundamentals is also a major theme in sports. In every major sport—baseball, football, basketball, soccer, cricket, rugby—the playing season is preceded by a training camp devoted largely to conditioning and practice in fundamentals. The most experienced veterans are, without exception, required to participate fully in training camp every year. And before the big games—the World Series, the Super Bowl, the league play-offs—media interviews with coaches and players are replete with references to fundamentals:

Sportswriter: "Tell us, coach, how do you see things shaping up for the big game?"
Coach: "Well, when two great teams like this are playing each other it usually comes down to which one is best able to execute its game plan, which one makes fewer mistakes."
Sportswriter: "How are you preparing for the big game?"
Coach: "The way we prepare for every game, by practicing fundamentals. You've got to be able to execute the fundamentals. If we execute the way I know we can, and avoid mistakes and injuries, we'll win."

When teams, or individual players, are having difficulty, the universal prescription from old hands is a return to fundamentals: Witness golfing legend

Ben Hogan advising a young pro with a putting problem, "Did you ever consider hitting it close to the hole?" Or baseball great Yogi Berra's tip to a batter in a slump: "Swing at the strikes."

Even as I write this I'm engaged in a battle with my eight-year-old son over the value of learning and practicing fundamentals. He doesn't want to continue piano lessons because he prefers to "play by ear." He and his friends are convinced that knowledge of proper fingering, reading music, and practicing scales will interfere with their creativity.

Then there was the participant in a recent workshop (forced by his boss to attend prior to being given an evaluation assignment) who responded to my opening sermon on the value of fundamentals with the comment, only half joking, "If Ronald Reagan can run the economy without any knowledge of economics, surely we can run a simple evaluation without any knowledge of evaluation." To which I replied, "That's fine, as long as you're prepared to end up with an evaluation that's in the same shape as the U.S. economy." But I'll spare the reader any further comparisons between surprise-side economics and evaluation.

Before closing this section on fundamentals two additional points should be added. First, there are often fundamental disagreements about which fundamentals are fundamental. Whether the field is painting, music, sports, politics, social science, religion, or evaluation, fundamentalists don't always agree among themselves about the basics. I once participated in a meeting of sociologists organized by a book publisher to identify fundamental sociological premises and concepts for a new introductory text. The meeting was a disaster, each participant vying to name his or her pet interest or speciality as most basic to all other sociological knowledge. To wit, the practical fundamentals presented in this book do not represent a consensus in the field, either in terms of which subjects I've chosen to discuss, or what I say about them. My selection of subjects and approach to those subjects is based on my own experiences in conducting evaluations, the premises that constitute the framework within which these fundamentals are grounded, and information from workshop participants about what they needed and wanted to know.

The second point has to do with the audience I have in mind as I write. This book is aimed at the hundreds of evaluators, part time and full time, who do relatively small-scale projects. While many of the issues raised in the book are relevant to the conduct of large-scale, national evaluations, my primary concern is with evaluators operating at local and state levels under severe resource constraints and with little supportive research infrastructure. For example, in education, the evaluation of ESEA Title I or Title IV-C programs "probably make up 90 percent of all the educational program evaluations undertaken locally today" (Alkin et al., 1979: 35). With the major changes taking place in the funding and implementation of human service and social action programs as a result of Reagan administration cuts, I expect small-scale, local evaluations to play an even more important role than they have in the past. I also expect more to be demanded of such evaluations, and of evaluators, who are using increasingly scarce funds for the purpose of improving programs and decision making about programs. It is particularly important that such evaluations be grounded in practical fundamentals that take seriously the criteria of excellence contained in the new standards, criteria specifying that evaluations be utilization focused, feasible, propriety conscious, and accurate.

PRACTICAL EVALUATION: PROCESS AND CONTENT

The mandate to be practical applies to two different aspects of evaluation: the evaluation process and the content that results from that process:

- Evaluation *process*—the way an evaluation is conducted, e.g., who is involved in the evaluation, how much it costs, how the evaluation is introduced into the program, the timelines involved, how feedback is handled, and so on.

- Evaluation *content*—the findings of a particular evaluation, including the data collected, interpretations made, and recommendations offered.

The distinction between process and content is a common one. In education, for example, the *process* is how one is taught (e.g., lecture, field experience, laboratory), and the content refers to what is taught (e.g., reading, math, history). In counseling, the process describes how the therapist works with a client (directive, nondirective, intimidating, supportive), and the content refers to the problem being worked on (e.g., marriage difficulties, sexual performance, professional confidence). In evaluation, a similar distinction can be made. The process is how the evaluation is implemented, while the content refers to what findings emerge from the process.

The new evaluation standards deal with both process and content, but by different names. The standards related to the evaluation process are grouped together as *feasibility standards* and *propriety standards*. In brief, these standards mandate that an evaluation process should be feasible (or doable), and that the evaluator should behave with propriety, i.e., in a legal, moral, responsible, fair, and professional manner. The standards that apply to the content of evaluations are in the criteria related to utility and accuracy. Evaluations should be useful and findings should be accurate.

With regard to the specific issue of practical evaluation, the standards on feasibility provide guidance in implementing a practical process, while the standards on utility are concerned with whether an evaluation serves the practical information needs of a given audience. The next two sections examine in more detail the standards related to practical evaluation processes and content.

Feasibility Standards: Making the Process Practical

The feasibility standards are intended to ensure that an evaluation will be realistic, prudent, diplomatic, and frugal. They are (as set forth by the Joint Committee, 1981: 51):

Practical Procedures

The evaluation procedures should be practical, so that disruption is kept to a minimum, and that needed information can be obtained.

Political Viability

The evaluation should be planned and conducted with anticipation of the different positions of various interest groups, so that their cooperation may be obtained, and so that possible attempts by any of these groups to curtail evaluation operations or to bias or misapply the results can be averted or counteracted.

Cost Effectiveness

The evaluation should produce information of sufficient value to justify the resources expended.

A practical evaluation process is one that can reasonably be implemented within the constraints of a particular situation. The constraints that must be dealt with include inevitable limitations of time, resources, and knowledge, and attention to political boundaries that can impinge on all aspects of an evaluation. A practical evaluation process is *doable*. It is manageable, understandable, feasible, and applicable within a given context.

Utility Standards: Making the Content Practical

Practical knowledge can be used to do something. Fritz Machlup, one of the world's most eminent authorities on knowledge (he is currently preparing an eight-volume work on the subject) distinguishes several types of knowledge that are not practical. "Intellectual knowledge" satisfies one's curiosity about or contributes to one's understanding of the world, but isn't directly applicable to doing things in the world. "Small-talk knowledge" consists of the myriad trivial facts and frivolous information that we accumulate daily. "Spiritual knowledge" includes what we "know" about the meaning of life, but can't "prove" (Machlup, 1962: 21-22). The priority in evaluation is on producing practical knowledge, i.e., knowledge that can be used to do something. The utility criterion in the new evaluation standards is aimed at this mandate to produce practical knowledge.

Utility, the first category, contains standards for guiding evaluations so that they will be informative, timely, and influential. These standards require evaluators to acquaint themselves with their audiences, ascertain the audiences' information needs, plan evaluations to respond to these needs, and report the relevant information clearly and when it is needed. . . .

Overall, standards of Utility are concerned with whether an evaluation serves the practical information needs of a given audience [Joint Committee, 1981: 13].

The Practical Connection Between Process and Content

There is a close relationship between the feasibility of an evaluation process and the utility of an evaluation's findings (content). Practical evaluation processes are most likely to generate practical and useful evaluation findings. But the mere fact that an evaluation is doable doesn't mean that it will be useful. In this regard, practical evaluation processes approach being a necessary, but not sufficient, condition for generating useful information. Practical evaluation processes fall short of being absolutely necessary to generate useful information because sometimes it's extremely useful to find out what can't be done. And sometimes the only way to find that out is to try to do it.

An example of how useful information can result from an impractical process may help clarify the distinction between process and content. The board of an infant food and nutrition program in a rural county wanted pre-and-post attitude and behavior data from all of their clients. They wanted the program staff to collect the preservice data on the very first home visit. The instrument designed for this purpose took about twenty minutes to complete. The board members participated in designing the instrument to make sure it included attitude and behavior changes in which they were particularly interested. After two months of implementation the evaluation process had to be significantly changed because it had proved to be impractical. In over 40 percent of the cases the preservice instrument could not be completed (or at least was not completed) because something interfered with data collection: an incessantly crying baby, a sick baby (or mother) who needed immediate service, a husband coming home and demanding attention ("Sorry, I've got to get supper now"), the presence of someone who made the asking of sensitive and confidential questions inappropriate, and/or a felt need on the part of the staff person to devote the little time available on a first visit to establishing rapport and trust, not to gathering objective data. For these same reasons the quality of the data that were collected was often suspect. It was simply impractical to have program staff collect data from *all* clients on a first visit. The evaluation was redesigned so that a nonstaff person collected preservice data from a random sample of potential clients. However, what was learned from the impractical evaluation process proved enormously useful. Board members got some valuable insights into the kinds of situations staff were encountering in the field. The need for flexibility and responsiveness in the provision of services was so apparent that the standardized, rigid, and lockstep program established for home visits was completely changed to permit staff to deliver whatever was needed when it was needed. It also became clear that staff needed training in how to better manage visits—how to handle interfering husbands, how to solicit information from clients, how to access client needs, how to politely carry on a visit when other people were in the home, and so on. In short, the delivery program was completely revised and a new staff training program was established based on what was learned from an impractical evaluation process.

Thus while practical evaluation processes (the primary focus of this book) are more likely to lead to useful evaluation information than are impractical processes, this relationship is far from certain. Impractical processes can generate quite useful and important information; practical processes can end up yielding nothing; and of course, impractical processes can, and usually do, yield big goose eggs. (A goose egg example: the decision by the Justice Department's Anti-Trust Division that its suit against IBM was "without merit" and would be dropped—after 13 years, 2500 depositions, and 66 million pages of documents. Sometimes, it seems, we human types have a bit of difficulty admitting that something just won't work.)

On balance, the odds would seem to favor going with the logical probabilities and betting evaluation time and moneys on the combination of practical (feasible) processes that yield practical (useful) content. But how does one decide what is practical?

DECIDING WHAT IS PRACTICAL

Judgments about the relative practicality of a particular evaluation process or evaluation finding can only be made with reference to a particular situation involving specific people, a specific program, and specific constraints. I feel comfortable stating absolutely that there can be no absolute judgment about what is practical. What is entirely feasible in one situation is entirely impractical in another. That's why it's impossible to respond in any absolute way to many of the kinds of questions I regularly get at workshops. My answers must inevitably be conditional and suggestive (like the suggestions throughout this book), rather than absolute and dogmatic.

Question: Is it practical to try to involve as many as twenty people in an evaluation task force?

Answer: It depends on the people, your skill in working with groups, and what you're trying to do with them. I prefer to work with at least three and no more than ten if the process is to be fairly intensive and lengthy. On occasion, however, and for certain steps in the evaluation process, I've worked with as many as a hundred.

Question: Is it practical to use a twenty-page questionnaire?

Answer: It depends on who will be answering the questionnaire (their motivation, their reading ability, their interest), the content of the questionnaire, the format you're using, and how the data will be collected. Generally speaking, the quality of responses is higher for shorter questionnaires, but I've had occasion to use lengthy questionnaires with highly motivated professionals where it was quite feasible to collect a large amount of consistently high quality data.

Question: Is it practical to do two-hour interviews?

Answer: It depends on whom you're interviewing, your interviewing skills, and what you're asking. With highly knowledgeable key informants who were much interested in the program being evaluated I've done ten hours of interviewing over two days. Interviews with four-year-olds in a nursery school begin to deteriorate after ten minutes.

Question: Is it practical to use statistical techniques like multiple regression analysis in evaluations to be used by people who are only high school graduates.

Answer: It depends on how you present the data, how much they trust you, why you're using regression analysis, what other data you're presenting, and what your high-school-educated information users want to do with the findings. I found that parents in rural North Dakota could interpret standardized regression coefficients when a set of such coefficients was presented in rank order with a simple (non-jargon-laden) explanation of what the coefficients represented. Of course, I didn't begin by telling them that they probably wouldn't understand the data; I didn't tell them it was a sophisticated statistical technique that is only taught in graduate schools; I didn't explain the derivation of the coefficients; and I didn't present the results as a set of simultaneous equations to impress the group with the output of stepwise forward and backward computer programs.

These examples illustrate why evaluators must be well schooled in fundamentals and able to adapt those fundamentals to specific situations. The new standards of evaluation—utility, feasibility, propriety, and accuracy—require situational responsiveness rather than implementation of standardized procedures. *Knowledge of and skill in applying evaluation fundamentals under these conditions requires ongoing analysis of specific situations and calculated judgments about what is possible, what is probable, and what just might be useful, given what is known and the people involved.*

PRACTICALITY IN PERSPECTIVE

This introductory chapter has been about the source of the mandate to be practical. The chapter opened with examples of complaints from evaluation clients and users about the practical problems evaluations often pose for them. This led to a broad definition of evaluation and an examination of how the professional practice of evaluation has changed over the last fifteen years, with particular emphasis on the emergence of new standards of excellence to guide evaluation practice. Methodological rigor is no longer sufficient. Evaluations are now to be judged according to their utility, feasibility, propriety, and accuracy. These standards explicitly include the mandate to be practical. Implementing the new standards will require situational responsiveness, methodological flexibility, multiple evaluator roles, political sophistication, and, probably, substantial doses of creativity. Yet situational adaptability and flexibility do not mean applying various techniques and tricks of the trade in a haphazard or will-o'-the-wisp fashion. Six basic premises were offered (to supplement the ten commandments) as a general framework for evaluation practice. These premises are the basis for a utilization-focused approach to evaluation. The mandate to be practical is part of the creative imperative in utilization-focused evaluation. Far from being mundane, mechanical, and simple, the conceptualization and implementation of practical evaluations challenge the evaluator to produce useful information under typically severe constraints of limited time, limited resources, limited knowledge, and seemingly unlimited politics. The elegance of practical solutions often disguises the creative work, skilled diplomacy, and disciplined talent contained therein.

The beginning point for practical evaluation practice is a firm grounding in evaluation fundamentals. The primary purpose of this book is to provide such a grounding within the framework of utilization-focused evaluation premises. The book will offer suggestions about both practical evaluation *processes* (feasible, doable evaluations) and the generation of practical *content* (useful evaluation findings), with the emphasis on the former as a usually necessary, but not sufficient, condition for the latter. The perspective offered here favors going with the odds and betting on the combination of practical processes that yield practical findings. At the same time, it is necessary to temper such a perspective with the recognition that (1) impractical processes can sometimes produce valuable information, (2) feasibility of implementation is no guarantee that practical findings will be generated (thus the need for a multiple focus on utility, feasibility, propriety, and accuracy), and (3) judgments about the relative practicality of a particular evaluation process or evaluation finding can only be made with reference to a particular situation involving specific people, a specific program, and specific constraints. Knowledge of and skill in applying and adapting evaluation fundamentals under these conditions require ongoing analysis of specific situations and calculated judgments about what is possible, what is probable, and what just might be useful, given what is known and the people involved.

To close this chapter and broaden the perspective on things practical (life, love, and prices on the stock market, not necessarily in that order), I offer a story from Halcolm concerning the Laws of Practicality.

LAWS OF PRACTICALITY

Over time the realities about sages and seers seem almost inevitably to become enmeshed with a certain mystique that suggests powers not ordinarily experienced by those of us who put on our robes one leg at a time. Such was the case with Halcolm. Myths about this sage teacher grew among his students and followers, myths that went beyond their usual commitment to steadfast empiricism, a commitment engendered by the sage himself. Rumors about these myths would eventually reach Halcolm and he used them, as was his wont, to further instruct and enlighten. But he always chose the time and place for such instruction, ever conscious, as was also his wont, of capturing the teachable moment.

Now it happened that the myth arose that Halcolm could walk on water. No one was quite sure from whence the myth originated, but there it was in all its avataric splendor. At the time Halcolm had been reflecting on how principles from physics related to enthalpy (total heat content of a system) and entropy (measure of the unavailability of a system's thermal energy for conversion into mechanical work) could be applied to evaluation. His students were having some difficulty grasping the practical relevance of such reflections. Being thus distracted, one particularly precocious youth decided to bring the discussion back down to earth—or actually water. As Halcolm paused amidst enthalpic and entropic reflections, the youth interjected, "Speaking of which, good sir, is it true that you can walk on water, and if so, might we not have a demonstration thereof?"

The others in attendance were aghast at the youth's impertinence and rudeness, but Halcolm smiled knowingly, and replied, "All in good time."

Thus it seemed to the gathering that the rumor was finally confirmed by the sage himself. The most dedicated students and devout followers immediately took it upon themselves to emulate their master, thereby to please him. Throughout the summer and fall of that year the wily observer would have seen students sneaking off to some isolated body of water, often under cover of darkness, to practice the art of walking on water. None succeeded, and winter gave rise to a new despair among those who failed that they would never succeed in emulating their master, and brought words doubting Halcolm's power to the lips of those who lacked the dedication or faith even to try. And still Halcolm had offered no actual demonstration that would finally confirm the myth and justify the ridicule experienced by those who proclaimed the sage's powers to doubting Thomases and Marys.

One cold winter's day the matter finally came to a head. Again distracted by the seeming irrelevance and impracticality of Halcolm's latest reflections on enthalpy and entropy, the same youth confronted the master with his doubts. "It would seem, good sir, that you would engage us in discussion on useless theories while we are to be permitted no resolution of a grave matter that casts doubt on your esteemed credibility: I refer of course, to the question of your walking on water."

Halcolm's momentary silence created an atmosphere of unprecedented tension in the usually peaceful atmosphere of the retreat. Never had the sage been so rudely confronted. Halcolm's reply, however, changed the air of tension to one of unprecedented expectancy. "How insightful of you to raise that question at this precise moment, for I was just about to provide a demonstration on just that issue."

With that, Halcolm headed for the nearby pond, walked across on the covering of ice, and returned to a much agitated gathering.

"But that proves nothing," scoffed the youth. "The pond is frozen."

"And of what does the ice consist?" asked Halcolm.

"Why, water, of course, but still . . ."

"Careful observation of the pond's total heat content through the practical application of enthalpy, and prudent measurement of corresponding entropy—that is, my system's availability of thermal energy for conversion into work, in this case walking across the pond—made it possible for me to adhere to your very proper request, that I demonstrate walking on water."

"Of such things are the laws of practicality derived:

What works, works, where and when it works. What is possible, is possible, except where and when it isn't. You can do what you can do. You can understand what you can understand.

"Be ever watchful that your own narrow definitions and limited vision of what is possible do not limit possibilities for others. And let not the doubts of others limit your own possibilities. What can be done, can be done."

And on that day a new myth was born, that Halcolm could instantaneously turn ice to water by the mere speaking of words.

PART II   *Issues and Options*

- *Early to bed and early to rise makes one a creature of habit.*

- *An outstanding success in conducting an evaluation has killed many an evaluator's flexibility.*

- *If you want an evaluation done based on the approach most in vogue at the moment, hire a second-year grad student.*

- *Were there not so many true believers, evaluation would not be so necessary.*

- *Leaders in modern society never do evil so completely and cheerfully as when they do it on the basis of "scientific" knowledge.*

- *On a clear day you can see even farther from a high place.*

- *Sometimes I can't remember which way it's supposed to be. Is life a metaphor for evaluation, or evaluation a metaphor for life?*

- *The hard part of speaking correctly is mastering all the exceptions to the rules. So, too, the mastering of practical evaluation.*

From Poor Halcolm's Almanac

CHAPTER 2   *Evaluation Issues in Practical Perspective*

> *I have yet to see any problem, however complicated,*
> *which, when you look at it the right way, did not*
> *become still more complicated.*
>
> Poul Anderson

I've had students in seminars and participants in workshops who were literally immobilized by their struggles with some of the complicated problems and issues in evaluation. Is what I'm doing *really* evaluation? Which model of evaluation is best? How do I handle my own values and biases? What's the appropriate role for me to play as an evaluator? How can I make sure that I select the best methods? How can I be sure the evaluation is used? How can I make sure the evaluation isn't misused?

Trying to deal with these kinds of questions can involve real anguish, for each question in its own way is part of the larger process of developing a personal and professional philosophy of practice and action, one that permits movement and occasional closure, however temporary, in a world filled to overflowing with uncertainty, ambiguities, competing perspectives, and conflicting roles. Some people seem able to function quite effectively without becoming entangled in a web of haunting questions and complex issues that threaten to undermine the ability to get on with the job. They do just that, they get on with the job, they stay busy, and let others think about the larger (or smaller) meaning of things. Perhaps they have learned to heed Oscar Wilde's warning that thinking, like cigarettes, can be downright hazardous to your health: "Thinking is the most unhealthy thing in the world, and people die of it just as they die of any other disease."

This chapter is directed at those who come to evaluation affected with the thinking disease, who find themselves afloat on what Charles Dickens described as the troubled seas of thought:

> Black are the brooding clouds and troubled the deep waters, when the Sea of Thought first heaving from a calm, gives up its Dead.

This chapter cannot provide definitive answers to tempestuous and troubling evaluation questions. I doubt that definitive answers exist. But the questions are real, the issues are serious, and for those who struggle with them, the modest purpose of this chapter is to join the struggle, to join in a search for practical perspectives that can harness philosophical thought and theoretical analysis to the service of day-to-day evaluation practice. The conceptual issues discussed in this chapter may, at first glance, seem like abstract concerns best reserved for those with an inclination toward mountaintop reflection or ivory tower navel gazing, but, far from being esoteric, I hope to show that these issues have important implications for evaluation work in the trenches.

WHAT IS EVALUATION?

Definitions are one of those things that are hard to live with and hard to live without. It is obviously necessary to define terms in order to communicate. It is also obvious that many ideas do not fit neatly into a narrow definitional pigeonhole. As the cartoon character Andy Capp once said, in an unusual fit of sober reflection, "The one thing I've learned above all others, mate, is that the only thing that fits in a pigeonhole well is a pigeon." The practice of evaluation does not fit comfortably into a single pigeonhole, a fact that leads to no small amount of confusion about just what evaluation is. Before suggesting a practical way of handling this definitional ambiguity and confusion, it will be helpful to explore a bit more the nature of the problem and how the problem affects day-to-day evaluation practice.

William J. Gephart's comprehensive effort at defining evaluation illustrates both the problem and one kind of solution. He begins with the assumption that no short, succinct definition will suffice. Single-sentence definitions usually contain a host of terms that need further definition to clarify the original definition. He proceeds to define evaluation in six different ways, different in that each represents a distinct approach to the definitional task. (1) His *classificatory* definition describes evaluation as a "problem-solving strategy" employed for establishing the relative or absolute worth of various choices. (2) His *comparative* definition likens evaluation to research, development, management, and other problem-solving strategies, pointing out similarities and differences with each. (3) His *operational* definition tells how an evaluation is conducted, from identification of the impending decision through data collection and analysis to information use. (4) His *componential* definition explains that evaluations include a problem, a situation involving choices, data on the worth of options, a context, a set of values, a time frame, and so on. (5) His *ostensive* definition gives examples of evaluations (e.g., deciding which dishwasher to buy). (6) His *synonym* definition includes such words as judgment and appraisal. He concludes that these six definitions, "taken together," form his concept of evaluation. He also notes that one of the difficulties encountered in sharing definitions is that, while there are at least six different ways of approaching the definitional task, "most of us fall into the habit of using only one of them" (Gephart, 1981: 250-255).

Gephart's effort shows that there are various ways of approaching the definitional task. Further complicating the problem is the fact that within any one or more approaches, the content of the definition can vary. A review of a few of the variations in the content of definitions of evaluation reveals important differences in what various evaluators emphasize in their work.

(1) The classic approach of Ralph Tyler (1949) was to emphasize goals and objectives, so for him (and for the thousands of educators and researchers schooled in his approach), evaluation is the process of determining the extent to which the goals and objectives of a program are being attained.

(2) Many social scientists emphasize scientific rigor in their evaluation models, and that emphasis is reflected in their definition of the field. For these social scientists, evaluation involves primarily the application of rigorous social science methods to the study of programs (e.g., Bernstein and Freeman, 1975; Rossi, Freeman, and Wright, 1979). These evaluators emphasize the importance of experimental designs and quantitative measures.

(3) Another common emphasis in evaluation definitions is on the *comparative* nature of the process: Evaluation is the process of comparing the relative costs and benefits of two or more programs. The principles and definitions that undergird evaluation models emphasizing the comparative nature of the process have emerged in part as a reaction to the narrowness of evaluation of a single program's goals (see Alkin and Ellett, forthcoming).

(4) Still another emphasis comes from evaluators who highlight the *valuation* part of evaluation. From this perspective evaluation is the process of judging a program's value. This final judgment, this ultimate determination of relative merit or worth, is the sine qua non of evaluation (see Worthen and Sanders, 1973: 22-26, 120-122; Guba and Lincoln, 1981: 35-36).

(5) Some evaluation practitioners focus on the generation of data for decision making and problem solving. This perspective goes beyond merely making judgments or assigning relative values. The emphasis is on choices, decisions, and problem resolution. It is quite possible to decide that one thing is better than another (e.g., program X versus program Y) without taking any concrete decision with regard to program X or program Y. When evaluation is defined as a problem-solving process (Gephart, 1981) or as a process that provides information for decision making (Thompson, 1975), some action process that goes beyond simply valuation is given primary emphasis in the definition.

(6) Finally, for the purposes of this discussion, there are those definitions that emphasize providing information to specific people. The broad definition I offered in the last chapter takes this approach.

The practice of evaluation involves the systematic collection of information about the activities, characteristics, and outcomes of programs, personnel, and products for use by specific people to reduce uncertainties, improve effectiveness, and make decisions with regard to what those programs, personnel or products are doing and affecting. This definition of evaluation emphasizes (1) the systematic collection of information about (2) a broad range of topics (3) for use by specific people (4) for a variety of purposes.

This definition is the basis for a "user-focused" approach to evaluation (Patton, 1981: 83-89), which places emphasis on the information needs and interests of specific people, such needs including, *but not limited to,* information relevant to making decisions, judgments, comparisons, or goal attainment assessments.

Now, then, we have six different types of evaluation definitions (classificatory, comparative, operational, componential, ostensive, and synonym) and six different emphases in various definitions (goals, methods, comparisons, value, decisions, and information users). Nor do these cover all the possibilities. For example, in the study of how evaluations are used that formed the basis for *Utilization-Focused Evaluation* (Patton, 1978), I began with a collection of 170 "evaluations" on file in the Office of Health Evaluation. Fewer than half of those 170 federal health studies could be considered "evaluations" using any of the definitions just reviewed. This was because a large number of those studies were nonempirical think pieces (i.e., they included no systematic data collection or analysis) or they focused on general social indicators without reference to any specific program. Still, they were filed (defined!) as evaluations.

Let me now make several observations based on the preceding discussion. First, no single-sentence definition will suffice to fully capture the practice of evaluation. Second, different definitions serve different purposes, one especially important function being to serve as a foundation for a particular model of or perspective on evaluation. Third, there are fundamental disagreements within the field about the essence and boundaries of evaluation. Fourth, people who propound a particular definition often have some ego investment in their special perspective, whether because they developed it, were trained according to it, or are part of a group in which that definition is esteemed; any critique of a definition, in such cases, can be taken as a personal attack, a good many people finding it difficult to separate criticism of their ideas from criticism of them personally. Fifth, people on the outside looking in (and many within the field) are often confused and uncertain about just what evaluation is. Sixth, there is no reason to expect an early end to either the disagreements or the confusion. As Samuel Butler explained the problem in "Higgledy—Piggledy,"

Definitions are a kind of scratching and generally leave a sore place more sore than it was before.

The practical question is what to do about the sore. My approach is to begin by finding out the perceptions and definitions of the people with whom I'm working. Before laying my definition on them (which they might reject, misunderstand, or yawn at), I want to know *their* preconceptions, *their* confusions, *their* expectations, and *their* beliefs about evaluation. I can then build on that knowledge to develop shared understandings about evaluation options and potential processes. It is often appropriate simply to ask people to associate freely in a stream-of-consciousness fashion with the word evaluation: "When you hear the word evaluation, what comes to mind?" This can be a verbal exercise or a written one, done in small groups or a large gathering. Notice, however, that I did not ask participants to *define* evaluation. The question, "Who can give me a definition of evaluation?" clearly implies a single right answer, and the wary participant will suspect that the evaluation trainer or facilitator will eventually pronounce the correct definition, but only after making several participants look stupid. *Definitions* are thus perceived as academic playthings to be used in a game at which the researcher is sure to win, so why participate? I'm not looking for skill at constructing or repeating definitions. I'm looking for perceptions and synonyms that will provide clues to tacit definitions held by people in the situation in which I'm working.

On some occasions, when I'm working with a group of people who seem relaxed with each other and who seem to be open to a more innovative style, I may use the metaphor exercise described in *Creative Evaluation* (Patton, 1981: 97-101). This exercise encourages participants to share their perceptions about and experiences with evaluation by constructing similes and metaphors using concrete objects I've brought to the session. Evaluation is like a camera . . . , a lock . . . , a rubber ball . . . , a paper bag . . . , a toy . . . , a chalkboard . . . , and so forth. They choose the object that they'll use to construct their metaphor, an object that permits the sharing of some notion about evaluation.

In a one-to-one consultation I begin with the same approach. I want to find out what a funder, decision maker, legislator, or client means by evaluation *before* I put myself in a pigeonhole to which they may have difficulty relating. The reason is quite practical. Working together effectively requires trust, shared understanding, and mutually held purposes. If a person defines evaluation as "measuring goal attainment," I'm not going to reply, "Well, that's a pretty narrow definition of evaluation. My own view is . . ." I'm going to respond with a respectful assurance that I understand what he or she means. Then, in the course of the interaction, I'll find out how much commitment the person has to a single, narrow definition (or a broad, diffuse one), where broadening (or narrowing) might occur, what other meanings exist in addition to the goal attainment one, and the origins of whatever definitions are offered (a book, a college course, a funding mandate, a friend or colleague, and so on). This is all very useful information that will help me communicate with a person or group throughout an evaluation process.

In my view, it is neither respectful nor practical to adopt a single definition of evaluation and then work at making the situations one encounters fit that definition. I therefore dissent from the usual advice to evaluation trainees that one of their tasks is to decide to which definition of evaluation they will pledge allegiance, or to come up with their own definition that will let the world know what they have to offer. Certainly there are times when one has to be prepared to state a preference, but such preferences can be presented in a framework that recognizes and respects other approaches. My own advice to trainees is to recognize the variations in and complexity of the field of evaluation. Situational responsiveness is built on such a recognition. The mandate to be situationally responsive includes having sufficient flexibility to understand which definition(s) of evaluation are appropriate and meaningful in a particular context, with a specific group of people. The next section elaborates this perspective with regard to formal evaluation models.

MODELS OF EVALUATION

In recent years there has been a great proliferation of evaluation models that prescribe what evaluators ought to do and explain how to conduct a particular type of evaluation. The discussion of definitions pointed to some of the varying approaches advocated by different evaluators. There is as yet no definitive classification scheme describing various models. Among recent efforts, House (1978) has developed one of the more comprehensive taxonomies of major evaluation models. He identifies eight separate models distinguishable by the audiences they address, what they assume consensus on, the outcomes they examine, the typical questions they ask, and the methods they employ. House's eight categories are: (1) *systems analysis,* which quantitatively measures program inputs and outcomes to look at effectiveness and efficiency; (2) the *behavioral objectives approach,* which focuses entirely on clear, specific, and measurable goals; (3) *goal-free evaluation,* which examines the extent to which actual client needs are being met by the program; (4) the *art criticism approach,* which makes the evaluator's own expertise-derived standards of excellence a criterion against which programs are judged; (5) the *accreditation model,* in which a team of external accreditors determine the extent to which a program meets professional standards for a given type of program; (6) the *adversary approach,* in which two teams do battle over the summative question of whether a program should be continued; (7) the *transaction approach,* which concentrates on program processes; and (8) *decision-making models,* in which the evaluation is structured by the decisions to be made.

Several major models are associated with prominent individuals. Goal-free evaluation is inextricably linked with Michael Scriven (1972). The connoisseurship model (art criticism in House's taxonomy) is associated with Elliot Eisner (1975). Discrepancy evaluation (comparing implementation and outcome ideals to actual achievements on an ongoing basis) is based on the work of Malcolm Provus (1971). Responsive evaluation is associated with Robert Stake:

> To emphasize evaluation *issues* that are important for each particular program, I recommend the *responsive evaluation* approach. . . . An educational evaluation is *responsive evaluation* if it orients more directly to program activities than to program intents; responds to audience requirements for information; and if the different value perspectives present are referred to in reporting the success and failure of the program [1975: 14; italics in original].

Responsive evaluation is "late-Stake." The countenance model is "early-Stake" (1967), the two "countenances" being description and judgment, each of which involved completion of a corresponding data matrix. Another well-known approach is the Stufflebeam et al. (1971) CIPP model, which called for data on context (C), input (I), process (P), and product (P) to conduct a comprehensive assessment in an educational setting. Illuminative evaluation (Parlett and Hamilton, 1976) is a methods-focused approach that emphasizes the value of qualitative methods, inductive analysis, and naturalistic inquiry.

So much for name dropping and model dropping. Clearly there are a number of distinct approaches to the practice of evaluation, at least forty by the count of one student who submitted a seminar paper to me on the subject. A practical approach to dealing with the population explosion in models can be derived from a few observations about models.

First, the names of models are seldom self-explanatory. Goal-free evaluation is not really goal *free* (Alkin, 1972), a point acknowledged by Scriven when he suggested in an interview that a better name might have been "needs-based" evaluation (Scriven and Patton, 1976). Responsive evaluation involves much more than simply being responsive to stakeholders. The responsive evaluation model, like most of the other models, includes a large number of steps and procedures that, taken together, provide coherence to the approach. Responsive evaluation includes the following parts:

(1) identification of issues and concerns based on direct, face-to-face contact with people in and around the program;
(2) use of program documents to further identify important issues;
(3) direct, personal observations of program activities *before* formally designing the evaluation to increase the evaluator's understanding of what is important in the program, and what can/should be evaluated;
(4) designing the evaluation based on issues that emerged in the preceding three steps, with the design to include continuing direct qualitative observations in the naturalistic program setting;
(5) reporting information in direct, personal contact through themes and portrayals that are easily understandable and rich with description; and
(6) matching information reports and reporting formats to specific audiences with different reports and different formats for different audiences.

The model's name, responsive evaluation, implies some, but not all, of these components. Reliance on the label attached to a model to reveal its specifications can be quite misleading and, at best, will provide only a partial understanding of the model's totality.

The second observation about models concerns their integrity and coherence. Model builders usually place considerable importance on the entire process. Picking and choosing only some parts of a model to apply may be perfectly appropriate and justifiable, but such selectivity means that one may no longer be able to claim to be following the model. If one faithfully includes the first three components of responsive evaluation, as outlined above, and then proceeds to design an evaluation that relies entirely on standardized tests, the results of which are reported only in written documents, one has *not* done a responsive evaluation, at least not by Stake's criteria.

Third, models are subject to Halcolm's Law of Discipleship. To wit:

> *Models, as understood and applied by the modeler, will be understood and applied otherwise by others.*

Discrepancies between original modeler intentions and the applications of followers arise not only through deliberate selectivity and deviations. Discrepancies and bastardizations occur because models are seldom, if ever, sufficiently detailed and comprehensive to cover all possibilities and all contingencies. Moreover, models are based on assumptions, principles, and philosophical traditions that are usually only partially made explicit in the writings of the modeler. In elaborating Stake's responsive evaluation model, Guba and Lincoln (1981: 33) found that they had to make "certain additions." Those who follow Guba and Lincoln will undoubtedly find it necessary to make still further additions. In the same vein, this book represents yet another elaboration of some of my own approaches. I regularly receive in the mail (and out of the blue) evaluation reports that are meant to be utilization-focused exemplars, but which leave me at a loss as to why, or how, they could be so designated. In subsequent chapters I shall respond to some of the more glaring misinterpretations of my approach. The point here is that relative faithfulness to a model is a matter of judgment that, like beauty, rests in the eye—and mind—of the beholder. Social scientists who study the diffusion of innovations, and evaluators who do implementation studies on adoption/adaptation of national programs at the local level, wrestle endlessly with the problem of determining how much variation there can be from the original before the supposed replication fails to qualify as a true adoption. When is an application so different in degree and kind that it no longer constitutes implementation of the model? There is no absolute answer. What we can be sure of is that there will be departures, modifications, adaptations, and distortions of original specifications, many of them entirely justified and deliberate, and many of them not.

The fourth observation may be the most important of all: model developers and model proponents seldom, if ever, implement their own models in any pure or ideal form. The major figures in the field demonstrate great adaptability and flexibility in their own work regardless of what particular formal model may be associated with their name. In 1977 a symposium session at the American Educational Research Association brought several major evaluation model builders (Worthen, Stake, Stufflebeam, Popham) together to consider the question, "Are synthesis and resolution of evaluation models possible?" The basic theme running through the comments of these evaluators was that their work is seldom guided by and directly built on specific evaluation models. Rather, each evaluation setting is approached as a problem to be solved—and the resulting design reflects their thinking about the problem as opposed to an attempt to follow carefully a prescriptive model. In effect, these experienced evaluators were describing how the *practice of evaluation research* requires more flexibility than is likely to be provided by any single model.

The same observation can be made about evaluation practice at the local level. Alkin et al. (1979) did intensive case studies of local educational evaluations in California. In their concluding chapter they observed that individual evaluator style, legal mandates, and local circumstances, not adherence to any formal evaluation models, were the kinds of things that determined how an evaluation was conducted.

> Use of a formal evaluation model—such as CIPP, CSE, adversary, goal-free, or the like—is one facet of the evaluator's approach that virtually demands attention, because so much of the literature on evaluation has been devoted to the presentation and elaboration of formal models. Nevertheless, none of the evaluators we studied attempted to apply any of the commonly known evaluation models to their evaluation task. This is not to say that they were unacquainted with these models—to the contrary, most were quite familiar with the major models—but they did not attempt to systematically apply any of them nor did they draw upon the concepts or procedures of the formal models in any specially significant, or readily apparent, way [Alkin et al., 1979: 240].

The fifth and final observation relates to the question posed at the 1977 AERA symposium: "Are synthesis and resolution of evaluation models possible?" Whether or not synthesis and resolution are *possible,* the evidence is that synthesis and resolution are not likely. Other fields of social science have shown no tendency toward such resolution, and evaluation models continue to proliferate as evaluators expand their horizons, take on new problems, and experience the inadequacies of existing models.

Nor is there any reason to believe that synthesis and resolution are desirable. Evaluation is a field made up of individuals with vastly different styles and backgrounds. Evaluations are conducted in all kinds of settings to provide information on all kinds of issues and problems, for all kinds of decision makers, stakeholders, information users, and audiences. Under these conditions, evaluation pluralism and the existence of multiple models strike me as altogether healthy. We have all the coherence and synthesis we need in Ernest House's (1980: 46-47) observation that the basic theme of all evaluation approaches is a commitment to liberal democracy and empiricism.

> The current models all derive from the philosophy of liberalism, with deviations from the mainstream being responsible for differences in approaches.
>
> Liberalism itself grew out of an attempt to rationalize and justify a market society which was organized on the principle of freedom of choice. Choice remains a key idea in the evaluation approaches although whose choice, what choices, and the grounds upon which choices are made are matters of difference. Consumer's choice is the ultimate ideal but who the consumer is is differently conceived.
>
> A second key idea of liberalism is that of an individualist psychology.
>
> Another key idea is the empiricist orientation.
>
> The evaluation approaches also assume a market place of ideas in which consumers will "buy" the best ideas. They assume that competition of ideas strengthens the truth. Ultimately, they assume that knowledge will make people happy or better in some way. So the evaluation approaches partake of the ideas of a competitive, individualist, market society. But the most fundamental idea is freedom of choice, for without choice, of what use is evaluation?

These five observations—that model names are not self-explanatory, that any given model has its own internal coherence, that followers of model prescriptions are seldom faithful to the original in actual practice, that most evaluators don't even try to base their practice on faithful adherence to a model, and that resolution of competing models is neither likely nor desirable—lead to some practical suggestions about the relevance and usefulness of evaluation models in practice.

Evaluation models are necessarily about generalities. Evaluation practice involves attention to details. As Alfred North Whitehead observed, "We think in generalities, we live in detail." We cannot expect the generalities of models to anticipate or be relevant to all the details of practice. In this regard, it is perhaps most useful to think of the models, not as either recipes or ideals, but as *ideas.* Knowing the limitations of models (e.g., they can't anticipate all details) and their potential as reservoirs of ideas, there are several ways of incorporating models into day-to-day practice.

One way to use models corresponds to my advice about how to use definitions. During initial contacts, find out what models, if any, seem to have influenced the thinking and expectations of the people with whom you're working. At the same time, avoid early identification with any particular approach until you know what that approach connotes to the people with whom you have contact. Consider the following scenarios taken from experiences workshop participants have reported to me. In each case an evaluation consultant is talking to a decision maker about a potential evaluation.

> **Evaluator:** "I'd be interested in knowing about any particular models or approaches you've considered using."
>
> **School Administrator:** "Well, I attended a session at a professional meeting where the CIPP model was explained."
>
> **Evaluator:** (anxious to impress and agree with the decision maker) "Oh, yes. Stufflebeam's stuff. That's one of the most widely used models there is. I wouldn't have any trouble working with you on a CIPP evaluation."
>
> **School Administrator:** "Actually I found it rather pedantic. I never can remember what the damn letters stand for. I even understand that Stufflebeam doesn't do CIPP anymore."
>
> *OR*
>
> **Evaluator:** "Are there any particular models of evaluation that have influenced your thinking so far?"
>
> **Funder:** "Well, I've been hearing a lot about—what's his name?—um, Scriven, yeah, Scriven's goal-free evaluation."
>
> **Evaluator:** "I'm very interested in Scriven's approach myself. I've been looking for an opportunity to conduct a goal-free evaluation. I think it has enormous potential."
>
> **Funder:** "My own view is that it's completely irresponsible to conduct an evaluation that doesn't measure directly and precisely program goals. How else is a program to be held accountable?"

Not only do you want to know the effect attached to a particular model, you also want to know what a person who names a model understands it to involve. Without revealing your own ignorance (in case you're not familiar with the model) or assuming that you know what the other person means (in case you are familiar with the model), you can always reply: "I understand there are several potential variations on that approach" (this is always true), "What aspects of it are of particular interest to you?" This open-ended approach allows one to get beyond model naming and name dropping to find out about issues of special interest and to begin the process of filling in situational details.

Attention to situational details, decision maker needs, and viable options permit an evaluator to draw on the *ideas* contained in models without making adherence to a model the driving force in an evaluation. The options open to evaluators have expanded tremendously in recent years. There are more models to choose from for those who like to follow models; there are legitimate variations in, deviations from, and combinations of models; and there is the somewhat model-free approach of problem-solving evaluators who are active, reactive, and adaptive in the context of specific evaluation situations and information needs. Given this pluralism, there would seem to be little of practical value to be gained by open and insistent allegiance to only one model. Although conducting an evaluation according to the logic and premises of a particular model may be practical in a specific situation, in my judgment it is not practical to base one's entire practice on a single model in the hope (or expectation) that said model will always work.

As a practical political maneuver, it is sometimes useful explicitly to conduct an evaluation within the general framework of a particular model, thereby enhancing its credibility by associating it with a nationally esteemed approach. I know of numerous situations in which local evaluators increased acceptance of innovative approaches (e.g., goal-free evaluation, qualitative methods) by drawing openly on the esteem, reputations, recommendations, and models of major figures in the field. Prophets not being accepted in their own county, it is sometimes useful to draw strength and esteem from more distant prophets. Of course, one wants to be sure first that that distant prophet is locally esteemed and that the model in question is adaptable to the local situation. Credibility being a matter of some considerable practical importance in potentially affecting how evaluations are used (Alkin et al., 1979: 245-247), credibility by association can be the beginning of establishing credibility on one's own record and merit.

Of course, in establishing credibility, there are also models from which one is well advised to distance oneself.

Evaluator: "Any particular models that are of special interest to you?"

Decision maker: "Yes, are you familiar with the Contrarian Approach?"

Evaluator: "What particular aspect of that approach interests you?"

Decision maker: "The part where the evaluator finds out what I want to know, and then gives me the exact opposite, under the assumption that as public officials we never know what we really need to know, only evaluators know what we need to know. You know that approach?"

Evaluator: "Sounds like a formalization of what academics have always done to policymakers."

Decision maker: "That's right. The Contrarian Model seems to be very big all over, not just with academics, but even with my own staff. That's the approach I *don't* want. I want just the contrary."

Finally, a useful way of thinking about models is to study your own practice and construct a formal model of how you typically operate. In *Creative Evaluation* I discussed at length the ease with which we fall into habits and ruts that interfere with situational flexibility and evaluation creativity. Studying one's own heuristics and modeling one's own processes may reveal ways of improving effectiveness in very practical ways. *Creative Evaluation* includes a number of suggestions for modeling one's own evaluation practice (see especially Chapters 2 and 5).

TYPES OF EVALUATION

Various evaluation definitions and different evaluation models reveal varying conceptualizations of and approaches to evaluation practice. Cutting across definitions and models are different types of evaluation. Whereas models are basically prescriptive, telling evaluators how they should conduct evaluations, the varying types of evaluation are descriptive. Different types of evaluations ask different questions and focus on specific aspects of the evaluative function. In this respect, different types of evaluations serve different purposes. A committee of the National Academy of Science has delineated different kinds of purposes to be served by evaluation, e.g.: (1) needs assessment, (2) basic research, (3) small-scale testing, (4) field evaluation, (5) policy analyses, (6) fiscal accountability, (7) coverage accountability, (8) impact assessment, and (9) economic analyses (Raizen and Rossi, 1981).

The Evaluation Research Society Standards Committee identified six categories of evaluation "defined both by the purpose of the evaluation effort and by the kinds of activities that tend to be stressed" (ERS, 1980: 3-4).

(A) *Front-end analysis* (preinstallation, context, feasibility analysis). These types of evaluations take place prior to installation of a program to provide guidance in planning and implementing the program as well as deciding if the program should be implemented.

(B) *Evaluability assessment:* This type of evaluation work includes activities aimed at assessing the feasibility of various evaluation approaches and methods. The scope of the evaluation, technical matters, design limitations, and cost parameters are established through evaluability assessment prior to undertaking a more formal evaluation, especially a causal evaluation of program outcomes.

(C) *Formative evaluation* (developmental, process): These evaluations are aimed at providing information for program improvement, modification, and management.

(D) *Impact evaluation* (summative, outcome, effectiveness): These evaluations are aimed at determining program results and effects, especially for the purposes of making major decisions about program continuation, expansion, reduction, and funding.

(E) *Program monitoring:* The ERS (1980: 7) statement says that "this is the least acknowledged but probably most practiced category of evaluation. . . . The kinds of activities involved in these evaluations vary widely from periodic checks of compliance with policy to relatively straightforward 'tracking' of services delivered and 'counting' of clients."

(F) *Evaluation of evaluation:* (secondary evaluation, meta-evaluation, evaluation audit). This category includes professional critiques of evaluation reports, re-analysis of data, and external reviews of internal evaluations.

These various types of evaluations are by no means mutually exclusive. Over time a particular program might be involved in activities from all six general categories. Some activities can go on simultaneously, e.g., program monitoring, formative evaluation, and impact analysis. Moreover, within each category there are numerous types of specific evaluations. Examples of common designations are listed below:

(1) Accreditation evaluation

Does the program meet minimum standards for accreditation or licensing?

(2) Appropriateness evaluation

What services should clients be receiving? To what extent are current services *appropriate* to client needs?

(3) Awareness focus

Who knows about the program? What do they know?

(4) Cost/benefit analysis

What is the relationship between program costs and program outcomes (benefits) expressed in dollars?

(5) Cost-effectiveness evaluation

What is the relationship between program costs and outcomes (where outcomes are *not* measured in dollars)?

(6) Criterion-referenced evaluation

To what extent has a specific objective been attained at the desired level of attainment (the criterion)?

(7) Decision-focused evaluation

What information is needed to make a specific decision at a precise point in time?

(8) Descriptive evaluation

What happens in the program? (No "why" questions or cause/effect analyses.)

(9) Effectiveness evaluation

To what extent is the program effective in attaining its goals?

(10) Efficiency evaluation

Can inputs be reduced and still obtain the same level of output or can greater output be obtained with no increase in inputs?

(11) Effort evaluation

What are the inputs into the program in terms of number of personnel, staff/client ratios, and other descriptors of levels of activity and effort in the program?

(12) Extensiveness evaluation

To what extent is this program able to deal with the total problem? How does the present level of services compare to the needed level of services?

(13) External evaluation

The evaluation is conducted by people outside the program in an effort to increase objectivity.

(14) Formative evaluation

How can the program be improved?

(15) Goal attainment scaling evaluation

To what extent do individual clients attain individual goals on a standardized measurement scale of 1 (low attainment) to 5 (high attainment)?

(16) Goals-based evaluation

To what extent have program goals been attained?

(17) Goal-free evaluation

What are the *actual* effects of the program on clients (without regard to what staff say they want to accomplish)?

(18) Impact evaluation

What are the direct and indirect program effects on the larger community of which it is a part?

(19) Internal evaluation

Program staff conduct the evaluation.

(20) Longitudinal evaluation

What happens to the program and to participants over time?

(21) Meta-evaluation

Was the evaluation well-done? Is it worth using?

(22) Needs assessment

What do clients need and how can those needs be met?

(23) Norm-referenced evaluation

How does this program population compare to some specific norm or reference group on selected variables?

(24) Outcomes evaluation

To what extent are desired client outcomes being attained? What are the effects of the program on clients?

(25) Performance evaluation

What are participants actually able to do as a result of participation in the program?

(26) Personnel evaluation

How effective are staff in carrying out their assigned tasks and in accomplishing their individual goals?

(27) Process evaluation

What are the strengths and weaknesses of day-to-day operations? How are program processes perceived by staff, clients, and others? What are the basic program processes? How can these processes be improved?

(28) Product evaluation

What are the characteristics of specific and concrete products produced by or used in a program? What are the costs, benefits, and effects of those products?

(29) Quality assurance

Are minimum and accepted standards of care being routinely and systematically pro-

	vided to patients and clients? How can quality of care be monitored and demonstrated?
(30) Social indicators	What routine social and economic data should be monitored to assess the impacts of this program (e.g., health statistics, crime statistics, housing statistics, employment statistics)?
(31) Summative evaluation	Should the program be continued? If so, at what level?
(32) Systems analysis	What are the available alternatives and, given those alternatives, what is the *optimum* way to do this program?
(33) Utilization-focused evaluation	What information is needed and wanted by decision makers, information users, and stakeholders that will actually be used for program improvement and to make decisions about the program?

This is by no means an exhaustive list of types of evaluation. In *Creative Evaluation* (Patton, 1981) I reported an additional one hundred types, some of which are problematic in value, but approaches that are nevertheless not uncommon.

Guesstimate approach	What do we *think* is happening to clients "without the pain and bother of actually collecting data"?
Personality-focused evaluation	Would program staff make good Scouts? Are they warm, friendly, clean, neat, trustworthy . . . , and do they do their best to do their duty to God, Country, and Program?
Quick-and-dirty evaluation	How can we do this as fast as possible at the lowest cost?
Weighty evaluation	How can we produce a thick evaluation report?

This list illustrates the difficulty of always making a distinct differentiation between "types" and "models." The distinction is not absolute. Also, this tentative listing of evaluation types illustrates yet again the complexity and diversity in the field. The observations that follow about the wide range of types suggest some practical implications for using a knowledge of alternative types in evaluation practice.

First, it is important to be aware that the field lacks a definitive lexicon. The same labels or words mean different things to different evaluators and decision makers. Effectiveness evaluation sometimes refers to a narrow focus on relative goal attainment; at other times it is used in a way that refers to the overall operations and processes of a program. Impact evaluation is sometimes synonymous with outcomes evaluation, implying an assessment of stated goals; at other times it is meant to include attention to unanticipated or unstated goals; and on other occasions it refers to measures of larger community impact, i.e., effects that go beyond direct program achievements.

Popular usage of some terms has led to other confusions. The summative versus formative distinction was originally made by Scriven (1967) to call attention to different evaluation *purposes.* Summative evaluations are done for the purpose of making judgments about the basic worth of a program. Formative evaluations are aimed at program improvement. Summative evaluations *tend* to focus on outcomes (though not necessarily to the exclusion of evaluating implementation), and formative evaluations *tend* to focus on program processes (though not necessarily to the exclusion of measuring outcomes). Over time these tendencies have led to an unfortunate deterioration in the precision of usage such that summative evaluation is sometimes taken to mean outcomes evaluation, and *only* outcomes evaluation, while formative evaluation is treated as equivalent to a process focus.

Needs assessment is another designation that is widely used with varying meanings. In many cases it has come to mean asking program clients, or potential clients, what they want, thereby making wants equivalent to needs. Others intend for the notion of needs assessment to include some independent assessment of genuine client circumstances and needs. The reference to needs is sometimes meant to encompass an assessment of the overall client situation, including strengths and assets, while others take it to refer only to determination of client deficiencies.

The practical implication of this observation is that evaluators must be quite careful to ensure that there are shared meanings for terms in a particular situation and context. One person's process assessment is another person's outcome (e.g., parent, staff, or client satisfaction). A finding that is meant to be formative may be interpreted, and used, in a summative fashion. It is helpful, as much as possible, to avoid dependence on references to categories, types, and labels when working with decision makers, stakeholders, and information users. Instead (or in addition), use a phrase that actually describes the type of evaluation to which one is referring: "This evaluation is aimed at providing information to be used for program improvement" rather than "This is a formative evaluation." Refer to *actual* outcomes, effects, or impacts instead of to their respective labels: "This evaluation will measure what children have learned" rather than "This is an educational outcomes evaluation."

This doesn't mean that evaluators should not know, and use, the developing lexicon of their field, particularly when talking with other evaluators. It does mean that evaluators should be careful not to lose sight of the actual (and varied) meanings of terms. Moreover, sensitive evaluators ought to be able to move easily back and forth between professional jargon and straight-forward descriptive references, depending on the situation. In introductory evaluation courses and workshops I encourage participants to learn and use some jargon. In advanced seminars and workshops for professional evalua-tors I often ban all use of jargon and insist that straightforward language be used. Different situations, different purposes, different people, different lan-guages.

A second observation about types of evaluation is that sometimes a deci-sion maker absolutely wants a particular type—and wants it explicitly la-beled as such. If a funding mandate calls for a summative outcomes evalua-tion, then the evaluator had better be prepared to produce such an animal, complete with a final report that includes that terminology right there on the front page, in big letters, in the title. The caveat here is that the evaluator, decision maker, and funder all need to be sure that they agree on what a summative outcomes evaluation is before the evaluation is conducted.

There are also situations in which a particular type of evaluation is an anathema, and in which reference to said evil is to be avoided at the risk of endangering one's health (or at least one's contract). To some people systems analysis conjures up images of the Pentagon and eighteen-star generals plan-ning the Vietnam War on Robert McNamara's computers. They want no part of it. I've worked in humanistic counseling and education settings where "there are no outcomes, there is only process." Process, however, turns out to include such things as how a person feels, what they think, what they know, and how they behave. The avoidance of any reference to outcomes is a philo-sophical/ideological position that states to the world (particularly program clients): There are no points of termination, short of death; we're constantly learning and changing. A meta-evaluation of actual data in these settings, however, would have turned up process statements that look suspiciously like outcome findings in more traditional settings.

Some evaluators would take the moral position that they have a responsi-bility to educate (convince) the people in such settings that what they call process is really outcomes. They will argue their own definitions and con-cepts with full conviction that winning that argument may be the most impor-tant outcome of the evaluation. My own preference is to avoid such battles, devoting my efforts instead to winning the utilization battle, to wit, getting people to look at and act on actual findings, regardless of whether they label those findings process statements or outcome results.

A third observation about types concerns the proliferation of evaluation terms and designations. There's hardly an issue of any of the major evaluation journals, or a session at the professional meetings, that doesn't include a paper expounding some new type, model, method, or approach. The lexicon is rapidly expanding, even as the traditional terms become more ambiguous. It's hard to keep up with the new confusions, much less the new terms. We can be assured that the lexicon will expand, and that major figures in the field will periodically lament that expansion, even as they offer some new term to synthesize and encompass old terms, thereby reducing proliferation through proliferation (evaluation's version of nuclear disarmament negotiations). All of which makes it incumbent to be clear about the terms one employs and the language one uses in day-to-day evaluation practice.

These commonsensical warnings about the overuse of jargon are certainly not new. Yet I regularly come across young evaluators who believe that the way to impress the uninitiated is to pepper their language liberally with big words and technical evaluation terms, thereby proving their professional competence to decision makers. This section is dedicated to the proposition that, in the end, it may be more impressive, and more useful, to speak clearly, simply, and practically.

I am also impressed by the ease with which academic language can become second nature to the point at which we're not even aware we're using exclusive terminology and technical jargon. It's important to keep reminding ourselves that just because we know what we're saying doesn't mean anybody else does. A case in point, I believe, is an important new book on naturalistic responsive evaluation by Guba and Lincoln (1981). From what I know of Guba, he is second to none in his commitment to produce useful, responsive evaluations sensitive to the needs and interests of information users. Yet I'm skeptical that Guba and Lincoln will realize their hope of reaching "members of the audiences for which evaluations are made, especially such stakeholders as funders, developers, and/or users of an evalu- and . . . , and consumers of evaluation reports" (1981: xii). The proliferation of technical terms and jargon makes the book heavy going for nonacademics. The term "evaluand" is certainly not common parlance outside academe (or even in it?). Describing our human ability to think quickly on our feet as "processual immediacy," or using the term "warrantability" for usefulness, will do little to reach evaluation consumers. I take such lapses into academic obfuscation as evidence of the difficulty of following a straight and narrow path bordered by simple, practical language. Such lapses by colleagues make me all the more aware of my own obfuscatory tendencies, and all the more anxious to help new practitioners avoid the habit.

The fourth, and final, observation is that we need technical evaluation terms to elucidate nuances of evaluation practice and to call our attention to evaluation options. The preceding observations were not meant to disparage evaluation terminology and typologies. The lack of definitive meanings for evaluation terms creates communications difficulties, but the absence of technical words for professional interactions would create even more difficulties. The proliferation of terms is a response to evaluators' perceived needs for greater clarity about the options available to them. The observation that some terms are avidly embraced by decision makers while others are an anathema only reinforces the point that all words, technical and nontechnical, should be used with deliberateness, consciousness, sensitivity, and acute attention to the need for sharing understandings and to the potential for misunderstandings. We have to know not only what we want to communicate, but also what we do *not* want to communicate, for as G. K. Chesterton observed, "a man does not know what he is saying until he knows what he is not saying."

Knowledge of the many different types of evaluation increases the options available for situational responsiveness. The trick is to master the terminology of types without becoming a slave to single meanings and absolute definitions. Situational flexibility is not enhanced by arguments over who has the correct definition of a term. The terms and types are meant to call our attention to important meanings and distinctions. The practical importance of different types of evaluation resides in the meanings, ideas, and distinctions behind the terms, not in the terms themselves. Professional practice requires a knowledge of both the terms and their varied meanings. If we were unable to distinguish among different types of evaluation, we'd be in the difficult position of Mrs. McCave.

> Did I ever tell you that Mrs. McCave
> Had twenty-three sons and she named them all Dave?
> Well, she did. And that wasn't a smart thing to do.
> You see, when she wants one and calls out, "Yoo-hoo!
> Come into the house, Dave!" She doesn't get *one*.
> All twenty-three Daves of her's come on the run!
> That makes things quite difficult at the McCaves!
> As you can imagine, with so many Daves!
> [Dr. Seuss, 1961: 36-41]

In the house of evaluation similar confusion would reign if we didn't have different names to distinguish among different types of evaluation.

CONCEPTUAL PRACTICALITIES

> *The sky starts at your feet.*
> *Think how brave you are to walk around.*
> Anne Herbert

Where the sky starts involves matters of definition and perception. The matter of practical importance is that we be able to walk around. Where evaluation starts (and ends) also involves matters of definition and perception. The important thing is that we be able to do it. This chapter has reviewed various definitions of "it," considered models of how to do "it," and made some observations about different types of "it," the "it" being *evaluation*.

I once asked Michael Scriven, who has probably identified and named more evaluation concepts, and developed more models, than anyone else in the field, how he came up with new ideas and concepts. He replied that he really didn't like "muddying up the field" with a lot of jargon and new terms, so he only created a term when he felt it was absolutely necessary. He said that as he noticed confusion about some issue or became sharply aware of some gap in the field, he would find it necessary to create some new terminology or to offer a new concept to help sort out the confusion and fill in the gap.

Recent experimental evidence demonstrates the practical importance of definitions, models, and typologies as mental mechanisms for making the world orderly and manageable. DeGroot (1966) showed complex chessboard displays from actual games to poor chess players and chess masters. After seeing the boards for only five seconds both amateurs and masters were asked to reconstruct what they saw. The masters were able to reproduce what they had seen almost perfectly, only occasionally making a minor error; the amateurs could scarcely place any of the pieces in the correct positions. In a second experiment the same two groups were shown new chessboards with the same number of chess pieces as before. This time, however, a new wrinkle was added to the experiment. Rather than arranging the pieces in positions taken from actual games, the pieces were arranged *randomly* on the board. Again the amateurs could scarcely place any of the pieces in the correct squares. *But neither could the masters.* The clear superiority of the chess masters over the amateurs disappeared when the masters were unable to conceptualize the patterns of a particular chess display because of the random ordering (the chaos) of the pieces. The problem for evaluators is to know when a new situation can be appropriately handled by prior conceptualizations and when to resist imposing order through familiar definitions and models, while taking the time to look for patterns unique to the circumstances at hand, circumstances that require some new conceptualization.

As concepts, definitions, and models order our world, they also tell us what things are important and what meanings to attach to the things we perceive through our conceptual screens. They direct our attention *to* certain things and direct our attention *away* from other things. We can only value (care about) things we are aware of, things we are capable of perceiving. To achieve conceptual flexibility evaluators will need to: (1) be aware of the major conceptual distinctions in the discipline, (2) be aware of their own personal conceptual predispositions, i.e., the concepts upon which they most often rely, (3) know how to broaden or adapt concepts and approaches in new situations, and (4) consider the possibility that an altogether new conceptualization or model is needed to do justice to a special situation.

I have been told by a number of evaluators that they're not interested in theoretical issues or conceptual discussions; they simply want to get on with the business of doing evaluations. The central point of this chapter is that *practice is inevitably undergirded by conceptual distinctions that are far from esoteric. Whether one is aware of it or not, practice is guided by—*

indeed, controlled by—the concepts, definitions, and models that order that world upon which one is "practicing." To ignore the conceptual distinctions that direct the day-to-day decisions taken in the field is to be controlled and limited by those conceptual predispositions. My primary concern in reviewing the conceptual issues in this chapter was to illustrate with concrete and specific examples how the ideas and definitions we take into the field can determine what we do in the field. The practical purpose of conceptual awareness and sensitivity is to increase clarity in communications so that evaluators and the people with whom they work will be able to be deliberate in considering various options and be more precise in arriving at mutual definitions of evaluation situations. The importance of such communications clarity was highlighted in a survey of nonacademic employers of social scientists conducted by Thomas Lyson (1981). Nonacademic people who employ social scientists identified as a major shortcoming the social scientists' "inability to communicate" with nonacademics. The next chapter continues these themes in considering how to work with decision makers and information users in an evaluation process.

COMMUNICATIONS CLARITY

One of Halcolm's students had the unfortunate experience of conducting an evaluation that ended in confusion. It turned out that, unbeknownst to either of them, the evaluator and decision maker held different expectations based on quite divergent definitions of evaluation. The extent of the differences only became apparent at the end. The student came to Halcolm to find out how to avoid misunderstandings and miscommunications in the future.

Halcolm: "So you wish to avoid all misunderstandings and miscommunications in the future. That is a lofty ambition, but an attainable one. I will tell you the secret, but you must agree to follow my instructions to the letter for at least one week."

The student agreed.

Other students, aware of the situation, were waiting outside to find out what Halcolm advised, for they too had encountered problems in communicating clearly. When the student emerged they crowded about, urging him to share Halcolm's wisdom. They were astounded when this normally affable young man pushed past them and went directly to his room.

For the next week the student took all his meals in his room, speaking to no one. His friends decided that Halcolm must have given him some deep meditative problem on which to reflect, so they anxiously awaited his reappearance. At the end of the week Halcolm assembled all students and sent for the young man. Halcolm then addressed the assembly: "During the past week has anyone here had any misunderstandings or miscommunications with this young man?"

No one spoke.

He turned to the young man. "During the past week, have you had any miscommunications or misunderstandings with anyone?"

The student shook his head, indicating he had not.

Halcolm then addressed the assembly. "If you would avoid all misunderstandings and miscommunications, do as this young man has done, and lock yourself away. Otherwise . . ."

And he left the assembly, leaving the students to ponder their choices.

CHAPTER 3

Collaborative Evaluation Practice With Groups

Working with people is difficult but not impossible.
Peter Drucker

This chapter is about working with decision makers and information users in a collaborative process aimed at increasing the utility—and actual use—of evaluation processes and findings. The first part of this chapter will establish a justification for using a collaborative, group approach in conducting evaluations. The second part of the chapter will present practical and concrete suggestions for implementing a utilization-focused process with an evaluation task force.

A collaborative approach is one in which the evaluator works directly and in partnership with a group of stakeholders (people who have a stake in how the evaluation comes out) to focus key evaluation questions, design the evaluation study, interpret results, and apply findings. The collaborative process is one of *shared* decision making about key aspects of the evaluation. The people who have a stake in the evaluation collaborate in solving evaluation problems and making research decisions. The evaluator is "active-reactive-adaptive" (Patton, 1978) in facilitating an evaluation process that addresses the concerns, interests, questions, and information needs of a group of stakeholders organized into some kind of evaluation task force. In facilitating the evaluation decision-making process, the evaluator helps task force members deal with the issues of utility, feasibility, propriety, and accuracy, but the evaluator does not decide unilaterally how these standards of excellence will be met.

A consultative, collaborative approach is not always possible, and may not always be desirable. This chapter will explore the strengths and weaknesses of such an approach, discuss alternatives, and suggest ways of using this strategy in practice.

A RATIONALE FOR CONSULTATIVE
EVALUATION PRACTICE

Let me begin by sharing some perceptions about typical evaluation practice. These perceptions are not based on any empirical study of evaluator behavior, but are drawn from my observations of and conversations with evaluation colleagues. Nor is the rationale for consultative evaluation practice that follows dependent on the accuracy of these perceptions. Rather, the purpose of sharing these observations is to establish a context for why the issues and strategies considered in this chapter are so important.

First, evaluators usually enter a program setting as research specialists where they expect, and are expected, to make all the major methodological decisions concerning the evaluation. They are given, and they assume, full responsibility for the conduct of the evaluation. When they meet with stakeholder groups, if they do so at all, it is to gather information so that the *evaluator(s)* can design the evaluation. Illustrative of this approach is responsive evaluation, which posits that "the major purpose of evaluation . . . [is] responding to an audience's requirements for information" (Guba and Lincoln, 1981: 36). Notice the use of the term "audience"—a reference to stakeholders that connotes a passive, receptive relationship to the evaluation rather than an active, involved participation. In the most complete description of responsive evaluation written to date, Guba and Lincoln make it clear that the evaluator is in control and makes all the major decisions about the conduct of the evaluation. In describing the steps for conducting a responsive evaluation (Guba and Lincoln, 1981: 25-26), the evaluator is clearly depicted as the key decision maker in the evaluation process.

(1) The evaluator talks with clients, program staff, and audiences—everyone in and around the program—to gain a sense of their posture with respect to the evaluand and the purposes of the evaluation.

(2) As a result of these conversations, the evaluator places limits on the scope of the program.

(3) The evaluator makes personal observations of what goes on in the name of the program.

(4) As a result of the preceding activities, the evaluator begins to discover, on the one hand, the purposes of the project, both stated and real, and, on the other hand, the concerns that various audiences may have with it and/or the evaluation.

(5) As he becomes more involved with these preliminary data, the evaluator begins to conceptualize the issues and problems that the evaluation should address.

(6) Once issues and problems have been identified, the evaluator is in a position to think about the design of the evaluation.

(7) Given these data needs, the evaluator selects whatever approaches are most useful for generating the data.

(8) The evaluator now proceeds to carry out the data collection procedures that he has identified.

(9) Once the data have been collected and processed, the evaluator shifts to an information-reporting mode.

(10) Since the evaluator cannot report on every problem, it is important that he winnow out those that will be reported.

(11) A final decision to be made by the evaluator has to do with the format to be used in reporting to each audience.

In short, evaluators typically control the evaluation process and make all major decisions about the conduct of the evaluation. Even when evaluators consult with decision makers about various problems, the evaluator typically reserves the right to make any final decisions as the person ultimately responsible for the evaluation. The collaborative approach presented in this chapter is quite different from this normal way of operating.

A second observation is that evaluator control of the evaluation decision making process is easier, less expensive, and more efficient than a task force approach that involves group decision making. Group decision making is time consuming and cumbersome. Indicative of the added cost of working with a group is the stance taken by a very successful, profit-oriented, and time-conscious evaluator I know. He charges a flat fee of $2,000 to design (not conduct) a straightforward outcomes evaluation for a local program in consultation with a single program administrator. He charges an additional $1,000 for each additional person whose views he must take into account in the design. It would cost a task force of eight people $10,000 to get a design that the program director can get alone for $2,000. In terms of the value he places on his own time, this evaluator figures he still loses money in doing group work compared to working with just one program administrator. Moreover, since *his* expertise is what is being purchased in both cases, and he uses a fairly standardized outcomes model, the $10,000 design would be likely to differ little, if at all, from the $2,000 design. The difference in price is to pay for his pain and trouble in having to work with more people.

A third, and final, prefatory observation is that evaluators are generally not very skilled at working with groups. Just as getting a social science Ph.D. in no way says anything about one's ability to teach, neither does it include any guarantee that one can be an effective consultant or work effectively with groups. Many evaluators lack the patience, sensitivity, and good humor to work with nonscientists. They also lack group facilitation skills. Knowledge of research methods is one kind of expertise; knowledge of group process techniques is another. Becoming an effective facilitator of evaluation groups requires training, sensitivity, and experience. Of course, some evaluators require more training than others; and for some, no amount of training is likely to help much. The collaborative, consultative style of evaluation practice isn't for everyone.

This chapter builds a case for collaborative evaluation practice as an approach likely to increase utilization of evaluation processes and findings. Skill in working with groups will be presented here as one of the fundamental competences that evaluators need to include in their repertoire to be truly situationally adaptable and responsive. In considering the collaborative approach, however, it is important to do so in the context of the following observations:

(1) Working with groups in a consultative fashion where evaluation decisions are shared is not the norm in current practice.
(2) Group processes are difficult and time consuming.
(3) Becoming an effective group facilitator requires training and practice.

Evaluator Role Options

It is clear that playing the role of collaborative facilitator is not the only option available to evaluators. This section considers some other options, and then looks at the particular strengths of a collaborative role. Gerald Barkdoll (1980), associate commissioner for planning and evaluation of the U.S. Food and Drug Administration, has identified three evaluator styles. The first style is the "surveillance and compliance" approach of aggressively independent and highly critical auditors committed to getting the goods on a program. In this type of evaluation, the evaluator is the Lone Ranger and program personnel are potential or suspected outlaws. The evaluator is on a mission of law enforcement. The second style of evaluation is epitomized by the aloof and value-free scientist who focuses single-mindedly on acquiring technically impeccable data. The objective scientist is on a mission seeking truth. Program personnel are research subjects to be labeled and studied in accordance with the rules of science. It is not so much a matter of the white hats against the black hats as it is of white laboratory coats against ordinary street clothes. The third style is where the evaluator works in a consultative, consensus-building process to help policymakers and program personnel cooperatively and openly clarify their information needs and use information to improve their effectiveness. In this approach, evaluators and information users are partners in the search for useful information.

Each approach is attractive in its own way. The auditor/detective style emphasizes justice. The scientific style emphasizes truth. The consultative style emphasizes utility.

In accordance with the premises of utilization-focused evaluation presented in the first chapter, the consultative style is here presented as the approach of choice. The reason is simple pragmatism. Little is gained by playing the Lone Ranger and identifying outlaws if the findings uncovered are ignored or discredited; the "guilty" are not likely to be brought to justice if the evidence is never used, is inadmissible, or never finds its way to the right court. (Plea-bargaining is more the norm in today's world anyway.)

Likewise, there is little point, other than self-satisfaction (no small consideration, to be sure), in discovering scientific truth if that truth is to be ignored or misused. The consultative process emphasizes collaboration as a pragmatic means of actively involving decision makers and information users in the search for knowledge and justice, thereby increasing utilization.

There are other practical considerations that weigh in favor of the consultative process where a concern for utility is the driving force in the interactive process. Program staff typically have an aversion to being treated as outlaws or research subjects. They have become sophisticated in ways of sabotaging evaluations. There are a multitude of ways of hampering data collection efforts, discrediting findings, disputing conclusions, and twisting interpretations. The evaluator *needs* the cooperation, goodwill, and interest of a variety of decision makers and information users to conduct a high-quality and useful evaluation. The consultative process of utilization-focused evaluation includes involving the people affected by evaluation results in a collaborative research effort for the purpose of program improvement.

The consultative style of evaluation described in this chapter is aimed at four practical accomplishments:

(1) getting decision makers and information users to share responsibility for the evaluation;
(2) getting decision makers and information users to care about the evaluation;
(3) making sure that decision makers and information users understand the evaluation process and evaluation findings; and
(4) increasing the personal commitment of decision makers and information users to actually use evaluation processes and findings.

The Stakeholder Assumption

The "stakeholder assumption" is the idea that key people who have a stake in an evaluation should be actively and meaningfully involved in shaping that evaluation so as to focus the evaluation on meaningful and appropriate issues, thereby increasing the likelihood of utilization. A consultative evaluation approach is based on the stakeholder assumption. In recent years, as evaluators have become increasingly concerned about utilization, the stakeholder assumption has received widespread attention. Doubts have been raised about the validity of the assumption. Nick Smith, for example, president of the Evaluation Network during 1980, wrote in his column in the *Evaluation Network Newsletter* that the assumption was being accepted without sufficient empirical evidence to support the supposed relationship between stakeholder involvement and utilization of findings.

Although this [the stakeholder assumption] appears to be a widely held belief, no one has bothered to test it empirically. From a recent 16-state study of local district school accreditation evaluations, I have found that data from school board members and administrators with first-hand experience in such evaluations do not agree with this assumption. These individuals do not want to be personally more involved in such studies, nor do they believe that their involvement will make the evaluation results more useful to them. In fact, for these school board members and administrators, the correlation between their level of involvement and their judgments of a past evaluation's utility to them was only 0.3, while there was a 0.7 correlation between their judgments of the evaluation's quality and its utility. Hardly strong support for the considerable effort now being expended at the local, state, and federal level to increase the involvement of various groups in evaluation [Smith, 1980: 39].

Smith's doubts about the validity of the stakeholder assumption provide an opportunity to clarify my own interpretations about what the stakeholder assumption means in practice. His critique includes some common misconceptions about the collaborative approach to utilization-focused evaluation.

First, there is the question of the nature of the relationship between stakeholder involvement and utilization. Smith states the relationship as a "necessary" condition. In the sentence preceding the excerpt quoted above, he said he was addressing "the currently popular assumption that increased involvement of clients and decision makers in evaluation activities will *necessarily* result in increased utilization of evaluation findings" (Smith, 1980: 39, emphasis added). From my point of view, the stakeholder assumption is somewhat overstated by Smith. I have never suggested, or heard others suggest, that increased stakeholder involvement in an evaluation will necessarily result in increased utilization. Nothing one can do, as near as I can tell, will guarantee utilization. The group process of utilization-focused evaluation is aimed at tipping the odds somewhat more in favor of utilization, odds that are typically loaded heavily against utilization (see Patton, 1978: 290-291).

Second, there is a hint of a tradeoff in Smith's skepticism implying that one must choose between stakeholder involvement and high quality data. Many evaluators assume that methodological rigor will inevitably be sacrificed if nonscientists collaborate in making methods decisions. This need not be the case. The ideal expressed in the new standards includes utility *and* accuracy. Other research confirms Smith's findings that decision makers are concerned about "quality" of data, but quality includes both "truth tests" (accuracy) and "utility tests," the latter being a concern for relevance and applicability (Weiss and Bucuvalas, 1980).

Third, Smith's point is directed entirely at the *quantity* of stakeholder involvement in an evaluation. The variable "level of involvement" is somewhat ambiguous, but the implication is that it refers to amount of involvement in terms of time. I want to make it clear that the emphasis in utilization-focused evaluation generally, and, more specifically, the emphasis in this discussion on working with task forces, is on careful selection of the people with whom one works and the *quality* of the evaluation group process. The quantity of group interaction time is often inversely related to quality, a point to which I will return in discussing how to implement a collaborative approach.

Fourth, while I expect Smith is correct in saying that there is a dearth of empirical evidence that "increased involvement" (if he means greater quantity) leads to greater utilization, there is substantial evidence that high-quality involvement of the right people contributes substantially to utilization. The massive diffusion of innovation literature (e.g., Havelock, 1971, 1973; Rogers and Shoemaker, 1971) is replete with relevant empirical evidence. The formal organizations, participatory management, and small group literatures in psychology and sociology provide substantial data relevant to this point (e.g., Hage and Aiken, 1970; Bennis, 1966; Azumi and Hage, 1972; Bennis et al., 1976; Argyris, 1972, 1974, 1976). These literatures document with empirical evidence the proposition that people are more likely to accept and use information, and make changes based on information, when they are personally involved in and have a personal stake in the decision making processes aimed at bringing about change. Most directly, there is a growing evaluation and policy analysis literature—*an empirical literature*—that supports the proposition that utilization of evaluation is enhanced by *high-quality stakeholder involvement in and commitment to the evaluation process* (e.g., Fairweather et al., 1974; Weiss, 1977; Patton, 1978; Alkin et al., 1979; Braskamp and Brown, 1980; Stevens and Tornatsky, 1980; Lynn, 1980; Dickey, 1981).

Fifth, evaluators should not expect much initial enthusiasm among stakeholders for the idea of participating actively in a research process. Past experiences are not likely to have been very positive. Most stakeholders are quite happy to leave evaluation to evaluators. They're also quite happy to ignore the resultant evaluation findings. Like a child who wants to avoid bad-tasting medicine (medicine, by definition, being bad tasting), stakeholders would typically prefer to avoid being subjected to distasteful doses of evaluation (evaluation, by definition, being distasteful), even if they believe it's good for them. The evaluation practitioner, like the medical practitioner, must often cajole and otherwise pursuade stakeholders to do what ought to be done. Getting cooperation and participation has to be worked at. Initial resistance is no reason to fall back on traditional patterns of operating alone, at least not if the evaluator is really committed to utilization. In my experience, if stakeholders won't get involved at the beginning of an evaluation, they probably won't pay it much heed at the end.

Sixth, and finally, it is important to clarify what utilization means. There are a variety of ways in which evaluation findings can have an impact. Evaluations can directly influence specific major decisions. Evaluations can be used to make minor adjustments in a program. Decision makers can use evaluations to reduce uncertainty, enlarge their options, increase control over program activities, speed things up, and increase their sophistication about program processes. Sometimes evaluations have more of a conceptual impact (i.e., they influence how stakeholders *think* about a program) than an instrumental impact (i.e., utilization manifested in concrete actions and explicit decisions). While the ideal of utilization typically centers on the ways in which major decisions are affected, a broader view of utilization reveals multiple layers of impact.

How one defines and thinks about utilization is important because it affects how one views the evaluation process. If utilization centers only on the use of specific findings to make concrete decisions, then stakeholder involvement can be narrowly limited to identifying relevant issues and reading final reports. But if utilization is viewed as *use of the evaluation process* and not just as final findings, then stakeholders must be involved in the entire process for the process to have the most impact. Much of the impact of evaluations on stakeholders comes through personal engagement in the difficult processes of goals clarification, issues identification, operationalizing outcomes, matching research design to program design, determining sampling strategies, organizing data collection, interpreting results, and drawing conclusions. These processes take stakeholders through a gradual awakening to program complexities and realities, an awakening that contains understandings and insights that will find their way into program developments over time, only some of which will be manifested in concrete decisions. Utilization begins as soon as stakeholders become actively involved in the evaluation because that involvement, properly facilitated, forces them to think about program priorities and realities. *The stakeholder assumption, then, includes the expectation that stakeholders need to expend time and effort to figure out what is worth doing in an evaluation; they need help in focusing on worthwhile questions; and they need to experience the full evaluation process if that process, which is really a learning process, is to realize its potential, multi-layered effects.*

This process-oriented approach to utilization and working with stakeholders is based on an empirical foundation of research about how programs operate and how decisions about programs are typically made. Organization studies reveal that there are few major, direction-changing decisions in most programming, and that evaluation research is used as one piece of information that feeds into a slow, evolutionary process of program development. Program development is a process of "muddling through" (Lindblom, 1959; Allison, 1971), and evaluation research is part of that muddling. Evaluation is part of what Weiss (1980) has called "knowledge creep and decision accretion." This view of evolutionary program development and evolutionary evaluation utilization, both occurring in small, creeping steps, is now well documented in the evaluation literature (see Weiss, 1977, 1980; Patton, 1978; Alkin et al., 1979; Delbecq and Gill, 1979; Young and Comtois, 1979; Larsen, 1980). The stakeholder assumption recognizes the need to provide a developmental process in which evaluation understandings can creep into stakeholder awareness, thereby making such understandings available for more direct, action-oriented use.

In short, *the practical view of utilization offered here broadens the notion of evaluation impact to include use of the entire evaluation process as a stakeholder learning experience, not just use of the findings in a report.* This distinction is parallel to that made in education between learning by doing versus learning by reading. Students can learn about science by doing science (actually conducting their own experiments) or by merely reading about and memorizing the results of scientific experiments conducted by others. The former has the more lasting impact. A consultative, collaborative process of working with stakeholders is the evaluation version of learning by doing, an experiential approach to evaluation research.

Why a Group Approach?

Evaluators can obviously work collaboratively with individual stakeholders. Since group facilitation requires special skills, it is worth considering some of the strengths and weaknesses of organizing and working with an evaluation task force.

This chapter began by acknowledging that there are good reasons why evaluators and other consultants resist sharing decision making with a group in an evaluation. Many of those reasons have to do with our stereotypes (with their grains of truth) about committees.

> *Committee—a group of the unwilling,*
> *picked from the unfit, to do the*
> *unnecessary.*
>
> Stewart Harroll

> *Committee—a group of men who keep minutes*
> *and waste hours.*
>
> Milton Berle

> *We always carry out by committee anything*
> *in which any one of us alone would be too*
> *reasonable to persist.*
>
> Frank Moore Colby

The connotations attached to committee work are largely negative. Committees are ridiculed as monsters with too many arms, too many legs, and most of all, too many heads (but not enough brains). Committees are reputed to be slow, inefficient, ineffective, indecisive, time consuming, and overly pervasive in contemporary society. It may well be that the only thing that takes more time than serving on committees is time spent avoiding serving on committees.

I was once in the office of a department chair who was known for his dictatorial style and dislike for committees. On his wall was a plaque that read:

God so loved the world that he didn't send a committee to save us. He sent us only one man.

As our discussion came to an end, with the chairman continuing to resist the idea of any kind of shared decision making on the project we were discussing, I pointed to the witticism on the wall, and asked,

Correct me if I'm wrong, but haven't you forgotten the rest of the story? It may be true that God so loved the world that He didn't send a committee. But as I remember the story, the first thing Jesus did in His ministry was set up a committee to help Him with His work.

My point was lost on this good gentleman who had set himself up as sole ruler (God?) in his own universe.

Parkinson (1957) has done as much as anyone to caricature committees. His "law of triviality" states that the complexity and importance of an issue vary inversely with the time that a committee will spend arriving at a decision. As an illustration of this law Parkinson reports on the deliberations of a university committee that had three items on its agenda:

(1) approving plans for an atomic reactor,
(2) building a bicycle shed, and
(3) deciding on refreshments for regular meetings.

The $10 million plans for the atomic reactor were approved without change in 2½ minutes. The bicycle shed plans involving about $2,000 were approved after 45 minutes of discussion that led to a modification saving $300. The decision about future meeting refreshments took 75 minutes and a final decision was deferred pending additional information. Any reader who has ever served on a committee can undoubtedly provide similar, if less dramatic, instances documenting operation of Parkinson's "law of triviality."

Because of all this bad press, I tend to avoid using the word "committee" in establishing an Evaluation Task Force. While the name change avoids a few of the negative connotations attached to the word "committee," the more important point relates to what actually happens in the group. Shared decision making, it seems to me, is one of those things that gets no press when things go well, and gets lots of bad press when things go poorly.

But, still, is it worth the bother?

The answer depends on what one hopes to accomplish. In the last section I suggested that the evaluation process can be viewed as a learning experience for stakeholders. This perspective goes beyond a concern that decision makers and information users learn about evaluation *findings*. The broader and fuller learning experience includes increasing conceptual clarity about program issues, activities, and goals; engendering a commitment to an empirical approach to the world; building up a willingness to subject beliefs and program assumptions to empirical examination; understanding the strengths and limitations of a data-based approach to program development; and developing competence in using data for decision making. This perspective on the larger meaning of the evaluation process follows from one of the premises of utilization-focused evaluation presented in the first chapter, to wit:

> Effective evaluators must also be effective trainers because every evaluation presents opportunities to train decision makers in evaluation processes and the uses of information.

A group approach is the most efficient way to operationalize this premise. It is highly inefficient to try to take a number of isolated stakeholders through the learning process. It takes time to work with a group. It takes considerably more time to train separate individuals. Of course, evaluators who incorporate the role of teacher in their collaboration must be prepared to deal with those stakeholders who are determined to follow Mark Twain's advice:

> Never learn to do anything: if you don't learn, you'll always find someone else to do it for you.

A second reason for working with an evaluation task force is the nature of group dynamics. Several things can be accomplished with a group that are less likely to occur with individuals.

(1) An environment of openness can be established to reduce suspicions and fears about what is going on in the evaluation. The key stakeholders who participate in the process know how decisions are made and who was involved in making them.

(2) Participants in the group process become sensitized to the multiple perspectives that exist around any program. They are exposed to divergent views, multiple possibilities, and competing values. Their view is broadened, and they are exposed to the varying agendas of people with different stakes in the evaluation. This increases the possibility of conducting an evaluation that is responsive to different needs, interests, and values.

(3) New ideas often emerge out of the dynamics of group interaction.

(4) A sense of shared responsibility for the evaluation can be engendered that is often greater than the responsibility that would be felt by isolated individuals. Commitments made in groups, in front of others, are typically more lasting and serious than promises made to an evaluator in private.

(5) An open forum composed of various stakeholders makes it difficult to suppress touchy questions or negative findings. Issues get raised and findings get publicized that otherwise might never see the light of day.

(6) The evaluator has an opportunity to observe firsthand the interactions among various stakeholders and to assess their interpersonal relationships. This information can be very helpful in developing utilization strategies.

(7) A certain momentum can often be established through group processes that helps reduce delays or roadblocks resulting from the attitudes or actions of one person.

(8) The evaluator(s) and stakeholders in a group process will often jell into a kind of support group. It's not the evaluator against the world. The other participants in the group can lend support, help, and understanding.

(9) The group will often continue to function after the evaluation is completed. Participants can develop a shared commitment to follow through on utilization of evaluation findings and recommendations. After all, in most cases the evaluator is present for only a limited period. Stakeholders stay with the program after the evaluation is over. A task force can become a repository for evaluation knowledge and carry forward an appreciation of evaluation processes. The members of the group can carry on what the evaluator helps to establish.

Of course, all of these outcomes of group dynamics assume an effective group process. The extent to which utilization is enhanced by a group process depends on (1) who participates in that process and (2) the questions dealt with by the group, i.e., the focus and quality of the process. The discussion later in this chapter on implementing a collaborative utilization-focused group process will emphasize these two points.

Any group of people rapidly becomes greater than the sum of its parts. Bringing together a group of incompetents seems to increase geometrically the capacity for incompetent and misguided action. On the other hand, bringing together a group of competent and creative people makes it possible for them to stimulate each other and create something that is more useful than any of them individually might have created. Shared decision making may mean compromise; it can also mean powerful chain reactions leading to increased energy and commitment, especially commitment to use evaluation findings in which group members have developed some *stake* through their involvement in the evaluation decision making process.

We return, then, to the question that opened this section, "Why work with a group?" Working with a group of carefully selected and caring decision makers and information users is only worth the bother *if you care about* utilization of evaluation processes and findings. I have never argued that an evaluation task force is more efficient, less painful, or more decisive than an evaluator working alone. What I have argued is that working alone increases enormously the likelihood that the evaluation will answer the wrong questions, be misunderstood, misused, underutilized, or altogether ignored. Working effectively with a group also provides an opportunity to incorporate a training role into the responsibilities of the evaluator. As both facilitator and trainer, the active-reactive-adaptive evaluator will be called on to walk a narrow line between providing too little direction and too much direction. I'll have more to say about the practical subtleties and nuances of working with a task force in later sections. For the moment, the wisdom of William Hazlitt will suffice:

> To get others to come into our ways of thinking, we must go over to theirs; and it is necessary to follow, in order to lead.

PRACTICALITIES OF IMPLEMENTING A COLLABORATIVE UTILIZATION-FOCUSED PROCESS

The preceding sections of this chapter have been aimed at establishing a rationale for collaborative evaluation practice with groups. The remainder of this chapter will discuss practical implementation issues beginning with a brief review of the steps in utilization-focused evaluation, followed by discussion of some fundamental procedural suggestions for making the process work in practice.

Utilization-Focused Evaluation

Figure 3.1 depicts the process of utilization-focused evaluation (Patton, 1978). This is a process for making decisions about the focus and content of an evaluation—but the content itself is not specified or implied in advance. Thus any of the major models in evaluation (see Chapter 2), or any of a full variety of methods, might emerge as the guiding direction in utilization-focused evaluation. The decision making process depicted in the flowchart does not preclude a priori any particular approaches, outcomes, measures, methods, typical questions, assumptions, or audiences. Utilization-focused evaluation is a strategy for making decisions about all of these things.

Utilization-focused evaluation begins with identification and organization of specific, relevant decision makers and information users (not vague, passive audiences) who will make decisions about the evaluation process, and who will use the information that the evaluation produces. The importance of gearing an evaluation to the interests, needs, and capabilities of particular people can fruitfully be thought of as "user-focused evaluation," an alternative way of labeling the process depicted in Figure 3.1. The evaluator works with the identified decision makers and information users to *focus* relevant evaluation questions. From these questions flow the appropriate research methods and data analysis techniques.

Utilization-focused evaluation plans for utilization *before* data are ever collected. The question that underlies and drives the ongoing interactions between evaluators and decision makers is, "What difference would *that* information make?" The evaluator asks: "What would you do if you had an

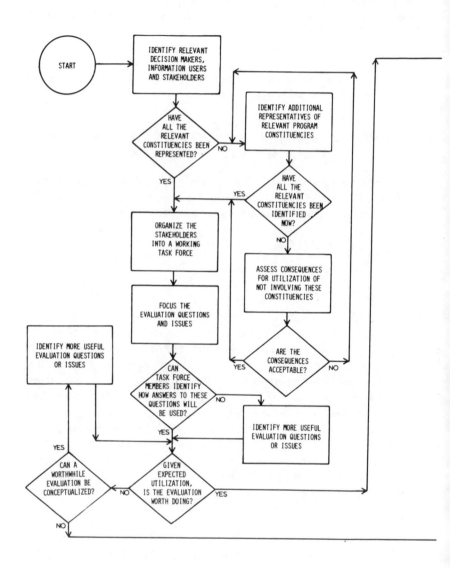

Figure 3.1   Utilization-Focused Evaluation Flowchart

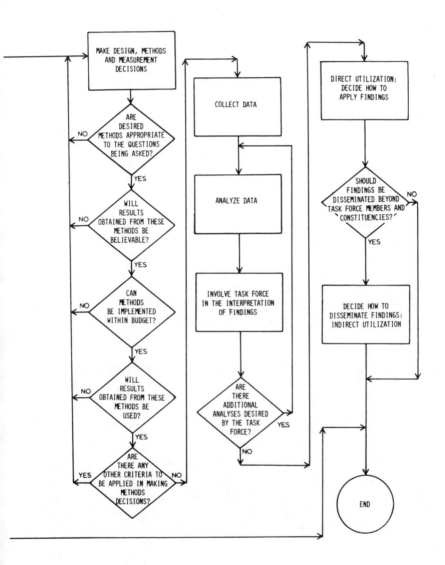

answer to *that* question?" Decision makers and evaluation task force members are expected to identify at least some ways in which answers to evaluation questions will be used before data are ever collected. If stakeholders can't specify how they expect to use information *before* the findings are in, there's little reason to expect that they'll be able to figure out how to use them *after* the findings are in.

Once questions are focused on relevant issues, methods decisions are made with special attention to questions of methods appropriateness, believability, feasibility, and data utility. Threats to utility are as important as threats to validity and reliability, a perspective reflected in the new standards of evaluation (see Chapter 1) and discussed at greater length in later chapters on methods and data collection in this book. Finally, the decision makers and information users are included in analysis, interpretation, and dissemination of findings, as well as in planning for further utilization processes.

Careful attention to the reiterative flow of arrows in the utilization-focused evaluation flowchart will put to rest any notion that this is a simple, linear process, e.g., (1) identify decision makers; (2) focus evaluation questions; (3) gather data; and (4) analyze data and feedback findings. The flowchart shows that any one of these steps can keep you going in circles for awhile. Nevertheless, there are strategic decision points at which one part of the process is brought to closure (at least *relative* closure) and the next part of the process is begun. For example, at some point you bring to an end the identification of decision makers and the organization of an evaluation task force, so that the process of focusing evaluation questions can begin. This doesn't mean that additional people may not join the group along the way; it just means that the evaluator has some responsibility to facilitate the process and keep it moving.

In training evaluators in the strategy of utilization-focused evaluation, I am often pressed to be specific about how I actually organize and consult with a group of decision makers, information users, and stakeholders. While my commitment to and belief in situational responsiveness makes me wary of laying out any single and absolute approach to organizing and facilitating groups, the realities of evaluation practice, especially time constraints and limited resources, have led me to develop some strategies for making the most of scarce consulting time. These experiences and ideas are shared in the hope that they help stimulate your thinking about your own consulting patterns (heuristics), while providing some practical suggestions that you may be able to adapt to your own style. In sharing these ideas, I am not recommending imitation of the specifics. Rather, I'm providing a description of one consulting pattern and style that can be used for making comparisons, drawing contrasts, and stimulating development of your own consulting style. The process I shall describe refers specifically to what I've called the active-reactive-adaptive style of utilization-focused evaluation aimed at facilitating the work of an evaluation task force.

Purpose of the Task Force

The reasons for organizing a task force in conducting an evaluation have already been discussed at some length in this chapter. A concise summary of purpose may be helpful, however, before going on. An evaluation task force is organized to make major decisions about the focus, methods, and purpose of the evaluation. The task force is a vehicle for actively involving key stakeholders in the evaluation. This helps guarantee that the evaluation is relevant, appropriate, and useful. Moreover, the very processes involved in making decisions about an evaluation will typically increase the commitment of stakeholders to the utilization of evaluation results while also increasing their knowledge about evaluation, their sophistication in conducting evaluation research, and their ability to interpret evaluation findings. Finally, the task force allows the evaluator to share responsibility for decision making and utilization by providing a forum for the political and practical perspectives that best come from those stakeholders who will ultimately be involved in the utilization of evaluation results.

Composition of the Task Force

Several criteria are important in attempting to form an evaluation task force. Not all of these criteria can be met to the same degree in every case, but it is helpful to have in mind a basic framework for the composition of the task force group. The members of the task force should:

(1) represent the various groups and constituencies that have an interest and stake in the evaluation findings and their utilization;
(2) have either authority and power to use evaluation findings in decision making or the ability to influence others who do have such power and authority;
(3) believe that the evaluation is worth doing;
(4) care how the results are used; and
(5) be willing to make a firm commitment of time, including a commitment to attend all of the evaluation task force meetings.

One of the things that causes the most problems in working with an evaluation task force is to have different people show up at different meetings, and to have such inconsistent attendance that the process never really moves forward, but has to be begun anew with each new meeting.

Size

The minimum number I would expect to have is three, in order to have some variation in viewpoints, and the most I would want to work with is ten. A group larger than ten begins to become quite cumbersome for decision making. For certain activities it may be appropriate and helpful to work with a much larger group. For example, I may do a goals clarification exercise with the entire program staff, or have a large meeting to discuss findings. These activities, however, are sponsored by the task force as part of the larger evaluation process. The task force participates in deciding when to hold larger group sessions and the purpose of such sessions.

The composition and size of a task force is limited for very pragmatic reasons. Not every stakeholder can or should participate, although an attempt should be made to represent all major stakeholder constituencies and points of view. The evaluator should be fair, but practical, in working with program administrators, funders, clients, program staff, and public officials to establish a task force (and imbue it with the necessary authority to make decisions). In this regard I find the advice of Guba and Lincoln (1981: 37) to be impractical when they assert that "it is unethical for the evaluator . . . to fail to interact with any known audience in the search for concerns and issues." They direct the evaluator to address "the broadest possible array of persons interested in or affected by the evaluand, including audiences that are unaware of the stakes they hold" (1981: 37). While evaluators need to take care that the interests of program clients and the powerless are represented, there are practical limits to identification and organization of decision makers and information users. Fairness and a healthy regard for pluralism are guiding lights in this regard.

Chairing the Task Force

I prefer to have one of the task force participants act as chair of the group. The chair's responsibility is to convene meetings, see that agendas for meetings are followed, and keep discussions on the topic at hand. Having a stakeholder chair the task force helps symbolize the responsibility and authority of the group. The evaluator is a consultant to the group and is paid to do the nitty-gritty staff work for the evaluation, but the task force should assume responsibility for the overall direction of the process. As facilitator, trainer, and collaborator, the evaluator will command a good deal of floor time in task force sessions. However, an effective evaluator can accomplish everything needed by working with the chair, rather than by being the chair.

Activities

In facilitating the work of the task force, the evaluator must be able to help focus the activities of the group so that time is well used, necessary decisions get made, and participants do not become frustrated with a meandering and ambiguous process. To make the best use of task force time, it is helpful to minimize time spent on decisions about the group process and maximize the time spent on decisions about substantive evaluation issues. Thus I recommend that the evaluator *not* begin by asking the task force members how they want to make decisions, but rather, that the evaluator provide the chair with an outline or agenda of the kinds of decisions that have to be made and then move the group through the process of decision making, *focusing at all times on substantive issues.* A lot of time can be wasted while people try to figure out how they're going to operate. When the group is convened, the facilitator should have a clear idea of how the group will operate so that participants can rapidly get down to business and accomplish the necessary tasks. This also means that each task force meeting should have definite closure so that members know what has been accomplished and what has to happen next. An inexperienced chair may need considerable preparatory help from the evaluator to keep the task force task oriented. What follows is a description of a barebones process. At a minimum I expect to hold four two-hour meetings with the task force.

(1) *Focus/conceptualization session.* The purpose of the first meeting is to establish the focus of the evaluation. This means the group must consider alternative evaluation questions, issues, problems, and goals to decide the purpose and direction of the evaluation. Some kind of group process is necessary to help participants consider alternatives or to generate options (e.g., Patton, 1978: ch. 5, 1981; Bertcher, 1979). In any case, the product of the first meeting is a focus establishing the basic direction for the evaluation.

(2) *Methods and measurement options.* The second meeting is devoted to consideration of different ways of conducting the evaluation, given the focus determined in the first meeting. The evaluator presents varying kinds of measurement approaches and different designs that might be used. Time considerations, resource considerations, staff considerations, and utilization possibilities are discussed with the clear intention of narrowing down the methods and measurement possibilities to those that are manageable, credible, and practical. Issues of validity, reliability, generalizability, and appropriateness are also discussed. What kinds of data are needed to answer the evaluation questions that emerged in the first meeting? What kind of design makes the most sense? What's an appropriate sampling approach? What comparisons should be made? The purpose of this second session is to provide clear direction for evaluation methods and measurement.

(3) *Design and instrument review.* Between the second and third meetings the evaluator will design the instruments to be used and write a concrete methods proposal specifying units of analysis, control or comparison groups to be studied, sampling approaches and sample size, and the overall data collection strategy. In reviewing the proposed design and instruments during the third meeting, the task force members should make sure that they understand what will be done and what *will not* be done, what findings can be generated and what findings *cannot* be generated, and what questions will be asked and what questions *will not* be asked. The third meeting will usually involve some changes in instrumentation—additions, deletions, revisions—and adjustments in the design. Basically, this meeting is aimed at providing final input into the research methods before data collection begins. The eval-

uator leaves the meeting with a clear mandate to begin data collection. The third meeting is also often a good time to do a mock utilization session where task force members consider specifically how various kinds of findings might be used given simulated evaluation results. "If we get these answers to this question, what would that mean? What would we do with those results?" If that question cannot be answered *before* data collection begins, then there is a good chance that that question will not be answerable when data collection is over—an indication that more work needs to be done on the utilization focus of the evaluation.

(4) *Data interpretation session.* The fourth and final meeting in this minimum scenario of task force activities focuses on data analysis, data interpretation, and recommendations. Following data collection, but before the writing of the final report, the evaluator assembles task force members to review initial findings. The evaluator has arranged the data and organized them so that the task force members can deal with them, understand them, and interpret them. However, at this point, the evaluator stops short of providing interpretations or recommendations. The purpose of this session is to allow task force members to get involved personally in the analysis and to consider the meaning of the findings. Out of this session will come recommendations about additional kinds of analyses that should be performed and insights about the meaning of the data. Recommendations will then follow from the findings. Later chapters of this book discuss in depth how to arrange data for decision makers' analysis and how to move from findings to recommendations.

I emphasize that this framework is the minimum for a task force. More than one meeting may be necessary at any of these stages, particularly for more complex and larger-scale evaluations. Sometimes larger meetings will be held to involve additional people at critical points in the process. There are a variety of activities and exercises that can be done with task force members to increase their understanding of evaluation options and processes. *Creative Evaluation* (Patton, 1981) offers a number of such approaches that go beyond the skeletal process outlined in the four meetings above. For local evaluations, however, I have found that it is possible to accomplish all that needs to be accomplished in these four two-hour sessions. Of course, between meetings a great deal of interpersonal contact may go on through phone calls, individual conferences, and memoranda. The evaluator may want to check out certain strategies with particular task force members and do the basic background work that allows task force meetings to flow smoothly. By conscientiously doing this groundwork, the evaluation task force members can accomplish the tasks set out at each meeting and play a meaningful role throughout the utilization-focused evaluation process.

The Consultative Process

> *My greatest strength as a consultant is to be ignorant*
> *and ask a few questions.*
>
> Peter Drucker

The flowchart, "Utilization-Focused Evaluation" (Figure 3.1), depicts a consultative process. The evaluator neither controls the task force decision making process nor is the evaluator *laissez faire* about what the task force decides. The evaluator, whether internal or external, is here being presented as playing a consultative role vis-à-vis the people who have primary responsibility for utilization and application of findings.

Management consultant Fritz Steele has incisively described the difficulty of deciding how directive to be in facilitating a group process. Part of the difficulty, he believes, is the extent to which the consultant may feel a need to demonstrate expertise and, in so doing, force the group unwittingly in a direction that matches the consultant's expertise and interests more than meeting the real needs and interests of the group. What Steele describes as ideal is a very creative consultative process.

> The problem, then, is this: if the consultant has no model or system for analyzing behavior, he is unlikely to be able to make much use of his immediate experience, nor is he likely to learn very much from it, since there will be no cumulative growth in understanding a particular area. Conversely, if he has a single, tightly organized, closed system for thinking about organizational behavior, he is also unlikely to learn very much, since he simply throws away or distorts those data which do not fit the system. The former situation is analogous, in perceptual terms, to *not being able to focus* enough on figure-ground relationships to see a pattern. The latter situation is akin to *staring* in an effort to make the pattern emerge (also unlikely to help the process very much). The process which is called for is one of real *seeing;* of having enough of a previous model so that perceptions can be organized, but being flexible enough to let patterns emerge and come into focus. My prediction is that the more anxious a consultant is about whether he will be able to see something in a group's process, the more likely he will be to stare (to try to guarantee in advance that he has something to report), and therefore the less likely he will be to see what is actually taking place or to learn from it [Steele, 1975: 16-17; emphasis in original].

Steele's analogy very much fits my own experience: Both lack of focus and "staring" at a group interfere with being able to *see* what is happening so as to be able to be truly active-reactive-adaptive. This means the consultant is always carefully observing, but only sometimes directing, and only sometimes laying back to let the group wander on its way. Useful solutions and directions are most likely to emerge from really *seeing* what is happening and what needs to happen. The trick is to be sufficiently directive to get the job done and sufficiently nondirective and open to allow task force participants to feel that their inputs have been meaningful and substantive.

Collaboration and Creativity

In the first chapter I suggested that finding practical solutions to situationally specific evaluation problems often requires considerable creativity. In *Creative Evaluation* (Patton, 1981), I discussed this perspective at length, offering a variety of ideas and exercises to use as ways of stimulating creative evaluation approaches. That book's discussion of the consultative group process gave the impression to some that the evaluator merely facilitates a group or task force in such a way that the group becomes creative; the evaluation consultant's job, it may appear, is to stimulate creativity in others, but the evaluator need not be particularly creative. I want to be sure that such an impression does not linger. The evaluator certainly works to unlock and stimulate creativity in others, but the primary responsibility for offering creative solutions to what the evaluator *sees* happening remains with the evaluator. The evaluator brings to the group experience, knowledge, skills, and insights that place on him or her the bulk of the responsibility for *seeing* creative possibilities. This is the *active* part of the active-reactive-adaptive trinity in utilization-focused evaluation. The evaluator then facilitates group *reaction* to the creative solution offered and adapts the solution accordingly. This is the heart of the creative evaluation process as an interactive, collaborative process.

Experimental evidence suggests that *the greater the need for a creative solution to a particular evaluation problem, the less able a group is to generate acceptable solutions.* A group process can generate ideas and establish the parameters for what would constitute an acceptable solution, but creative insight appears to be primarily an individual phenomenon. A creative insight can be sparked in a group, but some individual will usually need time alone to think and work out the details and full implications of a creative solution. This is what the evaluator does between meetings of the task force—and this is the reason I emphasized the need for tight organization and careful focus of task force meetings.

The experimental evidence to which I am referring involves observing how groups handle "Eureka" and "non-Eureka" types of problems. Eureka problems have unique and unambiguous solutions, whereas non-Eureka problems offer multiple possibilities for solution, none of which is obviously the single best possible choice. In evaluation, the selection of which statistical test to use in comparing test scores from two groups is a Eureka-type problem. How to overcome staff resistance to filling out routine evaluation forms is a non-Eureka problem. Michael Inbar (1979: 135) has summarized the research findings on how groups typically behave when faced with these two different types of problems:

> Specifically, when the problem is of the Eureka type (and is not too complex), the very fact that the problem has a unique and unambiguous solution also implies that mistakes are readily demonstrable. Under such conditions, group problem solving turns out to be more efficient because (1) mutual criticism rapidly uncovers errors, and this reduces the time spent on mistaken paths, and (2) this same process decreases the likelihood that a mistaken solution will be misconstrued by the group as being correct. Conversely, problems which are creative in the sense of accepting a variety of solutions (e.g., devising a cross-word puzzle), tend to have ambiguous cues for gauging the quality of efforts; moreover, this ambiguity is greater the further away one is from a solution—a fact which makes it difficult to evaluate the contribution that intermediate steps make to problem solving. As a consequence, the very same tendency to engage in mutual criticism noted above is instrumental for open-ended problems in breaking up trains of thought, more than it is in correcting "mistakes"; the result, not surprisingly, is a degradation of the quality of problem solving due to mutual interference by the participants.

Nor can evaluators rely on such group techniques as brainstorming to guarantee creativity. Richard Mitchell (1979: 116-117) is an incisive critic of this pervasively used "creative" group process.

> The term "brain storm" was coined in 1906 by Harry Thaw's lawyer. Clouds of witnesses had seen his client pumping bullets into Sanford White, so it seemed that the defendant would need something more than an alibi that would place him in a bowling alley in Union City that very evening. Accordingly, the cunning advocate convinced the jury that Thaw had suffered, that very evening, a violent fit of passing madness, a brain storm, which momentarily excused him from certain moral imperatives. Thus, Thaw escaped the electric chair.

Mitchell goes on to suggest that there is presumably no point in seeking justice for the crimes that result from committee brainstorming sessions since it would be impossible to get a conviction what with the Harry Thaw precedent and all.

In working with a group the evaluator cannot become dependent on the group to come up with all, or even most, of the answers. Sharing responsibility for evaluation decisions doesn't mean shirking responsibility. Creative evaluation requires creative evaluators, a central premise of my earlier book on the subject. The evaluator brings to a task force the knowledge and experience that undergirds the whole evaluation effort. This means that effective evaluators must be skilled group facilitators, must be able to identify what kind of problem has emerged in a particular situation, must be able to adapt the group process to fit the nature of the problem, and must have realistic expectations about how much can be accomplished in group settings. Most work will remain to be done outside the group where the evaluator's creativity is less encumbered by the group process. The group sets the basic direction and establishes the parameters within which the creative evaluator works. Creative, yet practical, evaluation solutions will still require the insights and hard work of individual creative evaluators. The integrity of the utilization-focused evaluation process depends on the evaluator's skill, creativity, and integrity in collaborating with others, and in doing the individual background preparation and homework that fuels the group process.

THE CONCERN FOR SCIENTIFIC INTEGRITY WHILE ESTABLISHING RAPPORT

One of the most common concerns I encounter in doing workshops on utilization-focused evaluation is worry that the evaluator may become co-opted by stakeholders during the collaborative process. How can evaluators maintain their integrity if they become involved in close, collaborative relationships with stakeholders? This is a serious question, one related to the propriety criterion in the new standards of evaluation.

The nature of the relationship between evaluators and the people with whom they work is a complex and controversial one. On the one hand, there is the tradition in social science that researchers should maintain a respectful distance from the people they study to safeguard objectivity and minimize the introduction of personal bias. On the other hand, there is the human relations perspective that emphasizes close, interpersonal contact as a necessary condition for building mutual understanding. Evaluators thus find themselves on the proverbial horns of a dilemma: Getting too close to decision makers may jeopardize scientific objectivity, but staying too distant from decision makers may jeopardize utilization of findings by failing to build rapport and mutual understanding. A program auditor at a U.S. General Accounting Office (GAO) workshop put the issue somewhat less delicately when he asked, "How can we get in bed with decision makers without losing our virginity?"

The answer, I believe, lies in keeping decision makers and stakeholders focused on the empirical nature of the evaluation process. In everyday life people operate on the basis of relatively unconscious assumptions and selective perceptions. They are not used to testing the validity of their assumptions and perceptions. Quite the contrary, they typically admit into their consciousness only that information which reinforces existing values, attitudes, and behavior patterns. People are socialized to operate in accordance with a fairly limited set of cultural patterns—strong patterns of behavior and perception that resist not only change, but even examination.

The empirical basis of evaluation involves making assumptions and values explicit, testing the validity of assumptions, and carefully examining a program to find out what is actually occurring. The integrity of an evaluation depends on its empirical orientation. Likewise, the integrity of an evaluation group process depends on helping participants adopt an empirical perspective. A commitment must be engendered to really find out what is happening, at least as nearly as one can given the limitations of research methods and scarce resources. Engendering this kind of commitment and helping task force participants adopt an empirical orientation involve the evaluator in the roles of teacher and trainer.

The evaluator begins building this empirical orientation at the very first task force meeting when the purpose of the evaluation is discussed and major evaluation questions or issues are clarified and identified. In *Utilization-Focused Evaluation* (Patton, 1978), I listed seven criteria for good evaluation questions, the first two of which emphasize the empirical nature of evaluation.

(1) It is possible to bring data to bear on the question.
(2) There is more than one possible answer to the question, i.e., the answer is not predetermined by the phrasing of the question.
(3) The identified decision makers *want* information to help answer the question.
(4) The identified decision makers feel they *need* information to help them answer the question.
(5) The identified and organized decision makers and information users want to answer the question for themselves, not just for someone else.
(6) They care about the answer to the question.
(7) The decision makers can indicate how they would use the answer to the question, i.e., they can specify the relevance of an answer to the question for future action.

The integrity of the evaluation rests firmly on the first two criteria. The relevance of the evaluation depends on the remaining five criteria. Emphasizing the empirical nature of evaluation doesn't mean that values are ignored. The making of judgments and decisions necessarily involves values. But value questions in and of themselves are not answerable empirically. It is critical, therefore, to separate the empirical question from the values question in the phrasing of the evaluation issue.

When stakeholders first begin discussing the purpose of an evaluation they will often do so in nonempirical terms. "We want to *prove* the program's effectiveness." Proving effectiveness is a public relations job, not an evaluation task. This statement tells the evaluator about that person's attitude toward the program, and it indicates a need for diplomatically, sensitively, but determinedly, reorienting that stakeholder from a concern with public relations to a concern with learning about and documenting actual program activities and effects. The evaluator need not be frightened by such public relations statements. It's best to get such inclinations out in the open. Then the work begins of moving toward an empirical process as, for example, in the scenario that follows.

Program Director: "We want to prove the program's effectiveness."

Evaluator: "What kind of information would do that?"

Program Director: "Information about how much people like the program."

Evaluator: "Does everyone like the program?"

Program Director: "I think most everyone does."

Evaluator: "Well, we could find out just how many do, and how many don't. So there's a reasonable evaluation question: 'What are participants' attitudes toward the program?' Later we'll need to get more specific about how to measure their attitudes, but first let's consider some other things we could find out. Assuming that some people don't like the program, what could be learned from them?"

Program Director: "I suppose we could find out what they don't like and why."

Evaluator: "Would that kind of information be helpful in looking at the program, to find out about its strengths and weaknesses so that perhaps you could improve it in some ways?" (This is a deliberately leading question to which it is very hard to say "No.")

Program Director: "Well, we know some of the reasons, but we can always learn more."

Evaluator: "What other information would be helpful in studying the program to find out about its strengths and weaknesses?" (Here the evaluator has carefully rephrased the original concern from "proving the program's effectiveness" to "finding out about the program strengths and weaknesses.")

In the dialogue above the evaluator chips away at the decision maker's biased public relations perspective by carefully allowing an empirical perspective to emerge. At some point the evaluator may want to, or need to, address the public relations concern with a bit of a speech (or sermonette).

> I know you're concerned about proving the program's effectiveness. This is a natural concern. A major and common purpose of evaluation is to gather information so that judgments can be made about the value of a program. To what extent is it effective? To what extent is it worthwhile?

> The problem is that if we only gathered and presented positive information about the program, it might lack credibility. You're sophisticated people. You know that if you read a report that only says good things about a program you figure something is being covered up. In my experience an evaluation has more credibility and usefulness if it's balanced. Everyone knows that no program is perfect, and I've never seen a program yet in which everyone was happy and everyone achieved all their goals. You may find that it's better to study and document both strengths and weaknesses, areas of effectiveness, and areas of ineffectiveness, and then show that you're serious about improving the program by presenting a strategy for dealing with weaknesses and areas of ineffectiveness. By doing that you establish your credibility as serious program developers who can deal openly and effectively with inevitable problems.

Sometimes the opposite bias is the problem. Someone is determined to kill a program, to present only negative findings, and to "prove" that the program is ineffective. In such cases the evaluator can emphasize what can be learned by finding out about the program's strengths. Few programs are complete disasters. An empirical approach means gathering data on *actual* program activities and effects, and then presenting those data in a fair and balanced way so that information users and decision makers can make their own judgments about goodness or badness, effectiveness or ineffectiveness. Such judgments, however, are separate from the data. In my experience, evaluation task force members will readily move into this kind of empirical orientation as they come to understand its usefulness and fairness. It's the evaluator's job to help them achieve that understanding and adopt that perspective.

In essence, the evaluator invites task force participants to enter into the culture of science. To most stakeholders science is a world quite different from their ordinary reality. The rules of procedure are different. The purposes are different. Certainly the language is different. And scientists are the alien creatures from that strange, different world. Scientists have typically worked in relative isolation from the general population. Several popular images symbolize the separation of scientists from the masses: the white lab coat, the image of the ivory tower, cartoons of scientists able to (and wanting to) communicate only with computers, the idea of the scientist working day and night in the isolation of the office or laboratory, jokes about the unintelligible rantings and ravings of mad scientists, and the absent-minded professor who is so absorbed in work that norms of simple etiquette and everyday grooming are ignored (e.g., no time for washing and combing of hair). Scientists have been known to play on these images, even to enhance them, so as to maintain and enlarge the scientific mystique, thereby engendering awe of and respect for Science and scientists. Thus evaluators, as scientists, are sometimes reluctant to invite stakeholders into the culture of science, for research may thereby lose its enigmatic magic. Those evaluators who do extend the invitation may find that, even as they are worrying about maintaining their integrity, the people with whom they're working are worrying about what kind of relationships they can risk with a science-type who, by definition, is likely to be arrogant, intolerant, and condescending. *Decision makers and information users also have concerns about maintaining their integrity.*

Social scientists who study the use and dissemination of scientific knowledge have formally acknowledged this traditional separation of scientists from nonscientists as a major factor explaining communications difficulties between the two groups. The Two Communities Theory of Nathan Caplan (1979) and colleagues (Caplan et al., 1975) at the Center for Research on Utilization of Scientific Knowledge, University of Michigan, attempts to explain how dissemination of scientific knowledge is hampered by differences in values, language, social contacts, and reward systems between members of scientific and nonscientific "communities." It is typically difficult to bridge this cultural gap between scientists and the general population.

Evaluators, as social science practitioners, are subject to the same communications impediments as other scientists when the issue becomes how to get nonscientists to use research processes and findings. The metaphor of two communities (Dunn, 1980) is helpful in thinking about the difficulties that can arise if one community wants to communicate effectively with the other community. Concern about evaluators working and communicating effectively with nonevaluators is central to the problem of working effectively with an evaluation task force. That's why I like the motif of dual communities or dual cultures. For both evaluators and nonscientists the shared task force experience can be a kind of cross-cultural one. When I invite task force participants to enter into the culture of science, learn some evaluation jargon, consider research options, and adopt an empirical perspective, I expect to reciprocate by learning about and experiencing the culture of the program and its staff—their language, their ideology, their world view. Cross-cultural exchanges always involve the possibility that the visitor will "go native." But evaluators cannot expect nonscientists to take the risk of adopting an empirical perspective unless they too are willing to take some of the reciprocal risks of cross-cultural exposure.

As I write this I'm living and working in Trinidad. It's Carnival season and the air is nightly filled with sounds of steel drums and calypso music. Masquerade bands are busy preparing their costumes. Rum shops are doing a brisk business. Carnival in Trinidad is not just a short festive season, it is a way of life, what people here refer to as the "Carnival mentality," sometimes pointed to as a matter of considerable cultural pride, and sometimes disparaged as symbolic of "what is wrong with Trinidad." In inviting Caribbean decision makers to experience the culture of science as we work together in planning and evaluation efforts, my credibility and effectiveness depend in part on my willingness to experience and show respect for local cultural patterns, particularly different orientations toward time, work, efficiency, and lifestyle, where they often *expect* to encounter intolerance based on past experiences. Their willingness to participate in and experience the culture of science (in which they are keenly interested) is directly proportional to their perceptions of my willingness to participate in and experience their culture.

While the Caribbean example represents a stark contrast to the culture of science, the same principle of cross-cultural sensitivity and need for intercultural communication (Asante et al., 1979) holds in less obviously divergent settings. A counseling center, a welfare program, an art group, a school, a corporation, a prison, a police academy, a health clinic are all "cross-cultural" settings in which I've worked as an evaluator. Each experience provided opportunities for mutual exchange as I worked to introduce an appreciation of the empirical perspective from the culture of science.

One other example may help illustrate the difference between an empirical and nonempirical orientation within the context of cross-cultural understanding. A common problem in an initial task force meeting is that evaluation questions and issues are stated in value-laden, nonempirical terms. For example, decision makers may want to study *improvements* brought about by a program. Are services improving? Are clients being helped? Are program participants doing better? Are staff becoming more effective?

Assessing improvement involves making a judgment about whether or not an observed impact is desirable or undesirable. It is important to separate the issue of improvement from the related but quite different issue of impact or change. Improvement involves a judgment about whether or not something is better, whereas impact involves the more limited question of whether or not something is different. An observed difference may or may not constitute improvement, depending on who is making the value judgment about whether or not the change is for better or worse. It is crucial throughout the evaluation process that empirical observations about program impact be kept separate from judgments about whether or not such impact constitutes improvement or effectiveness.

Questions of right and wrong, better or worse, are not simple empirical questions. To formulate evaluation questions solely in value terms can sabotage an evaluation from the beginning. The empirical question is not improvement but change, and the extent of change.

The evaluator must do two things when stakeholders suggest that the evaluation focus on such value-laden issues as improvement or effectiveness. First, the evaluator must work with stakeholders to determine what empirical information and data are needed to make judgments about improvement or effectiveness. Second, the evaluator must help make a shift from asking absolute, dichotomous questions ("Is the program effective?") to asking relative, continuum-based, and open questions ("To what extent and in what ways is the program effective?"). Thus the initial issue of proving the program's effectiveness becomes a set of empirical evaluation questions:

- To what extent and in what ways have clients changed?
- What are the attitudes of clients about the program?
- What is the relative strength of those attitudes?
- What do staff and clients do in the program?

These are empirical questions. When these kinds of questions are asked in an evaluation the evaluators have established a solid foundation for a credible process that has integrity. Answers to these questions can be used by a variety of people to make judgments about the program. Of course, decisions will still have to be made about specific issues for intensive study, what data to gather, and how to report findings. Continuing judgments are necessary to maintain balance, credibility, and fairness. Undergirding all such decisions is the evaluator's commitment to keeping the focus on the *empirical* nature of the evaluation process.

In closing this section on maintaining one's integrity while establishing rapport, I should probably explain why I have not emphasized (or even mentioned) the importance of objectivity. The concern about integrity usually goes hand-in-hand with a fear of losing objectivity, or at least of being accused of losing one's objectivity. A parallel concern is being sure that the evaluation gets at the Truth. Elsewhere I have discussed at greater length the illusiveness of truth and objectivity (Patton, 1978: 216-223, 1980: 267-283). Without going into a lengthy philosophical discussion, let me suggest that from a practical perspective, utilization-focused evaluation replaces the search for truth with a search for useful and balanced information, and replaces the mandate to be objective with a mandate to be fair and conscientious in taking account of multiple perspectives, multiple interests, and multiple realities. In this regard, Egon Guba (1981: 76-77) suggests that evaluators could learn a great deal by adopting the stance of investigative journalists.

> Journalism in general and investigative journalism in particular are moving away from the criterion of objectivity to an emergent criterion usually labeled "fairness." . . . Objectivity assumes a single reality to which the story or evaluation must be isomorphic; it is in this sense a one-perspective criterion. It assumes that an agent can deal with an object (or another person) in a nonreactive and noninteractive way. It is an absolute criterion.
>
> Journalists are coming to feel that objectivity in that sense is unattainable. . . .
>
> Enter "fairness" as a substitute criterion. In contrast to objectivity, fairness has these features:
>
> - It assumes multiple realities or truths—hence a test of fairness is whether or not "both" sides of the case are presented, and there may even be multiple sides.
>
> - It is adversarial rather than one-perspective in nature. Rather than trying to hew the line with *the* truth, as the objective reporter does, the fair reporter seeks to present each side of the case in the manner of an advocate—as, for example, attorneys do in making a case in court. The presumption is that the public, like a jury, is more likely to reach an equitable decision after having heard each side presented with as much vigor and commitment as possible.
>
> - It is assumed that the subject's reaction to the reporter and interaction between them heavily determines what the reporter perceives. Hence one test of fairness is the length to which the reporter will go to test his own biases and rule them out.
>
> - It is a relative criterion that is measured by *balance* rather than by isomorphism to enduring truth.
>
> Clearly, evaluators have a great deal to learn from this development.

Ultimately, there are no simple rules one can follow to guarantee evaluator integrity. Evaluators can expect to be attacked by those who don't like or may be hurt by evaluation processes and findings. Integrity is a matter of working out one's own personal and professional standards, and then working to adhere to them, while being ready to examine and learn from likely failings along the way. Then there's the advice on balance and fairness given by Halcolm to his students:

> *Being an evaluator is like being a fireplug in a dogpound. At times you can expect to be wet on from all sides. You don't really have to worry until one side starts getting cold.*

GETTING COLLABORATIVE EVALUATION CONTRACTS

One very real problem facing evaluators who adopt a utilization-focused perspective is how to get evaluation contracts. It is beyond the scope of this book to discuss the intricacies of consulting and contracting in detail. However, given the themes of this chapter two points can be made. Getting collaborative evaluation contracts depends on (1) selling evaluation funders on the applicability and usefulness of the utilization-focused evaluation process and (2) establishing one's credibility for facilitating and implementing that process. In short, both the process and the evaluator must be credible to evaluators. The new standards of evaluation include a statement on the importance of credibility (Joint Committee, 1981: 24):

Standard

The persons conducting the evaluation should be both trustworthy and competent to perform the evaluation, so that their findings achieve maximum credibility and acceptance.

Overview

Evaluators are credible to the extent that they exhibit the training, technical competence, substantive knowledge, experience, integrity, public relations skills, and other characteristics considered necessary by the client and other users of the evaluation reports. Since few individuals possess all of the characteristics needed for particular evaluations, it is often necessary that an evaluation be done by a team of persons who collectively possess those qualifications.

Evaluators should establish their credibility with the client and other users at the outset of the evaluation. If the confidence and trust of these audiences cannot be secured, the evaluators should seriously consider not proceeding. For, if they go ahead when they are not considered qualified by their audiences, they may find later that their findings and recommendations—however technically adequate— are ignored or rejected.

In conducting an evaluation, evaluators should maintain a pattern of consistent, open, and continuing communication with their client. They should also keep in mind that the fundamental test of their credibility will rest in an ability to defend the technical adequacy, integrity, utility, and practicality of their reports.

Alkin et al. (1979: 245-247) have discussed the importance of credibility as a factor in the utilization of evaluations.

> The trust that the user places in the evaluator is specific. That is, the evaluator is accorded trust and credibility only on certain matters, and this judgment of credibility is subject to change. Furthermore, different users often disagree in their judgments of the credibility of an evaluator. Some users may assign the evaluator high credibility in a wide range of areas; others, perhaps approaching the evaluation from a different vantage point, may assign the evaluator credibility on a narrowed range of topics.
>
> We refer to the fact that credibility is limited only to certain specific users and in certain areas as the *specificity* of an evaluator's credibility.
>
> Consideration of areas of credibility alone is not sufficient without also examining the specific audiences to whom the evaluator is credible.
>
> In discussing the evaluator's credibility to specific audiences and on specific matters we must also note that there is a *changeability* in the perceptions of an evaluator's credibility. As evaluators engage in their activities, they may come to be viewed as credible on a wider range of topics or credible to new audiences. Alternatively, the range of their credibility might stay relatively constant or even contract as a result of some action or event.
>
> In part, the evaluator's credibility is a function of the expertise he possesses. But changes in credibility can come about when the evaluator has opportunities to demonstrate his abilities and skills in relation to new issues and for new audiences.

Evaluation, like other professions, requires establishing a track record, cultivating potential clients and users of one's services, knowing how to find out what is needed, and being responsive to those needs. The most difficult problem in this regard is responding to requests for proposals. Under many bidding and contracting arrangements a formal and official document is published or distributed by an agency requesting evaluation proposals. These requests typically contain information about the program to be evaluated and parameters for the evaluation. If one wants to employ a utilization-focused approach that involves forming a task force to share in the making of evaluation decisions, it can be difficult to respond to requests for proposals with sufficient specificity to win the contract. What to do?

My own approach is to respond by describing the *process* I would use in conducting the evaluation and limiting the actual content to an indication of some of the major options and methods that would be considered in the process. I want to establish that I have specific ideas about how to conduct the evaluation, and these I would specify as methodological and measurement *possibilities*, but I also want to emphasize the importance of engaging in a collaborative process before bringing closure to the evaluation design. This means describing the purposes and nature of utilization-focused evaluation.

In short, it means selling the process while establishing methodological credibility through the description of design alternatives. (The utilization-focused evaluation flowchart presented earlier in this chapter was originally developed for use in responding to requests for proposals, to help describe the process being proposed.)

My own commitment to the collaborative process means that I am unwilling to specify general models or methods that can be applied across the board. Situational responsiveness cannot be optimized if one approaches an evaluation problem with a single, content-laden model in mind. Yet many program directors, evaluation funders, and evaluators still labor under the notion that there is some ideal design or model that is generally applicable across situations. A case in point was a special symposium sponsored by *Evaluation and Change* magazine to address the question of how to evaluate human services integration. The implication of the symposium topic was that there exists some single ideal design (methods and measurement) that can be applied generically to the evaluation of human services integration. In many ways, the symposium was like a request for proposals. My responses to the symposium questions posed by the editor of *Evaluation and Change,* Larry Kivens, illustrate how I attempt to focus attention on the collaborative process rather than on the specific content of an evaluation when I am asked how I would go about conducting an evaluation on some particular topic or for some particular program.

Kivens: To the extent that human services integration involves political balancing of power as well as administrative reorganization, by what standards should the effects of services integration be measured?

Patton: Standards for measuring the effects of services integration should be developed separately for each program based upon the information needs of specified decision makers and information users. There are no standards that can be applied across the board to all human services integration systems because systems will vary from place to place depending upon local needs and circumstances. Evaluation designs should be sensitive to those local variations and to the information needs of local decision makers.

Kivens: Given the complexity of organizational processes and arrangements in the integration of human services, what evaluation methods would be most suitable for determining the effects of services integration? Are existing measurement methods relevant, or do new ones need to be developed?

Patton: Just as it is impossible to specify universal outcomes or standards, it is also inappropriate to specify some universal set of measures or methods to be used in evaluating human services integration. The method selected should be appropriate for the kind of evaluation questions asked by local decision makers. Given the variety of methods currently available, it is unlikely that any new generic methods are necessary. Rather, what is necessary is that the methods and measurements used be credible, relevant, and appropriate. These criteria and their particular meaning should be developed through interactions with identified and organized decision makers and information users.

Kivens: Are there any special problems that you see as occurring in the conduct of the evaluation, and how would you go about dealing with them?

Patton: Given the framework I have outlined, the major problem to be anticipated is the large number of constituencies that need to be served through evaluation. This may mean that an evaluator would be faced with the problem of dealing with multiple and conflicting individuals or groups who have vested interests in particular evaluation findings. While it would take more evaluator time, I would deal with this problem by formation of an evaluation task force representing relevant constituencies. A variety of group process techniques are available for helping such a group reach consensus about the nature of information that is needed.

Kivens: What procedure should be employed in order to insure the integrity and accuracy of the evaluation?

Patton: The process used for formation of the evaluation task force is critical. The task force must be composed of people who can be seriously educated about evaluation options. A commitment to the conduct of a useful evaluation must be developed. As the evaluator interacts with members of the evaluation task force the evaluator's standards for what constitutes integrity and accuracy can be made explicit. The values of identified decision makers and information users concerning integrity and accuracy are also critical. In short, the precise meaning of "integrity" and "accuracy" should be made explicit as part of the negotiations engaged in by the evaluation research task force. All decisions made should be well reasoned, carefully documented, and quite explicit. Where constraints imposed by resources, politics, or time affect the evaluation design, these constraints should be made explicit. Finally, by exploring a variety of methods for collecting data on any particular evaluation questions or options, it is possible for the evaluator to show evaluation task force members how they can increase the integrity and accuracy of any evaluation through the use of multiple methods.

Kivens: Given the methods that you've described and the designs by which you would choose to implement them, how would you deal with the issue of causality—for example, between a policy change and a change in service delivery?

Patton: First, it is important to realize that many of the important information questions that may arise in designing the evaluation may not involve issues of causality. If local decision makers and information users want to monitor changes in attitudes or behaviors among staff, clients, funders, or other actors in a system, it is not necessary to presuppose that the collection of such information necessitates a causal framework. What decision makers and information users are looking for may well be information to guide them in making immediate and concrete decisions. Under such conditions they are concerned more with the meaningfulness of particular information about what is happening than they are with comprehensive, causal questions.

At the same time, it behooves an evaluator as part of the educational process involved in interactions with the evaluation task force to raise the level of sophistication about the difficulties and complexities of causal questions. In many cases, local decision makers and information users are already sophisticated about these issues. If local decision makers and information users decide to undertake an investigation of causal relationships, then it is the role of the evaluator to help them explore the most appropriate research design and measurement tools for investigating the issue of causality. The impetus for such an investigation, however, should come from the evaluation task force and should not be unilaterally imposed by the evaluator.

Kivens: Under what conditions would you participate in an evaluation such as you've described?

Patton: I would participate in such an evaluation when and if I were convinced that an evaluation task force could be formed of decision makers and information users who were committed to collecting useful information, and we were able to determine together how such information could affect program decision making, planning, and development.

Kivens: If an evaluation of the sort you recommend were conducted how would you decide whether or not it had been successful?

Patton: My major criteria for success would be the extent to which evaluation information was actually used by decision makers and information users. That is the crux of a utilization-focused approach to evaluation.

The thrust of these comments is that there can be no single model for evaluating services integration because the information needs of decision makers involved in integrating human services will vary from situation to situation. The processes of human services integration are not directed at any universal outcomes that can be imposed as evaluation criteria in any and all situations. The needs of decision makers for information about the relative attainment of specific outcomes will vary as the processes of integration change. The search for a single model of evaluation that can be applied to a broad range of human services integration is likely to distract evaluators from the task of providing information that is highly useful and relevant to a particular situation precisely because that information is relevant and useful in that particular situation. While it is neither appropriate nor desirable to specify a single model of evaluation for human services integration, particularly a model that specifies universal outcomes and inflexible ways of measuring those outcomes, it *is* possible to specify an ideal evaluation process. Such a process would involve active-reactive-adaptive evaluators in the conduct of utilization-focused evaluation. This same process orientation is appropriate in responding to requests for proposals.

AN EXAMPLE OF THE COLLABORATIVE PROCESS

This chapter has been about working with decision makers and information users in a collaborative process aimed at increasing the utility—and actual use—of evaluation processes and findings. The first part of the chapter built a rationale for employing a collaborative group approach. The second part of the chapter was a discussion of practical ways of actually working with an evaluation task force. To help ground these ideas in practical application this chapter closes with presentation of an extended example of utilization- and user-focused evaluation. Two themes have been central to this chapter, and those two themes are predominant in this example.

First, it's not the amount of time spent working with people that makes for an effective consulting process; it's the *quality* of time spent together that matters. Too often utilization-focused evaluation is interpreted as a demand that evaluators spend an enormous amount of time in interpersonal interaction with stakeholders. The point of this chapter is that it's what you do that's important, not how long it takes. A lot can be accomplished under severe time constraints.

The second key factor to successful consulting, in my opinion, is who you work with in an evaluation process. That's the whole point of careful identification of *relevant* and *interested* decision makers, information users, and stakeholders as the first step in utilization-focused evaluation. That's also the conceptual message in the phrase "user-focused evaluation." An effective collaborative effort depends on doing the right thing with the right people. The Caribbean example that follows emphasizes these points as they apply to a fairly complex project involving literally hundreds of people in eight different countries.

The Caribbean Agricultural Extension Project

The Caribbean Agricultural Extension Project (CAEP) is an evaluation and planning project aimed at improving extension services in nine English-speaking Caribbean countries. A brief description of the situation in the target countries will help establish a context for the analysis that follows: The nine nations and territories invited to participate in the project—Antigua, Barbados, Belize, Dominica, Grenada, Montserrat, St. Kitts/Nevis, St. Lucia, and St. Vincent/Grenadines—share common agricultural concerns despite their great differences in ecological conditions, cropping patterns, population densities, and land tenure systems. All are net food importers. The profitability and social prestige of agriculture are generally low. The very small size of most farms demands off-farm jobs, and part-time farming hinders the work of extension agents. Problems of training, personnel, transportation, interagency coordination, and politicization burden many extension programs. The coordinated efforts of the Caribbean Agricultural Extension Project are intended to help participating governments in designing and implementing more effective extension programs, and so improve the economic and social well being of the small-farm families.

While these countries are all basically agricultural and share the need for improved extension services, the diversity in the region is quite striking. Chief crops vary from sugar cane in St. Kitts, to hot peppers in Montserrat, arrowroot in St. Vincent, bananas in Dominica and St. Lucia, and cotton in

Nevis. Large areas of uncultivated land exist in Belize, but a scarcity of land prevails on many of the islands. Soils and ecological systems differ markedly throughout the islands. For example, although St. Kitts and Nevis are separated by only two miles at the nearest point, the soil on St. Kitts is fairly sandy, while that on Nevis has a much higher clay composition; the two islands, despite their proximity, have very different geological histories.

Land area, population size, and population density also depict a region of historical, cultural, and agricultural diversity. Belize has a land area of nearly 9,000 square miles and a population of 136,000; Barbados has nearly twice that many people (247,000) on 166 square miles; and Montserrat, the smallest of the islands (39 square miles), has a population of about 12,000.

The distances involved between Caribbean countries are enormous. The first principal of the University College of the West Indies wrote of the geographical problem of the area served by the University in the following terms:

> The British Caribbean colonies are sometimes thought of as a compact group like the Hebrides, but this is an illusion based on looking at small-scale maps. To translate the distances into European terms, let us place British Honduras (Belize), the most westerly of the Colonies, at London. Jamaica is then roughly at Danzig in the Baltic, Trinidad is at Odessa in the Black Sea, with the Windwards and Leewards stretching up north far to the east of Moscow and British Guiana is Asia Minor, almost at Batum. Or in other terms, British Guiana to British Honduras is as far as Cornwall is from Newfoundland. Yet in all these distances the population is only of the order of three million [Henderson, 1973].

In U.S. terms, if Belize were superimposed over southern Oregon and Northern California, Jamaica would lie in Eastern Wyoming; St. Kitts/Nevis would be islands in Lake Michigan, with the other Leeward and Windward islands extending down to the Kentucky/Tennessee border; Trinidad would occupy Northeastern Alabama, with Tobago to the Northeast in Tennessee; Guyana would extend from Southwest Georgia, across Northwest Florida, into the Gulf of Mexico.

Political diversity contributes to the complexity of the situation in the Caribbean. Five of the islands in the project have been independent countries for several years; two became independent in 1981; one is an Associated State under Britain, moving toward independence; and one is still a British colony. Political allegiances span the spectrum from left oriented to conservative.

In each participating country, a National Extension Planning Committee was established by the Minister of Agriculture to give local direction and meaning to the evaluation and planning processes. In effect, then, the Caribbean Agricultural Extension Project provides nine case examples of evaluation efforts, each of which involved different participants, information users, and stakeholders. In each case, the personal factor greatly affected the nature of the evaluation and planning process.

The positions involved

Our analysis begins with the seven key individuals who were initially involved in the evaluation planning process in each country:

(1) *Minister of Agriculture (MA)*—the elected member of Parliament whose portfolio includes, but is seldom limited to, agriculture. One minister with whom we worked managed at least seven portfolios (e.g., agriculture, tourism, energy, industry, lands, fisheries, transportation)

(2) *Permanent Secretary (PS)*—the senior civil servant (political appointment) in the ministry of agriculture with overall administrative responsibility for ministry affairs

(3) *Chief Agricultural Officer (CAO)*—highest-ranking technical official with overall managerial responsibility in the ministry

(4) *Director of Extension (DOE)*—highest-ranking extension specialist usually reports directly to the CAO

(5) *University of the West Indies (UWI) Outreach Professional*—a staff member of the Department of Extension, UWI, assigned to direct the project in an outreach area (e.g., Windwards, Leewards, or Belize)

(6) *MUCIA Project Associate*—a staff member of one of seven American universities in the Midwest Universities Consortium for International Activities (MUCIA) assigned to a UWI outreach office as counterpart of the UWI Outreach Professional

(7) *Liaison Officer*—a member of the extension staff of each participating country assigned to the project to coordinate and assist with national extension evaluation and planning activities

In each country the constellation of these seven key people represented a unique set of interactions. In some cases the minister of agriculture showed a great deal of personal interest in the project; in other cases the minister made the necessary public declaration of support, then quickly turned all responsibility over to others. Some ministers had an agricultural background, while some did not; some even had extension experience. Some had held office for several years; others were new to their position. Since the minister of agriculture was the key official who would have to approve plans based on evaluation findings, it became critical to the project that ways be found of soliciting each minister's views and getting his attention. How this was done, and the extent to which ministerial interest was maintained, varied from country to country, depending in large part on the relationship between the minister and the chief agricultural officer (CAO). In some cases the relationship was a close one of mutual trust and respect; in other cases the relationship was competitive or conflict laden; sometimes a power struggle was going on between these two powerful people; and in still other cases the CAO was the real power in the ministry, effectively controlling a weak or otherwise preoccupied minister of agriculture. While being aware of these various relationships and taking them into consideration throughout the process, it was critical that project staff adopt a stance of neutrality with regard to internal ministry power struggles. *Being sensitive to power struggles, personality conflicts, and feelings of mutual distrust or disrespect is not the same thing as taking sides.* As external consultants and advisers, we attempted to encourage expression of a full range of concerns and views without becoming aligned with any one perspective. We feel that our position in this regard was critical to overall project credibility when operating in often volatile political environments. It is important to be clear, then, that user-focused evaluation does not mean building alignments with one political group against another. Rather, it means being sensitive to, and respectful of, how political and personal predispositions affect the direction and utilization of evaluation processes.

Without attempting to fully elaborate all of the personal factors that affected the evaluation and planning process in each country, it may be helpful to illustrate at least a few additional nuances that made differences in what information was gathered and how it was used.

The experience, interest, and morale of directors of extension greatly affected their personal involvement in the project. In some cases directors of extension played an active and influential role; in other cases the directors of extension were background figures in the shadow of the CAO or some influential planning committee member.

The role of the liaison officer varied tremendously from country to country. Some liaison officers were highly committed to and enthusiastic about the project; others were difficult to motivate and involve. Some had evaluation and planning experience; others had no previous experience handling data. Some required a great deal of direct supervision; others showed unusual personal initiative and the ability to handle considerable responsibility. Thus it was impossible to write a uniform job description for all liaison officers (which they requested) because we wanted to adapt their roles and responsibilities to their backgrounds, capabilities, and interests.

Finally, the UWI and MUCIA professional staff who were serving as advisers and consultants to the national committees left their own marks on the evaluation and planning process. Such personal characteristics as their diplomatic sensitivity, their tolerance for ambiguity, their willingness to assume a background/supportive stance (as opposed to a foreground/controlling stance), their experience in handling data, their group process skills, and their writing ability all affected the outcomes and utilization of the evaluation and planning processes.

The point of these examples is to illustrate the importance of individuals—the personal factor—to an understanding of utilization dynamics. No uniform, standardized evaluation and planning process could be imposed on the kind of diversity—personal and situational—exemplified by the Caribbean Agricultural Extension Project. While the original project design paper set forth a fairly straightforward and routine set of procedures, the actual implementation of the project required considerable flexibility and individualization in response to situational and personal factor variations.

Project identification

Since a user-focused evaluation process requires active involvement of and sensitivity to specific users, it is desirable for the people who are to use the information being generated to relate to the project in some specific way. Two of the earliest problems we experienced in this regard were:

(1) establishing a unique and memorable identity for the project, and
(2) communicating the importance of the evaluation process, since government participants were universally anxious to get on with the actual delivery of services (and aid moneys), and often saw the 18-month evaluation and planning process as an unnecessary and undesirable delay.

The solution to both problems provides yet another perspective on the personal factor.

The Caribbean Agricultural Extension Project is one of those multiple-institution efforts that create special identification problems. The project is under the direction of the Department of Agricultural Extension in the Faculty of Agriculture at the University of the West Indies with technical and staff support from the Midwestern Universities Consortium for International Activities (MUCIA), which had designated the University of Minnesota as the "lead" university for MUCIA. The project was funded by the U.S. Agency for International Development (AID). Identification problems arose because the faculty of the University of the West Indies has multiple contacts and activities in the project countries; there are also many contacts and activities involving various U.S. universities, including individual MUCIA member institutions; and AID funds a number of projects, including many in agriculture in participating territories.

Further complicating the identification problem was the relatively large number of projects within these countries, and specifically within the ministries of agriculture. The Caribbean Agricultural Extension Project was an attempt to use the project approach as an initial springboard for encompassing the entire extension division in each country. Thus the project needed to establish a specific, visible, and recognizable identity that would simultaneously promote project objectives *and* ministry of agriculture objectives. This meant that what began through the stimulus of outside activity had to be internalized as a national project owned and operated by local people. The message we wanted to communicate was that this was *their* project, not *our* project. We were providing support, advice, and consultation for them to learn things *they* needed to know to evaluate and plan *their* own programs. This transference of project ownership and direction from the external "experts" to the local information users is critical to the user-focused evaluation process. It was, and often is, the most difficult part of that process.

Initially the project was described as a UWI or MUCIA or AID project. At the national level, however, we wanted the evaluation and planning process to be identified as a national effort with UWI support. The critical step in accomplishing this project identification was establishment of national extension planning committees with *real* responsibility for the evaluation and planning process. These committees, representing broad agricultural interests, were uncertain of their purpose and often skeptical about their tasks. From their past experiences, committee members seemed to expect the committees to be used in merely token ways with the external "experts" doing the real work and making the real decisions. To counter this impression we had to be firm and consistent in placing the center of responsibility with the committees and the ministry.

National extension planning committees

The members of the committees were appointed by the minister of agriculture and were expected to be responsible to the minister so that plans developed would be approved by participating governments. There was considerable initial confusion about these national planning committees. It took considerable explanation and repetition to firmly establish the idea that these were truly *national* committees responsible for deliberating on issues of national concern. They were not CAEP committees to be controlled (or even chaired) by CAEP staff. CAEP staff were to be support staff working for the committees, but not directing and/or controlling the committees.

In addition to producing a plan, an equally important reason for establishing national planning committees was to provide a mechanism for involving diverse segments of the agricultural community in the analysis and planning processes. *The national planning committees brought the private sector face to face with the public sector to discuss, analyze, and make decisions about agricultural development in general, and extension in particular.* In every participating territory, farmers were represented on the committee. Farmers were often the most outspoken critics of current extension practices on the committees. Where they existed, private extension organizations were represented on the committees, like the Organization for Rural Development in St. Vincent, the Banana Growers Association throughout the Windwards, and the Belize Agricultural Society in Belize. Banks, credit organizations, commodity associations, agricultural research professionals, marketing board representatives, estate managers (e.g., in Montserrat), nutritionists (e.g., in

Antigua), and extension staff were represented on various committees. The committee membership always included both private sector and public sector participants. All committees also included women, including women's desk representatives, where such an office existed (e.g., in Antigua and St. Lucia). The Montserrat Committee, for example, included the Farmer of the Year who, in 1981, was a woman.

Broad representation on national planning committees was considered critical to the success and legitimacy of the planning process. In cases in which initial ministerial appointments seemed overly narrow, CAEP staff requested additional appointments to the committees.

Committee processes: some lessons

The processes involved in getting the committees to take up their responsibilities revealed several patterns that we observed across country cases. These patterns are illustrative of the kinds of processes one can expect in planning and evaluation committees.

First, the substantive discussions flowed from general to specific. Each committee devoted some initial time to what we came to call "ventilation sessions" in which participants would share views, complain, pontificate, and offer solutions to a full range of agriculture and development problems (need for markets, lack of feeder roads, high costs and/or unavailability of productive inputs, and so on). These issues were often only marginally related to extension services, but we found that until these issues had been ventilated, participants were unwilling to get down to the specifics of extension evaluation and planning.

A second, and closely related, process was the establishment of territoriality around pet personal issues. Ventilation discussions were an opportunity for committee members to tell each other what they really cared about. In user-focused evaluation, when one is striving to build on the interests and competences of participants, it is especially important to be aware of, and sensitive to, the pet personal issues of those with whom one is working.

Third, and again closely related to the foregoing, was the process of establishing professional identity on the committee. Participants had been selected because of both their personal knowledge and their professional network connections. Some committee members would place great importance on their status as representative of others (farmers, extension agents, creditors or bankers, marketing board, commodity associations, cooperatives, and the like). Other committee members participated primarily representing themselves and their own personal views. To understand the political relevance of participant contributions, it was helpful to pay attention to whom participants felt they were representing, as well as to what ideas they most cared about (e.g., guaranteed markets).

A fourth pattern that was universal in its nagging consistency was the necessity of explaining the project over and over again. This relates to the basic problem of project identification discussed in the previous section. Project staff had to be careful *not* to assume that participants understood or remembered the precise nature of this particular project. In as little as a week's time many committee members might have contact with as many as ten to twenty different development projects. The higher the status and position of a participant, the more important it was to be mindful of the need to reexplain continually, but subtly, the project.

A fifth committee pattern that led to regular staff frustrations was the seeming impossibility of finding a "best" way to get information to participants. We mention this difficulty to alert students or planners/evaluators somewhat inexperienced in committee dynamics to the near universality of this motif. The problem has several manifestations:

(1) Failure to provide participants with papers, tables, reports, or literature in advance will lead to complaints that participants can't see how they can discuss the issues without having the opportunity to fully read the report or study the data in question. But . . .
(2) Giving out reports in advance doesn't lead to their being read in advance of a meeting. Whether a paper or report is given out in advance or distributed for the first time at a particular meeting, it will be necessary in *both* cases carefully to go over the document in the meeting. Documents should be prepared in such a way that key points are easy to locate and understand.

Finally, a sixth important pattern that can be critical to the ultimate effectiveness of a user-focused approach was the importance of talking with, interviewing, and soliciting the views of the committee participants on a one-to-one basis outside committee meetings. A user-focused approach requires sensitivity to individuals beyond what can be accomplished entirely in group meetings.

THE PROCESS AS AN END IN ITSELF

The usual emphasis and concern when discussing evaluation utilization is on the substantive decisions that are made as a result of planning and evaluation processes. However, the processes of planning and evaluation can be viewed as ends in themselves. From this perspective, particularly in the developing countries of the world, a project such as the Caribbean Agricultural Extension Project is important not only because of the plans produced and the decisions taken, but also because of the attitudes developed and skills learned by participants during the process. Participants learn the nature, potential, techniques, and important strengths and weaknesses of generating and using social science data for planning and decision making. To make the most of such learning opportunities, planners and evaluators who facilitate and work with participants in these processes must be attuned and sensitive to the individuals involved. Thus user-focused evaluation is aimed at enhancing the long-term utilization of planning and evaluation processes by training participants in those processes to more fully and effectively use data-based approaches.

This point about the educational nature of the collaborative group process has been a major theme of this chapter. The example of the Caribbean Agricultural Extension Project illustrates the potential importance of such a perspective. As I write this there is considerable doubt about continuation of AID funding for the project into its implementation phase at the regional level. The funding uncertainties have to do with new political priorities in the Reagan administration and international politics involving the relationship between Grenada, one of the participating countries, and the United States. But the international politics surrounding the project is another story that will have to await a different book. The point here is that even as we await word on the project's future, individual countries are maintaining their national planning committees and beginning their own individual implementation efforts. The process is being carried forward by the force of its own momentum. That is the real importance of the collaborative approach to evaluation research. In essence, this approach is a tribute to and illustration of the wisdom of the ancient Chinese proverb:

Give a man a fish and he eats for a day. Teach a man to fish and he eats for a lifetime.

The collaborative process of utilization-focused evaluation is aimed at making it possible for decision makers and information users to sup at the table of evaluation on a continuing basis, while making sure that the information they consume thereat is nourishing in accordance with their needs.

PART III   *Fundamentals*

- *If you see in the data only what everyone else sees, consider the possibility that you have become so attuned to and apart of the group that you are a victim of it.*

- *Only mad dogs and Englishmen go out in the noonday sun, . . . and social scientists studying mad dogs and Englishmen.*

- *Nothing is more beloved than a cheerful giver—unless it's negative feedback that's being given.*

- *All evaluations are valid. Some are simply more "exploratory" than others.*

- *Don't bite off more than you can analyze.*

- *In this world three things are certain: death, taxes, and program budgets considered too small by those conducting the program.*

- *Poor data yield long reports.*

- *Time is data.*

- *Data to the wise can open eyes.*
  Fools just want it done, then off they run,
  To do more of the same, in EVALUATION'S name.

From Poor Halcolm's Almanac

CHAPTER 4 *Practicing With and Without Goals*

Helping Alice Get Out of Wonderland

> *"Would you tell me, please, which way I ought to go from here?"*
>
> *"That depends a good deal on where you want to get to,"* said the Cat.
>
> *"I don't much care where—"* said Alice.
>
> *"Then it doesn't matter which way you go,"* said the Cat.
>
> *"So long as I get somewhere,"* Alice added as an explanation.
>
> *"Oh, you're sure to do that,"* said the Cat, *"if you only walk long enough."*

It is axiomatic in program development, planning, management, and related fields that if you don't know where you want to get to, then you will have great difficulty figuring out how to get there and you won't know if or when you've arrived. Goals and objectives serve the purpose of specifying where you want to get to. Had Alice not been in the unfortunate position of being short on cash she might have hired the Cat as a management consultant to help her clarify her goals and objectives.

This chapter offers some practical suggestions for working with program goals and briefly considers alternatives to goals-based evaluation. In *Utilization-Focused Evaluation* (Patton, 1978) I poked fun at the "goals clarification game" in evaluation in which program staff try to guess what the evaluator means by goals and, failing to guess correctly, the evaluator ends up writing the program's goals. The result may have little to do with what program staff are trying to accomplish, but at least the statements meet the evaluator's criteria for clear, specific, and measurable goals. Many readers have interpreted my sarcasm about the goals clarification game as an anti-goals statement. Actually, I was not attacking the idea of goals; rather, I was suggesting that the goals clarification process has become formalized in the minds of many evaluators as the primary task of evaluation research so that delineation of clear, specific, and measurable goals has become an end in itself rather than a means to the end of focusing program efforts and determining what information is needed by decision makers. The point, then, was that specification and clarification of goals is only one of many ways of focusing evaluation questions. Nick Smith (1980: 39) recently commented in the *Evaluation Network Newsletter* on the development of evaluation in this regard:

> In the middle and late sixties everyone in education assumed that you needed clearly specified objectives in order to do a good evaluation. What for some people was a statement of faith was in fact an empirically testable claim. Stake, Scriven, Walker, and many others have now shown us that one can conduct useful evaluations without ever seeing an instructional objective. Of course, many evaluators seem to now have adopted the fall-back position that although objectives are not strictly needed for good evaluation, they are probably needed for good development work—again, a claim open to empirical testing. What little research I know of on the use of objectives in instructional development is ambivalent but seems to suggest that objectives may lead to more explicit organization of material, but not necessarily to better student outcomes.

Goal-free evaluation (Scriven, 1972, 1979) and now "goal-free planning" (Clark, 1979) are strategies for situational responsiveness that avoid the routine heuristic of assuming that every evaluation and/or planning situation automatically requires the delineation of clear, specific, and measurable goals. Nevertheless, for political, organizational, programmatic, and management reasons, goals specification remains the most common way to focus evaluation and planning processes. This chapter is an attempt to provide some additional assistance to program people and evaluators who are struggling with the fundamental skill of goals clarification. Skill in working with decision makers and program staff in a goals clarification process is one of the fundamentals of evaluation practice referred to in the first chapter. Knowledge of alternatives to goals-based evaluation is also an important part of an evaluator's repertoire of fundamentals. This chapter offers some ideas about and guidelines for dealing with goals and alternatives to goals.

COMMUNICATING ABOUT GOALS

I have found that one of the most deadly ways to begin a program evaluation process is to ask program staff to engage in a "goals clarification process." Yet it remains true that without direction programs will flounder: If you don't know where you're going you won't know whether or not you've gotten there. Goals statements can be extremely helpful in focusing program activities and efforts.

Part of the difficulty, I am convinced, is the terminology. *Goals and objectives.* These words have taken on an awesome quality that strikes fear in the hearts of program staff. *Goals and objectives* become haunting weights that program staff feel they have to carry around their necks, burdening them, slowing their efforts, and impeding rather than advancing their progress. Helping staff clarify their purpose and direction may mean avoiding use of the term "goals and objectives."

I've observed on many occasions that I can have quite animated and interesting discussions with program staff about such things as: What are you trying to do with your clients? If you are successful, how will your clients be different after the program than they were before? What kinds of changes do you want to see in your clients? When your program works as you want it to, how do clients *behave* differently? What do they say differently? What would I see in them that would tell me they are different? Program staff can often provide quite specific answers to these questions, answers that reveal their caring and involvement with the client change process, yet when the same staff are asked to specify their *goals and objectives,* they freeze. Clearly, the formal terminology of evaluation carries connotations and authority that are intimidating to such staff members.

Under these conditions I find it is more helpful to stay with the questions about client changes, client differences, what the program can accomplish with clients, and other outcome-oriented questions that get at the content of what we mean when we talk about goals and objectives—but avoid actually using those sinister and terrifying words. After having worked with a group of people for a while, and after having obtained a clear picture of what kind of changes they are trying to bring about, I may then tell them that what they have been telling me constitutes their goals and objectives. This revelation often brings considerable surprise and more than just a little sense of satisfaction that they have actually, without knowing it, been able to specify what they were trying to do. Thus the sensitive and skilled evaluator can recognize statements of goals and objectives, and even measurement criteria, as program staff answer questions about client change, desired client progress, and differences to be brought about by the program.

On more than one occasion when I have reported back to program staff that what we've been talking about for the last half hour seems to me to constitute a statement of their goals and objectives, they react by saying, "But we haven't said anything about what we would count or any of the measures involved." This, as clearly as anything, I take as evidence of how widespread the confusion is between the conceptualization of goals and their measurement. Communicating meaningfully with program staff about what they are trying to do is a process that should not be encumbered by evaluative jargon or concerns about the state of measurement in social science.

Help program staff to be realistic and concrete about goals and objectives, but don't make them hide what they are really trying to do because they're not sure how to write a formally acceptable statement of goals and objectives, or because they don't know what measurement instruments might be available to get at some of the important things they are trying to do.

Separating the Concept from Its Measurement

As noted earlier, evaluation research is traditionally defined as measuring the extent to which program goals and objectives are attained. Such an approach requires specification of goals and objectives. The rules for such specification are quite explicit: Goals and objectives must be *clear, specific,* and *measurable.* This approach usually requires that the statement of the goal includes specification of how it will be measured, as, for example, in the statement:

> Student achievement test scores in reading will increase one grade level from the beginning of first grade to the beginning of second grade.

This statement is not, however, a goal statement. The goal is that children improve their reading. This is a statement of *how* that goal will be measured and how much improvement is desired (standard of desirability). Confusing the (1) specification of goals with (2) their measurement and (3) the standard of desirability is a major conceptual problem in many program evaluations.

The conceptualization of program direction in a statement of goals and objectives should be clearly separated from the specification of how those goals and objectives will be measured. The two things are quite different— the goal and its measurement. Conceptually, a goal statement should specify a program direction based on values, ideals, political mandates, and program purpose. Thus conceptually, goals make explicit values and purpose.

Measurement, on the other hand, provides data indicating the relative state of goal attainment. Measurement depends upon the state of the art of social science. Some things we know how to measure with considerable precision. In other areas our indicators are less precise, less clear, and less reliable. *Why should the goals and objectives of social programs be limited by the state of the art of measurement in social science?*

To require that goals be clear, specific, *and* measurable is to require programs to attempt only those things that social scientists know how to measure. Such a limitation is clearly unconscionable. It is one thing to establish a purpose and direction for a program. It is quite another thing to say how that purpose and direction is to be measured. By confusing these two steps, and by making them one, program goals can become quite limited, meaningless, and irrelevant to what program staff and funders actually want to have happen and do have happen.

To make the point, let me overstate the tradeoff in quite stark terms. In many cases program staff are given a choice between clear, specific, quantitatively measurable goals that are meaningless and irrelevant to what is actually going on in the program *or* broad, general, and "fuzzy" goals that express real program ideals but can only be measured or described with "soft" data. For my part, *I prefer to have soft or rough measures of important goals rather than have highly precise and quantitative measures of goals that no one really cares about.* In too many evaluations, program staff are forced to focus on the latter (meaningless but measurable goals) instead of on the former (meaningful goals with soft measures).

Of course, this tradeoff, stated in stark terms, is only relative. It is desirable to have as much precision as possible and, where appropriate, measures should be quite precise and quantitative. However, by separating the process of goals clarification from the process of goals measurement, it is possible for program staff to focus first on what they are really trying to accomplish and to state their goals and objectives as explicitly as possible *without regard to measurement,* and then to worry about how one would measure actual attainment of those goals and objectives. This makes it possible, over time, to keep the same goals and objectives but to change the measures as the state of the art of measurement progresses.

This recommendation comes out of experience with many programs in which staff have been constrained in their writing of goals and objectives by evaluators who told them they could only have goals and objectives whose measurement they could specify *in advance.* Thus program staff ended up beginning with the measures that were available and working backward to figure out what goals and objectives could be written from those measures. Given that they seldom had much expertise in measurement they ended up specifying goals and objectives that amount to nothing more than counting fairly insignificant behaviors and attitudes that they felt they could somehow quantify.

To summarize, rather than beginning with what can be measured and moving to a statement of goals, when I work with groups on goal clarification I have them write their statement of goals and objectives *without regard to measurement.* Once they have stated as carefully and as explicitly as they can what they want to accomplish, then it is time to figure out what indicators and data can be collected to monitor relative attainment of goals. In my experience, program staff understand and appreciate the importance of separating the concept—the goal—from its measurement. They are able to move back and forth between conceptual level statements and operational (measurement) specifications, attempting to get as much precision as possible in both areas without losing sight of the distinction, uniqueness, and importance of *both* the conceptual specifications and the separate measurement specifications.

A CONCRETE EXAMPLE

The preceding sections discussed some ways of helping decision makers and program staff specify their goals and objectives without using the awesome and intimidating terms "goals" and "objectives" and without confusing conceptual and measurement issues.

In this section I want to specify the criteria I use when program staff and decision makers have decided that they want to undertake a goals clarification process. To do so I shall use a real example.

In the midst of writing this book I got a call from a person who had attended a workshop I had done. She began as follows:

> I know that you are not all that hot on goals as the only way to do evaluation. But our board and the federal government are requiring us to come up with a formal statement of goals for everything we do in human services in the county. We've been working for months on this and it's still a mess. We just don't seem to be able to write down a decent statement of goals. You've said it shouldn't be all that difficult. Would you look at what we've got and help us?

We arranged a meeting a week later with all of the people involved in their goals clarification process. They had produced a document of 5 pages with 10 primary goals and 34 objectives. This particular set of goals and objectives was for only one division within the county. Similar statements were needed by all divisions.

The statements they had developed illustrate a number of the difficulties people can get into when they begin to write goals and objectives. These difficulties include: trying to put too much into the statement; using vague words that unnecessarily disguise what is intended; and getting overwhelmed by the exercise because they approach it as a mandate to produce something written in stone instead of developing a framework that is flexible enough to be changed over time as circumstances change. Let's look at the specifics.

GOAL I: To assure the maintenance and development of the county mental health system through a clear delegation of authority as a basis for:

      A.   educating providers, consumers, and the general public (e.g., community outreach and mental health forums);

    B.   determining need for contracting with or operating new and existing programs (i.e., defining client types);

    C.   determining the appropriateness of overall budget requests; and

    D.   developing interdivisional and interagency relationships/working agreements in order to provide essential services according to geographic distribution and special needs.

Objective 1. Define authority for mental health priorities and role of Division within the Department through the development of recommendations to the director.

Objective 2. Determine need for additional working agreements/goal definitions and with other Divisions and with other parts of the county.

It is clear that this statement mixes outcomes, implementation strategies, and organizational arrangements in such a way that it's very difficult to know exactly what is supposed to happen and what results are to be obtained from division activities. In a fully developed system it would be important to have clear statements of (1) goals and objectives, (2) the activities to be implemented to achieve those goals and objectives, and (3) evaluation criteria for all objectives and implementation activities that were to be evaluated. For our purposes here I will concentrate only on the statements of goals and objectives.

The place to begin is in taking apart and identifying the various elements in the complex statement that they had developed. The simplest way to do this is to identify a concrete product that is assumed or implied in each phrase and then to specify that product in such a way that one would know what one had if the product were actually attained or if the desired state were realized. Taking apart GOAL I, parts A, B, C, D, and Objectives 1 and 2, we can identify the following desired outcomes. (It is necessary to postpone the issue of measurement at this point; we are simply trying to identify potential discrete items.)

- a maintained mental health system
- a developed mental health system
- clearly delegated lines of authority
- educated providers
- educated consumers
- an educated general public
- a statement of needed new programs to be operated by the county
- a statement of needed new services to be provided through contracts with the county
- a statement of existing programs to be operated by the county
- a statement of existing programs to be operated under contract to the county
- appropriate budget requests
- interdivisional working agreements
- interagency working agreements

- developed interdivisional relationships
- developed interagency relationships
- essential services being provided
- geographically dispersed services being provided
- services to special needs populations being provided
- a statement specifying the division authority for mental health priorities
- a statement specifying the role of the division within the department
- a set of recommendations to the director
- a statement of the need for working agreements with other divisions
- a statement defining the role of the department in relation to other divisions

Having taken apart the pieces it is possible for the staff to examine the many different elements contained in that first goal and accompanying objectives. It is clearly a mish-mash. The focus on outcomes statements moves away from the participle verb forms that disguise what is to be attained. For example, GOAL I-B is "determining need for contracting with or operating new and existing programs." The participle form "determining" doesn't tell us exactly what is to occur. By asking the question, "If needs are determined what would we end up with?" we are able to identify that this statement is aimed at producing four things: new programs to be operated by the county, existing programs to be operated by the county, new programs to be operated under contract to the county, and existing programs to be operated under contract to the county. In order to attain clear statements with regard to each of these four areas it would be necessary to develop criteria in two areas—under what circumstances programs should be offered by the county and under what circumstances programs should be operated under contract to the county; and under what circumstances existing programs should be maintained and under what circumstances new programs should be added. These criteria, however, are not the end but rather the means to the end. The end desired is a comprehensive plan for the provision of mental health services in the county. The final statement, then, can read something like the following:

GOAL: A comprehensive plan will be written specifying the structural arrangements for offering county services.

Objective 1. Existing programs to be continued by the county will be specified in the plan.

Objective 2. New programs to be offered by the county will be specified in the plan.

Objective 3. Existing programs to be offered under contract to the county will be specified in the plan.

Objective 4. New programs to be offered under contract to the county will be specified in the plan.

Objective 5. Clear criteria for making decisions about which programs fall into each of the categories above will be specified in the plan.

Several things are noteworthy about the way that the statement has been rewritten. First, there is no complex grammar. Each statement is a simple sentence. Second, each statement involves only a single product or desired state. This is a basic rule in questionnaire writing and it is a basic rule in the writing of goals and objectives. Third, each statement begins with a specification of the product such that it is possible to tell exactly what is to be attained or obtained. Fourth, the statements are relatively understandable and sufficiently straightforward that it should be possible for someone to read the statements and know what is going to be done.

The issue here is not whether they were focusing on the appropriate goals, whether there are other goals that were left out that should have been included, or whether these goals and objectives can be measured. The issue here is simply the writing of reasonably well organized and understandable goals and objectives. Let me rephrase one other part of the original statement and then offer a set of criteria for the writing of goals and objectives.

GOAL I-A. Educating providers, consumers, and the general public.

The verb form "educating" implies that the outcome is education. Discussion of this item with program staff revealed that they were committed each year to determining some kind of educational focus that would be turned into a program for clients, staff, and the general public. At the division level the outcome would be an educational program. For those organizations and persons responsible for implementing the educational program the outcome would be changed knowledge, attitudes, and behaviors of people who were exposed to the educational program. But at the *division* level the outcome was an educational program not educated people. With this distinction in mind, then, it became possible to rewrite this item as follows:

GOAL: Each year an educational plan will be written specifying educational programs to be offered by the division.

> *Objective 1.* Educational programs will be provided to mental health providers.
>
> *Objective 2.* Educational programs will be provided to mental health consumers.
>
> *Objective 3.* Educational programs will be provided to the general public.
>
> *Objective 4.* In each case and for each target population the plan will specify:
>
> > a. the content of the educational program,
> > b. who will conduct the program,
> > c. the budget for each educational program,
> > d. evaluation criteria for measuring the impact of each program.

Criteria for Writing Goals

It is now clear for what the division is prepared to be held responsible. The division is not responsible for the educational outcomes of the eventual targets of the program but rather is responsible only for producing plans for educational programs. With these examples in mind I would offer the following criteria for writing statements of goals and objectives.

(1) Each goal and each objective should contain only one outcome. In other words, statements should be singular. This imposes a certain simplicity on the writing of goals and objectives because each item must stand alone. This has the additional advantage of making it possible to add or delete items without changing the entire structure of the statement of goals and objectives.

(2) With each statement one should be able to tell what is to be attained. This means that the statement must be written in product or outcomes language and that both nouns and verbs should be used in such a way as to make it clear that a particular thing is to result from the processes of program activity. The people who are engaged in working on and clarifying the goals and objectives have to keep asking themselves, "What would we end up with if we attain our goal?"

(3) It should be possible to conceptualize either the absence of the desired state or an alternative to it. If there is no way that the desired state cannot occur or if it is impossible to conceptualize some outcome other than that desired, then the goal is probably meaningless. This question arose in our example with regard to the first part of Goal I, which refers to "maintaining" the county mental health system. In an absolute sense whether the county system is formal or informal there will exist some system of mental health activity in the county. A maintained system without some specification of quality criteria or functioning level is a fairly meaningless goal. The addition of quality criteria can be specified as either part of the goal or as specific objectives. Phrases such as *individualized* system, *comprehensive* system, *professional* system, *well-organized* system, *well-managed* system, and the like include adjectives that suggest indicators of quality. These can be operationalized and evaluated, and go beyond simple maintenance as the desired state to be attained.

(4) The statement of goals and objectives should be understandable. It should not be necessary to read and reread each statement to figure out what is being specified. If the county board or funders is going to have to wade through difficult grammatical constructions and complex interdependent clauses to figure out what is supposed to happen in the division or program, then the staff may find that the specification of goals and objectives will cause them considerably more problems than having found some way of avoiding the exercise altogether.

(5) Nouns should be used to specify products. Verb forms should be stated

in the future tense and, wherever possible, active verb forms should be used. This increases the reader's ability to understand exactly what is to happen. Goals, after all, are intended future states.

(6) Adjectives, where used, specify quality criteria and functioning level, which modify the nouns that are the focus of the goal. The adjectives should elucidate, clarify, and add meaning to the nouns to help the reader understand what kind of desired state is being sought.

(7) Specification of how goals are to be attained, measurement criteria for evaluation, and other amplifications of goals and objectives should be written in separate columns, or in subsequent documents, so as to keep the actual statements of goals and objectives crisp and clear.

(8) The language used should make sense to the people who will be using and reading the goals and objectives. Program jargon that will not be understandable to persons not intimately familiar with the program should be avoided. Or, where program jargon is used, it should be fully explained at the point at which it is used.

(9) The statement of goals and objectives should contain all major points that are needed for staff focus and communication to others about that focus. Areas of program endeavor and activity that are of secondary importance should be excluded, with a brief paragraph explaining what is excluded. The writing of goals and objectives should not be a marathon exercise in trying to see how long a document one can produce. As human beings our attention span is too short to focus on pages and pages of goals and objectives. Only write them for the things that matter and for outcomes for which you intend to be held accountable.

(10) Thou shalt not covet thy neighbor's goals and objectives. Goals and objectives don't travel very well. They often involve matters of nuance. It is worth taking the time to construct your own goals so that they reflect your own assumptions, your own expectations, and your own intentions in your own language.

There are exceptions to all of these guidelines, particularly the last one. One option in working with groups is to have them review the goals of other programs both as a way of helping a staff clarify its own goals and to get ideas about format and content. Evaluators who work with behavioral objectives— for example, James Popham in education—often develop a repertoire of potential objectives that can be adopted by a variety of programs. The evaluator has already worked on the technical quality of the goals so program staff can focus on selecting the content they want. Where there is the time and inclination, however, I prefer to have a group work on its own goals statement so that participants have the experience of developing goals, know from whence they came, and understand what they do and do not contain. This can be part of the training function of evaluators, increasing the likelihood that staff will have success in future goals clarification exercises.

There are three options in this regard: (1) Staff may simply review and adopt another program's goals. (2) Staff may review another program's goals for ideas, but then adapt those goals or write their own. (3) Staff may begin by struggling with their own goals statement, then compare their goals to those of another program, thereby further clarifying their own statement. We used this latter approach in the Caribbean Agricultural Extension Project. First, each national extension service wrote its own goals, then goals statements were exchanged among countries. The exchange often led to additions or refinements, but each country ended up with its own unique statement of goals and objectives.

Practice

Becoming adept at helping a staff through a goals clarification process requires practice. For those readers who would like to practice clarifying goals and objectives, or attempt to apply the ten criteria offered above to a real situation, I have included as an appendix to this chapter the full draft statement of goals and objectives that I received from the county mental health program that served as an example earlier in this chapter (Appendix A). The reader is invited to exercise creativity tempered with tolerance and patience in working on these goals. I would hasten to add that this list is not an unusual one in any way. I have worked with initial documents that were much worse, and I have seen similar kinds of documents from all kinds of organizations at all levels of government and in the private sector. On the other hand, if you can make sense out of this set of goals and objectives, you can probably be of use to most any group in helping them clarify their goals and objectives.

GOALS AS ONLY ONE OPTION

I commented in the introduction to this chapter that focusing explicitly on goal attainment in evaluation is only one among many options available to planners and evaluators. Other ways of focusing and conceptualizing an evaluation are related to some of the varying definitions of evaluation discussed in Chapter 2.

(1) It is possible to focus on evaluation *questions*. The criteria for good evaluation questions were presented in Chapter 3. Questions are generated by asking decision makers and information users, "What questions would you like to have answered by the evaluation?" Questions should be empirical, relevant, meaningful, and directed at obtaining information, or answers, that will be used.

(2) Evaluations can be focused on concerns and issues, as in responsive evaluation (Stake, 1975; Guba and Lincoln, 1981): "A *concern* is a matter of interest or importance to one or more parties. It may be something that threatens them, something they think will lead to an undesirable consequence, or something

that they are anxious to substantiate in a positive sense (a claim requiring empirical verification). . . . An *issue* is any statement, proposition, or focus that allows for presentation of different points of view; any proposition about which reasonable persons may disagree; or any point of contention" (Guba and Lincoln, 1981: 33-35).

(3) Evaluations can be organized around program theories and rationales. The evaluation looks at the relationships among what staff believe, what they say they're doing, and actual program practice, thereby helping to clarify all three (Engel, 1981).

(4) Evaluations can be focused on decisions that are to be made or problems to be solved.

(5) Evaluation can be focused on client *needs*, assessing the extent to which participants in a program are being provided with services and programs that are meaningful and relevant. A program's goals and objectives may not address what clients really need (Scriven, 1972).

These options are derived from varying purposes of evaluation. In Chapter 3, different types and purposes of evaluation were discussed at length. Focusing on the relative attainment of a program's goals and objectives is only one type of evaluation. Goals and objectives specify desired program outcomes, so clear specification and measurement of goals are needed to conduct an outcomes or effectiveness evaluation. However, information users may need data only on program implementation or on some other aspect of program operations (e.g., appropriateness of service, unintended effects, community impact). These varying needs are one of the reasons there are so many different types of evaluation described in Chapter 3. What approach one uses in focusing an evaluation will depend on the mandate under which one does the evaluation (sometimes the funding mandate requires goals-based evaluation), the nature of the program, and the interests of decision makers and information users.

THE EOLITHIC ALTERNATIVE

The alternative ways of focusing an evaluation listed above are relatively straightforward in conceptualization. As discussed in Chapter 2, alternative conceptualizations are important and powerful because they direct our attention toward some things and away from other things, just as goals do. New conceptualizations can be helpful in opening our minds to potentially new ways of perceiving and experiencing the world. The eolithic alternative, *partly through the very strangeness of the term,* is meant to serve this thought-provoking, awareness-enhancing function. The notion of eolithism is meant to alert us to the limitations of goals-based evaluation designs, while making us aware of, not simply an alternative technique, but a totally different way of proceeding and perceiving.

The eolithic alternative was introduced into evaluation by David Hawkins (1976). In a highly provocative paper, Hawkins draws on the work of American engineer/novelist Hans Otto Storm to differentiate the principle of eolithism from the principle of design. The principle of design is fundamental to logical, rational, goals-based planning, and evaluation: One must know where one is going, have ways of measuring progress toward the specified goal(s), and select those means most likely to result efficiently in successful goal attainment. An evaluation design specifies a specific purpose and focus for the evaluation, methods to be used to achieve desired evaluation outcomes, measurements to be made, and analytical procedures to be followed. Proposals are usually rated, and funded, on the basis of clarity, specificity, efficiency, and rigor of design. The principle of design is logical and deductive in that one begins with goals (a purpose and desired outcomes) and then decides how best to attain those goals, given resources known in advance (at the design stage) to be available.

The principle of eolithism, on the other hand, directs the investigator to consider how ends can flow from means. One begins by seeing what exists in the natural setting and then attains whatever outcomes one can with the resources at hand. Storm adopted the term "eolithism" for this approach in order to focus our attention on the eoliths that are available all around us, but that are often overlooked in our preoccupation with attainment of preordinate goals and our commitment to follow paradigmatically validated designs. An eolith is "literally a piece of junk remaining from the stone age, often enough rescued from some ancient burial heap. . . . Stones, picked up and used by man, and even fashioned a little for his use" (Hawkins, 1976: 91). The important point here is that eoliths are discovered in modern times already adapted to and suggestive of some ancient end. More generally, and metaphorically, the principle of eolithism calls to mind a child (or stone-age human) happening upon some object of interest and pondering, "Now what could this be used for?"

There are two ways in which the principle of eolithism is important to creative evaluation, and therefore, important to include in the repertoire of creative evaluators. The principle is important first as a conceptual distinction for understanding how certain programs function. Evaluations of programs operating according to an eolithic principle may be best served by evaluation approaches other than the traditional, goals-based model of evaluation—at least in terms of the standards of utility, feasibility, and propriety. Second, the principle of eolithism is important as an alternative approach to evaluation, regardless of whether the program being evaluated is eolithic in orientation. We shall consider each of these sensitizing functions in more detail and then examine an actual example of eolithic evaluation applied in looking at an eolithic program.

Sensitivity to Eolithic Programs

Eolithic programs are those programs whose participants are guided by the principle of eolithism; i.e., they look around them to see what's available and then do whatever they can with whatever they find. What they do moves them toward emerging goals that are discovered in and grow out of the environment in which they find themselves, or are inherent in the materials available to them. In considering the point above, that eolithic-type programs may be best served by nontraditional (especially goal-free) evaluation approaches, it may be helpful to study and reflect on the experiences of David Hawkins as a subject (or object) of a traditional goals-based evaluation. As you read about his experience, you might consider how you would have approached evaluation of such a program. The excerpt that follows is fairly lengthy, but it's worth reading attentively and thoroughly as a powerful illustration of why evaluators need alternatives to goals-based approaches if they are to be situationally responsive.

> For two years I was completely involved in an effort of elementary school curricular innovation. From the wide range of the natural sciences there is a vast amount of concrete material, prized by scientists because of the intriguing and esthetically captivating phenomena associated with it which are, at the same time, intimately interwoven with the deeper laws and histories of nature which science has found. To survey this vast field and take from it materials which can be put in children's hands, to entrap their interest and to stimulate their capacity for wonder and inquiry, seems an important undertaking for this age when science, so interwoven into our lives, yet remains for most an alien and forbidden territory. During the time I was involved with the Elementary Science Study, and in the work some of us have tried to continue here since, there have been many times when we were called on to do something called stating our objectives. Now that is always a reasonable-sounding sort of request, if by someone who genuinely doesn't know what you are up to—and especially if you are asking him for financial support. But it gradually became clear to me that many people were not satisfied with the sort of answer I and my associates were prepared to give, and such as I have suggested above. I came to realize that it was somehow expected that we could lay down, in advance, a set of specifications as to what we hoped to accomplish, and by which our work could be—something called *evaluated.* The truth of the matter was that we were explorers working our way through the heterogeneous world of schools, children, teachers, and phenomena of science. There are the resources; what can you make of them? In short we were eolithicists being confronted, and literally "called to task" by the culture of the educational designers, being asked to show cause why we should not be classed with the junkman and his customers. Somehow one was supposed to be wise enough to define an all-encompassing set of ends before one had acquired the slightest bit of good sense about the nature and potentialities of the materials.

To all such questions our answers were characteristically, and I must confess for my own part deliberately, coy and evasive. We often said some general sayings, hoping to suggest that we knew what we were about. We said we hoped to make it easier for teachers to induct themselves and children into a frame of mind conducive to the enjoyment and close observation of natural phenomena, and then into the practical art of scientific investigation; that so far as we knew this could only be done by getting involved in that art, from the beginning. This meant designing inexpensive laboratory materials and apparatus, and in best eolithic fashion surveying the resources of wood and field and stream, of back alley and junk pile. We said that we therefore thought it best to try to *e*volve curricular materials and strategies out of repeated attempts to *in*volve children in inquiry, their inquiry. We were thus committed to be very opportunistic, that is to say very empirical, in selecting for further trial just those materials and strategies which did in fact best beckon to and absorb children of various ages and conditions. Nor did we believe that we could become final authorities on this subject. What we hoped, rather, was that in enlarging the store of materials and ideas available to teachers, we would help them in *their* proper task of helping children on the road to more competent choice and learning. That also meant giving teachers wider opportunities for choice and learning; not circumventing them with detailed curricular guidance which would substitute for their inventions and denigrate their professional role.

But often the demand for objectives was not satisfied with this kind of "vague, loose talk." What was expected often, whether from sheer habit or from anxiety or extreme narrowness of vision, was that we should produce a completely organized and sequenced guide for everybody who "adopted" our program. And that was where we stuck. We said we thought we were learning some of the *means* of good science teaching, but that we were not yet nearly wise enough to present what is vulgarly known in the trade as a complete package, with objectives spelled out, little texts, and words in teachers' mouths. We said we thought this should be left quite flexible and open to decision in the careers of particular schools, teachers, and children; open to significant choice. And then, of course, came the clincher: "Ah yes, but how can you evaluate your work if you don't state carefully defined objectives?" The phrase "behavioral objectives" had not yet come upon the scene, final expression of the primate dominance order which puts "design" on top, but we took the question to mean, as it typically does, a detailed setting forth of performance criteria related to subject matter and skill. And that, as I have said, we thought we should be more than a bit hesitant about. As I look back on that period I think we should have been less hesitant. We should not have *answered* the question about detailed objectives of subject matter and skill, but we should have explicitly *questioned* that question. Suarez said that it was the philosopher's job to question the questions, and answer the answers; to provide what a well-known mathematician, Stanislaw Ulam, once called "the necessary don't know-how." [Hawkins, 1976: 92-93].

The evaluators with whom Hawkins had contact operated from a goals-based, quantitative measurement paradigm of evaluation. By way of contrast, an eolithic evaluation approach would have involved saying to Hawkins and his colleagues, "Let's look at the things you have, the things you're doing, and see what we can learn about where they're taking you." Instead, the evaluators said: "Before we can look at what you have and what you're doing, we have to know where you're going. Moreover, your statement of where you're going has to meet our criteria of clarity, measurability, and specificity."

A user-focused approach to evaluation (see Chapter 3) would have begun by attempting to understand Hawkins's view of his program. The evaluation would then take that view into account, partly by avoiding talk of an evaluation "design." Program people to whom the word "design" has loaded and negative connotations are not helped by having a preordinate design foisted on them. It would have been possible, and might well have been appropriate, to focus the evaluation on a description of program activities, to document Hawkins's explorations of learning materials, and to inductively study the actual classroom effects and consequences of his approaches and materials. It might have been possible to take a phenomenological approach, to do a process evaluation, to use a goal-free model, or to undertake a connoisseur-ship evaluation (Eisner, 1975; Patton, 1980: 52). There are many possibilities. Unfortunately, what Hawkins described is the painful encounter of an eolithic program staff with a structured, goals-oriented evaluator. The result was pain on both sides and, at least in this case, a useless evaluation process from the perspective of program staff.

There are certainly times when an evaluator does a program a great service by pushing staff to think more clearly, concretely, and operationally about goals and objectives. Goals-based evaluations are likely to remain the norm for some time to come. But there are also times when a great disservice is done to programs by forcing on staff a goals-oriented model. The possibility of conducting practical, yet creative, evaluations is enhanced by having a sufficient repertoire of techniques and approaches that one can be truly situationally responsive and user-focused in developing evaluation strategies. The principle of eolithism can be part of such a repertoire.

While Hawkins was primarily concerned with how the principle of eolithism can enhance curricular development in educational programs, the principle of eolithism has many potential applications in evaluation. The probability is effectively zero that there should be two programs presenting the exact same evaluation challenges and opportunities. We have a choice in how we approach this diversity. We can approach each new program with the object of fitting it into one of a limited and preconceived set of categories such that the evaluation design is automatically determined by our categorization of the program and our preconceptions about the purpose of evaluation. Or, *we can approach each new program as if on a search for eoliths, looking for unique objects and activities of interest that suggest possible evaluation purposes and functions that are context and situation specific.* We can be "eolithic craftsmen," in Hawkins's terms, working from the principle that each evaluation opportunity is unique—its purpose, function, and possibilities to be *discovered,* rather than imposed or preordained.

Evaluation, and life in general, manifest and provide opportunities to employ both the principle of design and the principle of eolithism. While Hawkins began by emphasizing the differences between the two principles, he ended by recognizing their interrelationship:

> Clearly human life requires and exhibits an interplay of these two principles, which describe distinguishable but not separable phases of mind. . . . We seek goals and we set goals. As the seeking becomes routinized, we design mechanisms to help us. In seeking goals we encounter realities, however, which tempt and beckon, which bring us to redefine the goals we seek, and thus also to alter the direction of our seeking [Hawkins, 1976: 91].

The creative evaluator will find occasions to apply both the principle of eolithism and the principle of design in evaluation conceptualization, data collection, and analysis. Sometimes both principles may be applicable to the same evaluation. The challenge of eolithism is to understand the uses and functions of what may appear, on first glance, to be junk, while avoiding the collection of data that, because of design limitations and imperfections, end up being treated as junk.

I have included in Appendix B to this chapter an example of an eolithic evaluation. I do so to reduce the abstraction of the eolithic idea, and to show one way of proceeding without a statement of clear and specific goals. The example also illustrates the use of qualitative methods in evaluation. The most frequent request I've had since writing *Qualitative Evaluation Methods* (Patton, 1980) is for more examples of actual qualitative evaluation case studies. The example in Appendix B, then, serves the dual purpose of illustrating one result of doing an evaluation without attention to clear, specific, and measurable goals, while also providing a case example of using qualitative methods in evaluation. Chapter 7 discusses some of the issues involved in using qualitative methods.

ON GOALS, FORMS OF STUDY, AND OTHER REDUNDANCIES

One external reviewer of an early draft of this chapter doubted the need for a chapter on goals. He wrote the publisher:

> Fourteen pages on goals, written because Michael keeps running into people who have trouble with them. But what he says about goals has already been

said elsewhere [and better]. . . . Why does Michael think that writing it will help these individuals? My guess is that the people who read this won't need it, and those who need it won't be reading a thick book on evaluation.

In pondering this feedback, and considering whether to keep this chapter in the book (or publish the book at all for that matter, since the same critique could be made of all chapters, or of the redundancies among chapters) I came across a passage in which Sufi philosopher Idries Shah was answering a question about what form studies in search of truth should take. While he was not directly concerned with evaluation studies, Shah's response is applicable to evaluations, and particularly applicable to the question of whether all evaluations should be formed by attention to program goals. His answer also provides a rationale for including this chapter in the book despite whatever redundancies it may include.

Question to Shah: How can you explain the many forms in which people have attempted to teach and study? Since people believe in these forms, believe that they are true renditions of fact, they are enabled to reach truth through them. But is it that some are true and some are not? If certain forms through which studies are carried out are true, are all others false?

Answer: I must have answered this question several hundred times, both in speech and in writing. . . . The fact that such questions continue to be asked constitutes a quite remarkable demonstration of what questioners are like: some at least will ask questions even though they have been answered in accessible form dozens of times.

But this may mean that the questions need to be answered again and again until the answers penetrate.

The answers, once again, are:
(1) Truth has no form;
(2) The means through which people may perceive Truth have forms;
(3) All forms are limited. Some of the limitations are time, place, culture, language;
(4) Different forms are not necessarily antagonistic, for the above reasons;
(5) Forms have changed through the centuries in obedience to the external world to which all forms belong;
(6) When people believe that the form is more important than the Truth, they will not find truth, but will stay with form;
(7) Forms are vehicles and instruments, and vehicles and instruments cannot be called good or bad without context;
(8) Forms outlive their usefulness, increase or diminish in usefulness [Shah, 1978: 145-146].

Goals are one form of knowledge about programs. Goals-based evaluation is one form of evaluation. The form of an evaluation should follow its function, not vice versa, and evaluation has many functions, only some of which relate to goals. Now, say it again, say it again, louder, LOUDER. . . .

A CLOSING PERSPECTIVE

Evaluation sage Halcolm was noted for being concerned with both the mental and physical well-being of his students, and for relating the two in his teachings. The retreat included a running program. All students were to work up to five miles a day—a difficult, but attainable, goal. When all students had attained this goal, some more easily than others, he called them together for a new exercise.

"This morning I've laid out a level cross-country course for you to run. Don't worry about the distance. Run as far and as well as you can. Your stopping point will be recorded and your distance given to you afterwards. Run well now."

That evening, after food and rest, Halcolm again assembled the students. "Today some of you ran much farther than ever before. Most of you ran somewhere near the usual five-mile training distance. Some ran much less than five miles. What do you observe about these results?"

One student expressed surprise that several participants had run so much less than five miles since all had recently attained the five-mile training distance.

"Some people need specific, quantitative goals to aim at, to spur them on beyond what they would otherwise achieve. Others are limited by such goals, achieving only what is necessary rather than what is possible. Many are able to meet one target, revise it, and move on to new targets. Some need no targets to keep on progressing." Halcolm paused, then continued.

"The same diversity is true of programs. In running the course of an evaluation, goals affect programs in different ways. Sometimes they help, and sometimes they hinder."

"But how," asked a student, "can we know which programs, or people, need what? When do goals help and when do they hinder?"

"You can't always know," smiled Halcolm. "Sometimes you just have to play your hunches. Of course, some careful observation and experience with different situations can improve your hunches. Here, this may interest you."

Halcolm handed the student a small journal and departed. The journal was open to an entry dated the day before the students had run the cross-country course. Student names were arranged in three categories: those who Halcolm predicted would significantly exceed the five-mile standard; those who would run near that training norm; and those who would fall significantly short. Halcolm had correctly predicted in advance how every student would perform in the absence of a specific running goal. At the end of the entry was written a question: "When is a hunch not a hunch?"

APPENDIX A
PRACTICING WITH GOALS:
GOALS CLARIFICATION EXERCISE

What follows are the goal statements of an actual program. These goals are included here to provide an opportunity to practice the art and craft of goals clarification, and to apply the guidelines for goals clarification presented in this chapter.

Mental Health Division Goals

GOAL II: To assure coordination of information and utilization in the County Mental Health System across contracted and operated programs so that a minimum data base is available for planning and program development.

Objective 1: Negotiate with Director of Community Services Department to implement Mental Health Division Information System Package already developed by Mental Health Division, either through budget request, and/or through consultant contract, or any other visible means.

Objective 2: Develop format for implementation of time-limited study of current population in mental health service-delivery system.

GOAL III: To assure the current delivery of a broad range of community mental health services (e.g. preventive services, aftercare, clinical treatment) throughout the county to all residents of the county.

Objective 1: Through contracting with those mental health service providers whose services are compatible with Division priorities.

Objective 2: Through development of requests for proposal which outline sound program concepts and address specific mental health continuum/array of services needs to be addressed.

Objective 3: Continue to develop and update description of mental health services to be available by geographic distribution and special need.

Objective 4: Develop proposal/plan for a needs survey examining existing mental health needs of general population of the County, and secondly, formulate plan for meeting these specific needs. This objective will be coordinated with or extend from CSP needs assessment already begun.

Objective 5: Examine current program operation effectiveness through annual site visits and program audits of all Mental Health Programs (contracted or operated).

GOAL IV: To assure quality case management services to the chronically mentally ill through the facilitation of a unified community support system in the County.

Objective 1: Presentation and negotiation of CSP recommendations for future organization to Community Services Department Director.

Objective 2: Develop plan for implementation, including time frame/work plan based on results of Objective 1.

GOAL V: To assure the delivery of an integrated system of community mental health treatment for adolescents and children through the development of a continuum of care.

Objective 1: Define ideal continuum/array of service which should be available to serve the mental health needs of children/adolescents in the County.

Objective 2: Develop plan for assessing the current mental health system against the defined ideal continuum/array in order to define gaps.

Objective 3: Prepare work plan with time frame for budgetary requests and utilization of private sector for development of ideal continuum/array of mental health services to children/adolescents.

Objective 4: Consult with those mental health providers within the private and public sectors to assure integrated and effective service delivery to children/adolescents.

Objective 5: Develop a mental health consultation system for use by Social Service personnel in which mental health professionals from contract and operated programs within the county provide said consultative services.

Objective 6: Develop an RFP for Adolescent Day Treatment and an intensive treatment program for adolescents.

Objective 7: Bring on line a day treatment program for adolescents and an adolescent-intensive treatment program.

GOAL VI: To facilitate the development and utilization of new services and special projects based on defined mental health services essential within each geographic area.

Objective 1: To identify needs/special target populations as seen by existing appointed task forces, advisory committees, and the Council of Mental Health Programs through the development of a needs assessment to be applied to these groups.

Objective 2: Develop time frame and implementation plan compatible with Goal III, which will address the defined needs.

GOAL VII: To assure maximum usage of outside funding including medical assistance, insurance payments, and special grants.

Objective 1: To review Council recommendation for Division staff assignment to meet this goal and make recommendation and/or budget request as appropriate.

Objective 2: To research the status of rules and regulations affecting insurance reimbursement.

Objective 3: To establish liaison with local, state, and federal government officials responsible for effective reimbursements and mental health grants.

GOAL VIII: To assure the appropriate utilization of the state of the art through staff training and development and information exchange programs to develop quality treatment programming.

Objective 1: To develop plan/format for Information Exchange Forum to include Mental Health Division programs and other mental health programs.

Objective 2: To identify money available for mental health training within the jurisdiction/authority of the Mental Health Division.

Objective 3: To utilize the annual mental health program site visits as a means of information exchange through peer review.

GOAL IX: To assure cooperation and collaboration with other divisions of the Community Services Department, and with other resources, i.e., Crisis Intervention, Office of Planning and Development, County Commissioners, and so on.

Objective 1: To have Division staff participate on Community Services' Department and other Divisions/Departments/Bureaus/ Committees and Task Forces.

Objective 2: To develop work agreements with other Divisions/ Departments/Bureaus as is determined necessary.

Objective 3: To examine merit of holding annual Division "Open House" for purposes of information exchange, open communication, face-to-face meeting.

Objective 4: To assess feasibility and merit to increased mental health informational activity within Government Center and development of plan for implementation.

GOAL X: To assure high Division visibility through extensive community outreach and public information efforts.

Objective 1: To develop Division information package which can be made available at public forums, conferences, fairs.

Objective 2: To develop and circulate Mental Health Division Brochure to clients, other providers, interested persons, community leaders, federal and state officials.

Objective 3: To develop videotape of Mental Health Division Programs which would assist in education and training.

Objective 4: To examine methods of providing regular written information through newsletter, newspaper, media, and so on.

APPENDIX B
PRACTICING WITHOUT GOALS:
AN EOLITHIC EVALUATION
EXAMPLE IN THE WILDERNESS

In my first interactions with the staff of the Southwest Field Training Project it was as if they were reading a script prepared by David Hawkins, although at that time I had not yet come across Hawkins's essay on eolithic evaluation. Goals and objectives were purposefully vague. The idea of the program was to permit each person to use an experience in the wilderness to meet his or her own needs. There could be no universal goals because each person was perceived as unique, and each participant was expected to have a unique experience in the wilderness. The wilderness, the staff, and the program activities (climbing, backpacking, rafting, campfire discussions, journal writing, and the like) were things to be used by participants for their own purposes. The staff wanted to create an environment, a set of circumstances, and a program of activities that would begin an (undefined) change process that would then be taken over and continued by participants. The staff expected to evolve strategies as the program progressed and to involve participants in the evolution of those strategies.

In effect, the principle of eolithism describes quite nicely the basis from which program staff were operating. They had discovered the magnificence and splendor of the wilderness; they had some activities that were challenging and enjoyable; and they had some ideas about things to do with a group. The eolithic evaluation question was: In what ways, to what ends, and for what purposes could these things be put together? The evaluation strategy that evolved from our discussions was descriptive in focus and inductive in practice. I would join the program as participant observer with the task of watching what took place, participating, and interviewing participants to document how they used the experience, and to explore the issue of how they were affected by the experience, if at all.

In *Qualitative Evaluation Methods* (Patton, 1980), I used this program as illustrative of several aspects of fieldwork and various approaches to interviewing. Chapter 8 of this book includes a discussion of the participant interview chain used as part of the evaluation during the second year of this program. I am including in this appendix previously unpublished field notes from this evaluation in order to illustrate one approach to the analysis of eolithic data, and because I have had a number of requests to provide more examples of qualitative data and content analysis since the publication of *Qualitative Evaluation Methods.*

The data that follow are eolithic in the sense that they were discovered in my field note transcriptions and, once discovered, we asked if they had some meaning, purpose, or use. The data did not emerge from some prior conceptualization of what to look for, or of what would be important. We had to decide if the data were junk, or if they could tell us something.

Deciding what data mean is a common evaluation challenge. The data that follow provide examples of a particularly common kind of program data from which meanings and insights can be extracted. In looking through my field notes from the wilderness program, I discovered that the language of the participants was rich metaphors, analogies, and similes. This fieldwork experience increased my sensitivity to the extent to which the metaphors used by program participants can be important eolithic clues that reveal the real functions and effects of a program. In the process of taking field notes as a participant observer/evaluator in the project, I tried to record the ways in which people talked about their experiences in the wilderness. In looking through my notes I have been struck by the extent to which metaphors played an important part in the communication patterns among project participants. In organizing the fieldwork data from the evaluation I found it useful to focus on program metaphors as eolithic clues to the meaning of participant experiences. This case example also illustrates one way of gathering evaluative information without first generating a statement of clear and specific goals.

Of course, the whole project was, in many ways, a metaphor—it was an experimental acting out of what the world could be like. At its best the experiences in the wilderness became a metaphor for what was best in life, what was worth striving for, and what human relationships could represent. At other times the project became a metaphor for things that we seek to avoid, an intensification and exaggeration of some of our worst tendencies as human beings. In the examples that follow a variety of metaphor forms and functions are explored.

Group Identity Metaphors: Facilitating Cohesion

In both years of the project, metaphorical labels were created that helped facilitate cohesion among subgroups of participants. During the first year the *woodchucks* emerged. The imagery of the woodchucks included the notion that those who called themselves woodchucks were not the mightiest, or the most graceful, or the strongest, but that they got by all right and had a place in the environment. There were jokes about woodchuck merit badges, woodchuck tee shirts, and meeting of the royal order of woodchucks. The metaphor served to facilitate cohesion among the group of people who adopted it as descriptive of their approach to the wilderness.

During the second year the *turtles* emerged. The turtles consisted of a self-identified group who disdained anything that smacked of a gung-ho approach to the wilderness. The turtles hiked together at their own slow pace. They slept together, climbed together when possible, and basically provided support to each other in a go-slow approach that included both covert and overt resistance to the group process being facilitated by the staff. The turtles did not simply create an image that referred to their approach to the wilderness, but rather built an image that included their approach to the entire project and their participation in it.

The turtles emerged in contrast to another group, the *truckers,* who were the participants who tended to want to hike fast, climb to the highest elevation, and move quickly in the group process.

The Outward Bound staff provided a rich vocabulary of terms to describe what no one wanted to be—the losers and walking wounded of the world. These terms created some tension for fear that the label might be applied to oneself while at the same time creating a general sense of cohesion that none of us, as a group, were really part of the world that would be described as made up of *lamos, wuzs,* and *lillydippers.*

One function of metaphors, then, is to facilitate group identity and subgroup cohension. To be like a woodchuck, to be like a turtle, to be like a trucker is to belong and to have an identity. Conversely, to *not* be a lamo, a wuz, or lillydipper is also to have identity on a different level and in a different way. These kinds of group identity metaphors are clues to the evaluator about program interest groups and some of the political/interpersonal dynamics in a program.

Life Struggle Metaphors

The wilderness provided a rich medium for constructing life struggle metaphors. Life or work or relationships or learning could be compared to "carrying a heavy backpack up a steep and narrow path," (Photo 1) "trying to figure out where you are on the map when you don't know how to read the landscape," "searching for footholds on the way up," or "going with the flow" on the river (Photo 2). There was often some caution felt about using these kinds of metaphors because they seemed hokey or perhaps overly obvious.

Photo 1 Seeking the Upward Path

Yet despite this reluctance participants in both years laced their language with wilderness metaphors.

In some cases the metaphors had particular significance for particular individuals. In these cases, a specific metaphor served to crystallize a new insight. During the first year, while climbing in the Kofa Mountains, one woman shared a metaphor comparing the technical rope climbing process to a group support system and the need for support in work settings. After commenting on the difficulty of doing things without a mutual support system, she observed: "If you are always the strong one you are destined to climb without a rope."

The Southwest Field Training Project encouraged and stimulated reflection on the nature of life, work, relationships, and other facets of our existence. Different people found different parts of the wilderness environment that helped them make connections with their feelings about the nature of the world and their presence in it. Metaphor often played an important part in those connections. In the next few pages I have reproduced my notes from the debrief (postexperience discussion) at the end of the second field conference in the Kofa Mountains. You are invited to look for metaphors and think about what they tell you about this program and the participants in the program. At the same time, think about *the implications for evaluation* of what you learn about the program from the language and images used by participants in describing their experiences.

Final Kofa Debrief

A week of climbing, sharing, hiking, a week of wilderness experience in the Kofa Mountains of Arizona came to a close in a Phoenix motel conference room on a Tuesday morning. Each person was asked to share with the

Photo 2 The Evaluator "Going with the Flow"

group some moment of special significance from the week. Everyone was asked to close their eyes and remember back to the details of the path from camp to the spring in Kofa Queen Canyon where participants had been balayed up a particularly challenging climb.

Cliff: "I remember that climb as significant for me. I climbed it the first time the easy way, then I did it the harder way afterwards. Jane really helped. It was a real challenge. I needed to be pushed some to realize I had the resources to meet the challenge. I need to be pushed in other climbs in my life, not just rock climbs. I also need sometimes to be helped."

Karol: "For me, on solo, I constructed an analogy between climbing and life. It's the difference between climbing with ropes and without ropes, on living with support and without support. If you are the strong one, you are destined to climb alone."

Cory: "I didn't find unique significance in the trip and that was significant. I kept trying to change the trip to make it important and once I relaxed it became important to me. Sharing it with others was most important."

Charlene: "Walking out through the canyon *alone,* I put some pieces together and things began to mesh for me. I saw no one in front or behind and thought about getting lost. . . . I was looking for *one* right way out . . . and I realized that there are many ways. Alternatives. Alternative solutions. Finding *my* way to the goal. For me that was an enormously valuable realization—not just for use in walking out of canyons."

Tom: "During the week I came to understand the difference between education and training. In school I felt like an animal being formed. Over the course of my schooling and over the last several years I've felt there was something lacking. This week something came together for me. I thought we were doing rock climbing but people kept calling it education. I realized this week that the difference is in the processing. That will make a tremendous difference to me. It's closed a gap for me that has existed for years."

Cari: "The rope game showed me how I've been clutching my life too tightly. Climbing the second pitch I was really clutching. Clutching the rock . . . clutching my life . . . clutching people . . ."

Jeanne: "Two poles for me—wanting to do things myself and also wanting others to help me. I'm going to be very careful about looking for support, which anchors I choose. And I feel relaxed about not having to be anchored forever to my current workplace."

Carmen: "For me this was the week of being a woodchuck. Being a woodchuck. Being able to have fun, and not have to worry about the impression I make, but being able to enjoy myself."

Sturgis: "Listening to this final debrief is a real 'high' for me. It turns off the automatic pilot."

Jeanne: "This last debrief epitomizes for me the debrief and its value and I'll carry that into my work with me."

"I began the week thinking about it as a challenge, subconsciously, and on the first day I realized I was climbing it to conquer it. And it was a terrifying experience. I felt good at the top, but not good about the conquering. Then I was able to get in touch with the fluidity of the experience. I got rid of the outcomes orientation and I realized that that's how I have worked—ignoring the process."

Greg: "I had to stop and finish myself with the canyon yesterday. I started describing to myself the feelings I had and I relaxed and finished with the canyon. I learned the value of describing what's going on as a tool."

"At the start I was desperate for friendships. Somewhere validation through others lost its importance. I found I could validate myself. I learned how to envision power and strength in myself, like the power and strength of these mountains."

Process and Change Metaphors

While the wilderness provided a wealth of opportunities for metaphor construction about various facets of life, participants also constructed their own metaphors to describe the process of change involved in the Southwest Field Training Conference experience and related experiences. This sometimes involved entirely new metaphor construction. One of the most powerful metaphors that emerged during the first year was the "detoxification" and "retoxification" image. The idea that the project led to "detoxification," getting rid of the poisons from everyday life, emerged in the Kofas and became a natural part of the group's vocabulary in the San Juan River experience. The San Juan also saw the emergence of the "dropping out" and "moving on" metaphors as a focal point for discussing personal and professional changes.

Another metaphor emerged to describe the whole process of the Southwest Field Training Conference experience. The idea that the project could be compared to an "eddy" came from the San Juan field conference. The project was an eddy in the sense that it permitted one to get out of the current of life, over to the side, where you could see things and watch the river going by for a little bit, regain your strength, and develop a strategy for moving on down the river. Of course, as several participants noted, backwater eddies can be quite difficult to get out of.

The pages that follow are notes taken at the final San Juan debrief during the first year. Process and change metaphors are particularly prominent this debrief. Again you are invited to think about what you learn about the program from the language of participants, and the implications of what you learn for working with this group on an evaluation.

Final San Juan Debrief

The setting . . . a hanger blacktop outside the Cortez, Colorado, Airport terminal. The group is gathered together, oblivious of the wind and the occasional stares from departing passengers, for a final exchange after a river trip down the San Juan in southern Utah. Wind-burned and already beginning to make that often-difficult transition back to the city, the job, the family dog, we begin to talk about our week floating on the river, shooting the rapids, and living together on the San Juan. We drift from focusing on the past week to the past year we've spent together in the Learninghouse Southwest Field Training Project.

Sturgis: "It's remarkable. I transcended my cynicism. It's a really remarkable trip. The things that made it remarkable were . . . one, that we came together three times; that I could transcend my usual role of responsible leader; my personal realization that a Ph.D. is no road to happiness; other people's dedication to their professions, their jobs, and how your profession penetrates your entire life; and the most remarkable thing has been seeing you experience joy, seeing you get away from your professionalism, come out here and laugh and experience joy. It's important that we've all had a good time. What life's about is experiencing joy. This trip was designed for you to fall on your face—there was very little curriculum planning, very little direction from the wilderness staff—and you carried it off. Is the world like this project? Can it be? I don't know."

Lorri: "I'm usually the one to provide the experience for others and this has been instead a time for personal reflection and rejuvenation. I didn't have to do any stage-setting . . . it came out of the group."

Sturgis: "There's a stress factor: going home, having a chance to reflect— the petty things disappear and the important things remain. We come back refreshed. It offers more toward true growth because we can sort out and cull the bad and keep the good."

Henry: "We have had three chances to observe toxicity and detoxification, withdrawal and return, the insidiousness of that other environment and the real need to get it out of my system. To watch for the toxicity and attempt to learn from it."

Charlene: "This has been a time for me of studying both toxification and detox, a whole reflective process of being away."

Hal: "The project has been a source of discipline and a meditation on how I am with people. It has been a constant for me, and held my year together. I see myself through you. Each of you have helped me do my own growing, growing outside of the words, phrases, and abstractions. We're all nervy, having gotten into it. I'm grateful for your holding me accountable."

Peter: "I felt an incredible feeling of insignificance saying goodbye to the river. The river was a metaphor for the project and the insignificance of us in relation to that environment."

Henry: "It's nice not to have to get up in the morning and feel responsible for turning on the river or holding up the cliffs."

Carmen: (In reference to Malcolm's carving) "Each of us has had a chance to carve the figures of our own lives."

Lorri: "You all share things about who you are by the way you associate things—the metaphors. Everyone here is an open book. The cobwebs get ripped aside. It really works."

Cliff: "I see the river as a metaphor. Resistance—the wind, outside force; fear—of the hidden rock; excitement—of the rapids and coming as close as we can. Sometimes we get out of the river and take a side canyon. Sometimes we lazily float or walk on the water or in the mud and drudge to pull ourselves along. We can be alone in the kayak or in a group in the raft. All different aspects of life."

Jim: "Maybe one of the measures of detox is how seldom I thought of my work; the other measure is how many opportunities there were in seven days for poetry—to write, read, hear it. I'd say live it, but I don't want to sully it up by getting sentimental. How remarkable it was to take a shit 80 feet above the river and how that compares to the john in the Ute cafe in Cortez."

Greg: **"The challenge for me: It's really easy for me to retoxify. The feeling in my belly was there and I was back there in ten minutes—I'm already moving toward that now. I want to keep the process alive . . . I can see myself recollecting this trip, these people, the shitter above the river. Can I carry the meaning of the shitter with me? It's keeping the process alive."**

Karol: "It's really hard to know how to ward off retoxification. I want to keep the feelings longer that we've had here. We each have to find a way, like Peter putting the TV in the closet after the Kofa trip."

Jim: "There are a couple of ways. Use the telephone to call people. I'm going to put one of the snapshots of the river in front of my shitter at home."

Henry: "How much time there seems to be on the river. Somehow the days don't seem that long back in Denver. The time must be going somewhere."

Malcolm: "For the first time in my life I've found some peace. I've learned to carry the river with me. It's a choice and I've made it."

Lorri: "I don't think this can be kept. We experienced it, it's something inside me. My body is part river water. What I've really got is this experience and even that's gone. What's happening now is this conversation and when it's over, so is the experience of it. I think it's neat that we've created our own little island."

Charlene: "The group has an amazing ability to create community— wherever we are we are together . . . on the pavement at an airport we talk and create community."

Laura: "The meaning and value of the river is me . . . has shaped part of me."

Karol: "In the Gila I was waiting for the great debrief . . . this sense that all of us were going on blind faith and that finally we'll come upon the great debrief. Now I know we make our own meaning and don't have to be told what it meant. I have this image of the great debrief as Jim Reynolds in the Cortez Airport twirling his briefs. We don't have to be told what it means."

Giving Special Meaning to Things

Tom Robinson, the field director during the first field conference, began his instruction on backpacking in the Gila by saying: "Your backpack is your friend." Tom went on to explain what the friendship involved, the obligations on both sides, and the importance of giving special treatment to that friend, the backpack.

I remember struggling with that metaphor not more than ten minutes later as I found that my friend was cutting off the circulation to my legs and I was having difficulty walking. Indeed, the process of establishing that friendship was a difficult and painful one for me during the first two days of the Gila. A lot of adjustments had to be made in order for me to come to appreciate the qualities of my friend.

The "learning log" was another metaphor that allowed participants to attach special meaning to the brown notebooks they were given to use for the required project journal.

The rope that was used for climbing also took on other characteristics through the magic of metaphor. During the first year the participants engaged in an exercise in which they were asked to hold on to a rope and imagine that that rope was their lifeline, that it in fact represented their life flow. The exercise then involved experiencing the differences between holding on to the rope (our lives) tightly, holding on to the rope loosely, and trying to move from one place to another along the rope.

These kinds of metaphors permitted participants to attach special meaning to otherwise quite ordinary objects. Those special meanings allowed members to transcend the usual limitations of the meanings attached to those objects and make generalizations about things that were important to the group and the program.

Metaphors of Self

While metaphors in the project helped solidify group identity, crystallize ideas about life challenges, and provide images for process and change, metaphors were also useful in helping participants gain insights about themselves as individuals and to communicate those insights to others. Personal insight metaphors of self take the form: "I am like . . ."

During the second year the project leaders introducd an exercise that is the epitome of metaphor use. The exercise involved having participants construct representations of their "masks." This exercise turned out to be a particularly effective mechanism for facilitating interpersonal sharing and feedback. In the pages that follow I have reproduced selected notes from the mask session. Of particular interest are data about how people evaluated themselves in the project. Evaluation criteria are implicit in each mask. How can these criteria be used to enlighten a formal program evaluation process?

How, if at all, can these criteria be made explicit, systematized, and generalized?

Creating Images/Making Masks

This was the sixth and final field conference of the Southwest Field Training Project. It was the third and last field conference for the group of people participating in the second year of the project. The field conference involved rafting and kayaking some 70 miles down the San Juan River in Utah from Bluff, Utah, to Hall's Crossing just before the San Juan empties into Lake Powell. The river was at flood stage, the current swift (7-8 miles per hour) and the water level quite high (four times above the normal spring runoff level). The activity described here took place on the fifth day of the eight-day trip. The session was about "Masks and Images."

One of the staff members explained that he and several other people had been talking about how much of our interaction is conditioned by our images of each other, so they thought it would be interesting to explore how that occurred and what its implications are. He explained that in order to facilitate the discussion of images and masks he had brought along some material for people to use in actually making masks. He emptied out a bag that contained colored construction paper, masking tape, string, crayons, magic markers, small scissors, and transparent tape.

> Each person is going to have the opportunity here to make a mask of some part of yourself that you don't ordinarily show to other people, or some part of yourself that you keep hidden on the job, or some part of yourself, some mask, that you want to show people in order to say something about where you are, that will help you and us look at images of yourself. Then we're going to get into a couple of groups and discuss the masks.

People moved down toward the materials sorting through the paper, the tape, the crayons, to pick out what they needed for their own masks. There was no hesitation about the exercise.

I was near the end of the line because I had been taking photographs of people as they picked up the materials (Photos 3 and 4). I found that by the time I got my own materials many people were well under way in cutting and taping. I wanted to make a fairly simple mask, partly because I'm not skilled artistically and didn't want to get into something complex and partly because of my desire to continue taking photographs of other people working on their masks. As I was strategizing about the exercise, I noticed a piece of black construction paper that was still left. I immediately decided on a simple mask made of just a piece of construction paper. Black—with holes for eyes. I decided to represent the dark gloomy side of myself that I keep hidden from people at work or at home so that others don't know when I'm brooding about something, but I suspected that if I made a plain black mask people would respond to it in terms of my role as evaluator. "Aha, the evaluator's black

Photo 3 The Parade of Masks

Photo 4 Sharing Masked Meanings

mask: expressionless, foreboding, protective." I wondered if it would be possible for the group to respond to me outside of my role as evaluator. I doubted it, but decided to see what would happen.

The group was a half semicircle of eleven people. The director began by describing and talking about his own mask. He'd actually made two masks, one a cheerful, bright, smiling face and the other a mean, nasty face. He said that he hadn't really been able to make only one mask, that he found that he really needed to make both masks in order to feel complete with the masking exercise. He wore the masks so that when one was in front the other was behind and he could move them around so that the one that was behind came to the front. He said, "I show the nasty face most often but I'd like to show the cheerful face more."

Jane had made a red mask shaped somewhat like a kite with eyes and markings that gave the mask an oriental effect. There was no mouth on the mask.

> I didn't know what I wanted to portray so I just made the mask to see what it would represent. A mouth just didn't seem to fit. Maybe it's my silent self. Well-formed, but most of it may be the exotic, cross-cultural self that sounds to other people pompous and arrogant. I turned off that self in college when I became an all-American girl.

Jane's father was in the foreign service and she spent much of her youth outside the United States in the Orient and Brazil. Several people commented on the attractiveness of the mask. Most of the discussion, however, focused on the absence of a mouth. Some people liked it without the mouth, and others thought they would like it better with a mouth. They wanted to hear Jane speak. Phyllis asked, "What would the mask say if it had a mouth?" Jane said she didn't want to give the mask a mouth. She described how she had learned not to share her cross-cultural side with people when that side of her had not been reinforced in college. Until she made the mask, she explained, she hadn't really been aware of how much she'd shut that side of herself off.

Ellen talked next about her mask. Ellen's mask was made entirely out of natural material from the canyon rather than from the materials that had been provided. She had moved downstream a bit, removed her clothes and put mud, leaves and sticks on parts of her body and face, and in her hair.

> You asked me to show a part of myself that I don't show my clients. I became an ancient Indian woman. I came to this pool to purify myself. I don't think a lot about things, this is just my space. When people come here I use this space to heal them. I'm getting very centered and pure for this union that's about to occur. I'm very old and very young, very young and very old. Very concentrated. I have a lot of power. I'm preparing for a marriage ceremony and that's the reason that I'm here to purify myself for that ceremony.

> I went through a lot of changes thinking about doing this because I knew everyone else would have clothes on. I didn't want to use the paper and coloring and artificial materials. I wanted to be connected to the earth, a nature priestess.

The ensuring discussion focused on how Ellen's mask related to her clients. She explained that she had to be rather formal with her clients and that they couldn't see her in a natural state like this. Some day she hoped that as her confidence and credibility increased she might be able to engage in relationships with clients that were more natural, relationships where she could have them do precisely these kinds of things in wilderness settings where they could discover their own natural self.

Karl's mask was green construction paper with a black tree structure on it and small sticks taped on to the crayon tree.

> My mask is a tree. I've often had the sense of when I die of being buried at the foot of a tree in the Sierras. Being rooted in the earth, natural, being really organic, not speaking a lot (I put a mouth on reluctantly) but seeing and observing, and I sense just being instead of going someplace, doing something, being busy. This mask is the opposite of all that.

Malcolm responded that "it's a blossoming, branchy tree that already has its roots down. Your life is not a change but a branching/blossoming out." The branching out as a metaphor for personal and professional growth struck a resonant tone with the group as several people commented that they saw that process in Karl and liked what the mask represented.

Charlene made a clown mask on blue construction paper with yellow and red markings. It had a kind of smiling Buddha quality to it.

> I was delighted to be able to do this. Then my delight passed, and I didn't know how to do it. Then that passed and I wanted to do the part that is most valuable to me, that I don't use much. That's a part that is joyful, feeling, caring, knowing person. But I couldn't get knowing into the mask. Knowing is what I want to project. Joyful, feeling, caring people sometimes get ripped off. I wanted it also to be simple/primitive, but it didn't stay that way.

Phyllis immediately responded that throughout history the clown and fool has had to be the most knowing, and has been a reservoir of knowledge to the group. A couple of other people told Charlene that they saw that combination of knowing and joyfulness in her and that they thought that part of herself did show through.

Ramone made a multilayered mask where the top layers peel off to reveal other layers underneath.

> It became a very spontaneous process for me. I didn't think about it. I just did it. Lots of moods in my mask. Smiling, sad. This is what people see in me. Holes that go through my several masks connect them together. The second mask is a family mask. It's a mask that is very important to me but not often seen. The third mask is white—words. I want to be able to express in words my sadness, hurt, and pain. The fourth mask is a strong red. It shows a figure flying. It represents my outdoor spirit. The fifth mask is green. A lean-to in nature. Finally a commitment to all these things. In spite of my moods, in the first mask, I have a commitment to all these things. My moods mask that commitment.

There were several comments about the complexity and complicated intertwining, interweaving nature of Ramone's masks. One person suggested that that complicatedness and complexity was part of what Ramone struggled with.

Phyllis had made a jagged, off-centered mask cut out of pink construction paper with many colored lines running horizontally and vertically through the mask.

> I got a pink piece of paper. I don't own a single thing that is pink. I don't associate with pink. My mask is really seven masks in one. They're different facets of me. One part is ordered, the administrative part. One part is simple. One side here is complex and complicated. One part is sharp-edged. The pink is maybe a rebellion against stereotype.

A couple of the women comment on the color pink. They tell Phyllis that she would look great in pink. "Buy something pink when you get back. You'd really look great in pink, really." Phyllis kind of agrees that maybe she will buy something pink when she gets back, and there are some jokes about pink ruffled blouses and little girl look.

Brandon made a square red mask with orange parts on it, two eyes and a mouth.

> I made it simple to indicate what I think should be a rather simple part of my life. Social politics bums me out. I'd like to just be able to have simple social relationships. No real agendas. I get some of that here on these trips. I wish I could integrate that more, make that happen more in my other life. Just to be able to spend social time with people talking about simple things without heavy agendas, heavy politics. . . . Just simple time with people.

Jane responded: "I'm not sure what the expression is on your mask. That may tell more about my relationship with you than anything. I haven't really gotten to know you. I can't tell what you're thinking, what you're feeling when we're interacting."

Charlene adds: "I'm usually suspicious of that simplicity that you like. I don't trust it. But it's real. The simplicity is real. I like that. I can believe that in you."

Liz made a big purple mask, peacocklike, with a big colorful headdress.

> This colorfulness is a part of me that is very important to me, that I don't think people value in me. What people value in me is competence in work. The mask is my adventurousness, my artistic side.

A discussion ensues about why it is that Liz doesn't think her artistic side is valued with considerable affirmation from the group about their own valuing of her artistic and adventurousness side. She is urged to allow that side of herself to come out more so that people can know about it and value it.

I'm the last one to share my mask. The sharing has gone on for about 45 minutes, and it's clear that people are a little bit restless. I feel a bit nervous because I don't really want to get into a discussion about how the mask represents my evaluator self. I've kept my mask in my notebook so that when I take it out and put it on people see it for the first time. My mask is plain black construction paper with small eyeholes, no other features on the mask. When I put the mask on there is a clear reaction from the group. I hear people saying, "All right! That's it. Right on. That's the evaluator all right."

I explain that the mask represents, for me, my dark, gloomy side, a part of me that I keep hidden from people. Several people respond that that side of me is not hidden, that they can tell things are going on inside of me, but that it's hard to now when I'm being internally reflective as an evaluator and when I'm being internally reflective as a person. Several jokes are made about what this whole exercise would be like if done with a group of evaluators. "Imagine a whole room of people in black masks." There are screams of horror.

I've since used the exercise in evaluation workshops to help people focus on their perceptions of the roles, images, and masks of evaluators. It's a powerful exercise that can be added to the repertoire of creative evaluation workshop exercises I've described in other writings (Patton, 1981).

Using Eolithic Clues: Understanding Through Metaphors

> *Though analogy is often misleading, it is the least misleading thing we have.*
>
> Samuel Butler

Creative Evaluation (Patton, 1981) includes a chapter on metaphoric thinking as a way of communicating about and stimulating creativity in program evaluation. Smith et al. (1981) have used metaphors as a source of new methods in evaluation. The evaluation of this wilderness program illustrates how metaphors can be used to help evaluators understand programs. Metaphors can be eolithic clues to program mysteries, particularly the mystery of what a program is trying to accomplish, i.e., its goals.

In the early phase of an evaluation—whether conducting evaluability assessments (Rutman, 1980), helping with goals clarification, or just trying to get a feel for the program—the evaluator is essentially engaged in fieldwork. This fieldwork is aimed at developing a basic understanding of the program. The data collection process may be formal, as in an evaluability assessment, or informal, as in an initial get-acquainted site visit. In either case the evaluator is gathering data about the program to use in designing the study and in working with decision makers. Sensitivity to and awareness of program metaphors can provide a great deal of information about and insight into program philosophy, purpose, processes, and outcomes. As an example of how sensitivity to metaphors, analogies, and similes can provide insights about a program, this chapter presented some of my field observations about the Southwest Field Training Project.

I have identified five different kinds of metaphors that seemed to me to emerge in the Southwest Field Training Project: group cohesion and identity metaphors, life challenge metaphors, process and change metaphors, metaphors of self, and giving special meaning to things. My purpose in reflecting on how metaphors became an important part of the communication patterns during the project has been to make more accessible these eolithic clues. By consciously paying attention to the metaphors we use, by listening carefully to the metaphors that others use, and by looking for opportunities to construct and facilitate the construction of metaphors, we can be more deliberate about our communications and more effective both in sharing our perspective with others and in understanding the perspectives of others. The ability to hear, interpret, and use metaphors to understand programs can be an important skill for evaluators—a creative data collection skill well worth practicing and developing. Halcolm's observations and advice are quite incisive in this regard.

> Programs,
> like people,
> wear masks.
>
> It is the job of evaluators
> to lift the program veil and
> uncover the program mask
> long enough for the people
> involved to see what's underneath.
>
> They may like what they see.
> They may be horrified by what they see.
> They may decide to change what they see.
> They may refuse to see.
> But one of their choices should be
> to put the mask back on
> exactly as it was.
> This means that
> in uncovering a program mask,
> an evaluator must be extremely careful
> not to tear it to shreds.

> from *Halcolm's Evaluation Thoughts*

CHAPTER 5 *Thoughtful Questionnaires*

> *Judge a man by his questions rather than by his answers.*
>
> Voltaire

If survey respondents ever begin to heed Voltaire's advice, questionnaire response rates will plummet. Voltaire would certainly have counted himself proudly and righteously among the nonrespondents in most surveys.

During the past ten years I have spent a considerable amount of time reviewing questionnaires, helping people revise specific items, and trying to make sense out of survey results. As often as not my services would be requested *after* the survey had been conducted when those responsible for analyzing the results had reached a deadend trying to make sense out of what they had. Usually their confusion was justified—the questions they were analyzing were essentially impossible to interpret.

There certainly is no shortage of errors one can make in constructing questionnaires: plural instead of singular items, jargon-laden questions, too much verbiage, poor grammar, overly complicated syntax, obtuse wording, and violation of any or all of Stanley L. Payne's 101 rules set forth in *The Art of Asking Questions* (1951). But these are the technical problems in questionnaire construction, and though such problems are commonplace, they are also relatively easily corrected. Experience, practice, careful pilot testing, and technical training can improve the technical quality of questionnaires. *The more serious problems are conceptual in nature.* In thinking back over the hundreds of questionnaires I have reviewed (not to mention the ones on which I've been a respondent), it is conceptual errors and thoughtless questions that stand out in my mind.

This chapter is about some of the fundamentals of questionnaire writing, particularly conceptual fundamentals. By no means is this chapter a complete guide to questionnaires or survey research. Readers interested in a more complete and technical treatment should consult special books on the subject (e.g., Dillman, 1978; Alwin, 1978; Henerson et al., 1978; Berdie and Anderson, 1974). This chapter focuses on some of the more practical and basic issues in putting together a questionnaire for small-scale evaluations in which there is not pretense of doing sophisticated research and no intention of carrying out sophisticated statistical analyses of questionnaire responses. The purpose of this chapter is to increase the likelihood that simple questionnaires will yield information that is worth using.

One doesn't need a doctorate to write questionnaires. What one does need is some clear thinking about the kind of information that is needed and an understanding of what kinds of questions to ask to get the needed information. I would hazard a guess that questionnaires are probably employed more often than any other technique in evaluation. Questionnaires also probably generate more worthless data than any other technique in evaluation. Greater attention to a few fundamentals of questionnaire writing would improve immensely the quality of data being generated by many local evaluations. Moreover, the issues discussed in this chapter with regard to improving the quality of questionnaires are also relevant to the more general issue of carefully clarifying overall evaluation questions. Well-focused evaluation questions are necessary to design useful evaluation questionnaires.

COLLABORATIVE QUESTIONNAIRE DESIGN

Where do the questions come from for evaluation questionnaires?

If one is engaged in the kind of collaborative evaluation practice described in Chapter 3, the decision makers and information users with whom one is working are the major source of questions for the evaluation *and* for specific questionnaires. Sometimes evaluation task force members are sufficiently interested in questionnaire design that I'll do a half-day workshop on the subject before getting down to the task of writing specific items for their evaluation. That workshop basically covers the material in this chapter on how to write questionnaire items. Most typically, however, there is neither time nor inclination for a survey research workshop, so I'll simply work with task force members on identifying the information they want from a survey. I'll begin by identifying with them the likely categories of questions, e.g., a section on what program participants have actually done in the program, a section on what they've gotten out of the program, a section on ways the program can be improved, a section on respondents' backgrounds, and so on. For a large group of evaluation task force members I'll break them into smaller groups and have each small group write potential items for a section. For a smaller task force we'll simply begin moving through section by section. For each section I first ask each individual participant to write five items; then items are shared by reading them in the group. Agreement is reached on which items are most important. During these discussions the focus is on what information is needed and how results would be used, *not* on writing technically correct and rigorous items. Once the important information that is needed has been identified, the evaluator has the responsibility for translating that information into technically correct items that are clear, understandable, and arranged in a proper format and sequence. These technical issues are the focus of most of this chapter.

Another important source of questionnaire items is fieldwork in the program prior to a survey. By spending time in a program observing what is happening, talking with program participants, learning their concerns, interests, and even special language (i.e., how they refer to staff, program components, and so on), the evaluator can develop insights that will make it possible to "ground" a questionnaire in the realities of firsthand, direct program experience (see Glaser and Strauss, 1967, for a discussion of "grounding"). The point here is that in working with the evaluation task force members in collaborative questionnaire design, the evaluator's collaborative input will be enhanced through direct program observations and experiences that can provide insights into information that will be useful and relevant to decision makers and information users. The evaluator doesn't just facilitate task force members in their efforts to decide what questionnaire items ought to be asked. The active-reactive-adaptive evaluator participates in that process as a contributor.

A third source of questionnaire items is other questionnaires that have been used for similar purposes. Borrowing items from other instruments is especially important when one wants to do comparisons. For comparisons to be completely valid, comparison items should be identical. However, I prefer not to introduce borrowed instruments or items to task force members until after they've struggled some themselves with what they want to find out. The process of figuring out what should be asked on a questionnaire is a process that lays the foundation for later analysis and utilization of findings. Even though it may mean some recreating of the wheel (i.e., duplicating the questionnaire design efforts of others), I prefer to hold back on review of similar questionnaires until the people with whom I'm working have decided for themselves what kinds of questions are worth asking.

Once the basic content of the questionnaire has been decided, the evaluator works alone on the technical writing of specific items. When a draft instrument is ready, the task force members meet again to review the instrument. At this meeting the evaluator will need to be prepared to explain why questions have been asked in a particular way using a particular format. The later sections of this chapter focus on the reasons for arranging and writing items in a particular way. Still, the evaluator needs to remain open to suggestions and revisions offered by task force collaborators.

Involving stakeholders in questionnaire design is based on the assumption that the potential for utilization is enhanced if users believe in, understand, and have a stake in the data. Understanding is enhanced by direct involvement in the painstaking process of making decisions about what data to collect and how to collect them. Decision makers who acquiesce to the expertise of the evaluator may later find that they neither understand nor believe in evaluation data. By the same token, evaluators can expect resistance to using findings if they rely on the mysticism of their scientific priesthood to establish the credibility of data rather than relying on the understanding of decision makers directly involved with the evaluation.

CONCEPTUAL CLARITY IN QUESTIONNAIRES

Once the evaluator knows the kind of information that is needed on a questionnaire, the design challenge is communicating clearly to respondents so that they too know what information is needed and wanted as they fill out the questionnaire. The kind of problem that can arise when respondents receive a questionnaire that is not conceptually clear is nicely illustrated by the reactions of grammarian Richard Mitchell (1979: 3-5) to a survey he received.

> A colleague sent me a questionnaire. It was about my goals in teaching, and it asked me to assign values to a number of beautiful and inspiring goals. I was told that the goals were pretty widely shared by professors all around the country.
>
> It spoke of a basic appreciation of the liberal arts, a critical evaluation of society, emotional development, creative capacities, students' self-understanding, moral character, interpersonal relations and group participation, and general insight into the knowledge of a discipline. Unexceptionable goals, every one.
>
> Instead of answering the questionnaire, I paid attention to its language; and I began by asking myself . . . how a "basic" appreciation was to be distinguished from some other kind of appreciation. I recalled that some of my colleagues were in the business of *teaching* appreciation. It seemed all too possible that they would have specialized their labors, some of them teaching elementary appreciation and others intermediate appreciation, leaving to the most exalted members of the department the senior seminars in advanced appreciation, but even that didn't help with basic appreciation. It made about as much sense as blue appreciation.
>
> As I mulled this over, my eye fell on the same word in the covering letter, which said, "We would appreciate having you respond to these items." Would they, could they, "basically appreciate" having me respond to these items? Yes, I think they could. And what is the appropriate response to an item? Would it be a basic response?
>
> Suddenly I couldn't understand anything. I noticed, as though for the first time, that the covering letter promised "to complete the goals and objectives aspect of the report." What is a goals aspect? An objectives aspect? How do you complete an aspect? How seriously could I take a mere aspect, when my mind was beguiled by the possibility of a basic aspect? Even of a basic goals and basic objectives basic aspect?
>
> After years of fussing about the pathetic, baffled language of students, I realized that it was not in their labored writings that bad language dwelt. *This*, this inane gabble, this was bad language. Evil language. Here was a man taking the

public money for the work of his mind and darkening counsel by words without understanding.

Mitchell is clearly a tough respondent. He has dedicated himself to increasing the clarity of the language people use, thereby hoping to increase the clarity of communications. Some improper use of language results from ignorance of what is proper and poor training in how to speak and write. Much improper usage, however, results from the simple failure to think about what is really being said. That's the reason this chapter is entitled "Thoughtful Questionnaires." Clarity results from careful deliberation and thoughtfulness. This chapter isn't about technical formulas for survey design. It's about being conscious of what questions mean so as to avoid the more obvious inanities that so outrage a Richard Mitchell, or may simply turn off a questionnaire respondent, or confuse evaluation results. Mitchell's final evaluation of the questionnaire he received contains both a warning and a challenge:

> Who speaks reason to his fellow men bestows it upon them. Who mouths inanity disorders thought for all who listen. There must be some minimum allowable dose of inanity beyond which the mind cannot remain reasonable.
>
> This man the [survey researcher] had offered me inanity. I had almost seized it. . . . People all around you are offering inanity and you are ready to seize it, like any well-behaved American consumer dutifully swallowing the best advertising pill. *You are, in a certain sense, unconscious.*
>
> *Language is the medium in which we are conscious.* The speechless beasts are aware, but they are not conscious [Mitchell, 1979: 5].

The point of this chapter is that reason, deliberation, and consciousness are essential to practical questionnaire writing. The sections that follow discuss the most common conceptual weaknesses I run into when consulting on evaluation questionnaires. The chapter closes with some suggestions about alternative ways of designing and administering questionnaires.

CONCEPTUAL ISSUES IN CONDUCTING SURVEYS

A great way for an evaluator simultaneously to impress, intimidate, and indurate a program staff is to begin by stressing the importance of establishing "a theoretically sound conceptual framework" for the evaluation. A theoretically sound conceptual framework sounds like something *The Music Man* would sell to the good people of River City to keep their children out of pool halls.

Conceptualizing an evaluation questionnaire doesn't require some grandiose theoretical framework or a voluminous and vortiginous vocabulary. That grand old measurement savant Rudyard Kipling provided all the conceptual framework one needs to construct questionnaires.

> I keep six honest serving men
> They taught me all I knew:
> Their names are What and Why and When
> And How and Where and Who.

I find that the people with whom I'm working warm quickly to the task of conceptualizing the evaluation when I recall for them Kipling's "conceptual framework for measurement."

What . . . . . ?	What do we want to find out?
Why . . . . . . ?	Why do we want to find that out?
When . . . . . ?	When do we need the information?
How . . . . . . ?	How can we get the information we need?
Where . . . . ?	Where should we gather information?
Who . . . . . . ?	Who is the information for and from whom should we collect the information we need?

What Do We Want to Find Out?

Not counting background or demographic items, there are four major kinds of questions that are commonly asked on evaluation questionnaires.

Behavior questions ask about what a person does or has done. These questions are aimed at descriptions of actual program experiences, activities, actions by participants, and respondent behaviors that would have been observable had the evaluator been present when the behavior took place.

Opinion questions are aimed at finding out what people *think* about something, usually about various aspects of a program in which they have participated. Opinion questions tell us about people's goals, intentions, desires, and values.

Feeling questions elicit information about the emotional responses of people to their experiences and thoughts. Feelings occur inside people. They are their natural, emotional responses to what they experience. Feelings tap the affective dimensions of human life and program experience.

Knowledge questions are asked to find out what factual information the respondent has. The assumption in asking knowledge questions is that certain things are considered to be known or true. These things are not opinions, they are not feelings, and they are not actions. Rather, they are things that one *knows*, the facts of the case. Knowledge about a program may consist of reporting on what services are available, who is eligible, the characteristics of clients, who the program serves, how long people spend in the program, the rules and regulations of the program, how one enrolls in the program, and so on. Knowledge questions may also ask about specific things the respondent is expected to have learned in the program. While from a philosophical point of view it is possible to argue that all knowledge is merely a set of beliefs rather than facts, the issue here is to find out what the person being questioned considers to be factual.

The key conceptual issue is designing a program evaluation questionnaire is to determine precisely what information is needed about participants and/or staff behaviors, opinions, feelings, and knowledge. Then, having decided what it is important to find out, the questionnaire must be designed so as to clearly distinguish between knowledge, opinion, feeling, and behavior questions. The wording and format of questions should clearly communicate to the respondent what kind of question is being asked. Confusion on this issue is a major conceptual flaw in many evaluation questionnaires.

Clearly Focused Questions

Having decided what we want to find out from a survey, it is essential that the questionnaire be carefully designed and clearly focused to communicate to respondents what we are asking them. This means that response categories or scales should be consistent with the type of information being sought. Knowledge questions imply true/false answers. Opinion questions request respondents to agree or disagree. Behavioral items ask what the respondent has actually experienced. Feeling questions should tap emotional states.

Now let us look at how confusion arises about what is being asked. Suppose we're evaluating a sexual fulfillment workshop for couples. A preworkshop questionnaire is to be used as part of the evaluation. The following item is part of the questionnaire:

The pleasure sensations of sexual intercourse are more emotional than physical.

Is this question asking about my knowledge, my opinion, my experience, or my feelings? It depends on what scale I use for response categories.

Knowledge cue: "The pleasure sensations of sexual intercourse are more emotional than physical."

True	False	Don't Know

This question implies that there is known, research-based, right or wrong answer to the question. I am being asked if I know the correct answer.

Opinion cue: "The pleasure sensations of sexual intercourse are more emotional than physical."

Strongly Agree	Agree	Disagree	Strongly Disagree

This question implies that there may not be a right or wrong answer. I am being asked for my opinion, for my assessment of the situation based on my own logical or illogical deductions—what do I think rather than what do I know.

> *Experience cue:* "The pleasure sensations of sexual intercourse are more emotional than physical."

Always for me	Often	Sometimes	Seldom	Rarely	Never for me

Here the format tells me that I'm being asked about my own experience. An answer implies that I've had sexual intercourse, that I've examined my experience, and that I can report on the nature of those experiences.

> *Feeling cue:* "During sexual intercourse what sensations do you usually feel?"

intense emotional sensations	___	___	___	___	___	___	intense physical sensations

This semantic-differential format helps to gain access to feelings by providing contrasting types of feelings and asking the respondent to report the relative balance between them. The question cues the respondent to a feeling response rather than a knowledge, opinion, or frequency of behavior response.

Admittedly these are matters of nuance. But of such nuances are good questionnaires made. Matching the response categories to the type of question being asked and the kind of information needed is essential to obtain valid and reliable results. The empirical results of the questionnaire as well as the meaning of those results will be different depending on how one cues the respondent. All too often, however, evaluators adopt a true/false or agree/disagree format for all the items on a questionnaire regardless of whether the information being solicited taps knowledge, opinion, behavior, or feelings. Consider how the interpretations of the items below are changed by altering the scales used.

(1) This workshop is for everyone.

True	False	Don't know	(factual cue: Is it open to and aimed at the general public?)
Agree	Disagree	No Opinion	(open cue: Should it be open and available to the general public?)

(2) IRS income tax audits are fair.

True	False		(factual cue: Someone has studied IRS audits and determined their fairness.)

Agree	Disagree		(opinion cue: What attitude do I have based on whatever I may have heard?)
a. My experience was fair.			(experience cue: Presumes I've been involved in at least one IRS audit.)
b. My experience was unfair.			

(3) Students in schools today are disciplined less than students a generation ago.

True	False	Don't know	(knowledge cue: facts are known to someone.)
Agree	Disagree	No opinion	(opinion cue)

Compared to me, my children are:

a. disciplined less   (experience cue)
b. the same
c. disciplined more

The lines between knowledge, opinion and behavior are often fuzzy. There are opinions and feelings about knowledge and behaviors. There is knowledge about opinions, feelings, and behavior. Experience can be, and often is, the basis for knowledge, feelings, and opinions. But it is precisely because these things are so easily confused that the evaluator must provide clear cues to questionnaire respondents about what is being asked. Without clear cues different respondents will interpret questions in different ways, questions won't make much sense to respondents, and data analysis will show the results to be uninterpretable. The following items taken from actual evaluation questionnaires illustrate the problem of an inappropriate match between item and scale.

Example	Comment
(1) Staff in this progam must have a college degree. Agree Disagree	The question was meant to tap client knowledge about staff qualifications but many clients interpreted the question as asking for their opinion about what qualifications staff should have.
(2) Children in kindergarten can go the full school day without a nap. True False	Many parents interpreted this as a knowledge question asking about their knowledge concerning state laws regulating naps for kindergarten children. Actually, the program staff wanted to get parents opinions about the need for naps in full-day kindergarten.

(3) I participate in making decisions here.

   True   False

The true/false dichotomy makes the questions difficult to answer in cases where participating is not clear cut. A better scale would be: always, often, sometimes, seldom, rarely, never *or* all decisions, many decisions, some decisions, few decisions, no decisions.

Cues for Respondent Comparisons

> *"Take some more tea," the March Hare said to Alice, very earnestly.*
> *"I've had nothing yet," Alice replied in an offended tone: "so I can't take more."*
> *"You mean you can't take less," said the Hatter: "it's very easy to take* more *than nothing."*
>
> Lewis Carroll

Another frequent source of problems in questionnaire construction is conceptual confusion about what kinds of comparisons and judgments are to be made by respondents. In working with school administrators to design personnel evaluation forms for school principals, I collect over sixty such forms from districts throughout the country. In over three-fourths of the forms we reviewed, a scale something like the following was used:

Overall, this person's performance is . . .
   a. excellent
   b. good
   c. average
   d. needs improvement
                OR
Overall, this person's performance is . . .
   a. outstanding
   b. above average
   c. adequate
   d. poor
   e. inadequate
                OR
Overall, this person's performance is . . .
   a. superior
   b. adequate
   c. below average

All of these examples mix criterion-based and norm-referenced scales. A criterion-based scale asks for a comparison against the respondent's own absolute criteria for performance: excellent, good, fair, or poor. The respondent is being asked to think about what constitutes "excellent" performance and to use that criterion of excellence in answering the question. A norm-referenced scale, on the other hand, asks that the comparison be made with some reference group in mind: the person is then above average, average, or below average in comparison to that reference group.

When parts of criterion-based and norm-referenced scales appear in the same item in the respondent has mixed cues about what kind of comparison is being requested. It is quite possible for a person to be both a "poor" teacher and an "average" teacher if most of the teachers in the reference group are poor. (College student ratings of their professors regularly confirm that a teacher can be both poor *and* average.)

The same admonition holds for all kinds of ratings, not just personnel ratings. Ratings of workshops, training sessions, program activities, instructional materials, facilities, policies, and so on can all be rated according to ideal criteria or normative criteria. In many cases both criteria will be requested. In no case, however, should both criteria be mixed in a single scale.

It is also helpful to respondents if one specifies explicitly the appropriate basis for comparison, especially normative comparison.

> Compared to other workshops you have taken, how would you rate this workshop?
>
> Compared to your expectations when you arrived, how would you rate the workshop?
>
> Compared to other speakers at this workshop, how would you rate the presentation by _____ ?
>
> Compared to your usual sources of information, how valuable was this workshop as a source of information?
>
> In comparison to your own personal ideals for what you should get out of a workshop, how would you rate this workshop session?
>
> Compared to other learning experiences offered by this university, how would you rate this workshop?

This wording of a questionnaire item should tell the respondent precisely what the evaluator wants to find out. Ambiguous questions and response scales that mix criteria seriously reduce the validity and usefulness of survey data.

The Odd-Even Question

Should response scales be even-numbered (e.g., four or six response categories) or odd-numbered (e.g., three or five response categories)? It doesn't seem like such a big thing, actually, but I've seen evaluators on both sides of the question go at each other with the vehemence of Marxists versus capitalists, osteopaths versus chiropractors, or physicists who believe that light consists of particles versus those who believe in the wave theory of light. What's all the ruckus about? It's about whether or not to give people a midpoint on questionnaire items. In conducting workshops on evaluation instrumentation it is the most common question I get: "Should we give people a midpoint?"

An even-numbered scale has no midpoint.

Strongly Agree		Agree		Disagree		Strongly Disagree
Always	Usually	Often	Sometimes	Rarely		Never
		True	False			
Very Satisfied		Somewhat Satisfied		Somewhat Dissatisfied		Very Dissatisfied

Active ____ ____ ____ ____ ____ ____ Passive

Excellent	Good	Fair	Poor
A great deal	Somewhat	Not too much	Not at all
	Yes	No	

Ugly   1   2   3   4   5   6   7   8   9   10   Beautiful

An odd-numbered scale has a midpoint, a neutral position, a balance point, or just a plain old "don't know."

Strongly agree	Agree	Undecided or No opinion	Disagree	Strongly disagree
Always	Often	About half the time	Seldom	Never
	True	Don't know	False	
Very satisfied	Basically satisfied	In-between: both satisfied and dissatisfied	Basically dissatisfied	Very dissatisfied

Active ____ ____ ____ ____ ____ ____ ____ Passive

Excellent	Good	Fair	Poor	Unacceptable
A great deal	A fair amount	Somewhat	A little	None
	Yes	Maybe	No	

Ugly   0   1   2   3   4   5   6   7   8   9   10   Beautiful

Even-numbered scales force people to lean in one direction or the other (although a few will circle the two middle responses creating their own midpoint if not provided one by the investigator). Odd-numbered scales allow the respondent to hedge, to be undecided, or, in less kind terms, to cop out of making a decision one way or the other, or yet again, to be genuinely in the middle.

One of the best descriptions of a genuine middle ground is Thomas Hardy's description of Farmer Oak in *Far From the Madding Crowd:*

> Upon the whole, he was one who felt himself to occupy morally that vast middle space of Laodicean neutrality which lay between the Communion people of the parish and the drunken section,—that is, he went to church, but yawned privately by the time the congregation reached the Nicene creed, and thought of what there would be for dinner when he meant to be listening to the sermon. Or, to state his character as it stood in the scale of public opinion, when his friends and critics were in tantrums, he was considered a rather bad man; when they were pleased, he was rather a good man; when they were neither, he was a man whose moral colour was a kind of pepper-and-salt mixture. . . . His features adhered throughout their form exactly to the middle line between the beauty of St. John and the ugliness of Judas Iscariot.

One thing about questionnaires is clear: If given a midpoint many respondents will use it. Not given a midpoint, almost all respondents will still complete all items, leaning one way or the other.

"Which one is best?" I'm regularly asked at workshops. "Should respondents be given a midpoint?" Having carefully considered the arguments on both sides of the issue, having analyzed a large number of questionnaires with both kinds of items, and having meditated on the problem at great length, I find that I am forced to come down firmly and unwaveringly right smack in the middle. It depends. Sometimes odd-numbered scales are best and sometimes even-numbered scales are best.

The issue is really conceptual, not statistical or methodological. What do you want to find out? Will the information you want be more useful if people are forced to lean in one direction or the other, or do you really want to know what proportion of people are undecided or "don't know." What's your own theory about the human mind (or better yet, the theory held by the decision makers who will use the survey information)? Do you (or they) believe that "down deep inside" everyone really leans one way or the other, or do you believe that some people are genuinely in the middle on the issues you are measuring? Do you want to encourage people to guess on true/false questions (omitting the "don't know" response has that effect) or do you really want to know if they "don't know"?

For those of you who can't make up your minds (the "not sure" position on this weighty issue of odd versus even), I recommend the six-point scale. A six-point scale has the virtue of permitting both kinds of analysis. You can dichotomize the data to see what proportion lean in one direction or the other.

strongly agree	mostly agree	slightly agree	slightly disagree	mostly disagree	strongly disagree
% agreeing			% disagreeing		

You can also trichotomize the data to compare the more strongly opinionated with those who lean toward the middle, thus ending up with a midpoint in the analysis (including those who circled both middle responses on the questionnaire).

strongly agree	mostly agree	slightly agree	slightly disagree	mostly disagree	strongly disagree
% more strongly agreeing		% tending toward neutrality		% more strongly disagreeing	

There is also the question of whether a scale is really odd or even. For example, it is possible to treat a "don't know" response on a true/false questionnaire as a midpoint. In weighting the responses in this way one is making the judgment that respondents who know that they "don't know" deserve a higher score than a respondent who answers the true/false question wrong. Thus, for example, one way of adding a series of true/false questions to obtain an overall knowledge score is to add one for a correct response, subtract one for a wrong response, and count a "don't know" response as a zero. Conceptually, this is the same as treating the "don't know" response as a midpoint. At least that is my opinion. Nick Smith, in personal correspondence, argues that "a midpoint is not the same as a 'don't know.' A midpoint is a position on a continuum, while a 'don't know' signifies that the respondent cannot place him or herself on the continuum at all—not the same as being in the middle." From this perspective, a true/false scale is an even scale and the "don't know" response indicates missing data, or is counted separately from the true and false responses. Smith's point is an important one, identifying as he does an important issue of conceptual debate. The debate, in my opinion, is not empirically resolvable. It is a conceptual issue that must be resolved situationally by deciding what a response *means* in a particular context, for a particular group of respondents, on a particular set of items, and given particular information needs of the people who will use and interpret data from the questionnaire. Sometimes it may make conceptual sense to treat a "don't know" or "undecided" response as a midpoint; at other times such an interpretation would not make sense.

Here again is the recurring theme of situational responsiveness. The point is to get away from standard formulas and rigid rules in evaluation, including questionnaire writing, so that the practical evaluator develops the heuristic of automatically *not* doing things automatically, or even routinely. Deliberate choice and conscious selectivity are the order of the day.

By way of closing this section on item construction, it may be worth noting that there is yet another way of expanding a true/false scale beyond a mere two points while adding considerable conceptual clarity to a questionnaire, particularly in instances in which a knowledge item is poorly, ambiguously, or incorrectly worded. The technical suggestion that follows comes from *Peanuts* cartoonist Charles Schultz via that eminent methodologist Peppermint Patty. In the midst of a test using a true/false format, Peppermint Patty raises her hand and asks the teacher: "Ma'am, what do we do if we come across a half-truth?"

I've seen (and have been a respondent to) a number of questionnaires that would have been more valid if the true/false format had been supplemented with a "half-truth" option. Indeed, there are occasions when an entire evaluation report might be so labeled, based on the quality of the questionnaire data reported in the evaluation.

Face Validity of Questionnaire Items

This chapter places high value on the "face validity" of questionnaires. Face validity concerns "the extent to which an instrument looks like it measures what it is intended to measure" (Nunnally, 1970: 149). One of the best ways to facilitate stakeholder understanding of and belief in evaluation data is to place a high value on face validity. Social science technicians prefer to emphasize statistically based forms of validity: predictive validity, concurrent validity, and construct validity (Nunnally, 1970). These concerns are appropriate for basic research and larger-scale evaluations aimed at generalizable results. For local evaluations aimed at getting simple and straightforward information from participants in a program, and where results will not be generalized beyond the local setting, I shall argue that the concern for face validity is not only sufficient, but is, indeed, the priority. Face validity simply means that local people can look at a questionnaire item and tell what the question asks, and what the answer means. Using their commonsensical judgment, they have reason to believe that the questions and answers are valid.

Thus, this chapter doesn't discuss ways of constructing trick questions or projective items. Anyone who has taken a psychological inventory is familiar with projective questions:

On a typical Saturday night would you rather
  (a) go to a wild party,
  (b) swim a moat and storm a castle in search of adventure, or
  (c) stay home with a quiet book?

In this question it's not altogether clear what any particular answer means, so the meaning has to be projected and inferred. A question with more face validity would go like this:

What kind of person are you in new social situations?
- (a) a person who meets people easily and is comfortable in new social settings
- (b) a more shy person who is uncomfortable in new social situations
- (c) a kind of in-between person.

Projective questions have played an important part in psychological research. For certain situations decision makers may prefer and need to ask a series of projective questions. This chapter, however, is aimed at those evaluation situations in which a high premium is placed on the gathering of straightforward, practical, and understandable information from questionnaires.

KALEIDOSCOPIC INSTRUMENTS AND DESIGNS

> *Master Fuketsu:* "*If there is movement—there is*
> *no progress;*
> *if there is standstill—there is*
> *stagnation.*
> *This no-movement-no-standstill,*
> *should one be mindful of it?*
> *Should one be unmindful of it?*"
> *Pupil Bokushu:* "*Not to cut when one should*
> *cut invites disorder.*"
> *Master Fuketsu repeats his anthem and his question.*
> *He adds, "If I keep after you in this way, how will you*
> *answer?*"
>
> *The pupil slaps his master once.*
>
> Zen Koan

A slight turn of a kaleidoscope when you're looking through it and you get a different view of things. The image changes. If you turn the kaleidoscope a great deal the image changes substantially or even completely. If you turn the kaleidoscope only slightly, however, the image changes only slightly, being built partly upon that at which you were looking initially.

The same possibilities hold in the design of questionnaires. The usual procedure is to work toward a single, fixed instrument. Once revisions have been made in a questionnaire and final changes have been incorporated as a result of pilot testing, it is fundamental in traditional survey research that the instrument must not subsequently be changed. The ideal is for the questions to be exactly the same for all respondents: the color of the paper should be the same, the print should be the same, the length should be the same, and, as near as possible, the time at which respondents receive the instrument should be the same for everyone in the sample. The purpose of all this sameness is to improve the meaningfulness and validity of generalizations. Any changes in the instrument constitute threats to the reliability and validity of the questionnaire or interview.

To make progress in the uses of questionnaires for evaluative purposes it may be necessary to slap gently the face of methodological masters who repeat this anthem that a research instrument, once designed, must never be changed lest we reduce the validity and reliability of subsequent data. In evaluation practice we are constantly making tradeoffs among the various things we want to accomplish. What tradeoffs compete with the value obtained from fixed questionnaires?

One practical problem is that evaluators and decision makers often want to ask program participants more questions than can reasonably be incorporated into a single instrument. Long questionnaires can understandably reduce return rates. Might it not be possible, then, to send some respondents only some of the questions? This reduces the ability to generalize those items to the entire sample. On the other hand, it means being able to obtain considerably more information about a larger variety of questions.

Another reason for changing items on successive questionnaires is the information one can learn from earlier versions of a questionnaire to redesign, improve, or go in new directions in obtaining later responses. I have hardly ever worked on an evaluation or instrument where we didn't discover at the end some additional questions that we wished we had asked or some finding that needed additional questions to really clarify what respondents meant. Perhaps if we sent questionnaires out in waves, fifty at a time for a sample of three hundred, we might be able to analyze each wave and revise the next questionnaire wave based upon preliminary findings.

In both of these examples of kaleidoscopic instrument adjustments, we are making slight changes in the instrument to get at a different image or perspective. In sending out a questionnaire to three hundred people in waves of fifty we would end up with a basic core of questions answered by the entire sample of three hundred plus a subset of questions answered in each case by only fifty people. The generalizations in the smaller subsamples are weaker, to be sure, but for certain issues and interests powerful generalizations may not be needed. Moreover, many questions turn up quite marked patterns such that further confirmation is likely to make only minimal changes in the results. For example, if participants are being asked:

How helpful were staff to you personally?

| Very helpful | Somewhat helpful | Not too helpful | Not at all helpful |

In analyzing the first fifty questionnaires, 90 percent of the respondents reply "very helpful." Now in constructing the questionnaire it was very difficult to choose among such dimensions as helpfulness, courteousness, respect for clients, attentiveness, flexibility, caring, approachableness, and so forth. There is a long list of staff characteristics that one might be interested in posing to clients for their rating of staff. Given the marked response from the first fifty respondents (randomly sampled), the next wave of questionnaires might ask about a different characteristic since the findings on staff "helpfulness" are fairly clear. Indeed, by changing the terminology with the next fifty questionnaires one gets a much better sense of what clients actually meant by "helpfulness' since the results on some related but different characteristics might turn out either the same or different, thus allowing one to validate, amplify, and better understand those initial responses.

Another variation on this same theme is simply to do kaleidoscopic instrument design from the very beginning. If time is an issue such that it's not possible to take six months to send out six consecutive waves of fifty questionnaires each, then six different instruments might be sent out all at once each with a common core of questions for generalization to the entire sample and each with a subset of questions for generalization only to the subsample. This permits any given instrument to be relatively shorter while gaining considerably more information from the total sample. Unfortunately, the solution most often chosen to the problem of getting as much information as possible from respondents is to send out very long questionnaires. The response rate often suffers and one ends up with a weak generalization in any case. (For ways of obtaining high response rates on long questionnaires, see Dillman, 1978.) It may be better to send out much shorter questionnaires to begin with, thereby increasing the response rate and getting a more powerful generalization for the core of items as well as very useful information on the less generalizable subset of items.

Scriven has made a similar recommendation with particular focus on being able to add questions to interviews and observation schedules when certain findings turn up midway through the project. He notes that by adding a new interview question halfway through the fieldwork one reduces the generalizability of the information obtained, but to ignore the need to attempt some systematic verification of unanticipated consequences and side effects that may be discovered during fieldwork is worse than changing the instrument. He particularly recommends such adjustments for formative evaluation.

Let us think for a moment about the purpose of a formative evaluation. It's a digging expedition—in part—a search, an investigation, an exploration, a probe, a trouble-shooting trip. It's not just a survey. You are looking for gold, not making a comprehensive map. So you must be able to follow up on leads, not just report them. What this means in practice is changing interview (or observation) forms in mid-stream—not just once, but possibly several times.

The assumption that one can think of all the right questions to ask in advance is pretty dumb. Indeed, even pilot-testing the questionnaire is not going to pick up more than a fraction of these responses that interviewees are reluctant to produce. I see no way in which one can avoid going through this "adjustable instrument methodology."

[T]here may be cases when the question or questions to be asked are perfectly clear in advance, vitally important, and you're not on a "fishing expedition" as well. But as I look at evaluation designs with "instrument adjustment methodology" in mind, I have recently been finding very few that wouldn't have benefitted from this. I am sure that it should be added to our tiny stock of procedures for coping with potentially serious side effects [Scriven, 1979: 36-37].

One of the things I like most about this approach is that it makes clear from the very beginning that evaluators do not have perfect foresight. If one knew exactly how the data were going to come out and knew all the important questions to ask, then it would probably not be necessary to conduct the evaluation. By building in flexibility from the beginning the evaluator is making clear that no single image in the kaleidoscope provides all the desired perspectives so it may be necessary to turn the kaleidoscope slightly now and then in order to increase the number of images and perspectives available to decision makers in their efforts to improve their programs.

One final advantage of this approach is that it forces evaluators to deal with the issue of analysis before all the data have been collected. All too often one doesn't discover just how bad certain questionnaire items are until analysis is begun. Questions that appear to be perfectly clear and focused can suddenly become ambiguous when subjected to actual analysis. Conducting such an analysis on the first wave of questionnaires would still leave time to get rid of bad questions and improve the instrument at each step along the way and with each new wave of questionnaires. When several versions of the same instrument are sent out at the same time the use of multiple questions keeps one from having to put all the interpretation eggs in a single-item basket.

Finally, it can get pretty boring looking at the same kaleidoscopic image all the time. Slight turns in and adjustment to the instrument can give one new and often more interesting perspectives.

DESCENDING UPON THE PRIVATE REGIONS

Questionnaires are an importance source of evaluative information. They are also intrusions into people's lives. In working with a group to design a questionnaire I urge them to imagine being on the receiving end of the survey. To assist them in taking the stance of the poor, beleaguered survey respondent, I'll read the following poem. It was submitted anonymously to N. J. Demerach III and Kenneth G. Lutherman in lieu of a response to an anonymous questionnaire they sent out in their study of student values and campus religion at the University of Wisconsin.

A Note from the Underground
by Respondent No. 5542

The little men in untold legions
Descend upon the private regions.
Behold, my child, the questionnaire,
And be as honest as you dare.

"As briefly as possible, kindly state
Age and income, height and weight.
Sex (M or F); sex of spouse
(or spouses—list).

Do you own your house?
How much of your income goes for rent?
Give racial background, by percent.
Have you had, or are you now having
Orgasm? Or thereunto a craving?
Will Christ return? If so, when?
(kindly fill this out in pen)
Do you masturbate? In what style?
(fill and return the enclosed vial)
Feces? Whose?

And were you beaten?
Was your mother? Sister? Dog?
(attach descriptive catalogue)
Have you mystic inspiration?
Our thanks for you co-operation."

Distended now with new-got lore,
Our plump and pleasant men-of-war
Torture whimsey into fact,
And then, to sanctify the act.
Cast in gleaming, ponderous rows,
Ingots of insipid prose
A classic paper: Soon to be,
Rammed down the throats of such as we.

Thoughtful questionnaires are also sensitive questionnaires, sensitive to the intrusion being made into the lives of respondents, sensitive to the good-will needed to obtain valid and useful responses. Sensitivity and conceptual clarity go hand in hand.

The importance of conceptual clarity in instrument design is the theme running through all these sections on questionnaire construction. Whether the issue is matching the scale to the type of question being asked, deciding whether to ask for criterion-based or norm-referenced comparisons, making a decision on odd versus even scales, or adjusting an instrument through several iterations, *the underlying theme is that you first have to know what you want to find out and then design the items to give you the information you need. Good measurement depends on clear conceptualization of evaluation issues.* And so we return to Kipling's "conceptual framework for measurement."

> I keep six honest serving men
> They taught me all I knew:
> Their names are What and Why and When
> And How and Where and Who.

CHAPTER 6   *Thoughtful Interviewing*

The reason why we have two ears and only one mouth
is that we may listen the more and talk the less.

Zeno of Citium
300 B.C.

Most people approach questionnaire writing with some notion that there are probably some ways of going about the task that one ought to know before plunging in. This doesn't keep them from plunging in, nonetheless, but at least they're aware that if they had the time and inclination they could probably benefit from some training on the matter. Such seems not to be the case with interviewing. Every babe who has ever sat at a mother's knee learning the mother tongue seems to think that skill at interviewing is equivalent to knowing how to talk and listen. They are thus little inclined to spend time training in and practicing the fine art of interviewing. The results are there in hundreds of inane evaluation reports for all to see.

Skill at interviewing is a fundamental evaluation requisite. The themes of conceptual clarity and sensitivity that ran through the chapter on questionnaires are also the themes of this chapter. These themes are especially important here because so many interviewers seem to want to jump into the field without having thought through what they need to find out and how they ought to go about asking questions to find it out. Data can certainly be generated in this way. It's the utility and analyzability of such data that are in question. Such enthusiastic interviewers pay a steep price when it comes time to organize and analyze their interviews.

I feel strongly about this issue because the validity of open-ended interview data is so often (and rightly) called into question as a result of sloppy and thoughtless fieldwork. Yet qualitative interviewing is rich with possibilities. Unfortunately, this approach to gathering evaluative information is too often relegated to exploratory studies in which evaluation questions have not been clearly focused, so open-ended interviewing is adopted as a way of going ahead despite a lack of clarity about the purpose of the evaluation or the data-gathering exercise.

This chapter is a condensation of a much longer chapter on qualitative interviewing in *Qualitative Evaluation Methods* (Patton, 1980). It is included here to call attention to the importance of interviewing as a fundamental evaluation skill, and to emphasize some practical ways of using interviews in an evaluation. The end of the chapter includes some interviewing exercises to emphasize the need for practice and training if one is to become a skilled evaluation interviewer, not just for data-gathering purposes, but also for interacting with and interviewing decision makers and information users in the process of focusing evaluation questions.

Finally, it should be noted that this chapter is mostly applicable to open-ended interviewing. Reading a respondent a closed questionnaire is not the kind of interview discussed in the pages that follow.

INNER PERSPECTIVES

The purpose of interviewing is to find out what is in and on someone else's mind. The purpose of open-ended interviewing is *not* to put things in someone's mind (e.g., the interviewer's preconceived categories for organizing the world), but rather, to access the perspective of the person being interviewed. We interview people to find out from them those things that we cannot directly observe. The issue is not whether observational data are more desirable, valid, or meaningful than self-report data. The fact of the matter is that we cannot observe everything. We cannot observe feelings, thought, and intentions. We can't observe behaviors that took place at some previous point in time. We can't observe situations that preclude the presence of an observer. We can't observe how people have organized the world and the meanings they attach to what goes on in the world—we have to ask people questions about those things. The purpose of interviewing, then, is to allow us to enter into the other person's perspective. The assumption is that perspective is meaningful, knowable, and capable of being made explicit.

It is the responsibility of the interviewer to provide a framework within which people can respond comfortably, accurately, and honestly to open-ended questions. The task undertaken by the interviewer is to make it possible for the person being interviewed to bring the interviewer into his or her world. The quality of the information obtained during an interview is largely dependent upon the interviewer. The purpose of this chapter is to discuss ways of obtaining high-quality information by talking with people who have that information.

This chapter begins by discussing three different types of interviews, three basic approaches to qualitative interviewing. Later sections consider the content of interviews: what to ask questions about and ways of phrasing interview questions. The chapter ends with a discussion of how to record the responses obtained during interviews.

VARIATIONS IN QUALITATIVE INTERVIEWING

There are three basic approaches to collecting qualitative data through open-ended interviews. The three approaches involve different types of preparation, conceptualization, and instrumentation. Each approach has strengths and weaknesses, and each serves a somewhat different purpose. The three choices are:

(1) the informal, conversational interview,
(2) the general interview guide approach, and
(3) the standardized, open-ended interview.

The differences among these three approaches lie in the extent to which interview questions are determined and standardized *before* the interview occurs.

The Informal, Conversational Interview

The informal, conversational interview relies entirely on the spontaneous generation of questions in the natural flow of an interaction, typically an interview that occurs as part of ongoing participant observation fieldwork. During an informal, conversational interview, the persons being talked with may not even realize they are being interviewed. Most of the questions will flow from the immediate context. No predetermined set of questions is possible under such circumstances, because the observer does not know beforehand precisely what is going to happen and what it will be important to ask questions about.

The data gathered from informal, conversational interviews will be different for each person interviewed. In many cases, the same person may be interviewed on a number of different occasions using an informal, conversational approach. This approach is particularly useful where the investigator can stay in the situation for some period of time, so that he or she is not dependent on a single interview to collect all the information needed. Interview questions will change over time, and each interview builds on the other, expanding information that was picked up previously, moving in new directions, seeking elucidations and elaborations from various participants in their own terms. The interviewer must "go with the flow."

The strength of the informal, conversational approach to interviewing is that it allows the interviewer to be highly responsive to individual differences and situational changes. Questions can be individualized to establish in-depth communication with the person being interviewed and to make use of the immediate surroundings and situation to increase the concreteness and immediacy of the interview questions and responses.

The weakness of the informal, conversational interview is that it requires a great amount of time to get systematic information. It may take several conversations with different people before a similar set of questions has been posed to several respondents. The informal, conversational interview is also more open to interviewer effects in that it depends on the conversational skills of the interviewer to a greater extent than do more formal, standardized formats. The conversational interviewer must be able to interact easily with people in a variety of settings, to generate rapid insights, to formulate questions quickly and smoothly, and to guard against asking questions that impose interpretations on the situation by the structure of the questions. Data obtained from informal, conversational interviews are also difficult to pull together and analyze. Because different questions will generate different responses, the interviewer has to spend a great deal of time sifting through responses to find patterns that have emerged at different points in different interviews with different people. By contrast, interviews that are more systematized and standardized facilitate analysis but provide less flexibility in terms of being able to be responsive to individual and situational differences.

The Interview Guide

An interview guide is a list of questions or issues that are to be explored in the course of an interview. An interview guide is prepared in order to make sure that basically the same information is obtained from a number of people by covering the same material. The interview guide provides topics or subject areas within which the interviewer is free to explore, probe, and ask questions that will elucidate and illuminate that particular subject. The issues in the outline need not be taken in any particular order and the actual working of questions to elicit responses about those issues is not determined in advance. The interview guide simply serves as a basic checklist during the interview to make sure that all relevant topics are covered. The interviewer is thus required to adapt both the wording and sequence of questions to specific respondents in the context of the actual interview. The interviewer remains free to build a conversation within a particular subject area, to work questions spontaneously, and to establish a conversational style—but with the focus on a particular subject that has been predetermined.

The advantage of an interview guide is that it makes sure that the interviewer has carefully decided how best to use the limited time available in an interview situation. The interview guide helps make interviewing across a number of different people more systematic and comprehensive by delimiting the issues to be discussed in the interview. The interview guide approach is especially useful in conducting group interviews. A guide keeps the interaction focused, but allows individual perspectives and experiences to emerge. Interview guides can be developed in more or less detail, depending on the extent to which the researcher is able to specify important issues in advance and the extent to which it is felt that a particular sequence of questions is important to ask in the same way or in the same order to all respondents. John Lofland (1971), in his book *Analyzing Social Settings*, provides a number of examples of interview guides that have been used in the conduct of sociological research. What follows is an example of an interview guide used with participants in a manpower training program (Patton, 1980: 201).

Interview Guideline For
Manpower Program Evaluation

What has the trainee done in the program: activities? interactions? products? work performed?

What are the trainee's current work skills? What things can the trainee do that are marketable?

How has the trainee been affected by the program in areas other than job skills—feelings about self? attitudes toward work? aspirations? interpersonal skills? spinoffs?

What are the trainee's plans for the future—work plans? income expectations? lifestyle expectations/plans?

What does the trainee think of the program—strengths? weaknesses? things liked? things disliked? best components? poor components? things that should be changed?

This interview guideline provides a framework within which the interviewer would develop questions, sequence those questions, and make decisions about which information to pursue in greater depth. The interviewer would normally not be expected, however, to go into totally new subjects that are not covered within the framework of the interview guide. The interviewer does not ask questions, for example, about previous employment or education, how the person got into the program, how this program compares with other programs the trainee has experienced, or trainee's health.

The flexibility permitted by the interview guide approach will become clearer after reviewing the third strategy of qualitative interviewing.

The Standardized, Open-Ended Interview

The standardized, open-ended interview consists of a set of questions carefully worded and arranged for the purpose of taking each respondent through the same sequence and asking each respondent the same questions with essentially the same words. Flexibility in probing is more or less limited, depending on the nature of the interview and the skills of interviewers. The standardized, open-ended interview is used when it is important to minimize variation in the questions posed to interviewees. This reduces the possibility of bias that comes from having different interviews for different people, including the problem of obtaining more comprehensive data from certain persons while getting less systematic information from others. A standardized, open-ended interview may be particularly appropriate when a large number of people are to conduct interviews on the same topic and the social scientist wishes to reduce the variation in responses due purely to the fact that, left to themselves, different interviewers will ask questions on a single topic in different ways. By controlling and standardizing the open-ended interview, the investigator obtains data that are systematic and thorough for each respondent, but flexibility and spontaneity are considerably reduced.

In many cases when conducting a study it is only possible to interview participants for a very limited period of time. Sometimes it is only possible to interview each participant once. At other times it is possible and desirable to interview participants before they enter an experience, when they leave the experience, and again after some period of time (e.g., six months) after they have completed the experience. Because of limited time, and because it is desirable to have the same information from each person interviewed, a standardized, open-ended format may be used. The interview questions are written out in advance *exactly* the way they are to be asked during the interview. Careful consideration is given before the interview about how to word each question. Any clarifications or elaborations that are to be used are written into the interview itself. Probing questions are placed in the interview at appropriate places.

The basic purpose of the standardized, open-ended interview is to minimize interviewer effects by asking the same questions of each respondent. Because the interview is systematic, interviewer judgment during the interview is reduced. The standardized, open-ended interview also makes data analysis easier because it is possible to locate each respondent's answer to the same question rather quickly, and to organize questions and answers that are similar. In addition, by generating a standardized form other social scientists can more easily replicate a study in new settings, using the same interview instrument with different subjects. They will then know exactly what was previously asked and what was not previously asked.

The standardized, open-ended interview also reduces variation among interviewers. Some studies use volunteers to do interviewing; at other times key informants may be involved in doing some interviewing; and in still other instances interviewers may be novices, students, or people who are not professional social scientists. When a number of different interviewers are used, variations in data created by differences among interviewers will become particularly apparent if an informal conversational approach to data gathering is used or even if each interviewer uses a basic guide. The best way to guard against variations among interviewers it to word questions carefully in advance and to train the interviewers to stick with the interview. The data collected are still open ended, in the sense that the respondent supplies his or her own words, thoughts, and insights in answering the questions, but the precise wording of the questions is determined ahead of time.

The weakness of this approach is that it does not permit the interviewer to pursue topics or issues that were not anticipated when the interview was written. Constraints are also placed on the use of different lines of questioning with different people based on their unique experiences. Therefore, a standardized open-ended interview approach will reduce the extent to which individual differences and circumstances can be taken into account.

Style Combinations

It is possible to combine an informal, conversational approach with an interview guide approach. It is also possible to combine an interview guide approach with a standardized, open-ended approach. Thus a number of basic questions may be worded quite precisely in a predetermined fashion, while permitting the interviewer more flexibility in probing and more decision-making flexibility in determining when it is appropriate to explore certain subjects in greater depth, or even to undertake whole new areas of inquiry that were not originally included in the interview instrument. It is even possible to have a standardized, open-ended interview format for the early part of an interview and then to leave the interviewer free to pursue any subjects of interest during the latter parts of the interview. Another combination would include the using of the informal, conversational interview early in the research project followed midway by an interview guide, and then closing the study with a standardized, open-ended interview to provide systematic information from a sample of subjects at the end of the experience or when conducting follow-up of participants.

Summary of Interviewing Strategies

The common characteristic of all three qualitative approaches to interviewing is that the persons being interviewed respond in their own words to express their own personal perspectives. While there are variations in strategy concerning the extent to which the wording and sequencing of questions ought to be predetermined, there is no variation in the principle that the response format should be open ended. The interviewer never supplies and predetermines the phrases or categories that must be used by respondents to express themselves. The purpose of qualitative interviewing in social science research is to understand how people in a setting view the setting, to learn their terminology and judgments, and to capture the complexities of their individual perceptions and experiences. This is what distinguishes qualitative interviewing from the closed interview, questionnaire, or test typically used in quantitative research. Such closed instruments force respondents to fit their knowledge, experiences, and feelings into the evaluator's categories. *The fundamental principle of qualitative interviewing is to provide a framework within which respondents can express their own understandings in their own terms.*

Table 6.1 summarizes the basic variations in evaluation research interview instrumentation. In reviewing this summary table it is important to keep

TABLE 6.1 Variations in Evaluation Research Interview Instrumentation

Type of Interview	Characteristics	Strengths	Weaknesses
Informal, conversational interview	Questions emerge from the immediate context and are asked in the natural course of things; there is no predetermination of question topics or wording.	Increases the salience and relevance of questions; interviews are built on and emerge from observations; the interview can be matched to individuals and circumstances.	Different information collected from different people with different questions. Less systematic and comprehensive if certain questions don't arise "naturally." Data organization and analysis can be quite difficult.
Interview guide approach	Topics and issues to be covered are specified in advance, in outline form; interviewer decides sequence and wording of questions in the course of the interview.	The outline increases the comprehensiveness of the data and makes data collection somewhat systematic for each respondent. Logical gaps in data can be anticipated and closed. Interviews remain fairly conversational and situational.	Important and salient topics may be inadvertently omitted. Interviewer flexibility in sequencing and wording questions can result in substantially different responses, thus reducing the comparability of responses.

(continued)

TABLE 6.1 (Continued)

Type of Interview	Characteristics	Strengths	Weaknesses
Standardized, open-ended interview	The exact wording and sequence of questions are determined in advance. All interviewees are asked the same basic questions in the same order.	Respondents answer the same questions, thus increasing comparability of responses; data are complete for each person on the topics addressed in the interview. Reduces interviewer effects and bias when several interviewers are used. Permits decision makers to see and review the instrumentation used in the evaluation. Facilitates organization and analysis of the data.	Little flexibility in relating the interview to particular individuals and circumstances; standardized wording of questions may constrain and limit naturalness and relevance of questions and answers.
Closed quantitative interviews	Questions and response categories are determined in advance. Responses are fixed; respondent chooses from among these fixed responses.	Data analysis is simple; responses can be directly compared and easily aggregated; many questions can be asked in a short time.	Respondents must fit their experiences and feelings into the researcher's categories; may be perceived as impersonal, irrelevant, and mechanistic. Can distort what respondents really mean or experienced by so completely limiting their response choices.

Source: Patton (1980).

in mind that these are presented as pure types. In practice any particular study may employ several of these strategies or combinations of approaches.

THE WORDING OF QUESTIONS

An interview question is a stimulus that is aimed at creating or generating a response from the person being interviewed. The way a question is worded is one of the most important elements determining how the interviewee will respond. As Stanley L. Payne (1951) put it, asking questions is an art. For purposes of qualitative measurement, good questions should, at a minimum, be open-ended, neutral, sensitive, and clear. Each of these criteria will be discussed below.

Asking Truly Open-Ended Questions

The basic thrust of qualitative measurement is to minimize the imposition of predetermined responses when gathering data. When using qualitative interviewing strategies for data collection it is critical that questions be asked in a truly open-ended fashion. This means that the question should permit the person being interviewed to respond in his or her own terms.

The standard questionnaire item in quantitative measurement provides the respondent with a categorical list of response possibilities.

How do you feel about the program? Would you say that you are (a) very satisifed, (b) somewhat satisfied, (c) not too satisfied, (d) not at all satisfied.

It is clear in this instance that the question is closed and that the respondent has been provided with a limited and predetermined set of alternatives. The response possibilities are clearly stated and made *explicit* in the way in which the question is asked. Many interviewers think that the way to make a question open-ended is simply to leave out the structured response categories. Such an approach does *not,* however, make a question truly open ended. It merely makes the predetermined response categories implicit and disguised. Consider the following "open-ended" question:

How satisifed are you with this program?

On the surface this appears to be an open-ended question. Upon close inspection, however, it is clear that the dimension along which the respondent can answer the question has already been identified. The respondent is being asked for some degree of satisfaction. It is true that the interviewee can use a variety of modifiers for the word satisfaction, e.g., "pretty satisfied," "kind of satisifed," "mostly satisfied." But in effect the response set has been narrowly limited by the wording of the question. The desired dimension of response is identified in the wording of the question such that the typical answers are only slightly different from those that would have been obtained had the categories been made explicit from the start.

The truly open-ended question does not presuppose which dimensions of feeling, analysis, or thought will be salient for the interviewee. The truly open-ended question allows the person being interviewed to select from among his or her full repertoire of possible responses. Indeed, in qualitative measurement one of the things the social scientist is trying to determine is what dimensions, themes, and images/words people use among themselves to describe their feelings, thoughts, and experiences. Examples, then, of truly open-ended questions would take the following format:

How do you feel about the program?

What is your opinion of the program?

What do you think of the program?

The truly open-ended question permits the person being interviewed to take whatever direction and use whatever words he or she wants to in order to represent what he or she has to say.

Clarity of Questions

It is the responsibility of the interviewer to make it clear to the interviewee what is being asked. Asking questions that are understandable is an important part of establishing rapport. Unclear questions can make the person being interviewed feel uncomfortable, ignorant, confused, or hostile. Asking focused questions helps a great deal to make things clear. There are a number of other factors that contribute to clarity.

In preparing to do an interview, find out what language the people you are interviewing use in talking about the setting being studied. Use language that is understandable and part of the frame of reference of the person being interviewed. This means taking special care to find out what language the person being interviewed uses to describe the setting, people in the setting, special activities, or whatever else the interviewer is interested in talking about. Learning the interviewee's language also occurs during the interview. The interviewer then uses the language provided by the interviewee in the rest of the interview. Those questions that use the respondent's own language are question that are most likely to be *clear* to the respondent.

Being clear about what you are asking contributes to the process of establishing and maintaining rapport during an interview. Using words that make sense to the interviewee, words that are sensitive to the respondent's context and world view, will improve the quality of data obtained during the interview.

Neutral Questions

As an interviewer I want to establish rapport with the person I'm questioning, but that rapport must be established in such a way that it does not undermine my neutrality concerning what the person tells me. Neutrality means that the person being interviewed can tell me anything without engendering either my favor or disfavor with regard to the content of the response. I cannot be shocked; I cannot be angered; I cannot be embarrassed; I cannot be saddened; indeed, nothing the person tells me will make me think more or less of him or her. In short, I am neutral about the content of the responses.

At the same time that I am neutral with regard to the *content* of what is being told to me, I care very much that that person is willing to share with me what he or she is saying. *Rapport is a stance vis-à-vis the person being interviewed. Neutrality is a stance vis-à-vis the content of what that person says.* Rapport means that I respect the person being interviewed, so what that person says is terribly important because of who is saying it. I want to convey to the interviewee that his or her knowledge, experiences, attitudes, and feelings are important. Yet the content of what is said to me is not important.

One kind of question wording that can help establish neutrality is the *illustrative examples format.* When phrasing questions in this way I want to let the person I'm interviewing know that I've pretty much heard it all. I've heard the bad things and I've heard the good things and so I'm not interested in something that's particularly sensational, particularly negative, or especially positive. I'm really only interested in what that person's experience has really been like. An example of the illustrative examples format is provided by a question taken from interviews we conducted with juvenile delinquents who had been placed in foster group homes. One section of the interview was aimed at finding out how the juveniles were treated by group home parents.

Ok, now I'd like to ask you to tell me how you were treated in the group home by the parents. Some kids have told us that they felt that they were treated like one of the family in the group home; some kids have told us that they got knocked around and beat up by the group home parents; some kids have told us about sexual things that were done to them; some of the kids have told us about a lot of recreational and hobby kinds of things; some kids have felt they have been treated really good and some kids have been treated really bad. When you think about how *you* were treated in the group home, what kind of things come to mind?

A closely related kind of format is the *illustrative extremes format.* With this format I attempt to let the interviewee know that I've heard it all by giving examples only of extreme kind of responses.

How much dope did you use while you were in the group home? I know that some kids have told me they were doped up the whole time they were in the home, they smoked or dropped stuff every day and every night, while other kids have said that they decided to stay completely straight while they were in the home. How about you?

The critical thing to avoid in both the illustrative examples format and the illustrative extremes format is the asking of a *leading* question. Leading questions are the opposite of neutral questions. Leading questions give the interviewee hints about what would be a desirable or appropriate kind of answer. Leading questions "lead" the respondent in a certain direction.

An example of a typical leading question that might be asked of juveniles is:

We know that most kids use a lot of dope because that's part of what it means to be young, so we figure you use it too—right? So what do you think about everybody using dope?

This question has a built-in response bias that communicates the interviewer's belief that drug use among the young is legitimate and universal. The question is leading because the interviewee is led into acquiescence with the interviewer's point of view.

It is important in giving examples that the examples cover several dimensions and are balanced between what might be construed as positive and negative kinds of responses. My own preference is to use these illustrative formats only as clarifying questions after having begun with a simple, straightforward, and truly open-ended question where the response was not constrained or influenced by any kinds of examples: "What has been your experience with the use of drugs in the group home?"

Sensitivity

It is the interviewer's responsibility to be sensitive to how the interviewee may be affected by different questions and various question formats. It is not possible here to review all possible variations in how to ask questions. A few examples of sensitive question formats are provided here to illustrate the point that *how* the question is worded can make a great deal of difference in the quality of the response received.

One stylistic technique that shows sensitivity to the interviewee is providing a context for a question. This can have the effect of making a particularly probing question less personal and intrusive. Consider the two questions below:

How do you sneak dope into the prison?

(versus)

Suppose someone you trusted asked you how to sneak dope into the prison, what would you tell him?

The first question comes across like an interrogation or inquisition. The second question is softened and has more of an informal and sensitive tone to it. Despite the fact that the content is the same for both questions, the second question has the psychological effect on the interviewee of permitting the interviewer to be dissociated from the question. While this technique can be overused and can come across as a phony or trick question if the intonation with which it is asked is hesitating or implies awkwardness, used sparingly and with subtlety this format can ease the asking of difficult questions and can permit the interviewer to obtain high-quality information.

Simulation questions provide a context in a different way. The simulation question asks the person being interviewed to image him- or herself in some situation about which the interviewer is interested.

Suppose I was present with you during one of your group therapy sessions. What would I see happening? What would be going on? Describe to me what one of those sessions is like.

In effect, these kinds of questions ask the interviewee to become an observer. The observer is asked to simulate for the interviewer some situation that has been experienced. In most cases, a response to this question will require the interviewee to visualize in his or her head the situation to be described. When the interviewee is able to move fully into and experience the simulated situation through a visualization, the interviewer may observe that the person being interviewed takes on a far-away expression as if he or she were someplace else. That's the point of the question. Don't try to bring him or her back, but rather, encourage him or her to describe to you what is happening in the simulation. I frequently find that the richest and most detailed descriptions come from a series of questions that ask a respondent to reexperience and/or simulate some experience.

Probes and Follow-Up Questions

Probes are used to deepen the response to a question, to increase the richness of the data being obtained, and to give cues to the interviewee about the level of response that is desired. The word "probe" itself is usually best avoided in interviews. "Let me probe that further . . ." can come across like you are about to perform surgery on the respondent or are conducting an investigation of something illicit or illegal. Quite simply, a probe is an interview tool used to go deeper into the interview responses. As such, probes should be conversational, offered in a natural style and voice, and used to follow up initial responses.

One natural set of conversational probes consists of *detail-oriented* questions. These are the basic questions that fill in the blank spaces of a response.

When did that happen?

Who else was involved?

Where were you during that time?

What was your involvement in that situation?

How did that come about?

Where did that happen?

These *detail-oriented* probes are the basic "who," "where," "what," "when," and "how" questions that are used to get a complete and detailed picture of some activity or experience. There are times, as in the probes suggested above, when *particular* details are elicited through follow-up questions.

At other times an interviewer wants to keep a respondent talking more about a subject. In such cases *elaboration* probes are used. Elaboration probes encompass a variety of ways to cue the person being interviewed that you'd like them to keep talking.

There are times when you want the interviewee to say more because you haven't fully understood an answer. If something has been said that is unclear, ambiguous, or an apparent non sequitur, a *clarification probe* may be useful. Clarification probes tell the interviewee that you need more information, or a restatement of the answer, or more context. A clarification probe should be used quite naturally and gently. It is best for the interviewer to convey the notion that the failure to understand is the "fault" of the interviewer and not a failure by the person being interviewed. The interviewer does not want to make the respondent feel inarticulate, stupid, or muddled. After one or two attempts at achieving clarification, it is sometimes best to leave the particular topic that is causing the confusion and move on to other questions, perhaps returning to that topic at a later point.

A major characteristic that separates probes from general interview questions is that probes are seldom written out in an interview. Probing is an art and skill that comes from knowing what you are looking for in the interview, listening carefully to what is said and what is not said, and being sensitive to the feedback needs of the person being interviewed. Probes are always a combination of verbal and nonverbal cues. Silence at the end of a response can indicate as effectively as anything else that you would like the person to continue. Probes are used to communication with the interviewee about what you, the interviewer, want. More detail? Elaboration? More clarity? Probes, then, provide guidance to the person interviewed. They also provide the interviewer with a way to maintain control of the flow of the interview, a subject discussed in more detail in a later section.

Support and Recognition Responses

Effective interviewing feels to both the interviewer and the interviewee like there is a two-way flow of communication going on. Interviews should not be simply interrogations during which the interviewer intensively pursues a set of questions and the respondent provides the answers. The interviewer has a responsibility to communicate clearly about what information is desired and why that information is important, and to let the interviewee know how the interview is progressing. These things constitute the interviewer's communication to the person being interviewed.

Previous sections have emphasized the wording of questions so that what is being asked is clear and so that it is possible to get detailed responses from persons being interviewed. The purpose of the overall interview and the relationship of particular questions to that overall purpose are important pieces of information that go beyond the simple asking of questions. While the reason for asking a particular question may be absolutely clear to the interviewer, such purposes are not always clear to the respondent. The interviewer communicates respect for people being interviewed by giving them the courtesy of explaining why questions are being asked. Understanding the purpose of the interview will increase the motivation of the interviewee to respond openly and in detail.

The other part of this process of maintaining communication with the interviewee is giving out clues about how the interview is going. One of the most common mistakes in interviewing is a failure to provide reinforcement and feedback to the person being interviewed about how the interviewer perceives the interview progressing. This means that it is necessary, from time to time, to let the interviewee know that the purpose of the interview is being fulfilled. Words of thanks, support, and praise will help make the interviewee feel that the interview process is worthwhile.

"It's really helpful to get such a clear statement of what this community is like. That's just the kind of thing we're trying to get at."

or

"We are about half-way through the interview now and I think a lot of really important things are coming out of what you're saying."

or

"I really appreciate your willingness to express your feelings about that. That's really helpful."

The point here is that the interview is an interaction. The interviewer provides stimuli to generate a reaction. That reaction from the interviewee, however, is also a stimulus to which the interviewer responds. The flow of communication back and forth occurs in the context of the whole interaction. The interviewer must maintain awareness of how the interview is flowing, how the interviewee is reacting to questions, and what kinds of feedback are appropriate and helpful to maintain the flow of the interview.

Maintaining Control of the Interview

Time is precious in an interview. Long-winded responses, irrelevant re-marks, and getting side-tracked in the interview will reduce the amount of time available to focus on critical questions. This means that the interviewer must maintain control of the interview. Control is maintained by (1) knowing what it is you want to find out, (2) asking the right questions to get the kind of answers you want, and (3) giving appropriate verbal and nonverbal feedback to the person being interviewed.

Knowing what one wants to find out in the interview means that one is able to recognize and distinguish appropriate from inappropriate responses. It is not enough just to ask the right questions. The interviewer must listen carefully to make sure that the responses received provide answers to the questions that are asked. Consider the following exchange:

Q: What happens in a typical interviewer training session that you lead?

A: I try to be sensitive to where each person is at with interviewing. I try to make sure that I am able to touch base with each person so that I can find out how they're responding to their training, to get some notion of how each person is doing.

Q: How do you begin a session, a training session?

A: I believe it's important to begin with enthusiasm, to generate some excitement about interviewing.

In this interaction the interviewer is asking descriptive, behavioral questions. The responses, however, are about beliefs and hopes. The responses do not actually describe what happened. Rather, the responses describe what the interviewee thinks ought to happen. Since the interviewer wants descriptive data, it is necessary to first recognize that the responses are not providing the kind of data desired, and then to ask appropriate questions that will lead to behavioral responses.

Interviewer: Okay, you try to establish contact with each person, and you try to generate enthusiasm at the beginning. What I'd like you to do now is to actually take me to a training session. Describe for me what the room looks like, where the trainees are, where you are, and tell me what I would see and hear if I were right there in that session. What would I see you doing? What would I hear you saying? What would I see the trainees doing? What would I hear the trainees saying? Take me into a session so that I can actually experience it.

It is the interviewer's responsibility to work with the person being inter-viewed to facilitate the desired responses. At times it may be necessary to give more direct feedback about the kind of information that has been re-ceived and the kind of information that is desired.

Interviewer: I think I understand now what it is you try to do during an interview training session. You've explained to me what you hope to accomplish and stimulate, now I'd like you to describe to me what you actually do, not what you expect, but what I would actually see happening if I were present at the session.

It is not enough simply to ask the right initial question. Neither is it enough to have a well-planned interview with good, on-target basic questions. The interviewer must listen carefully to the kinds of responses supplied to make sure that the interview is working according to plan. I've seen many well-written interviews that have resulted in largely useless data because the interviewer did not listen carefully to the responses being received and did not recognize that the responses were not providing the kind of information needed. The first responsibility, then, in maintaining control of the interview is knowing what kind of data one is looking for and directing the interview in order to collect that data.

Giving appropriate feedback to the interviewee is essential in pacing an interview and maintaining control of the interview process. Head-nodding, taking notes, "uh-huhs," and silent probes (remaining quiet when a person stops talking to let them know the interviewer is waiting for more) are all signals that the person being interviewed is on the right track. On the other hand, it is often necessary to stop a highly verbal respondent who gets off the track. The first step in stopping the long-winded respondent is to cease giving the usual cues mentioned above that encourage talking: stop nodding the head; interject a new question as soon as the respondent pauses for breath; stop taking notes, or call attention to the fact that one has stopped taking notes by flipping the page of the writing pad and sitting back, waiting. When these nonverbal cues do not work, it becomes necessary to interrupt the long-winded respondent.

Let me stop you here, for a moment. I want to make sure I fully understand something you said earlier. (Then ask the question aimed at getting the response more targeted.)

or

Let me ask you to stop for a moment because some of what you're talking about now I want to get later in the interview. First I need to find out from you . . .

Interviewers are sometimes concerned that it is impolite to interrupt an interviewee. It certainly can be awkward, but when done with respect and sensitivity, the interruption can actually help the interview. It is both patronizing and disrespectful to let the respondent run on when no attention is being paid to what he or she is saying. It is respectful, of both the person being interviewed and the interviewer, to make good use of the short time available to talk. It is the responsibility of the interviewer to help the interviewee understand what kind of information is being requested and to establish a framework and context that make it possible to collect the right kind of information.

One example of how this can be done is to tell the interviewee quite explicitly that you, as the interviewer, may have to interrupt a response to keep the interview moving along so that all questions are covered in the time available. This announcement about the interviewer's role will help legitimate subsequent interruptions. Thus, I might say something like the following:

(Interviewer interrupting a long-winded response)

Excuse me a moment here. Let me interrupt at this point to be sure I'm following you. I find myself feeling very conscious of how many questions I still need to ask you, and how quickly interview time can pass. What I'd like to do is move on through the next sections of the interview, and then come back to fill in more detail if we have time at the end. I'm anxious to get your responses to all the questions, so I hope you'll forgive me if I interrupt some of your more detailed responses and hold those for later. Okay, the next question I'd like to ask is . . .

Asking focused questions in an appropriate style to get relevant answers that are useful in understanding the interviewee's world is what interviewing is all about. Maintaining focus on information that is useful, relevant, and appropriate requires concentration, practice, and the ability to separate that which is foolish from that which is important. In his classic *Don Quixote,* Cervantes describes a scene in which Sancho is rebuked by Don Quixote for trying to impress his cousin by repeating deeply philosophical questions and answers that he has heard from other people, all the while trying to make the cousin think that these philosophical discourses were Sancho's own insights.

"That question and answer," said Don Quixote, "are not yours, Sancho. You have heard them from someone else."

"Whist, sir," answered Sancho, "if I start questioning and answering, I shan't be done til tomorrow morning. Yes, for if it's just a matter of asking idiotic questions and giving silly replies, I needn't go begging help from the neighbors."

"You have said more than you know, Sancho," said Don Quixote, "for there are some people who tire themselves out learning and proving things that, once learned and proved, don't matter a straw as far as the mind or memory is concerned" [Cervantes, 1964: 682].

Regardless of which interview strategy is used—the informal conversational interviews, the interview guide approach, or standardized, open-ended interviews—the wording of quesitons will affect the nature and quality of responses received. Constant attention to the purpose of specific interviews and to the ways in which questions can be worded to achieve that evaluation purpose will reduce the extent to which, in Cervantes's words, evaluators "tire themselves out learning and proving things that, once learned and proved, don't matter a straw as far as the mind or memory is concerned."

RECORDING THE DATA

The primary data of in-depth, open-ended interviews are quotations. What people say, what they think, how they feel, what they've done, and what they know—these are the things one can learn from talking to people, from interviewing them. The purpose of qualitative interviewing is to understand the perspective and the experience of the people being interviewed. But no matter what style of interviewing is used, and no matter how carefully one words interview questions, it all comes to naught if the interviewer fails to capture the actual words of the person being interviewed. The raw data of interviews are the actual quotations spoken by interviewees. There is no substitute for these data.

Tape Recording Interviews

A tape recorder is part of the indispensable equipment of researchers using qualitative methods. Tape recorders do not tune out of conversations, change what has been said because of interpretation (either conscious or unconscious), or record more slowly than what is being said. (Tape recorders, do, however, break down and malfunction.) In addition to increasing the accuracy of data collection, the use of a tape recorder permits the interviewer to be more attentive to the interviewee. The interviewer who is trying to write down everything that is said as it is said will have a difficult time responding appropriately to interviewee needs and cues. The pace of the interview can become decidedly nonconversational. In brief, the interactive nature of in-depth interviewing is seriously affected by the attempt to take verbatim notes during the interview.

The major justification given to the interviewee for using a tape recorder is that:

> I'd like to tape record what you have to say so that I don't miss any of it. I don't want to take the chance of relying on my notes and thereby miss something that you say or inadvertently change your words somehow. So, if you don't mind, I'd very much like to use the recorder. If at any time during the interview you would like to turn the tape recorder off, all you have to do is to press this button on the microphone, and the recorder will stop.

The use of the tape recorder does not eliminate the need for taking notes. Taking notes can serve at least two purposes: (1) Notes taken during the interview can help the interviewer formulate new questions as the interview moves along, particularly where it may be appropriate to check out something that was said earlier; and (2) taking notes about what is said will facilitate later analysis, including locating important quotations from the tape itself. The use of a tape recorder does *not* mean that the interviewer can become less attentive to what is being said. This is important regardless of whether a standardized, open-ended interview format is used, or the more informal, conversational approach is the basis for data collection.

> One's full attention must be focused upon the interviewee. One must be thinking about probing for further explication or clarification of what he is now saying; formulating probes linking up current talk with what he has already said; thinking ahead to putting in a *new* question that has now arisen and was not taken account of in the standing guide (plus making a note at that moment so one will not forget the question); and attending to the interviewee in a manner that communicates to him that you are indeed listening. All of this is hard enough simply in itself. Add to that the problem of writing it down—even if one takes shorthand in an expert fashion—and one can see that the process of note taking in the interview decreases one's interviewing capacity. Therefore, if conceivably possible, *tape record;* then one can interview [Lofland, 1971: 89].

Transcribing Interviews

Since the raw data of interviews are quotations, the most desirable kind of data to obtain would be full transcriptions of interviews. Unfortunately, transcribing is enormously expensive. Despite the costs, full transcriptions are the most desirable kinds of data to obtain. Transcripts can be enormously useful in data analysis or, later, in replications or independent analyses of the data.

Where resources are not sufficient to permit full transcriptions, the interviewer can work back and forth between interview notes and sections of the tape; only those quotations that are particularly important to take from the tape for data analysis and reporting need be transcribed. In any case, it is critical that the tape recording be of high quality technically. Few things are more distressing in the collecting of qualitative data than to find that the tape is blank or that background noise is so severe that the tape is virtually worthless. In the first large-scale interviewing project with which I was involved, *nearly 20 percent of the data was lost because of poor quality recordings.*

Note Taking During Interviews

When a tape recorder is being used during the interview, notes will consist primarily of key phrases, lists of major points made by the respondent, and key terms or words shown in quotation marks that capture the interviewee's own language. While most interviewers will not know how to take technical shorthand, it is enormously useful to develop some system of abbreviations and informal shorthand to facilitate note taking. Some important conventions along this line include: (1) only use quotation marks during note taking to indicate full and actual quotations; (2) develop some mechanism for indicating interpretations, thoughts, or ideas that occur to you during the interview, e.g., the use of brackets to set off your own ideas from those of the interviewee; and (3) keep track of what questions you ask and what answers you receive.

When it is not possible to use a tape recorder because of some sensitive situation, interviewee request, or tape recorder malfunction, it is necessary for note taking to become much more thorough and comprehensive. Again, it is critical to gather actual quotations, as much as possible. This may mean that from time to time, when the interviewee has said something that strikes you as particularly important or insightful, it may be necessary to say: "I'm afraid I need to stop you at this point so that I can get down exactly what you said, because I don't want to lose that particular quote. Let me read back to you what I have and make sure it is exactly what you said."

With practice and training, an interviewer can learn to use notes for later expansion into more comprehensive detail of what was said in the interview. To do this with accuracy and reliability means expanding the notes taken during the interview *immediately following the interview.*

After the Interview

The period after the interview is critical to the rigor and validity of qualitative measurement whether the methods used involved interviewing or observation. The period following an interview is a time for guaranteeing the quality of the data. The first thing to be done after an interview that has been recorded on tape is to check the tape to make sure that it was functioning properly. If for some reason a malfunction occurred the interviewer should immediately make extensive notes of everything that he or she can remember. Even if the tape functioned properly, the interviewer should go over the interview notes to make certain that what is written makes sense, to uncover areas of ambiguity or uncertainty, and to review the quality of information received from the respondent. Did you find out what you really wanted to find out in the interview? If not, what was the problem? Poorly worded questions? Wrong topics? Poor rapport?

It is at this point immediately following the interview that observations are written down about the interview itself. The interviewer should note where the interview occurred, who was present, observations about how the interviewee reacted to the interview, observations about the interviewer's own role in the interview, and any additional information that would help establish a context for interpreting and making sense out of the interview. This period after the interview is a critical time of reflection and elaboration. *It is a time of quality control to guarantee that the data obtained will be useful, reliable, and valid.*

On occasion this process of immediately reviewing the interview will reveal areas of ambiguity or areas of uncertainty where you're not really sure what the person said or meant. As soon as these areas of vagueness turn up, the interviewer should check back with the respondent to clarify what was meant. This can often be done over the telephone as a simple way of checking out the accuracy of the interview. In my experience, people who are interviewed appreciate such a follow-up because it indicates the seriousness with which the interviewer is taking the responses of the person who was interviewed. Guessing at what the person said is absolutely unacceptable. If there is no way of following up the comments with the respondent, then those areas of vagueness and uncertainty simply become missing data.

This period after an interview or observation requires great discipline. Interviewing can be exhausting. It is easy to forgo this time of reflection and elaboration, put it off, or neglect it altogether. To do so is to undermine seriously the rigor of qualitative methods. Interviews and observations should be scheduled so that sufficient time is available for this time of data clarification, elaboration, and evaluation. This is also the beginning of analysis because, while the situation and data are fresh, insights can occur that might otherwise have been lost. Thus ideas and interpretations that emerge following an interview or observation should be written down and clearly marked as such.

PERSONAL REFLECTIONS ON INTERVIEWING

This chapter has attempted to suggest some ideas about how to go about doing interviews. There is no one right way of interviewing, no single correct format that is appropriate for all situations, and no single way of wording questions that will always work. The particular research situation, the needs of the interviewee, and the personal style of the interviewer all come together to create a unique situation for each interview. Therein lies the challenge of in-depth interviewing.

I find that interviewing people can be invigorating and stimulating. It's a chance for a short period of time to try to get inside another person's world. If participant observation means "walk a mile in my shoes," then in-depth interviewing means "walk a mile in my head." A good interview lays open thoughts, feelings, knowledge, and experiences not only to the interviewer, but also to the interviewee. The process of being taken through a directed, reflective process affects the person being interviewed and leaves them knowing things about themselves that they didn't know, or at least were not aware of, before the interview.

I'm personally convinced that to be a good interviewer you must like doing it. This means that you are interested in what people have to say. You must yourself believe that the thoughts and experiences of the people being interviewed are worth knowing. In short, you must have the utmost respect for this person who is willing to share with you some of his or her time to help you understand their world.

Certainly there are uncooperative respondents, people who are paranoid, respondents who seem overly sensitive and easily embarrassed, aggressive and hostile interviewees, timid people, and the endlessly verbose who go on at great length about very little. When an interview is going badly it is easy to call forth one of these stereotypes to explain how the interviewee is ruining the interview. Such blaming of the victim (the interviewee), however, does little to improve the quality of the data. Nor does it improve interviewing skills.

A different approach is to believe that there is a way to unlock the internal perspectives of every interviewee. It is the task and responsibility of the interviewer to find which interviewing style and which question format will work with a particular respondent. It is the responsibility of the interviewer to establish an interview climate that facilitates open responses. When the interview goes badly, it is the responsibility of the interviewer, not the fault of the interviewee. A Sufi story makes this point quite nicely.

An Interview with the King of the Monkeys

A man once spent years of his life learning the language of monkeys so that he could personally interview the king of monkeys. Having completed his studies he made careful inquiries to find the king of the monkeys. In the course of searching for the king of the monkeys he had to talk to a number of monkey underlings. He found that the monkeys he spoke to were generally, to his mind, neither very interesting nor very clever. He began to doubt whether he could learn very much from the king of the monkeys either.

Finally he located the king of the monkeys and arranged for an interview. Because of his doubts, however, he decided to begin with a few basic questions before moving on to the deeper questions in which he was really interested.

"What is a tree?" he asked.

"It is what it is," said the king of the monkeys. "We use trees to swing on."

"And what is the purpose of the banana?"

"They are to eat."

"How do animals find pleasure?"

"By doing things they enjoy."

At this point the man decided that the monkey's responses were rather shallow and uninteresting, and went on his way, severely disappointed. Soon afterwards an owl flew into the tree next to the king of the monkeys. "What was that man doing here?" the owl asked.

"Oh, he was only another silly human," said the king of the monkeys. "He asked a bunch of simple and meaningless questions so I gave him simple and meaningless answers."

PRACTICE EXERCISES

As noted at the beginning of this chapter, qualitative interviewing is a skill that requires practice. To emphasize this point, this chapter closes with some practice exercises.

Pick some topic on which you would like to interview people for about a half hour. Identify nine people whom you can interview. With three of the interviewees, use an informal, conversational approach to interviewing. With a different three interviewees design and use an interview guide. With the final three interviewees write a structured, open-ended interview and follow those questions exactly as you have written them in conducting the interview. Once you have conducted all nine interviews compare your experiences in using the three different approaches. How was the interview affected by the kind of interviewing approach used? How was your style as an interviewer affected? How was the quality of the data affected? Reflect on what you have learned about interviewing from engaging in this exercise.

Option 1

This option involves practice in writing different formats for interview questions. Pick some highly focused topic that you would like to study. Once you have selected the topic write single questions, or a series of questions, that illustrate different question formats. Write a structured interview section to study the topic you have picked using five different approaches in wording your questions. In effect, you would be asking questions about the same topic but using different interview questions to elicit responses from interviewees on that topic. Once you have written the five different questions or question sequences, conduct interviews with at least ten people so that you can apply each type of questioning to at least two different people. How did the wording of the question affect the answer you received? How did the wording of the question affect how you asked the question? What are the strengths and weaknesses of different question formats based on your experience with this exercise? Reflect on what you have learned about how the wording of questions affects the data you receive in in-depth interviewing.

Option 2

This exercise is aimed at practicing conducting the informal conversational interview. It is also aimed at further developing your understanding of different kinds of interview questions. Four people are needed for the exercise. One person will be the interviewer; one person will be the interviewee; one person will keep track of and write down the questions asked; and the fourth person will write down the answers received to the questions asked. Pick a topic for the interview and conduct an informal, conversational interview that lasts about a half hour. At the end of the interview the interviewer should write a summary of what the interviewee said. The interviewee should write a summary of what he or she said in response to the interviewer's questions. The person recording the answers should also write a summary. The person recording the questions should analyze the kinds of questions that were asked throughout the interview. For each question asked identify its type and look for the structure clues that will help you identify what question format was used in each item. The three people who wrote summaries should then compare their summaries and discuss any differences among summaries, especially substantial differences in meaning or content. The person who kept track of the questions should present a summary of what was learned from analyzing the questions. The group should then discuss both the questions and answers with particular focus on how the nature of the questions affected the answers, with attention to the issue of the quality of the interview notes taken by all participants in the exercise.

Answer the following questions either in the discussion or in writing:

(1) Describe your experience in taking notes during the interview and reflect on what you have learned about note taking.
(2) How did the questions asked affect the answers received?
(3) Describe the style of the interviewer and the style of the interviewee in responding to the interviewer's questions. Reflect on how personal style affects information received.
(4) Overall, what did you learn about the interviewing process in this exercise? What did you learn about yourself as an interviewer or an interviewee from this exercise? What did you learn about your skills in note taking in this exercise?

Option 3

Repeat the last exercise using the interview guide approach and then using a standardized, open-ended interview format. Take turns being the interviewer, the interviewee, and the observers. Include in your discussion questions, after all three types of interviews have been conducted, consideration of how the different interview approaches affected the interview and the data obtained.

CHAPTER 7   *Thoughtful Methods Decisions*

> *Habit is habit, and not to.be flung out of the window,*
> *but coaxed downstairs a step at a time.*
>
> Mark Twain

A prominent and recurring theme throughout this book has been that much evaluation practice is based on habit rather than on situational responsiveness. In nothing is this more true than in making methods decisions. Routine heuristics and paradigmatic blinders constrain methodological flexibility and creativity by locking practitioners into unconscious patterns of perception and behavior that disguise the habitual nature of their methods "decisions."

This chapter carries forward the theme of thoughtfulness in evaluation decision making that undergirded the previous two chapters on questionnaires and interviewing. Making thoughtful and practical methods decisions means using methods that are appropriate to the particular nature of an evaluation and the specific context in which the evaluation is conducted. The new standards of evaluation emphasize the importance of contextual sensitivity in making methods decisions (Joint Committee, 1981: 104):

> The context in which the object of an evaluation exists is the combination of the conditions surrounding the object that may influence its functioning. These conditions include the geographic location of the object, its timing, the political and social climate in the region at that time, relevant professional activities in progress, the nature of the staff, and pertinent economic conditions.
>
> These and other contextual factors must be examined to assure that the evaluation can be designed, conducted, and reported in relation to them. Maintaining an understanding of the context is necessary if the evaluation is to be designed and carried out realistically and responsively.

Author's Note: An earlier version of this chapter appeared in *Evaluation and Program Planning* as an article entitled "Making Methods Choices" (Patton, 1980a).

Another theme carried forward from previous chapters is the importance of conceptual clarity in evaluation practice. As applied to the making of methods decisions, conceptual clarity concerns how one understands and thinks about methodological alternatives and options. The past several years have witnessed an intensive debate among evaluators about methodological alternatives and methods paradigms. This chapter reviews that debate and suggests a practical way of thinking about methods options. I shall also use the opportunity of this review to respond to critics of some of my previous writings about methods paradigms by way of clarifying and elaborating my position in the debate about methods. I shall not, however, attempt to provide a full discussion of the epistemological and philosophical underpinnings of alternative evaluation paradigms (for such a discussion see Patton, 1978: 199-238; Rist, 1977; Cronbach, 1975; Patton, 1980; Reichardt and Cook, 1979; and Guba and Lincoln, 1981).

In the second chapter I made the point that conceptual discussions of the kind found in this chapter are far from esoteric. How we conceptualize evaluation alternatives very much affects the practical decisions we make in the field. How we think about evaluation affects what we do. This chapter is about both the thinking and the doing.

THE PARADIGMS DEBATE

Concern about methodological prejudice led me to compare two alternative paradigms of evaluation measurement and design in *Utilization-Focused Evaluation* (Patton, 1978). That comparison included a lament about the dominance of one paradigm over the other.

Evaluation research is dominated by the largely unquestioned, natural science paradigm of hypothetico-deductive methodology. This dominant paradigm assumes quantitative measurement, experimental design, and multivariate, parametric statistical analysis to be the epitome of "good" science. This basic model for conducting evaluation research comes from the tradition of experimentation in agriculture, which gave us many of the basic statistical and experimental techniques most widely used in evaluation research.

By way of contrast, the alternative to the dominant hypothetico-deductive paradigm is derived from the tradition of anthropological field studies. Using the techniques of in-depth, open-ended interviewing and personal observation, the alternative paradigm relies on qualitative data, holistic analysis, and detailed description derived from close contact with the targets of study.

The hypothetico-deductive, natural science paradigm aims at prediction of social phenomena; the holistic-inductive, anthropological paradigm aims at understanding of social phenomena. From a utilization-focused perspective on evaluation research, neither of these paradigms is intrinsically better than the other. They represent alternatives from which the active-reactive-adaptive evaluator can choose; both contain options for identified decision makers and information users. . . . *The problem from a utilization-focused approach to evaluation is that the very dominance of the hypothetico-deductive paradigm with its quantitative, experimental emphasis appears to have cut off the great majority of its practitioners from serious consideration of any alternative evaluation research paradigm or methods.* The label "research" has come to mean the equivalent of employing the "scientific method," of working within the dominant paradigm. There is, however, an alternative [Patton, 1978: 203-204, 207].

In their recent article entitled "Beyond Qualitative *Versus* Quantitative Methods," Reichardt and Cook (1979) attack this kind of conceptualization of alternative paradigms because it offers evaluators only two mutually exclusive options: *either* qualitative/naturalistic methods *or* quantitative/experimental methods.

Let me begin this discussion by responding to the attacks on paradigmatic perspectives made by Reichardt and Cook (1979). They suggested that "part of this current debate over qualitative and quantitative methods is not centered on productive issues and so is not being argued in as logical a fashion as it should be" (1979: 8). The problem, from my point of view, is that Reichardt and Cook apply a purely logical analysis to what is largely an empirical phenomenon. They argue that evaluators *don't have to* work only within one paradigm or the other. Logically, they are correct. By the same token, I have argued throughout this book that evaluators *don't have to* be constrained by routine heuristics and paradigmatic blinders. But the assertion that evaluators are often so constrained is not based on logic. It is based on *observation* of how evaluators and other scientists typically behave. Logic and rhetoric are not at issue. It is certainly logically possible to be methodologically flexible. Moreover, the rhetoric advocating such flexibility is widespread, not least of all in the evaluation standards discussed in Chapter 1. Evaluators are widely encouraged to be situationally responsive and flexible in matching research methods to the nuances of particular evaluation questions and the idiosyncrasies of specific decision maker needs (see Young and Comtois, 1979). Evaluators are encouraged to use multiple methods (Reichardt and Cook, 1979).

The problem is that this ideal of evaluators being situationally responsive, methodologically flexible, and sophisticated in using a variety of methods to study any particular evaluation questions runs headlong into the realities of the evaluation world. Those realities include limited resources, political considerations of expediency, and the narrowness of disciplinary training available to most evaluators, which imbues them with varying degrees of methodological prejudice.

THE DIFFERENCE BETWEEN COMPETING AND BEING INCOMPATIBLE

Part of the confusion in the paradigms debate has come from a failure to distinguish between alternative paradigms as *competing* world views and alternative paradigms as *incompatible* world views. This confusion is illustrated by Heilman's article in *Evaluation Review* (1980) aimed at disputing my perspective. Heilman correctly quotes me as writing that in "a very real sense these are opposing and competing paradigms" (Patton, 1978: 209). He then concludes: "[I]f the methodological division Patton describes is truly paradigmatic, evaluators and program administrators should consciously see themselves as confronted by an either/or choice of research procedures" (Heilman, 1980: 702). But to say that adherents of the two paradigms *compete* for research funds, credibility, and students is not to say that the paradigms are incompatible, or that evaluators and stakeholders are faced with an either/or choice. Reichardt and Cook draw a similar conclusion from the subtitles of my original piece on paradigms, e.g., induction versus deduction, qualitative versus quantitative methods, objectivity versus subjectivity, distance from versus closeness to the data, holistic versus component analysis, fixed versus dynamic systems, reliability versus validity, and uniformity versus diversity. They interpret these as "forced choices" (Reichardt and Cook, 1979), but what I meant to suggest was that these dimensions describe variations in *emphasis* when choosing methods, and the virtues of these relative emphases compete for evaluators' attention. I was also describing research findings about how decision makers and information users actually approach methods decisions. They are viewed as opposing paradigms and competitive perspectives. I further noted that the eight competing perspectives just listed were stated in the form of oppositions "in the hope of releasing social scientists from unwitting captivity to a format of inquiry that is taken for granted as the naturally proper way in which to conduct scientific inquiry" (Blumer, 1969: 47). I went on to state that "this heuristic technique of comparing ideal-typical methodological paradigms is aimed at making both approaches accessible to evaluators and decision makers. The real point is not that one approach is intrinsically better or more scientific than the other, but that evaluation methods ought to be selected to suit the type of program being evaluated and the nature of decision makers' questions" (Patton, 1978: 210-211).

It is possible to build a logical case showing that the competing paradigms are incompatible. Guba and Lincoln (1981) have built such a case showing that the "scientific" and "naturalistic" paradigms contain incompatible assumptions about the nature of reality, the inquirer/subject relationship, and the nature of truth statements. For example, the scientific paradigm assumes that reality is "singular, convergent, and fragmentable" while the naturalistic paradigm holds a view of reality that is "multiple, divergent, and inter-related" (Guba and Lincoln, 1981: 57). These opposite axioms about the nature of the universe embrace much more than methods. The issue for them is not so much methods alternatives as it is more fundamental axioms about the nature of reality. The issues about which there can be no middle ground are issues about one's view of the universe. Lincoln (1982) explains:

> The fundamental axioms of competing paradigms are sufficiently incompatible and mutually exclusive so as to *force* a choice on paradigms (naturalistic vs. scientific) on a situation-by-situation (or evaluation-by-evaluation) basis. One cannot, in the same evaluation framework, simultaneously believe that reality is singular and fragmentable into tiny pieces (called variables) and at the same time believe that reality is wholistic and incapable of being separated into something called variables. The two beliefs are not only competing, they are also incompatible. And this is only one example of one axiom on which there are strong incompatibilities between the scientific and naturalistic paradigms.

I don't disagree with Lincoln's logic in pointing out that the competing paradigms contain incompatible axioms. Where we disagree is on the implications of these incompatible axioms for practical evaluation situations. I believe that the flexible, responsive evaluator can make mind shifts back and forth between paradigms within a single evaluation setting. In so doing, this evaluator can view the same data from the perspective of each paradigm, and can help adherents of either paradigm interpret data in more than one way.

This kind of flexibility begins at the design stage. Consider the following situation. An evaluator is working with a group of educators, some of whom are "progressive, open education" types and some of whom are "back-to-basics" fundamentalists. The open education folks want to frame the evaluation of a particular Title IV program within a naturalistic framework. The basic skills people want a rigorous, scientific approach. Must the evaluator make an either/or choice to frame the evaluation within either one or the other paradigm? Must an either/or choice be made about the kind of data to be collected? Are the views of each group so incompatible that each must have its own evaluation?

I've been in precisely this situation a number of times. My approach is *not* to try to resolve the paradigms debate. I try to establish an environment of tolerance and respect for different, competing viewpoints, and then focus the discussion on the actual information that is needed by each group: test scores? interviews? observations? The design and measures must be negotiated. Multiple methods and multiple measures will give each group some of what it wants. The naturalistic paradigm educators will want to be sure that test scores are interpreted within a larger context of classroom activities, observations, and outcomes. The scientific paradigm educators will likely use interview and observational data to explain and justify test score interpretations. My experience suggests that both groups can agree on an evaluation design that includes multiple types of data, and that each group will ultimately pay attention to and use the "other group's" data. In short, a particular group of people can arrive at agreement on an evaluation design that includes both qualitative and quantitative data without resolving ultimate paradigmatic issues. Such agreement is not likely, however, if the evaluator begins with the premise that the paradigms are incompatible, and the evaluation must be conducted within the framework of either one or the other paradigm.

I tend to emphasize the methods implications of the paradigms debate, not because the competing paradigms can be reduced to contrasting methods, but because methods distinctions are the most concrete and practical manifestation of the larger, more overarching paradigmatic frameworks.

Perhaps an analogy will help here. A sensitive, practical evaluator can work with a group of people to design a meaningful evaluation that integrates concerns from both paradigms in the same way that a skillful teacher can work with a group of Buddhists, Christians, Jews, and Muslims on issues of common empirical concern without resolving which religion has the correct world view. Another example is the project on which I've been working in the Caribbean. It includes social scientists and government officials of varying political persuasions. Despite their theoretical differences, the Marxist and Keynesian economists and sociologists had little difficulty agreeing on what data were needed to understand agricultural extension needs in each country. Their interpretations of those data also differed less than I expected. Thus the point I'm making about the paradigms debate extends beyond methodological issues to embrace a host of potential theoretical, philosophical, religious, and political perspectives that can separate the participants in an evaluation process. I am arguing that, from a practical perspective, the evaluator need not even attempt to resolve such differences. By focusing on and negotiating data collection alternatives in an atmosphere of respect and tolerance, the participants can come together around a commitment to an *empirical* perspective, i.e., bringing data to bear on important program issues. As long as the empirical commitment is there, the other differences can be negotiated in most instances. The bridge between the naturalistic and scientific paradigms, to use the labels of Guba and Lincoln (1981), or between the hypothetico-deductive paradigm and the holistic-inductive paradigm, to use my own terms, is a common commitment to *empirical* evaluation.

Debating paradigms with one's clients, and taking sides in that debate, is different from debating one's colleagues about the nature of reality. I doubt that evaluators will ever reach consensus on the ultimate nature of reality. But the paradigms debate can go on among evaluators without paralyzing the practice of practical evaluators who are trying to work responsively with decision makers and information users to get answers to relevant empirical questions. The belief that evaluators must be true to only one paradigm or the other in every situation is an extremely narrow and limiting perspective that underestimates the human capacity for handling ambiguity, duality, and mind shifts. In short, I'm suggesting that evaluators would do better to worry about understanding and being sensitive to the world views of their clients than in unilaterally resolving the paradigms debate, or working within only one perspective.

Thus I am indebted to Reichardt and Cook for calling my attention to the ease with which my previous writings about paradigms could be interpreted as one-sided advocacy of one paradigm over the other. My purpose in elaborating methods alternatives and competing paradigms has been to call attention to the methodological blinders that can result from narrow research training experiences and to increase the options available to evaluators, *not* to replace one limited paradigm with another limited, but different, paradigm. With that purpose still primary (namely, to increase the real methods options available to evaluators) this chapter will examine in some detail assumptions about the linkage between paradigms and methods. First, however, one other distinction is necessary, a distinction between alternative paradigms and alternative consulting styles.

ALTERNATIVE CONSULTING STYLES

Before examining in more detail alternative ways of thinking about paradigms and methods distinctions, let me ask the reader's forbearance in clearing up another area of confusion about my perspective. *Evaluation Review* is one of the major, most widely read journals in the field, so when one's writings are wrongly represented in such an eminent forum, the wrong bears being put right. One hopes that such dialogues, over time, contribute to greater clarity of practice.

The ideal-typical paradigms discussed here contrast hypothetico-deductive (quantitative/experimental) research with holistic-inductive (qualitative/naturalistic) research. The latter I called the "alternative paradigm" with reference to the relative dominance of quantitative/experimental approaches in evaluation research. The alternative methods paradigm is *not* the "active-reactive-adaptive" approach to evaluation consulting I described in Chapter 3 on collaborative evaluation practice and in *Utilization-Focused Evaluation*. Heilman (1980: 698-702) makes the error of confusing the two, and equating them, in his critique of the paradigm debate. He describes the alternative to the hypothetico-deductive paradigm as the "active-reactive-adaptive" approach. However, the active-reactive-adaptive approach is a consulting style, not an evaluation paradigm. It is a strategy for making evaluation decisions including, but not limited to, methods decisions. Active-reactive-adaptive consulting can lead to any of a variety of methods, based on (one hopes) attention to decision maker information needs, situational constraints, and attention to the evaluation standards of utility, feasibility, propriety, and accuracy. An active-reactive-adaptive consulting approach could well lead to selection of an experimental design and quantitative methods (and often has in my own practice). Thus Heilman's conclusion that the active-reactive-adaptive approach is compatible with the hypothetico-deductive paradigm does not represent any refutation of my position. I agree. What I take issue with is his allegation that I ever said there was any incompatibility.

The ideal-typical opposite of the two-way information flow and collaborative approach epitomized by active-reactive-adaptive consulting is evaluator authoritarianism and dogmatism in one-way, one-sided communication patterns from evaluation expert to passive stakeholders. Chapter 3 discussed alternative consulting styles. This chapter is about methods alternatives.

Finally, the views and counterviews just reviewed illustrate how easily communications difficulties arise in evaluation practice, a point discussed at length in Chapter 2. If evaluators have difficulty understanding each other, as clearly they do, it is even more difficult for evaluators to communicate clearly with decision makers and information users, thus the need for a process of developing shared definitions and meanings in the context of a specific evaluation.

ASSUMPTIONS ABOUT THE LINKAGES BETWEEN PARADIGM AND METHOD

After reviewing what Reichardt and Cook call the "shopping list of attributes which are said to distinguish the qualitative and quantitative world views" (1979: 9), they expose the two basic assumptions that they believe undergird conceptual arguments about methodological paradigms.

Such paradigmatic characterizations are based on two assumptions which are of direct consequence to the debate over methods. First, it is assumed that a method-type is irrevocably linked to a paradigm so that an allegiance to a paradigm provides the appropriate and sole means of choosing between method types. That is, because they see the world in different ways, researchers must use different methods of inquiry. If one's theory of evaluation is more closely related to the attributes of paradigm A than to the attributes of paradigm B, one should automatically favor those research methods that are linked to paradigm A.

Second, the qualitative and quantitative paradigms are assumed to be rigid and fixed, and the choice between them is assumed to be the only choice available. That is, the paradigms are considered to be cast in stone so that modifications or other options are not possible.

These two assumptions ultimately lead to the conclusion that qualitative and quantitative methods themselves can never be used together. Since the methods are linked to different paradigms and since one must choose between the mutually exclusive and antagonistic world views, one must also choose *between* the method-types [Reichardt and Cook, 1979: 10-11].

The problem is that Reichardt and Cook treat what are meant to be *descriptive* paradigms as prescriptive. The purpose of describing alternative evaluation research paradigms is to sensitize evaluators to the ways in which their methodological prejudices, derived from their disciplinary socialization experiences, may reduce their methodological flexibility and adaptability. The purpose of *describing* how paradigms typically operate in the real world is to free evaluators from the bonds of allegiance to a single paradigm. This is quite different from prescribing that evaluators should *always* operate within one or the other paradigm.

The fallacies in the Reichardt and Cook assumptions reside in the absolute and overstated conditions they attach to paradigm choices and distinctions. In order to illustrate the difference between *descriptive* assumptions and *prescriptive* assumptions, allow me to reword the Reichardt and Cook assumptions from prescriptive statements to descriptive statements. Their prescriptive assumptions, reproduced from the preceding quote and supposedly derived from the literature on qualitative and quantitative paradigms, are presented exactly as they stated them, thus the quotation marks. My descriptive assumptions, which present my interpretation of what writers on the paradigmatic nature of evaluation methods actually mean, are presented on the right side of the page. I have italicized the key word changes necessary to move from prescription to description.

Reichardt and Cook Prescriptive Assumptions

Revised Descriptive Assumptions

1. "First, it is assumed that a method-type is *irrevocably* linked to a paradigm so that an allegiance to a paradigm provides the appropriate and *sole* means to choosing between method-types." (p. 10)

1. First, it is assumed that a method-type is *typically* linked to a paradigm so that a *basically unconscious* allegiance to a paradigm is usually *the major* (but not the only) basis for making methods decisions.

2. "Because they see the world in different ways, researchers *must* use different methods in inquiry." (p. 10)

2. Because they see the world in different ways, researchers *typically will* use different methods of inquiry.

3. "If one's theory of evaluation is more closely related to the attributes of paradigm A than to the attributes of paradigm B, one *should automatically* favor those research methods that are linked to paradigm A." (p. 10)

3. If one's theory of evaluation is more closely related to the attributes of paradigm A than to the attributes of paradigm B, one *will usually* favor those research methods that are linked to paradigm A.

4. "The qualitative and quantitative paradigms are assumed to be *rigid and fixed,* and the choice between them is assumed to be *the only choice* available." (pp. 10-11)

4. The qualitative and quantitative paradigms are assumed to be *ideal-types; real world choices* are assumed to vary in the extent to which they epitomize any particular ideal-type, but

most methods choices will tend to exemplify more closely the attributes of one or the other paradigm.

5. "The paradigms are considered to be *cast in stone* so that modifications or other *options are not possible.*" (p. 11)

5. The paradigms are considered to be *ideal-types* so that *practical* modification, or other options, would *typically lead to deviations from the ideal type* while still tending to exemplify more closely the attributes of one or the other paradigm.

6. "Qualitative and quantitative methods themselves can *never* be used together." (p. 11)

6. Qualitative and quantitative methods have *typically* not been used together.

7. Since the methods are *linked to* different paradigms and since one must choose between the *mutually exclusive and antagonistic* world views, one *must* also choose between the method-types." (p. 11)

7. Since methods are *typically imbedded in* different paradigms and since one will *typically feel more comfortable* operating closer to the world view of one or the other paradigm, one will *typically* choose between method-types.

MAKING METHODS CHOICES

The basic thrust of the assumptions on the right-hand side is that most evaluators are not fully aware of the extent to which the methods choices they make follow from methodological biases and paradigmatic assumptions. The purpose, then, of elaborating the alternative paradigms is to help make evaluators more aware of their methodological biases and paradigmatic assumptions so that they *can* make flexible, sophisticated, and adaptive methodological choices. Contrary to what Reichardt and Cook assert, the purpose of describing paradigmatic ideal-types is *not* to advocate one paradigm over the other in all situations and for all types of evaluations. In *Qualitative Evaluation Methods* (1980) I followed the *description* of the two alternative evaluation paradigms with advocacy of a new paradigm—"a paradigm of choices"—which recognizes that different methods are appropriate for different situations.

> The issue of selecting methods is no longer one of the dominant paradigm versus the alternative paradigm, of experimental designs with quantitative measurement versus holistic-inductive designs based on qualitative measurement. The debate and competition between paradigms is being replaced by a new paradigm—*a paradigm of choices*. The paradigm of choices recognizes that different methods are appropriate for different situations [Patton, 1980: 19-20].

In all fairness it is true that many articles on qualitative methods include descriptions of the two contrasting paradigms that may give the appearance that the qualitative/naturalistic paradigm is being advocated as better than the traditional experimental/quantitative paradigm, or even that the former paradigm should be used exclusively. In most cases, I believe, the appearance of such advocacy is merely a function of the defensiveness of qualitative methodologists about their use of alternative approaches and a tendency to overstate the case in an effort to be heard at all.

More importantly, the real issue is *how* to be flexible in making methods decisions that are appropriate to various evaluation situations. The problem is the elusiveness of choice. In practice, paradigms operate to reduce the necessity for painstaking choice by making methods decisions routine and obvious. Paradigms tell practitioners what is important, legitimate, and reasonable. As such, paradigms are normative and largely implicit, telling evaluators what to do without the necessity of long existential or epistemological consideration. The purpose of making paradigms explicit and contrasting is to reduce the likelihood that evaluators' decisions about methods will be like the bear's "decision" to like honey or the mouse's "decision" to like cheese.

From my perspective, one of the useful purposes served by elaborating the various dimensions that distinguish the methods paradigms is to make methods options more explicit. Of course, the real options are much more complex than a simple choice between "qualitative" and "quantitative" paradigms. In any given study there are a host of methods choices.

(1) *Measurement options:* What kinds of qualitative data should we collect? What kinds of quantitative measures should we use?

(2) *Design options:* How much should we manipulate or control variance in the settings under study? (Options vary from controlled experiments to naturalistic field studies with a lot of variation in between.)

(3) *Personal involvement options:* What kinds of interpersonal contacts, if any, should the researchers have with the subjects under study?

(4) *Analysis options:* To what extent should the study be open to whatever emerges (inductive analysis) and to what extent should prior hypotheses be examined (deductive analysis)?

These questions illustrate only a few of the many options evaluators can consider. The issue in the discussion about methodological paradigms is not whether certain options *should* automatically be avoided; the issue is the extent to which certain options *are* automatically eliminated by paradigmatic blinders that keep evaluators from even considering the potential of methodological alternatives. We shall return to this empirical question after further consideration of the logical propositions discussed by Reichardt and Cook.

METHODS VARIATIONS

Descriptions of the contrasting paradigms represent ideal-types. Rarely are actual studies completely pure and comprehensive in methodology. Just as few evaluations exemplify double blind experiments, so too, there are few that exemplify the anthropological ideal of long-term participant observation. Compromises in methods result from limited resources, limited time, practical considerations, and political limitations. One function served by comprehensive descriptions of paradigmatic ideal-types is alerting researchers to the extent to which they approximate or depart from the ideal-types. Consider the interpersonal interaction dimension.

In *Utilization-Focused Evaluation,* I suggested that the two paradigms differ in their emphasis on "distance from versus closeness to the data." The quantitative/experimental paradigm emphasizes distance in order to guarantee neutrality and objectivity. This component has become increasingly important with the professionalization of the social sciences and the educational research establishment. Scientific objectivity connotes cool, calm, and detached analysis without personal involvement.

The qualitative/naturalistic inquiry paradigm questions the necessity of distance and detachment, assuming that, with empathy and sympathetic introspection derived from personal encounters, the observer can gain insight into the varied meanings of human behavior. Understanding, in this case, comes from trying to put oneself in the other person's shoes, from trying to discern how others think, act, and feel. John Lofland (1971) explains that methodologically this means: (1) getting close to the people being studied through attention to the minutiae of daily life, through physical proximity over a period of time, and through development of closeness in the social sense of intimacy and confidentiality; (2) being truthful and factual about what is observed; (3) emphasizing a significant amount of pure description of action, people, and so on; and (4) including as data direct quotations from participants as they speak or from whatever they might write.

> The commitment to get close, to be factual, descriptive, and quotive, constitutes a significant commitment to represent the participants *in their own terms* [Lofland, 1971: 4].

Reichardt and Cook take up this issue by asking, "Do quantitative methods necessarily insulate the researcher from the data?" (1979: 13). Their answer is "no," thereby showing that logically this paradigm distinction is untenable. As an example of how quantitative methodologists *can* get close to the data they cite the case of Fienberg "sending his graduate students to spend a couple of nights riding around in a patrol car so as to be better able to design a quantitative evaluation of police activities" (Reichardt and Cook, 1979: 13). Fienberg's approach in this instance does involve some degree of closeness to the subjects under study, but "a couple of nights" riding in a police car is far from the ideal of the qualitative/naturalistic paradigm. Closeness involves "attention to the minutiae of daily life, through physical proximity over a period of time, and through development of closeness in the social sense of intimacy and confidentiality" (Patton, 1978: 221). Fienberg is quoted as finding it "astonishing that getting close to the data can be thought of as an attribute of only the [qualitative] approach" (Reichardt and Cook, 1979: 13). It is perhaps indicative of the difficulty of communicating across paradigms that Fienberg, Reichardt, and Cook believe that "a couple of nights" in a police car constitutes qualitative closeness. Perhaps an analogy will help here: *A couple of nights of fieldwork is to a full qualitative study what a "one-night stand" is to mutually satisfying and deeply intimate love making.*

The point here is that methods options vary along continua. The construction of ideal-typical and opposing methods paradigms is a heuristic device that serves the purpose of bringing into stark contrast the nature of the alternative strategies available. Seldom do actual studies exemplify all the ideal characteristics of either paradigm. There is a lot of real-world space between the ideal-typical endpoints of paradigmatic conceptualizations.

The Fienberg example also illustrates the difficulty of really combining paradigmatic perspectives. So long as qualitative approaches are considered mostly "exploratory," secondary, or merely supportive of quantitative approaches, a true merger of methods will not be possible. We shall return to these difficulties in merging methods later. First, it may be helpful to look at another of the questions raised by Reichardt and Cook where complex issues need elaboration if evaluators are to learn how to use multiple methods.

FROM SIMPLICITY TO COMPLEXITY

The complexity of real-world methods decisions is unfortunately concealed by the simplistic questions considered by Reichardt and Cook. They ask: "Are qualitative measures necessarily naturalistic, and are quantitative measures necessarily obtrusive?" (1979: 12). Again they answer "no," and again they have demonstrated that *logically* methods/paradigm linkages are not automatic. Yet their question is confusing because it implies a single continuum from naturalistic inquiry to obtrusive inquiry. In fact, however, the extent to which inquiry is naturalistic and the extent to which measurement is obtrusive are conceptually separate dimensions. To treat these two dimensions as a single continuum is to confound complex measurement and design issues. Separating measurement from design issues is an important first step in making methods choices more flexible, sophisticated, and situationally appropriate.

Naturalistic inquiry is distinguished from experimental inquiry by the extent to which the investigator or evaluator attempts to avoid controlling or manipulating the situation, people, or data under study. The extent to which any particular investigator engages in naturalistic inquiry varies along a continuum (Guba, 1978). It is certainly possible for an investigator to enter a field situation and try to control what happens just as it is possible for the experimentalist to control only the initial assignment to groups, then to watch what happens "naturally." The important distinction is between relative degrees of *calculated* manipulation. A naturalistic inquiry strategy is selected in which the investigator wants to minimize research manipulation by studying natural field settings; experimental conditions and designs are selected where the evaluator wants to introduce a considerable amount of control and reduce variation in extraneous variables.

Obtrusiveness of measurement is a different issue from naturalistic inquiry. Obtrusiveness concerns the extent to which data collection creates reactions in the subjects under study. It is clear that unobtrusive measures are possible in a wide variety of designs that involve more or less investigator manipulation (that is, that are more or less naturalistic or experimental in design). Furthermore, participant observation as a data collection strategy can be used in both naturalistic designs and in experimental designs. Participant observation can be more or less obtrusive depending on the nature of the situation, the kind of data to be collected, the skill of the participant observer, and a variety of other factors.

The point is that the nature of the intrusions experienced by research subjects or program participants is different when qualitative data collection is undertaken than when quantitative data collection is undertaken. Different kinds of data collection involve different kinds of reactivities. The issue here, then, is not one of more or less intrusion with either quantitative or qualitative methods; the issue involves different kinds of intrusions with different effects and different consequences for data interpretation.

Unfortunately, none of this complexity is captured or even hinted at in the simplistic question posed by Reichardt and Cook: "Are qualitative measures necessarily naturalistic, and are quantitative procedures necessarily obtrusive?" A negative answer to that question (an answer with which I agree, by the way) tells us very little about real-world methodological practices and options.

DICHOTOMOUS CHOICES

Reichardt and Cook accuse those of us who have elaborated the contrasting paradigms of forcing people into the position of making dichotomous choices—either one method or the other. Throughout their article they present a series of dichotomous choices that they believe represents the alternatives being imposed on evaluators by those of us who have described alternative paradigms. Unfortunately, their interpretations represent serious distortion of the complex issues under discussion. Below I have reproduced some more of the questions posed by Reichardt and Cook. Next to each of their questions I have posed what I consider to be the real issue, the descriptive rather than the purely logical issue, with my own answer. The reader will see, I believe, why absolute answers to the simplistic logical questions posed by Reichardt and Cook illuminate very little. Again, I have italicized the critical word differences in each set of questions.

Questions from Reichardt and Cook

Revised Questions

1. "Is the researcher who uses quantitative procedures *necessarily* a logical positivist, and conversely, is the researcher who uses qualitative procedures *necessarily* a phenomenologist?

Certainly not . . ." (p. 12)

1. Is the researcher who uses *primarily* quantitative procedures *usually* a logical positivist, and conversely, is the researcher who uses *primarily* qualitative approaches *usually* a phenomenologist?

Usually.

2. "Are qualitative procedures *necessarily* subjective and quantitative procedures *necessarily* objective?" (p. 12)

No.

2. To what extent are evaluators employing qualitative methods *likely to emphasize* the value of documenting and presenting subjective insights while evaluators employing quantitative procedures are likely to *deemphasize* and discount such insights? By contrast, to what extent are quantitative methodologists *likely to emphasize* the objective nature of their findings, while qualitative methodologists doubt that objectivity?

To a considerable extent in both cases.

3. "Do quantitative methods *necessarily* insulate the researcher from the data?"

"It is clear that the quantitative researcher need not be isolated from the data." (p. 13)

3. Are quantitative researchers *likely* to distance themselves from the people they study and, by contrast, are qualitative methodologists likely to value the insights generated by close, personal contact with the people they study?

Yes, though it is clear that distance from or closeness to research subjects varies considerably among both qualitative and quantitative researchers.

4. "Are qualitative procedures *necessarily* grounded, exploratory, and inductive whereas quantitative procedures are *always* ungrounded, confirmatory, and deductive?" (p. 13)

"The logic of description and inference cuts across methods." (p. 14)

4. Are qualitative approaches *usually* inductive while quantitative data are *usually* generated through deduction?

Usually.

5. "Must qualitative procedures *only* be used only to measure process, and must quantitative techniques *only* be used to detect outcome?"

"The logic of the task cuts across method." (p. 14)

5. Are qualitative approaches *particularly useful* in studying program processes?

Yes, detailed description is particularly useful for understanding program processes.

Do quantitative methodologists *tend to* focus on program outcomes as their primary dependent variables in statistical analysis?

Only about 95% of the time—give or take a few percentage points.

6. "Are qualitative methods *necessarily* valid but unreliable, and are quantitative methods *necessarily* reliable but invalid?" (p. 14)

No.

6. Do the writings of qualitative methodologists *tend to* focus a great deal on the validity of their data and observations while the writings of quantitative-methodologists *tend to* focus a great deal on reliability estimates and coefficients?

While such tendencies are unfortunate in both cases since both validity and reliability are important issues, the empirical tendency, I believe, is clearly manifest in the directions described in the above question.

7. "Are qualitative methods *always* limited to the single case and therefore ungeneralizable?

Statements that assert the affirmative are wrong." (pp. 14-15)

7. In contrast to their quantitative counterparts, do qualitative methodologists *tend* to focus more on case study data in order to understand the particular characteristics of whole situations and thus to worry less about making generalizations?

Such a tendency exists because the purpose of qualitative studies is *usually,* though not always, quite different than the purpose of quantitative studies (the purpose of the latter often being precisely one of making generalizations).

What I find particularly interesting is that it is possible to completely agree with the answers to the questions in both columns above. There is no logical contradiction because the questions and issues are different in each case. I agree with the answers provided by Reichardt and Cook to their questions. What I dispute is the meaningfulness, relevance, and importance of the questions they have asked.

The point, I hope, is clear to the reader. Reichardt and Cook have set up a simplistic logical structure that forces us to respond "no" to each of the questions they pose because they word the questions in absolute and dichotomous terms. It is clear that for virtually any question one might ask about human beings that took the form "Must people always . . . ?" or "Must people necessarily . . . ?" behave in a certain way, the answer would *always* or *necessarily* be "No!" People do not always and necessarily develop a strong affection for their children—but they usually do. Evaluators do not *always* and *necessarily* allow methodological bias and narrow paradigmatic blinders to affect their methods decisions—but they *often* do.

EMPIRICAL ISSUES IN THE PARADIGMS DEBATE

Throughout their article Reichardt and Cook assert that they are dealing with logical distinctions. The problem is that the paradigms are not simply logical phenomena. They are also empirical phenomena. The issue is not simply whether one can *logically* employ qualitative and quantitative methods together. Of course, one can. The issue is *not* whether one *must* choose to operate within one paradigm or the other. Of course one need not logically and universally and consistently make such a dichotomous choice.

Two empirical issues are central in the paradigms debate. First, to what extent do the alternative paradigms describe actual methodological tendencies among evaluators? In practice, are the dimensions that describe methodological options correlated such that clear and significant patterns emerge along the lines predicted by the paradigm ideal-types? In other words, to what extent do evaluators *tend to* conduct studies that are either primarily experimental in design, quantitative in measurement, logical-deductive in conceptualization, inferential in statistical analysis, and outcomes oriented *or* to conduct studies that are primarily naturalistic in design, based on collection of qualitative data, holistic-inductive in conceptualization, descriptive in analysis, and process oriented?

Second, if the empirical tendencies predicted by the alternative paradigms actually describe evaluator patterns, to what extent are those tendencies explained by methodological bias, disciplinary prejudice, and narrow professional socialization? It is possible that methods tendencies in evaluation practice are the result of careful consideration of alternatives and appropriate match of methods to situations. The evidence, I believe, lends little support to this rival explanation. Nevertheless, the point here is that the real issues in the paradigm debate are empirical not logical.

Reichardt and Cook end their article by briefly referring to these empirical issues. Their observations appear to lend support to the proposition that the paradigmatic contrasts describe real evaluator tendencies. They appear to recognize that the two methods paradigms do actually *describe* real differences among evaluators and that paradigms exercise considerable influence over evaluators' choices of methods.

Of course, some wisdom is revealed by the linkage, which exists in practice, between paradigms and methods. Researchers who use qualitative methods do subscribe to the qualitative paradigm more often than to the quantitative paradigm. Similarly, there is a correlation between the use of quantitative methods and adherence to the quantitative paradigm. . . . Such linkages may be the result of an adaptive evaluation reflecting the fact that all else being equal, qualitative and quantitative methods often are best suited for the separate paradigmatic viewpoints with which they have come to be associated [Reichardt and Cook, 1979: 16-17].

Heilman (1980: 702) also finds that the evidence of actual evaluation practice fits the pattern of alternative paradigms. He regrets, as I do, the necessity felt by so many evaluators to limit their practice to a single approach, and he questions, as I do, the desirability of limiting oneself to extreme and pure paradigmatic alternatives, but he admits the *descriptive* accuracy of paradigmatic contrasts.

The next section provides additional evidence on this issue.

RECENT TENDENCIES IN EVALUATION PRACTICE

Since I agree with Reichardt and Cook that there are no logical reasons why qualitative and quantitative approaches cannot be used together, let us consider in more depth the empirical paradigmatic questions posed above. What are the recent tendencies in evaluation methods?

The evidence is mixed. To be sure, the dominant hypothetico-deductive paradigm no longer seems as ominous today as it seemed when I first described my view of the two paradigms in 1975. Recent meetings of the Evaluation Research Society and the Evaluation Network have devoted substantial program time to consideration of qualitative methods as valuable both in their own right and in combination with quantitative approaches. The Reichardt and Cook work is a contribution in this regard.

Donald Campbell and Lee Cronbach, considered major proponents for the quantitative/experimental paradigm in the past, have advocated the appropriateness and the usefulness of qualitative methods. Ernest House, in describing the role of "qualitative argument" in evaluation research, notes that "when two of the leading scholars of measurement and experimental design, Cronbach and Campbell, strongly support qualitative studies, that is strong endorsement indeed" (House, 1977: 18). In my own work I have found increased interest in and acceptance of qualitative methods in particular and multiple methods in general. I would guess that the empirical tendency to operate largely within only one paradigm has diminished during the last decade.

On the other hand, it is clear that qualitative methods are still the poor relative of quantitative approaches. The requirements for evaluation by many federal agencies reflect the continued dominance of quantitative methods to the virtual exclusion, in any meaningful way, of qualitative data. A case in point is the Joint Dissemination Review Panel (JDRP), the body that passes judgment on the value of educational programs based on review of evaluations of those programs. The JDRP, established by HEW in 1972, reviews products and practices developed in federally supported programs, and decides which ones merit the endorsement of the Education Division. The chosen projects are designated "exemplary," and school systems throughout the nation are urged to look them over and try them. Federal funds are used to provide the "fanfare" and support dissemination activities. To earn the JDRP's seal of approval, the panel must be persuaded that a program is effective. The panel is made up of 22 experts in education and evaluation, 11 from the National Institute of Education, and 11 from the Office of Education. The JDRP criteria of evaluation excellence represent one important set of government standards for judging success in educational interventions. Judgment by JDRP determines whether or not programs are funded for dissemination purposes. It controls considerable amounts of money. It has enormous power in deciding which innovative programs in the United States will be considered legitimate, effective, and suitable for dissemination and public attention. *Its guidelines, its procedures, and its composition virtually eliminate evaluations using qualitative methods.* It insists on experimental designs; it insists on standardized tests and quantitative instruments; and it insists on statistical analysis using significance tests. I have personally been involved in reviewing the reports that are submitted to the JDRP for judgment and, in my opinion, the parsimony required in those reports make it impossible to include qualitative data or to report in any meaningful way about program context, nuance, or process. The influence of these methodological biases is felt in the state departments of education throughout the country and affects the evaluation predispositions of program personnel and evaluators at the local level in school districts throughout the United States. Similar scenarios exist for agencies in criminal justice, health, housing, and welfare.

Another recent example of continued ignorance about the important role qualitative methods can play in evaluation research is the widely used new textbook, *Evaluation: A Systematic Approach,* by Rossi et al. (1979). Students being taught with that widely adopted book would come away with no real exposure to more than a single, dominant, and traditional quantitative evaluation paradigm. (They wouldn't even know that there was a debate going on about evaluation methods.)

MULTIPLE CHOICES

The point of these remarks is not advocacy of one set of methods over another, but greater awareness of the multiple choices available. By way of expanding on that theme, while showing how the qualitative/quantitative options can be merged with other options, the next section presents a matrix of data options that I have used in working with decision makers and information users to expand their awareness of the multiple options available (for a discussion of the purposes and limitations of a matrix approach in working with stakeholders, see Patton, 1981: 123-144).

A MATRIX OF DATA COLLECTION OPTIONS

If evaluators are to be active-reactive-adaptive in working with decision makers, information users, and stakeholders to focus evaluation questions and select appropriate methods, it is necessary that evaluators be able to simplify the options available to the people with whom they are working. Nonevaluators will seldom have mastery of a full range of methodological alternatives. By identifying some critical dimensions along which choices must be made, the evaluator can facilitate the input of others into the evaluation process, thereby increasing their commitment to and understanding of that process. (For a more elaborate discussion of how evaluators can work with decision makers to make methods decisions see the section on working with an evaluation task force, Chapter 3.)

A matrix approach to methods options involves selecting a couple of relevant methodological dimensions and crossing them to create cells that represent the actual options. In the example below (Table 7.1) two dimensions are identified: a qualitative/quantitative data dimension and a standardized/individualized design dimension. The first dimension refers to the options of collecting qualitative data (open-ended interviews, narrative observations, and document analysis) and quantitative data. The decision maker is not faced with having to choose *either* qualitative *or* quantitative data since in many cases a combination of types of data will be desirable. Rather, this dimension highlights the range of choices among types of data.

The second dimension (standardized/individualized designs) refers to the extent to which the same data are systematically gathered from each respondent or from each setting (standardized approach) in contrast to an approach in which different data are collected from different individuals based on the circumstances of those individuals and what can be learned from them of interest to the evaluation. The advantage of standardized data collection is that reliability is enhanced by systematically and carefully providing each

TABLE 7.1   Data Collections Options

	Quantitative Data	*Qualitative Data*
Standardized Design	standardized questionnaire or test; routine management information system	standardized interview guide or observation schedule; same data gathered from each person or setting
Individualized Design	goal attainment scaling; kaleidoscopic questionnaire or adjustable instrument methods	case studies emphasizing uniqueness of each individual or setting

respondent with the same stimulus; analysis is facilitated because all the data appear in the same form; and all the information desired is collected from each person or setting in the study. The advantage of an individualized approach is that it permits the collection of in-depth information from some persons and settings (depending on particular things that can be learned in those cases), while gathering less information from other people and places.

By crossing these two dimensions we obtain Table 7.1. The most common combinations consist of standardized collections of quantitative data and individualized collections of qualitative data. The former is the usual type of statistical information while the later is the most common kind of qualitative design obtained through naturalistic inquiry. It is possible, however, to collect qualitative data in a standardized fashion with the use of a standardized, open-ended interview guide or interview schedule (Patton, 1980). The most unusual case is that of combining an individualized design with quantitative data. From my point of view, this is precisely what goal attainment scaling accomplishes (Kiresuk and Lund, 1978). Goal attainment scaling is a technique for quantifying a wide variety of individual goals in such a way that statistical analysis can be performed on the resulting scales. (Another variation on this theme is the kaleidoscopic questionnaire approach or adjustable instrument methods discussed in the next chapter.)

While this simple matrix is a great simplification of the many options available in evaluation research, it can serve as the beginning point in discussing with decision makers, information users, and stakeholders their values and interests with regard to the degree of standardization desired in designs and the types of data to be collected in the evaluation. As those ideas and values become clear it is possible to pose additional options aimed directly at the specific questions raised by the people with whom one is working. This kind of matrix of methods options, then, is a starting point rather than an ending point, and as such it makes it possible to begin the important discussion of data alternatives.

MERGING QUANTITATIVE AND QUALITATIVE PERSPECTIVES

When qualitative and quantitative approaches are used together, the data are very often difficult to integrate, and when doubts are raised or conflicts emerge it is the qualitative data that most often bear the larger burden of proof. An excellent article by M. G. Trend (1978) described the difficulties of getting fair consideration of qualitative data in a major Abt Associates study. The Trend article is an excellent description of what my experience suggests is quite typical: Qualitative data are rejected if they do not support quantitative findings.

The 1980 meetings of the Society for Applied Anthropology in Denver, Colorado, included a symposium on the problems encountered by anthropologists participating in teams where both quantitative and qualitative data were being collected. The experiences of those anthropologists and the problems they shared were stark evidence that many of the adherents of the dominant hypothetico-deductive (quantitative) paradigm, who control most of the resources in evaluation research, are still prepared to give only token attention to qualitative data. When qualitative data support quantitative findings, that's icing on the cake. When qualitative data conflict with quantitative data, the qualitative data are often dismissed or ignored. (Let me hasten to add for the benefit of Reichardt and Cook that the qualitative data must not *always* and *necessarily* be ignored; I am describing what usually happens under much current team evaluation work.) Such experiences also explain why so many qualitative methodologists prefer to conduct studies where theirs are the only data (and the only paradigm).

While there are some very positive signs that evaluators have become much more sophisticated about the complexities of methodological choices, much of the evidence suggests that integrating quantitative and qualitative methods will be a difficult task. To understand those difficulties it is necessary to understand the paradigms that separate evaluators who tend in one direction or the other. The paradigms make communication, understanding, and cooperation difficult because narrow socialization into one paradigm or the other typically involves adoption of a world view that limits the kinds of questions that are asked and the strategies used to answer those questions. Thus much of the cooperation between quantitative and qualitative methodologists continues to be like the proverbial cooperation between the alligator and the fox.

The Alligator and the Fox

Often, while sunning himself on the river bank, the alligator would observe the hunting skills of the fox. Over time the alligator came to appreciate the slyness of the fox and so one day he called to the fox: "Renard, come closer here and let us work together for our common good."

The fox was much taken with this unusual offer from the alligator. But the fox was wary because he had been brought up to believe that alligators were his natural enemies.

The alligator understood the caution of the fox, but he persuasively explained the advantages of their cooperation. "I have watched your cunning in hunting. You move quickly and stealthily across the land. I move silently and stealthily through the water. By combining your skill on the land with my strength in the water we would be invincible. Let me show you."

The alligator invited the fox to climb on his back and the alligator would take him to the other side of the river. It took a bit more persuading but in the end the fox agreed to a trial period of cooperation. He climbed on the alligator's back and they started to cross the river. As they moved out into the deep water of the river the fox found more and more of the alligator's back submerged in the water. He had to move up the alligator's back and closer to his head. This made him increasingly uncomfortable with their union and so he said to the alligator, "I'm not so sure this is working out quite right. Please take me back to the shore."

The alligator wanted to continue. They began to argue, all the time the alligator becoming more and more submerged in the water and the fox moving higher and higher on the neck and head of the alligator. As it became clear that the two could not agree, the alligator said, "I'm sorry, my dear Renard, I'm sorry you don't see it my way." With that the alligator flipped the fox into the air, grasping him in his powerful jaws as he fell. After devouring the fox the alligator returned to bathing contentedly in the warmth of the sun and said to himself: "We made quite a team there for awhile, that fox and I. That was actually quite a good beginning. I'll have to cooperate more with my fellow foxes. We work real good together I think."

BEYOND METHODS HABITS TO CREATIVE PRACTICE

In my opinion, the development of the evaluation profession in accordance with the standards of excellence that call for studies that are useful, feasible, ethical, and accurate will best be facilitated if we become more creative in matching methods to particular situations and specific decision makers, thereby more flexibly applying the large and rich repertoire of possible methods. Paradigm debates play an important role in helping move toward these ideals by calling to our attention some of the tendencies and practices that limit real flexibility and situational responsiveness. By way of closure, then, let me present a series of conclusions that I hope will clearly separate logic, prescription, and description to summarize my current thinking about methodological paradigms.

(1) *Assumption:* The methodological practices of evaluators can usefully be described along a series of dimensions whose polar ends constitute the characteristics of ideal-typical qualitative/naturalistic and quantitative/experimental paradigms.

(2) *Description:* Evaluators tend to feel more comfortable operating within the world view of one or the other paradigm, and their methods decisions are influenced accordingly.

(3) *Logical assertion:* It is possible to combine various elements of the paradigms and various components of methods, measurement, and analysis along the different dimensions used to describe and contrast the paradigms.

(4) *Logical assertion:* Because evaluators are largely unaware of their methodological prejudices and paradigmatic biases (description), it is necessary to make them aware of those biases and prejudices through elaboration of the contrasting paradigms in order to free them from the bondage of narrow paradigmatic blinders.

(5) *Prescription:* Evaluators should be flexible, sophisticated, and rigorous in matching research methods to variations in program situations, the nuances of particular evaluation questions, and the idiosyncrasies of specific decision maker needs. *Qualitative Evaluation Methods* (Patton, 1980) describes sixteen conditions under which qualitative methods are particularly appropriate in evaluation research. Sometimes quantitative methods alone are most appropriate. In many cases both qualitative and quantitative methods should be used together. Certainly, triangulation of methods is ideal.

(6) *Prescription:* Wherever possible multiple methods should be used. Where multiple methods are used the contributions of each kind of data should be fairly assessed. In many cases this means that evaluators working together in teams will need to work hard to overcome their paradigmatic tendency to dismiss certain kinds of data without first considering seriously and fairly the merits of those data. Then, we can move out from under the "shadow of the dominant paradigm" (Patton, 1981: 220).

CHAPTER 8

Practical and Creative Evaluation Data Collection

So simple, to create the world;
I could do it in a week.
And my world would have everything—except the moon;
I would not have thought of that.
My so simple world would perish nightly.

Cosmogony
by Hal Lenke (1978)

This chapter explores the symbiotic relationship between pragmatism and creativity in evaluation practice with special reference to problems of design and measurement. In the first chapter I suggested that the mandate to be practical is contained in and is part of the creative imperative in utilization-focused evaluation. Fulfilling the mandate to be practical may sound like a rather mundane, simplistic, and uncreative process. Quite the contrary, my experience suggests that finding feasible solutions to enormously complex problems with limited resources is the epitome of the evaluation challenge, requiring hard work, flexibility, and all the pains and insights of creative problem solving grounded in evaluation fundamentals.

This chapter will *not* review fundamentals of design and measurement. Such a review is beyond the scope of what can be handled in the limited space available here. (Writing, like evaluation, is subject to contraints and limitations. For design and measurement fundamentals in evaluation see Rossi et al., 1979; Rutman, 1977; Fitz-Gibbon and Morris, 1978; Wright, 1979; and Campbell and Stanley, 1963.)

The design and measurement ideas presented in this chapter are all deviations from standard practice. Each idea is subject to misuse and abuse if applied without regard for ways in which the quality of data collected can be affected because of threats to reliability and validity. I have not discussed such threats and possible errors at any length because I believe it is impossible to identify *in the abstract and in advance* all the tradeoffs involved in balancing concerns for accuracy, utility, feasibility, and propriety. For example, having program staff do client interviews in an outcomes evaluation *could:* (a) seriously reduce the validity and reliability of the data, (b) substantially increase the validity and reliability of the data, or (c) have no measurable effect on data quality. The nature and degree of effect would depend on staff relationships with clients, how staff were assigned to clients for interviewing, the kinds of questions being asked, the training of the interviewers, attitudes of clients toward the program, and so on. Program staff might make better or worse interviewers than external evaluation researchers depending on these and other factors. An evaluator must grapple with these kinds of data quality questions for all designs, particularly the kinds of nontraditional designs discussed in this chapter.

Practical but creative data collection consists of using whatever resources are available to do the best job possible. There are many constraints. Our ability to think of alternatives is limited. Resources are always limited. This means that data collection will be imperfect, so dissenters from evaluation findings, who want to attack a study's methods, can always find some grounds for doing so. A major reason for actively involving decision makers and information users in making methods decisions is to deal with weaknesses in the design, and consider tradeoff threats to data quality, *before* data are generated. By strategically calculating threats to utility, as well as threats to validity and reliability, it is possible to make practical decisions about the strengths of creative and nonconventional data collection procedures. It is also necessary, at the design stage, to consider threats to feasibility: Can the proposed evaluation design actually be implemented?

It is important to review critically the evaluation designs presented in this chapter. Anderson (1980), in work on problem-solving approaches, has reported that "critical" thinking and "creative" thinking are seldom found operating simultaneously. The critical thinker assumes a stance of doubt and skepticism; things have to be proven; faulty logic, slippery linkages, tautological theories, and unsupported deductions are the targets of the critical mind. Evaluators are trained to be rigorous and unyielding in critically thinking about research methods. Therein lies the adherence to the "accuracy" part of the standards of evaluation. Creativity is no justification for research findings that lead to incorrect, unjustified, and inaccurate findings. The creative designs reviewed in this chapter are subject to the same careful scrutiny that would be applied to conventional designs. Readers are urged to pay particular attention to potential problems of subject reactivity, ways of checking for data quality, and limitations on generalizability. In considering the practical data collection ideas presented in this chapter, readers are urged to keep in mind the accuracy standards that are aimed at safeguarding evaluation procedures in data collection. Among the most relevant standards for the issues presented in this chapter are the following (Joint Committee, 1981):

Described Purposes and Procedures

The purposes and procedures of the evaluation should be monitored and described in enough detail, so that they can be identified and assessed.

Defensible Information Sources

The sources of information should be described in enough detail, so that the adequacy of the information can be assessed.

Valid Measurement

The information-gathering instruments and procedures should be chosen or developed and then implemented in ways that will assure that the interpretation arrived at is valid for the given use.

Reliable Measurement

The information-gathering instruments and procedures should be chosen or developed and then implemented in ways that will assure that the information obtained is sufficiently reliable for the intended use.

Systematic Data Control

The data collected, processed, and reported in an evaluation should be reviewed and corrected, so that the results of the evaluation will not be flawed.

Objective Reporting

The evaluation procedures should provide safeguards to protect the evaluation findings and reports against distortion by the personal feelings and biases of any party to the evaluation.

PARTICIPANT INTERVIEW CHAIN

As a participant observer in the wilderness training program for adult educators described in Appendix B (Chapter 4), I was involved in: (1) documenting the kinds of experiences program participants were having and (2) collecting information about the effects of those experiences on their regular work situations. In short, the purpose of evaluation was to provide formative insights that could be used to help understand the personal, professional, and institutional outcomes of intense wilderness experiences for these adult educators.

During the first year of this program the two of us who were doing the observations conducted follow-up telephone interviews with all the participants three weeks after each ten-day wilderness experience. The limited resources available for evaluation meant that it was possible to do only one follow-up interview for each experience and that those interviews, being conducted over the telephone to people all over the United States (including

Hawaii), could last no longer than one-half hour. Such data collection procedures were sufficient to give us an overview of the kinds of experiences they
were having, but the data lacked depth and detail about the ongoing effect of
the experiences over time. Sufficient evaluation resources were not available
to permit us to increase our own data collection efforts. Therefore, we began
discussing with the program staff ways in which the participants might become involved in the data collection effort to meet both program needs and
evaluation needs. The staff liked the idea of involving participants in systematic data collection, thereby introducing them to observation and interviewing as ways of expanding their own horizons and perceptions.

During the second year there were to be twenty participants who would
participate in three different wilderness experiences of ten days each about
three months apart: an intensive backpacking experience in New Mexico; a
rock-climbing expedition in Arizona; and a river trip in Utah. The initial
backpacking field experience would be organized in two groups of ten participants each. We used this fact to design a data collection approach that
would fit with the programmatic needs for sharing of information between
the two groups. Participants were paired for interviewing each other. At the
very beginning of the first trip, before people knew each other, all of the
participants were given a short, open-ended interview of ten questions. They
were told that each of them, as part of their project participation, was to have
responsibility for documenting the experience of their pair-mate throughout
the year. They were given a little bit of interview training, a lot of encouragement about probing, and told to record responses fully—thereby taking responsibility for helping to build this community record of individual experiences. They were then sent off in pairs and given two hours to complete the
interviews with each other, recording the responses by hand.

At the end of the ten-day experience when the separate groups came back
together, the same pairs of participants, consisting of one person from each
group, were again given an interview outline and sent off to interview each
other about their respective experiences. This served the program need for
sharing of information and an evaluation need for the collection of information. The tradeoff, of course, was that with the minimal interview training
given the participants and the impossibility of carefully supervising, controlling, and standardizing the data collection, the resulting information would
be of variable quality. On the other hand, there were not sufficient evaluation
resources for the two evaluators to conduct twenty in-depth interviews with
all of the participants, nor was there time at both the beginning and the end of
the experiences to allow such data collection to occur. This mode of data
collection also meant that confidentiality was minimal and certain kinds of
information could be expected to be lost.

On the subsequent two field experiences the same people were paired to
again interview each other, although the nature of the questions asked in each
interview changed somewhat to fit the circumstances and timing of the data

collection. Most of the participants enjoyed the interviewing though they enjoyed taking notes on the interviews less, and most of them did a quite conscientious job of taking down verbatim quotes and getting detailed information. A few of them became very interested in applying similar types of data collection in their home educational settings. The data proved quite useful in documenting and understanding the experiences participants were having and the effects of those experiences on their personal and professional situations. The costs of collecting the information were minimal, and far from interfering with the program, the evaluation became integrated into program activities, increasing both the usefulness of the evaluation process and its credibility to participants and staff.

A plan to have the participants write up case studies of their pair-mates fell through because the participants were simply not willing to spend the time and make the effort to write up detailed case studies. There are limitations to how far one can push client involvement in data collection and analysis. But before those limits are reached, there is a great deal of useful information that can be collected by involving participants in a program in the actual data collection process.

DATA COLLECTION BY PROGRAM STAFF

Another resource for data collection that is often overlooked is the program staff. Raising the possibility of involving program staff in data collection immediately raises objections about staff subjectivity, data contamination, losses of confidentiality, the vested interests of staff in particular kinds of outcomes, and the threat that staff can pose to clients or students from whom they are collecting the data. Balancing these objections are the things that can be gained from staff involvement in data collection: greater staff commitment to the evaluation, greater staff understanding of the data collection process, training staff in data collection procedures, increased understanding by staff of clients' and students' perceptions, and cost savings in data collection.

One of my first evaluation experiences was studying a program to train teachers in open education at the University of North Dakota. Faculty were interested in evaluating that program, but there were almost no resources available for a formal evaluation. There certainly was not enough money available to bring in an external evaluation team to design the study, collect data, and analyze the results. The main data collection consisted of in-depth interviews with student teachers in 24 different schools and classrooms throughout North Dakota, and structured interviews with 300 parents who had children in those classrooms. The only evaluation moneys available would barely pay for the transportation and the actual mechanical costs of data collection. The interviewers were staff and students at the university. Structured interview forms were developed for both the teacher and parent interviews; a full day of training was given to all of the interviewers; and a highly structured system of assigning interviewers to geographical areas was worked out so that no staff were collecting data from their own student teachers. The in-depth interviews with student teachers were tape recorded and transcribed. The parent interviews involved a precoded, structured instrument. I did follow-up interviews with a 5 percent sample of the parents as a check on the validity and reliability of the student and staff data.

After data collection, seminars were organized for staff and students to share their personal perceptions based on their interview experiences. It was clear that the interviewing had had an enormous impact on both staff and students. One major outcome was the increased respect both staff and students had for the parents. They found the parents to be perceptive, caring, and deeply interested in the education of their children. Prior to the interviewing, many of the interviewers had held quite negative and derogatory images of North Dakota parents. The systematic interviewing had put them in a situation in which they were forced to listen to what parents had to say rather than tell parents what they (as educators) thought about things, and in that listening it was clear that they had learned a great deal. The formal analysis of the data yielded some interesting findings about the program; the evaluation was used to make some changes in the program; and the data provided a source of case materials used in training future program participants. But it is very likely that the major and most lasting impact of the evaluation were the actual experiences of students and staff, who learned a great deal by participating in the data collection. That experiential impact was more powerful than the formal findings of the study.

By the way, had the interviewers been paid at the going commercial rate the data collection would have cost at least $10,000 just in personnel costs. As it was, there were no personnel costs in data collection and a considerable human contribution was made to the university program by both students and staff.

INTERACTIVE RESEARCH

The involvement of program staff or clients as colleagues in evaluation research changes the relationship between evaluators and staff. The relationship becomes interactive and cooperative, rather than one-sided and antagonistic. William Tikunoff (1980) has used this "interactive research" approach in educational research and development projects. He found that putting teachers, researchers, and trainer/developers together as a team increased both the meaningfulness and the validity of the findings, because teacher cooperation and understanding of the research made the research less intrusive, thus reducing rather than increasing reactivity.

The problem of how research subjects or program clients will react to staff involvement in an evaluation, particularly involvement in data collection, needs careful scrutiny and consideration in each situation in which it is attempted. Reactivity is a potential problem in both conventional and non-conventional designs. Breaches of confidence and/or reactivity-biased data cannot be justified in the name of creativity. On the other hand, as Tikunoff's experiences indicate, interactive designs may increase the validity of data and reduce reactivity by making evaluations less intrusive and subjects or clients less resistant or suspicious.

The previous two examples of nontraditional data collection approaches have focused on who collects the evaluation data. By contrast, the next section is one solution to the problem of locating a good, but inexpensive, sample of people from whom data can be collected.

A READY AND WILLING COMMUNITY SAMPLE

There is great interest these days in community surveys. Health programs, criminal justice programs, education programs, and community planning efforts of all kinds are attempting to conduct community surveys as parts of needs assessments, evaluations, and planning efforts. Such surveys can be quite costly because of the difficulties of constructing a reasonable sample frame, drawing a random sample, and getting interviewers out and about the community to collect the data. In addition to being expensive, the organization of such projects usually involves fairly lengthy time horizons of several months, often a year or more.

In considering the time and cost involved in community surveys, one county planning department in Minnesota came up with a quite creative solution. It occurred to them that there is a ready and willing sample of people who represent a broad cross-section of the community and who, because they happen to have a considerable amount of time on their hands, are likely to be quite willing interview respondents. *This sample consists of people who have been called for jury duty and are waiting for an actual jury assignment.*

Jury participants are drawn from voter lists. While the resulting sample is not entirely random because many people get out of jury duty for one reason or another, it represents a not altogether unattractive proxy for a random sample with the advantages that no expensive sampling procedures are necessary and the interview respondents are all gathered together at one place in time so that they are easily accessible to interviewers. Moreover, the length of time needed to plan such a study is fairly minimal because no time has to be devoted to the lengthy process of identifying and constructing a sampling frame, drawing the sample, and matching interviews to sample respondents. All you have to do is write your instrument and go down to the courthouse to conduct the interviews. My experience has been that people awaiting jury duty are quite willing to be interviewed because they have nothing else to do while they are waiting. Relatively large samples can be obtained in this way at low expense allowing the planning department to get some basic ideas about how the more active citizens in the county (registered voters) are thinking about major issues of the day.

Of course, one has to get the approval of relevant county officials and judges to do such interviewing. Our experience has been that the judges know how boring it is to be waiting for jury duty. They are quite happy to have prospective jurors entertained, even providing a useful public service, while they are standing by to perform the public service that has brought them to the courthouse. Even if one were not to use this sample for a full study, it represents an excellent group for doing pilot studies, for testing out intruments, and for carrying out exploratory research.

TEACHING INSTEAD OF DOING

Many demonstration projects in education, chemical dependency, health, criminal justice, and other areas of human service programming are so small that their evaluation budgets, even if they consist of as much as 5 percent of program funds, allow the purchase of no more than a few days of an evaluator's time. For example, many of the Title I and Title IV-C programs in schools involve evaluation budgets of $500, $1000, or sometimes as much as $2000. Because of the limited funds involved many of these evaluations end up consisting entirely of a one- or two-day site visit by an evaluator at one or two times in the course of the project year, resulting in a fairly minimal description of what is happening in the program.

One way of making use of these limited evaluation funds (particularly in the early formative years of the project before the full credibility of an external evaluator is needed for summative purposes) is to have the evaluator train people in the program to collect evaluative data, and to work with them in setting up their own evaluation system, rather than collecting the data directly. This strategy follows the ancient proverb. "Give a man a fish and he eats for a day; teach him to fish and eats for a lifetime."

In a number of instances we have found that it is possible to integrate evaluation into the program in such a way that the evaluation becomes part of the learning experience of program participants. Perhaps the best example in this regard was an evaluation of a "school service" project. The purpose of the project was to develop new approaches to creating student learning experiences that contributed to the school and the community. These "school service" projects thus served a dual role: (1) they allowed the students to get practical experience while they were learning something, and (2) they allowed the students to provide a needed service as part of their learning experience. The evaluation design called for doing some case studies of actual "school service" projects. If the evaluation moneys were spent for professional evaluator time to collect data for the case studies, it would have been possible to look at no more than three school service projects. As an alternative, we suggested creating a school service experience through the evaluation project. A group of students would be trained by the evaluator to conduct case studies and the students, as their school service learning, would actually collect the data and write the case studies. In this way it was possible to construct a much larger number of case studies while providing some practical benefits to the program as part of the evaluation. The quality of the resulting case studies were considerably lower than those that would have resulted had the professional evaluators constructed the cases based on their own data collection. However, the quality was sufficient to serve the minimal purposes for which data were collected and the much larger number of cases made it possible to understand a greater variety of school service experiences than would have been possible with two or three cases done solely by the evaluator.

AN *N* OF ONE

Sampling tradeoffs can be one of the most difficult issues to deal with in an evaluation, particularly where resources are quite limited. I once attended a congressional hearing at which a researcher was being hounded by a congressman about the small sample size in his study. The congressman didn't like the results so he was playing the "evaluation á la Machiavelli" game (see Patton, 1981: 112) and attacking the study's sample size to reduce its credibility. Finally, in frustration and with minimal diplomacy, the researcher retorted:

> I yield to your judgment, Congressman. Sampling is just no damn good. In fact, the idea of generalizing from a small sample is so unreasonable that the next time you go for a physical check-up I hope you'll insist that they take *all* your blood—not just a sample.

It is worth remembering that some of the major breakthroughs in knowledge have come from studies with small sample sizes. Freud's work was based on a few clinical cases. Piaget significantly changed educational thinking about how children learn with an in-depth study of two children—his own. There are even rumors that Newton's major contributions in physics began with the study of a single apple (of course he had the precedent of Adam and Eve to follow).

In *Qualitative Evaluation Methods* (Patton, 1980) I discussed a number of "purposeful" sampling approaches that involve small samples selected for their high information payoff. One type of purposeful sampling—"the critical case"—involves an *n* of one.

Critical cases are those that can make a point quite dramatically or are, for some reason, particularly important in the scheme of things. A clue to the existence of a critical case is a statement by a decision maker to the effect that "if the program doesn't make it there, it won't make it anywhere." Perhaps, then, the focus of the evaluation should be on understanding what is happening in *that* critical program. Another kind of clue would be a statement to the effect that "if that program is having problems then we can be sure all the programs are having problems." Looking for the critical case is particularly important where resources may limit evaluation to the study of only a single site. Under such conditions it makes strategic sense to pick the site that would yield the most information and have the greatest impact on decision maker actions and understanding.

While studying one or a few critical cases does not technically permit broad generalizations to all possible cases, logical generalizations can often be made from the weight of evidence produced in studying a single, critical case. Physics provides a good example of such a critical case. In Galileo's study of gravity he wanted to find out if the weight of an object affected the rate of speed at which it would fall. Rather than randomly sampling objects of different weights in order to generalize to all objects in the world, he selected a critical case—the feather. If in a vacuum, as he demonstrated, a feather fell at the same rate as some heavier object (a coin) then he could logically generalize from this one critical case to all objects. His findings were enormously useful and credible.

There are many comparable critical cases in social action programming—if one is creative in looking for them. For example, suppose national policymakers want to get local communities involved in making decisions about how their local program will be run, but they are not sure that the communities will understand the complex regulations governing their involvement. The first critical case is to evaluate the regulations in a community of well-educated citizens; if they cannot understand them, less-educated folks are certain to find the regulations incomprehensible. Or conversely, one might consider the critical case to be a community consisting of people with quite low levels of education: "If *they* can understand the regulations, anyone can."

A variation of the critical case strategy involves selecting (or sometimes avoiding) a politically sensitive site or unit of analysis. For example, a statewide program may have a local site in the district of a state legislator who is particularly influential. By studying carefully the program in that district evaluation data may be more likely to attract attention and get used. This does not mean that the evaluator then undertakes to make that site look either good or bad, depending on the politics of the moment. This is simply an additional sampling strategy for trying to increase the usefulness and utilization of information where resources permit the study of only a limited number of cases.

Identification of critical cases depends on recognition of the key dimensions that make for a critical case. As noted in the last paragraph the critical dimension may be political sensitivity or visibility. A critical case might be indicated by the financial state of a program; a program with particularly high or particularly low cost-per-client ratios might suggest a critical case. A critical case might come from a particularly difficult program location. If the funders of a new program are worried about recruiting clients or participants into a program, it may make sense to study the site where resistance to the program is expected to be greater to provide the most rigorous test of the possibility of program recruitment. If the program works in that site, "it could work anywhere."

INSTRUMENT VALIDATION A LA MOTHER MEASUREMENT

Critical case sampling is a technique for making logical generalizations. Evaluators are more often involved with and concerned about making empirical generalizations. The extent to which one can have confidence in empirical generalizations depends partly on the validity and reliability of the data collected in the evaluation. This section reproduces a creative solution to the validity and reliability problem. The solution is from *Discrepancy Digest* (February 1980), the Evaluation Training Consortium newsletter from the Evaluation Center, Western Michigan University.

Dear Mother Measurement:

I have a question regarding the assessment of validity and reliability of instruments which I presently use to evaluate participant satisfaction with inservice workshops. The real problem is that the content and format of each workshop is different. Consequently, I must use a new and completely different instrument for each workshop. This means I am never able to re-use instruments to get data concerning validity and reliability. I realize that instrument validation can be complex, but is there something easy I can do that will solve my problem!

I. M. Unsatisfied

Dear Unsatisfied:

Yes, there are a number of procedures that can be used for instrument validation that range from simple procedures to a major evaluation effort. The procedure I will describe is ideal for your situation, and it can also be used if you are planning to use an instrument more than once and want an indication of its validity before you actually begin using it at workshops.

You will need a small group of individuals that you can administer your instrument to prior to each workshop. Here is the procedure you should follow. Generate three different short scenarios concerning how participants might react to your workshop. For example, the first scenario might read something like this: "The workshop you just attended was tremendous, met all of your needs and was extremely beneficial. etc. . . ." The second would read something like this: "The workshop you attended was alright. You learned some new information, but felt lukewarm about the experience, etc. . . ." The third scenario: "The workshop you just attended was a disaster, poorly organized and boring; you got nothing from attending, etc. . . ."

Using the small group of individuals you have selected, randomly assign them to three groups, each group being given a different scenario. They will be instructed to assume that they are participants in a just completed inservice workshop and the printed scenario they have been given is how they actually felt about the workshop experience. The subjects are then given your workshop evaluation form, and told to mark at the top the number of the scenario card they have. They are then told to complete the instrument using only the scenario card to guide their responses to the questions.

The overall scores on the completed instruments should fall into three distinct groups congruent with the scenario the individual had. A high positive correlation between scores on the instrument and assigned scenarios would indicate your instrument was sensitive in differentiating among these three possible outcomes to your workshop. Additionally, you can evaluate responses to individual items to determine those questions that do or do not differentiate among the three possible workshop outcomes.

Love,

Mother

The *Discrepancy Digest* is a consistent source of creative evaluation ideas. Indeed, evaluation is blessed with a large numer of excellent journals and newsletters that serve to inform, stimulate, and provide a forum for sharing creative evaluation thoughts. Many of them are provided without cost. The newsletters of the Evaluation Network and the Evaluation Research Society are provided with membership in those organizations. I've listed here addresses for three of the center newsletters I find most stimulating and creative. All are available at no cost.

Discrepancy Digest
Evaluation Training Consortium
Western Michigan University
Kalamazoo, Michigan 49008

Using School Evaluations
Center for the Study of Evaluation
UCLA
Los Angeles, California 90024

Research on Evaluation Program Newsletter
Northwest Regional Educational Laboratory
410 S.W. Second Ave.
Portland, Oregon 97204

DATA COLLECTION TRADEOFFS

Each of the examples in this chapter involves an attempt to optimize the use of limited resources while serving both the program and the need for evaluation. Each example also involves tradeoffs between data quality, data credibility, varying roles for the evaluator, different threats to validity and reliability, and evaluation costs. By discussing the options with the relevant decision makers in each case, it was possible to arrive at designs and data collection procedures that served more than one purpose and built a constructive foundation for future evaluation efforts.

Every evaluation situation presents options. The evaluator's task is to identify creatively those options, assess the strengths and weaknesses of each approach, and work with decision makers to come up with a design that is appropriate to the situation at hand. Far from being a deterrent, the fact that you come up with a design or approach that, to the best of your knowledge, has never been tried before, may be as good a reason as any to try it.

COST-EFFECTIVE EVALUATION

In Trinidad "liming" is a word for the fine art of hanging out somewhere doing absolutely nothing; "scrunting" is a word describing a difficult struggle against impossible odds; "wining" is an especially provocative dance done during Mardi Gras Carnival; and "evaluation" is something you do several days after Carnival when you've begun to recover from all the parading and partying. It's quite an intriguing approach to evaluation: making sure of the benefits before *counting the costs.*

From *Halcolm's Evaluation Travels*

Thinking along the lines suggested in the preceding sections assumes a commitment to conduct cost-effective evaluations. Cost-effective evaluations are those where the benefits to the program are worth the cost of conducting the evaluation. Michael Scriven (1976) has referred to such evaluations as "cost-free" evaluations. They involve no cost to the program in the long run because what is added to the program exceeds the cost of the evaluation, or, in many cases, the savings to the program or to program funders exceeds the cost of doing the evaluation. Given increasingly limited resources for the development of programs and the conduct of evaluations, there is every likelihood that evaluators will be called on more and more to demonstrate the cost-effectiveness of their work. Evaluators can expect to be held accountable both for utilization and for showing that the evaluation results were justified in terms of the cost expended on research.

Scriven's concerns about cost-effective evaluations are reflected in his recent work on what he has called "responsibility evaluation," as exemplified in the "school evaluation profile." A number of principles of cost-effective evaluation are illustrated in Scriven's description of responsibility evaluation:

1. In responsibility evaluation you start by asking: If we ignore all the variance of all factors over which there is no manipulable control, is there enough variance left to be worth fooling around with? You identify the factors over which there is no control and ignore them.

2. For whatever remains, can we identify the actor(s) who have control over these factors?

3. Third, can we get measure of these factors?

4. Then, can these measures be obtained cheaply? As we all know schools are pressed for funds. The economy issue is important.

5. Finally, will the measures be interpretable? We must avoid using measures or indicators that are so complex or esoteric that they are not comprehensible by school personnel [Scriven, 1979a: 50].

Cost-effectiveness analysis is not simply something to be undertaken after an evaluation has been completed. Indeed, if an evaluation is to be cost effective, a careful assessment of potential benefits and expected costs should be carried out *before* data collection, and such discussions should take place in the context of a real consideration of creative alternatives *including the alternative of not doing the evaluation at all* (see the utilization-focused evaluation flowchart in Chapter 3 to see how the cost-effectiveness decision fits into the overall evaluation decision making process). The next section provides a concrete example of how cost-benefit criteria can affect an evaluation approach.

INTERNAL-EXTERNAL EVALUATION COMBINATIONS

Internal evaluations, where people in the program collect the data themselves, are typically less expensive than evaluations conducted by external evaluators. External evaluation, however, tends to have more credibility and legitimacy than internal evaluation. In workshops I am often asked to compare the tradeoffs between internal and external evaluation, or what are euphemistically called "in-house" evaluations and "out-house" evaluations.

The problem with the way in which the question is typically posed to me is that it sets up an artificial dichotomy. The question usually concerns the advantages and disadvantages of internal *versus* external evaluation. Actually, there are a good many possible combinations of internal *and* external evaluations that may be more desirable and more cost effective than either a purely internal *or* purely external evaluation.

Accreditation processes are a good example of an internal-external combination. The internal group collects the data and arranges them so that the external group can come in, inspect the data collected by the internal group, sometimes collect additional information on their own, and pass judgment on the program. There are many ways in which an evaluation can be set up so that some external group of respected professionals and evaluators guarantees the validity and fairness of the evaluation process while the people internal to the program actually collect and/or analyze the evaluation data. The cost savings of such an approach can be substantial while still allowing the evaluation to have basic credibility and legitimacy through the blessing of the external review committee.

I have been working for several years with one of the leading chemical dependency programs in the country, the Hazelden Foundation of Minnesota. They have established a quite rigorous evaluation process that involves data collection at the point of entry into the program and then follow-up questionnaires six months, twelve months, and eighteen months after leaving the program. Hazelden's own research and evaluation department collects all of the data. My responsibility as an external evaluator is to monitor that data collection periodically to make sure that the established procedures are being followed correctly. I then work with the program decision makers to identify the kind of data analysis that is desirable. They perform the data analysis with their own computer resources. They send the data to me and I write the annual evaluation report. They participate in analyzing, interpreting, and making judgments about the data, but for purposes of legitimacy and credibility the actual writing of the final report is done by me. This internal/external combination is sometimes extended one step farther by having still another layer of external professionals and evaluators pass judgment on the quality and accuracy of the final report through a *meta-evaluation* process— evaluating the evaluation.

There are limitations to this kind of process. One of the limitations is that the external group may impose unmanageable and overwhelming data collection procedures on the internal people. I saw this happening in an internal-external model with a group of school districts in Canada. The external committee was asking for a "comprehensive" data collection effort by the local schools that included data on learning outcomes, staff morale, facilities, curriculum, the school lunch program, the library, parent reactions, the perceptions of local businessmen, analysis of the school bus system, and so on. After listening to all of the things the external committee thought the internal people should do, the internal folks renamed the evaluation approach. They suggested that the model should not be called the "Internal-External Model" of evaluation but rather the "Internal-External-Eternal Model" of evaluation.

Evaluations should have clear closure points; they should not go on eternally. Evaluations are often

> *hellish, occasionally heavenly, but they should not be*
> *eternal in duration (or seemingly eternal).*
>
> From *Halcolm's Evaluation Bible*

THREATS TO DATA QUALITY

This chapter has presented some alternative and nonconventional approaches to data collection. The first example illustrated one approach to
interactive research, as exemplified by the participant interview chain. The
subsequent suggestions for actively involving program staff in data collection provided yet another perspective on interactive research. I then discussed the potential of using people who are awaiting jury duty as a ready,
willing, inexpensive, and easily accessible sample for pilot and exploratory
studies, or for community surveys. Purposeful and small samples were considered as alternatives to random sampling. There was also a section on
teaching people to do their own data collection for evaluation purposes. The
chapter included a selection from "Mother Measurement" on a creative instrument validation approach. Data collection tradeoffs, cost-effective evaluation, and responsibility evaluation á la Scriven were discussed. Finally, I
presented some alternative ways of structuring and organizing data collection and analysis: internal-external evaluation combinations.

The purpose of presenting this diverse range of data collection alternatives has been to illustrate the possibilities for creative solutions to all kinds
of practical design and measurement problems. These examples have been
offered in the hope that they will stimulate thinking about practical methods
options.

This chapter only scratches the surface in relation to the full range of
creative designs that are possible in evaluation. In the last several years my
evaluation work and consulting have brought me into contact with hundreds
of evaluators. While much of the tone of this book may come across as
critical of standard evaluation practice, I know from direct observation that
there is a great deal of creative work being done by evaluators in all kinds of
difficult and challenging situations. My observations suggest that what these
evaluators have in common is a commitment to do the most and best they can
with the resources available, the short deadlines they face, and the intense
political pressures they feel—all of which constitute the context for their
work. They share a belief that *doing something is better than doing nothing,
so long as one is realistic and honest in assessing and presenting the limitations of what is done.*

This last caveat is important. I have not attempted to delineate all the
possible threats to validity and reliability that may be posed by the design
alternatives in this chapter. This is not a methods, measurement, and design
text. My purpose has been to stimulate thinking about alternatives, not to
repeat the design analyses of Campbell and Stanley (1963), on which most

social scientists cut their teeth. Moreover, as I noted in the introduction to this chapter, I believe that it is impossible to identify *in the abstract and in advance* all the tradeoffs involved in balancing concerns for validity, reliability, utility, feasibility, propriety, and accuracy that will need to be considered in any particular situation. Even when faced with the reality of particular circumstances and specific evaluation problems, it often is not possible to determine in advance precisely how a creative design or measurement approach will affect the quality of the data collected. Both "truth tests" (whether data are believable and accurate) and "utility tests" (whether data are useful) are important to decision makers, information users, and stakeholders (Weiss and Bucuvalas, 1980). One is obligated to think about and deal with threats to validity that may reduce the utility of data, just as one is obligated to consider threats to utility that may result from overly elaborate and too-sophisticated designs aimed at reducing threats to validity. One is obligated to take validity and reliability constraints into consideration in data analysis, as those constraints become known in the process of data collection and analysis. One is obligated to be forthright in reporting on the quality of data in an evaluation. But, what one is *not* obligated to do is return the technical, validity-reliability-accuracy criteria to a position of predominance and ascendancy as the primary standards against which an evaluation is judged. As the emergent standards of evaluation make clear (see Chapter 1, and Stufflebeam, 1980), technical concerns for data accuracy should be made in conjunction with concerns for utility, feasibility, and propriety. There is a lot of room for creative data collection approaches to meet the spirit and challenge of these standards. Indeed, there is a substantial need for creative evaluation approaches to evaluation to meet the spirit and challenge of these standards. It is in that spirit, and in the face of the challenge represented by the new standards, that the ideas in this chapter have been presented.

A CLOSING PERSPECTIVE

Designing practical, but creative, evaluations, means not forcing new situations into old molds—in this case, traditional research designs. To do so is to make the error of the traveler who came across a peacock for the first time, a story from Halcolm:

A traveler to a new land came across a peacock. Having never seen this kind of bird before, he took it for a genetic freak. Taking pity on the poor bird, which he was sure could not survive for long in such deviant form, he set about to correct nature's error. He trimmed the long, colorful feathers, cut back the beak, and dyed the bird black. "There now," he said, with pride in a job well done, "you look more like a standard guinea hen."

CHAPTER 9　　　　*Managing*
Management
Information Systems

> *When action grows unprofitable,*
> *gather information; when*
> *information grows unprofitable, sleep.*
> Ursula K. LeGuin

The single most common question I am asked at evaluation workshops is how to use management information systems for program evaluation. Actually, it is not quite accurate to say that I am asked questions in this regard. Rather, I infer this question from assorted rantings and ravings about, and hostilities toward, management information systems. The question usually never quite becomes explicit because the cynicism about, and frustrations with, these information systems are so deep and longstanding that the people expressing their rage—and the rage is quite real—can no longer entertain the possibility that the management information system might actually be somehow useful.

The dissatisfaction occurs at all levels. Case workers, line staff, probation officers, counselors, health professionals, agricultural extension agents, energy conservation workers, manpower trainers—the list goes on and on—are fed up with the useless paperwork and the meaningless diversion from real service delivery. They openly admit to falsifying information, filling out all the forms for a month at one sitting, making up data when they can't remember what actually happened, and otherwise "coping" with the paperwork demands of the system. Even those, and I suspect they are the large majority, who try to take the systems seriously, do the paperwork conscientiously, and complete their forms on time are embittered that their valuable time is wasted.

Program administrators, agency directors, and supervisory personnel complain that they send all the data off but never get anything back. They charge that data move from the local level to the state and on to the federal government but nothing of any value comes back down the pipe. When something does come back the output generated is too late to be useful and is aggregated in ways that don't make much sense or are too difficult to decipher. The categories in which data are collected are decided either by programmers who understand computers but don't understand human service delivery systems, or by state and federal officials who are taking care of their accountability needs without any sensitivity to the demands they place on local programs. Then there is the great frustration with impossible formats on forms, and the frequent necessity of filling out separate forms for different state and federal agencies, or completing different forms for county accountability, state monitoring, and federal audits. "Why can't somebody coordinate this mess?"

The management systems' developers and computer programmers are frustrated because they can't get program staff and administrators to talk with them about their data needs. They charge that program people don't understand the system constraints and refuse to treat computer personnel as people and colleagues. "All program staff do is complain, complain, complain . . . , instead of really trying to improve things."

The state and federal officials are frustrated that they can't get better quality data. They are subjected to constant demands from state legislators and members of Congress who seem to have an endless capacity for thinking up new kinds of data that are "crucial" for agency accountability. State and federal officials explain that they have to produce reports showing they are monitoring carefully the programs for which they have responsibility. They have to be able to account for dollars spent, for clients served, for affirmative action, for accessibility to the handicapped, for serving poor people; the list goes on and on. "We can't meet accountability and monitoring responsibilities and worry at the same time about providing useful information to programs." "We have trouble getting out our own reports much less putting data together to send back down to local programs."

Somewhere in all these complaints—complaints and frustrations from caring, conscientious, and competent people who are trying to do a reasonable job under difficult circumstances—somewhere in this morass there's a question trying to get out. That question has something to do with how it may be possible to manage management information systems and make them useful for a variety of purposes, including program evaluation.

I always feel compelled to begin a response to these issues by noting the obvious: There's no simple and single solution to the complex set of issues and problems involved in managing management information systems. In particular, there is certainly no set of solutions that can be applied to all situations and all frustrations. Given these general (and standard) disclaimers, it *is* possible to move to a discussion of some specific cases. Those workshop discussions lead me to make some observations about the patterns that are common to many of these complaints and some simple recommendations that may constitute at least a starting place for bringing information systems under control.

ASKING QUESTIONS OF THE SYSTEM

*He had never outgrown the feeling that a quest for
information was a series of maneuvers in a game
of espionage.*

                                        Mary McCarthy

We are not talking here about how to design a useful management information system from scratch. That is a quite separate issue and the process I
would recommend in that case is the same I would recommend in designing
any evaluation. Decision makers, information users, and stakeholders should
come together with computer programmers to plan, design, implement, and
pilot test a system with focus on the usefulness and utilization potential of the
data to be collected. This kind of process was described in Chapter 3.

What we are talking about here is coping with and attempting to use
systems that are already in place and/or systems that have been imposed from
above and into which one has had no input. The place to begin is to realize
that management information systems and routine data collection procedures for monitoring purposes are *not* program evaluation. These systems
collect data and information. To use those data for evaluation purposes one
has to ask questions of the data. The data have to be processed and organized,
arranged and analyzed, studied and interpreted to be useful for evaluation
purposes. To know how many males and females are in a program, or how
many participants are in low-income categories, is relatively meaningless
data by itself. To make the data meaningful one has to have a question: Are we
serving as many males (or females) as we should be? Has the ratio of males to
females changed significantly in the last six months? Is the proportion of
low-income people in the program representative of the proportion of low-
income people in the total population? As I talk with people who are frustrated with management information systems I note that commonly they
have approached the data without any questions and yet they complain that
the data don't tell them anything. *If there is nothing you are trying to find out,
there is nothing you will find out.*

Of course, no routine data collection system will be able to answer all of
one's questions. It can only answer questions for which data are routinely
collected. The place to begin is with getting the answers that are already
there. What can we learn from what is available? What questions are appropriate given the limitations of the data? Having determined that, the second
step is to identify important questions that may be raised by the data but not
answered by the data. If the proportion of males to females has changed
significantly, why has it changed? If low-income participants are not representative of their proportion in the total population, why not? Answers to
these questions may require more intensive study. *The management information system, then, is not an endpoint but a beginning point in raising significant issues for additional, more in-depth study.*

Asking questions of the system is only a first step. The data have to be organized and arranged in some way to provide answers to the questions being asked. In some cases such organizing and arranging of the data will have to be done manually (this is usually relatively easy given the raw data) because software packages are not available or the writing of specific programs for organizing and arranging the data is a cumbersome or bureaucratically difficult (impossible) process. Regardless of how it is done, the raw data from the system have minimum utility. Those raw data have to be put into comparative frameworks that permit interpretation. Many different standards of comparison are possible. It is possible to compare this month's data with last month's data; to compare this month's data with data from the same month a year ago; to compare data aggregated by quarters; to compare data aggregated annually; to compare data for particular periods to a goal or an identified need. It is also possible to combine questions on the system so that low-income participants are broken down by sex and age. But here again all of these possibilities for comparisons imply that questions are being asked of the data. The permutations and combinations are enormous. It doesn't make sense simply to arrange the data in all possible ways and to make all possible comparisons. *Use of the system begins by asking questions of the system.*

While such a recommendation is so simple and straightforward that it appears almost trivial, my experience in talking with hundreds of people who feel burdened by useless systems suggests that they don't approach these systems with questions, and they are not quite sure how to go about formulating appropriate questions. This is where evaluators can be particularly helpful. Evaluators should have the kind of questioning skills that can help program personnel and administrators formulate questions to ask of their management information systems. Evaluators can then help them figure out how to order and arrange the data to answer their fundamental questions. But regardless of who asks the questions and who arranges the data, the fundamental point remains the same, and, at the risk of being tediously redundant, I find myself repeating over and over in workshop after workshop: *You have to ask questions of the data. If you don't ask questions, you won't get answers.*

DECISION RULES

Another technique that can help make management information systems more useful is the formulation of decision rules for acting on the data. A decision rule is part of a framework that can be applied to routine data to indicate when some significant threshold or action point has been reached. The decision rule is like the red light that flashes on a boiler when too much pressure has built up. It tells the machine operator that it is time to relieve the pressure, that some action is indicated. Routine monitoring systems for all kinds of machinery and chemical systems specify acceptable ranges of activity as well as danger points that indicate when the system needs special attention. Decision rules for management information systems serve this same purpose.

Consider, for example, routine data on caseloads. When a system is set up or even after it has been running for awhile, a decision rule should be formulated that says: When caseloads get to this level we know we have a problem. When caseloads get to be too high (and the level that is "too high" must be specified in advance), then we either have to add staff, limit intakes, or initiate some other action to make the program more manageable. In hospitals a decision rule is needed about the number of empty beds that can be tolerated without creating crisis. In programs of all kinds decision rules are needed. How many dropouts constitute an acceptable level and when has a dropout rate reached unacceptable levels? What proportion of low-income people in a program is unacceptable, either because the proportion is too low or too high? What is the acceptable ratio between males and females? *When one has decision rules to use to examine the data the examination process takes on considerably more meaning and interest than it does when one simply looks at the data month after month without having a firm framework for interpreting trends.*

This approach to interpreting data from a management information system is much like the system that experienced financial people use in playing the stock market or the commodities market. Successful financial people formulate decision rules. When the market reaches a certain level they buy. When the market reaches another level they sell. Different people use different indices to tell them when to buy and sell. Some use the Dow Jones Industrials. Some use the Standards and Poor Index. Some use volume indices. Technicians in the market have one set of rules; brokers who follow market fundamentals have a different set of rules; many people use a combination of indices. The point is that no person can absorb and make sense of all the financial data that are available about the stock market and about companies on the stock market without some framework for interpreting those data and some decision rules to tell them when action is appropriate.

What is particularly interesting about the stock market analogy is that research on investor behavior suggests that people who lose money in the market—and apparently that encompasses most of the people who play the market—get into trouble for one of two reasons: (1) they haven't carefully specified decision rules in advance and so they play the market day by day, allowing their emotions and intuitions to be their guide, or (2) they fail to act upon the decision rules that they have set for themselves. This latter group knows the importance of formulating decision rules in advance, but then as the market or particular index they are following moves toward the point of decision, they find various rationalizations for holding off a little bit to see if the situation changes, thereby ignoring the decision rules they set for themselves (Dreman, 1977, 1979).

I am not suggesting here that one arbitrarily set decision rules and then blindly follow them come hell or high water. But at a minimum, when the data indicate some threshold has been reached on the basis of carefully pre-determined criteria, then it is at least necessary to call together the key people in the program to consider action alternatives and decide what kind of action, if any, ought to be taken.

Sometimes, delays in following decision rules can lead to disaster. On August 19, 1981, an airliner crashed in Saudi Arabia because a pilot failed to heed a warning light. The crash killed 301 people. The civil aviation investi-gation committee report said that the captain and crew wasted "precious minutes" checking automatic fire warnings when they should have immedi-ately turned the plane back to Riyadh.

> Seven minutes after the plane took off, a flashing light and bell in the cockpit signaled smoke in the compartment below the tail. The pilot should have turned back immediately and prepared for an emergency landing. Instead, the cockpit crew chose to make sure that the alarm was correct. Thus, five precious minutes were lost. By the time the plane did land, the fire already was spread-ing through the cabin and the crew had to try to battle the flames with frantic passengers rushing the doors to get out [UPI].

Decision rules related to program management are unlikely to carry such dramatic consequences. Program disasters resulting from failure to heed data-based warnings tend to kill off programs more slowly than is the case with airline crashes.

John Ross (1980) has written a helpful article on "Decision Rules in Pro-gram Evaluation." He notes that there has been little discussion and real use of decision rules in evaluation. He lists several advantages of decision rules:

(1) Decision rules focus evaluators' attention on important questions.
(2) The tendency to generate masses of useless information is reduced.
(3) The difficulty of analysis is reduced.
(4) The probability of data use is increased.
(5) Decision rules provide a framework for reporting information to decision makers.
(6) Explicit specification of decision rules help protect against biased interpreta-tions of data.

To the extent possible key decision makers, including funders, should be involved in setting these decision rules and interpreting them. It is often easier to get funders to agree well in advance that a certain level of caseload activity clearly indicates a problem and a need for action than to get those same people to act under crisis conditions when caseloads have been allowed to mount, have gotten out-of-hand, and the program is in turmoil. Funders don't like being forced to act under the gun and in response to crisis. Crisis reactions, whether in the stock market or in human services programs, are emotion laden and subject to arousal of strong political feelings. While decision rules will by no means completely avoid these situations, calm and serious discussions of what constitutes threshold levels for action in advance of reaching those threshold levels will allow for anticipation of crisis and mobilization of contingency plans in a less than chaotic climate.

One final note: My experience suggests that *if people in a program are unable to specify in advance what constitutes a decision threshold, they will probably be unable to recognize such a threshold if it actually occurs— despite careful attention to the data.* I am responding here to a reaction that sometimes comes from the suggestion to formulate decision rules:

> I don't see how we can decide what the unacceptable levels are in advance. All we can do is follow trends in the data and see what develops and then decide when a problem has emerged. We don't want to get locked into guessing at critical thresholds too far in advance.

The practical problem here is that without a decision rule it is easy to postpone action for months and months while waiting to see if the trend continues and then planning to act "next" time. There are always lots of reasons for postponing decisions at a particular moment in time. The function of setting decision rules in advance is to increase the pressure to take action when it logically and rationally should be taken rather than being seduced by endless postponement until a full crisis has emerged. Moreover, it is important to keep in mind that there are different kinds of decision rules. Some decision rules are of the order: "We are approaching a critical stage and we need additional information to inform action." Other decision rules are of the order: "We are at a critical point; action must be taken now!" Then, of course, there are the post hoc decision rules that say (after the system has already blown from the pressure build up): "Gee, I guess we should have acted."

TAKING TIME TO STUDY THE DATA

Sometimes, after listening to the rantings and ravings of people frustrated with their management information systems, I'll ask them how much time they have actually spent trying to make sense of the data they receive from the system. They often respond that, "The stuff comes across my desk and I take a quick look at it, but it just doesn't make any sense." Additional probing usually reveals that they haven't really devoted any serious amount of time to trying to make sense out of the available data. They approach the data with the expectation that it won't make sense; they give the process of making sense out of the data a minimum amount of time; and, not surprisingly, *their expectation that the data won't make any sense is fulfilled.*

Making sense out of data and interpreting findings takes time. The quick glance in that rare spare moment just isn't sufficient. Staff and administrators who are serious about trying to use the system need to set aside a block of time, a minimum of two or three hours, to periodically take a close look at the data and to consider its implications. This can be done individually or in small groups, but without some concentrated attention almost any set of data will appear obscure. The old axiom that you get out of something what you put into it is applicable here. Sure, the measures used may not be the best, the quality of the data may be suspect, and the classification systems may be less than appropriate, but the best of systems will be underutilized unless program staff and administrators take the time to really look carefully at what is there, approaching the data with questions and decision rules, and giving the process a fair amount of time to work.

TRANSLATION AND PROJECTION

The problems of multiple forms, duplicate systems, and layer on top of layer of data collection is quite real. The paperwork loads are quite incredible in many systems. One way to begin to deal with this problem in some situations is to construct a single data collection form or to use the most comprehensive of the various duplicate forms, and then to translate or make projections from that basic data base to file the reports required by other agencies and other levels of government. Many programs simply blindly add to their already existing data collection system each new form that comes from every new funding source. Eventually the people at the bottom of the service delivery hierarchy are faced with redundantly filling out form after form. *Careful review of forms by administrators and managers to sort out duplications and set up translation and projection systems may make it possible to meet multiple reporting requirements without duplicating data collection efforts.*

In some cases the translations from one set of categories to another may not be exact; the translations or projections may introduce error. But the error introduced by translation and projection may well be less than the errors introduced from paperwork loads that are too high, leading to falsification of data or filling out all the forms in retrospect at the end of the month. It may be better to have a single form with items that have to be manipulated to meet multiple reporting requirements, thus introducing some error through statistical manipulations, than to have a complete set of data for each separate funder where the validity of the data is suspect at the point of origin.

This may also mean devising forms where the single data collection system may include a large number of categories that can be collapsed to meet the different classification systems of different agencies. For example, one program with which I worked had to report income statistics on clients to ten different funding sources. The county had a system; three state agencies had different systems; and six federal programs had different reporting requirements. The income categories required by each funding source were somewhat different. Some funding sources asked for data to be reported in increments of $3000. Another funding source wanted the data reported in a classification of increments of $4000. Still another wanted to know how many clients had incomes below $7500. Some systems wanted income data for individuals and others wanted family income statistics. At the point I began working with the program, case workers were filling out ten separate forms to meet the reporting requirements for all ten funding sources. Those who were filling out the forms conscientiously were spending an inordinate amount of time doing so; those who were not filling out the forms conscientiously were spending an inordinate amount of time falsifying and avoiding. By reviewing all the forms we were able to come up with a single form that reported both individual and family income in thousand dollar increments. On a monthly basis these data could be aggregated into the various categories to meet the requirements of all the different sources. For the agency that wanted data reported in a category of $7500 it was necessary to perform some statistical extrapolations. This introduced some error. But the errors introduced by extrapolation were trivial compared to the errors introduced at the point of actual data collection under the system of multiple forms.

SAMPLING

Another way of reducing the paperwork load is to use some sampling techniques so that complete data are not gathered on every client. Some kinds of basic monitoring information may be necessary to collect on each person, for example, basic demographic statistics that are relatively easy to gather at intake into the program. More complete and in-depth information, however, may be obtained with great validity and reliability from a sample, rather than from the entire program population.

In evaluation of an energy hotline, we set up a system where detailed information on callers was collected on every fifteenth caller because collecting data on every single person was unmanageable—and not really necessary. In another program in a mental health center we established some random time periods during which detailed data would be collected on all clients in the system at that time with only minimal collections of data going on at other times. This not only reduced the amount of data being collected so that the information system was manageable to those who filled out the forms, but it also meant that there were fewer data in the system as a whole; the total information load was reduced and program staff and administrators found the entire system more manageable and more useful. They were willing to look intensively at the results that came out of the selected time periods in a way that they were not willing to look at results gathered routinely all the time.

Another way to reduce the paperwork load is through item sampling. Where a great deal of information is desirable about the total client population it may not be necessary to gather all of those data from every single client. Different forms can be constructed so that some forms contain some kinds of information and other forms contain only other kinds of information. All the forms contain the basic background and demographic information needed on clients, but particular items are available only for subsamples of the total population. These subsamples are large enough to allow generalizations and provide detailed information about questions of special interest without taking the time to gather all the data from all the clients. This, of course, is the system used in the U.S. Census with its short form, completed by everyone, and its long form, completed by only a sample of people.

Staff and administrators need to take a careful look at what data are needed from all clients and what data needs can be satisfied through sampling. A variety of sampling approaches are possible—time samples, samples of individuals, item sampling—but data carefully collected from samples may be considerably more accurate than data collected from *all* clients at *all* points in time and on *all* times collected such that the system bogs down under its own weight.

ADDING TO AND SUBTRACTING FROM THE SYSTEM

One common problem in management information systems is that the system is designed in such a way that it is not easy or even possible to make additions and deletions. It is desirable to leave some space at different points in the file or on the disc so that information can be added. It is not necessary for management information systems to be set up at one point in time and thereby written in stone forever. At particular points in the history of a program it may be helpful to gather data about special issues for a period of six months. Once the questions related to those data are answered, those questions can be omitted from the forms and deleted from the system. Indeed, one way to generate interest in management information systems is to consciously provide some space that is available for staff to ask questions of special interest for short periods of time. Even in a system that is geared largely toward meeting reporting requirements of people at higher levels, some space devoted to local program concerns can reduce hostility about the overall system.

OVERALL REVIEW

The suggestions in this chapter for managing management information systems are only coping mechanisms. They are ways of trying to deal with the demands for information that occur at all levels of program funding. No single management information system designed at a particular point in time will meet the information needs of everyone involved in the system for long periods of time. Certainly there is no substitute for designing useful systems from the very beginning. But given the imposition of systems from above and the inheritance of ongoing systems from others, such coping strategies can help alleviate some of the burdens.

As programs and situations change, the management information system should be periodically reviewed to make sure that it still serves at least the purposes for which it was originally designed. Because such reviews can be costly, they shouldn't be done every six months. But when the systems are designed or when someone inherits a system, they should attempt to establish a decision rule about when a complete system review should be done to revise, update, and overhaul the management information system. Such reviews should be done infrequently enough so that any given system has a chance to make a return on its initial costs but often enough to keep the system from becoming completely outdated.

THE HUMAN CAPACITY TO MANAGE INFORMATION

> *Everybody gets so much information all day long that*
> *they lose their common sense.*
>
> Gertrude Stein

The problems discussed in this chapter are not limited to human service and education programs. Large and small corporations face the same difficulties. Writing for *The Wall Street Journal,* William Blundell (1981) has documented management information system problems in industry and commerce. He quotes a private management information system consultant as offering a practical solution to many of these problems: "The greatest thing that could happen would be to cut their data processing budgets 75%." He attributes a multitude of typical information-processing problems to the fact that people don't know how to manage management information systems. After describing these missed opportunities and waste, he concludes:

> The thing people wanted from computers they're just not getting. And they could have it. They could have it.

What computers are doing is making it possible to store enormous amounts of information. The "knowledge explosion" seems an inadequate way of referring to the fact that the amount of information in the world now doubles every ten years (Price, 1963). This doesn't mean we *know* more. Reilly believes that "as knowledge mounts, ignorance increases" (1974: 22) because people don't know how to use masses of information. She argues persuasively that more is not simply better when the issue is knowledge. It's the kind of knowledge one has that matters, and what one does with it. Less may really be more, and small amounts of information can be beautiful, if the information is appropriate and relevant. Thus Reilly might well be sympathetic to the view expressed by some participants in a national conference on evaluation and policy. They suggested that evaluators should strive for a "reduction in data" so that only the necessary *minimum* is collected, not the maximum.

Every time you start measuring somebody and collecting information, you're interfering with some other process. Given that it's necessary to do that, it's also necessary that we interfere as little as we can to do whatever job is necessary. First of all, the information should be appropriate to the level of decision making, second relevant and third minimal—the actual minimum that's possible [Far West Lab, 1976: 27].

In designing and using management information systems it is important to keep in mind limitations on the human capacity to use information. Computer hardware, storage capacities, and software packages have moved well beyond the basic human capability to absorb all the information that such systems can provide. Government systems that purchase computers and hire programmers to manage their systems often get caught up in a compulsion to fill up all the storage space on the computer. Our capacity to think up items and devise classification schemes into which people can be pigeonholed is far greater than our capacity to retrieve those data in an orderly manner for analysis and interpretation. *Management information systems should not be judged by their size, comprehensiveness, or storage capacity. They should be judged by their ability to provide useful information within the constraints of limited human energy, limited time, and limited ability to absorb information.*

SUMMARY MIS POINTS

(1) Management information systems provide information only. You don't have an evaluation system until someone does something with the information.

(2) If there is nothing you are trying to find out, there is nothing you will find out. You have to ask questions of the system.

(3) The MIS can be a beginning point in raising significant issues for additional, more in-depth study.

(4) Raw data have minimal utility. The data have to be organized and arranged in some way to provide answers to the questions being asked.

(5) Raw data have to be put into comparative frameworks to permit interpretation; many different standards of comparisons are possible.

(6) Decision rules are needed to interpret routine data so that appropriate actions can be taken when the system indicates a need for action.

(7) If people in a program are unable to specify in advance what constitutes a decision threshold, they will probably be unable to recognize such a threshold if it actually occurs—despite careful attention to the data.

(8) Making sense out of data and interpreting findings takes time. Set aside a block of time periodically to study data from the MIS and consider their implications for the program.

(9) Careful review of forms to sort out duplications and set up translation and projection systems may make it possible to meet multiple reporting requirements without duplicating data collection efforts.

(10) Carefully selected and rigorously implemented sampling techniques can im-

prove the quality of information in a system and reduce the burdens of paperwork and data collection. A variety of sampling approaches are possible—time samples, samples of individuals, item sampling.

(11) Systems should be constructed so that they can be changed; short-term additions and deletions can increase a data collection system as well as making the system more useful.

(12) Periodic and comprehensive reviews of an MIS should be done to revise, update, and overhaul the system. Input from all the people who use the system should be sought during such reviews.

(13) Management information systems should not be judged by their size, comprehensiveness, or storage capacity. They should be judged by their ability to provide useful information within the constraints of limited human energy, limited time, and limited ability to absorb information.

POSTSCRIPT: THE KARNAK APPROACH TO MIS

The epitome of the management information system that is out of control is one that can produce literally volumes of statistics on virtually every aspect of a set of programs but the people who generate those data have no idea of how to arrange the data for use or even what questions they are answering. This puts the evaluator in a role similar to that of the Karnak character played by Johnny Carson on the *Tonight Show.* "Karnak the Magnificent" is the all-knowing seer, sage, and soothsayer who divines the answers to unknown questions sealed in an envelope. Having determined the answer, the envelope is opened to determine the question. In the Karnak Approach to MIS the management information system contains the answers and the evaluator, given these answers, tries to figure out what the questions are. I recently spent several days working with a group of people in a major county helping them sort through their reams of statistics trying to figure out what questions they had answers to. When systems are designed without specific questions in mind, the Karnak approach to data interpretation may be the only hope for using the information in the system.

> *Solutions to problems*
> *are easy to find:*
> *the problem's a great*
> *contribution.*
> *What is truly an art*
> *is to wring from your mind*
> *a problem to fit*
> *a solution.*

Piet Hein

CHAPTER 10 *Fundamental Principles of Data Analysis*

You and I are forever at the mercy of the census-taker and the census-maker. The impertinent fellow who goes from house to house is one of the real masters of the statistical situation. The other is the man who organizes the results.

Walter Lippman

Evaluator competence in using statistics consists of two critical components: the ability to analyze data in appropriate ways to guarantee the integrity and accuracy of findings, and the ability to help nonstatisticians (decision makers and information users) understand the meanings of evaluation data. This chapter deals with both of these fundamental skills. In so doing, the focus is on analytical thinking, not statistical formulas. The discussion will concern practical ways of thinking about and presenting data.

This is not a statistics text. Indeed, the principles presented in this chapter are so basic that they are often ignored in statistics courses because statistics professors assume students will already understand these fundamentals, and because statistics professors are seldom concerned with their students' ability to communicate with nonstatisticians. As a result, many students come out of statistics courses able to manipulate numbers, but they remain unschooled in elementary statistical reasoning. Yet without a foundation in statistical reasoning, statistical manipulations can hinder, rather than increase, the capacity to make sense of data in ways that permit real utilization and application of findings.

The fundamental principles of data analysis covered in this chapter include the kinds of things I cover in workshops with program staff, decision makers, and information users at the data analysis stage of an evaluation. The collaborative evaluation approach described in Chapter 3 emphasizes decision maker and stakeholder involvement in data analysis. My purpose in working with workshop and evaluation task force participants to increase their understanding of these fundamentals is to enhance their feelings of competence in being able to analyze and interpret evaluation findings. I don't want them to rely blindly on my analysis. This direct, personal involvement of decision makers and information users in the analysis process is predicated on the stakeholder assumption that people are more likely to use findings they have worked with, believe in, and understand.

At the same time, it is important to maintain the integrity of the evaluation. The integrity of the evaluation rests ultimately on the integrity of the information that emerges from the evaluation. Users of evaluation data are concerned about both the utility and the accuracy of findings (Weiss and Bucuvalas, 1980). Recent discussions of ways of increasing utilization have been tempered by concern for the misutilization of evaluation information—the abuse, distortion, and misuse of evaluation data and findings (Cook et al., 1980). Thus in working with decision makers and information users, the evaluator is again guided by multiple standards: attention to the utility, feasibility, propriety, and accuracy of any given analysis. The collaborative analysis process is aimed at elucidating both the strengths and limitations of the data, thereby enhancing the potential for utilization while guarding against misutilization.

In considering the analysis points made in this chapter, the framework provided by the standards on accuracy is particularly relevant. Among the specific standards that bear on issues in this chapter are the following:

Accuracy Standards

The Accuracy Standards are intended to ensure that an evaluation will reveal and convey technically adequate information about the features of the object being studied that determine its worth or merit.

Analysis of Quantitative Information

Quantitative information in an evaluation should be appropriately and systematically analyzed to ensure supportable interpretations.

Guidelines

A. Choose an analysis procedure that is appropriate to the evaluation's questions and quantitative information.

B. Report potential weaknesses in the data collection or analysis design—e.g., violation of assumptions—and describe their possible influence on conclusions.

C. When feasible, collect and analyze independent sets of data to bolster what might otherwise be a weak quantitative analysis.

Pitfalls

A. Allowing data collection and analysis considerations to reduce the questions under study to a false simplicity.

B. Assuming that statistically significant results are always practically significant, and that statistically insignificant results are always practically insignificant.

(Joint Committee, 1981: 97, 127-128).

THE SUBCULTURE OF STATISTICS

In Chapter 3 I described how I often begin an evaluation by inviting participants into the culture of science. This cross-cultural metaphor is meant to emphasize that science involves a special world view grounded in attention to and study of *empirical* reality. One part of that worldview, one subculture of science, if you will, has to do with measurement and statistics. Elsewhere in this book I have discussed qualitative approaches to understanding the world. Qualitative methods comprise one subculture of science. Statistical methods comprise yet another subculture, one that has its own important practices and worldview. For decision makers and information users to use quantitative data and evaluation findings based on quantitative data effectively, they need to be able to enter into the scientific subculture of statistics, not as practicing statisticians, not even as long-term residents, but at least enough to develop an appreciation of and respect for statistical reasoning as one way of understanding and analyzing the world.

There is often some resistance to statistical experiences. Participants in an evaluation process will often say, "Don't bother us with the numbers. Just tell us what you found out. We can't understand the statistics anyway. Just tell us what the results mean." It is tempting to take on the role of expert at this point, let the details of the analysis stay shrouded in scientific mystery, and spare these poor people the hard work and agony of dealing directly with the data. My own graduate students have regularly proved quite obstinate in this regard. It makes some sense to them to involve stakeholders in specification of relevant questions, but certainly the evaluator must completely control the analysis and interpretation of data.

In resisting the temptation to bear alone the burden of analysis and interpretation, the evaluator is again viewing the evaluation process as a training opportunity through which decision makers and information users can become more sophisticated about the potential of data-based decision making approaches over the long term. H. G. Wells anticipated the importance of making statistical thinking accessible to nonstatisticians when he observed:

Statistical thinking will one day be as necessary for efficient citizenship as the ability to read and write.

For evaluation task force members that day is now. But incorporating a training perspective in the evaluation process will mean being prepared to deal with resistance to statistical reasoning.

Many program staff and clients have developed psychological blocks to dealing with numbers. This is part of the familiar "I-can't-even-balance-my-checkbook" routine. I reply to this routine with the firm suggestion (all the while smiling in a most friendly fashion) that if one is to be a serious participant in making crucial decisions about a program, perhaps it's time one learned to balance one's checkbook. The problem is usually more a psychological than an arithmetic one, perhaps based on early difficulties (or perceived and laid-on difficulties) with arithmetic or algebra in school. An evaluation experience can be just the right occasion to finally overcome the bad experiences of third grade math or high school geometry. At the analysis stage the evaluator may have to display considerably more belief in participants' basic arithmetic skills than they themselves display.

Other participants in the evaluation process will be found to have adopted a kind of cynicism about statistics that gives them an excuse for refusing to participate in the analysis of data, and later may give them an excuse to ignore altogether evaluation findings. This cynicism is based on popular notions that statistics can be used to prove anything, a repetition in more polite form of Mark Twain's observation that "there are three kinds of lies: lies, damned lies, and statistics." Mrs. Robert A. Taft expressed the feeling of many decision makers and information users when she said:

> I always find that statistics are hard to swallow and impossible to digest. The only one I can remember is that if all the people who go to sleep in church were laid end to end they would be a lot more comfortable.

It does little good to argue about such feelings. Resistance to statistics is seldom based on a carefully thought out and well reasoned position. These are *feelings* we're talking about—feelings of fear, insecurity, incompetence, suspicion, uncertainty, and distrust. I don't expect to convince people by argument that participation in an analysis process is possible and worthwhile. As participants in the culture of science and the subculture of statistics, I simply want to get them to participate in the analysis process as an empirical test of the worthwhileness and possibility of such an exercise. Rather than arguing about analysis in the abstract, I prefer to begin by acknowledging the prevalence of negative, or at least ambiguous, feelings about statistics—such feelings often being quite justified given the widespread abuses of statistics in advertising, politics, and yes, even research. Having acknowledged the understandable resistance many may feel, I then want to get on with the task of engaging in an analytical experience that is empowering and confidence building, a cross-cultural experience in the subculture of statistics ready made for wary tourists.

Just as there is a wariness about statistics, there is also a fascination with them. This makes for a kind of approach-avoidance reaction to participating in data analysis. One wants to embrace the precision and parsimony of numbers, but avoid being misled and made a fool of. The powerful attraction of numbers as a basis for proving "truth" is also the source of much of the abuse of statistics. Consider the following example. As I write this, the Moral Majority is getting a great deal of press. One major figure in that movement is the Reverend Donald Wildmon, Chief of the National Federation for Decency. In 1981, he and his organization published statistics on the decadent nature of the Phil Donahue television show, a talk show that discusses controversial topics with special guests. The press release reported the results of research showing that 3.7 out of every 5 Donahue shows devoted 16 out of every 22 minutes to licentious urgings that ultimately wreck the lives of 4 out of every 7 children under 12. After protests from Donahue and network officials, the good Reverend Wildmon publicly apologized and admitted that the numbers were based on no data analysis whatever (Boulder Daily Camera, September 30, 1981: 2). The numbers had simply been used to make a point in a powerful way, for a "good" purpose, since statistics are so often used for evil purposes by the powerful.

Since evaluators operate in a climate in which statistics are regularly subject to abuse, and where there is a solid basis for cynicism and distrust, it is all the more important that decision makers and information users know as directly as possible the basis for evaluation findings. When inviting evaluation participants into the culture of science and the subculture of statistics, I deal with the avoidance part of the approach-avoidance duality by making the following three points.

(1) Numbers must be interpreted to have meaning. Numbers are not bad or good, they're just numbers. Judgments have to be made about the accuracy and meaningfulness of numbers. Interpretation means thinking about what the numbers mean and how they ought to be applied. There are no magic formulas for making interpretations. Statisticians have no corner on the ability to think and reason. Interpretation is a human process, not a computer process. The best guideline may be Einstein's dictum that "the important thing is to keep on questioning."

(2) Numbers, particularly those generated in program evaluations, are usually indicators or estimates of what the world is like. Just as a map is not the territory it describes, the statistical tables on a program are not the program. They are indicators of what the program is like, but they are not the program. Thus statistics are a means of increasing understanding about a program; generating statistics is not an end in itself.

(3) As indicators and estimates subject to interpretation, statistics contain varying degrees of error. Thinking within the framework of the culture of science involves probabilities, not absolutes. The switch from absolute judgment (things are or are not) to probabilistic thinking (things are more or less likely) is fundamental to entry into the subculture of statistics.

It is necessary to return to these three points, and the related principles discussed throughout this chapter, time and time again as one deals with actual evaluation data, thereby reducing the initially abstract nature of these ideas. Evaluators, for whom statistical reasoning is usually second nature, may underestimate the extent to which these simple principles represent a significant departure from stakeholders' ordinary ways of thinking.

The shift to probabilistic reasoning involves evaluators in helping decision makers understand that complete precision and error-free data are impossible in the real world of research. It can be helpful in this regard to recall the experiences of Gulliver in Laputa, the moving island in the sky. The good residents of that country were so obsessed with the quest for precision that even tailors, when measuring for a suit, used a sextant and compass to assure greater accuracy.

A certain amount of poetic license is appropriate, and often needed, in moving from the quest for absolute accuracy to a quest for basic understanding. The experience of Alfred Lord Tennyson with Cambridge mathematician Charles Babbage illustrates this point. Tennyson published a poem which included the lines:

> Every minute dies a man,
> Every minute one is born.

Babbage, as occupant of the Lucasian chair of mathematics at Cambridge, disputed the accuracy of Tennyson's reflections. He wrote Tennyson that, in fact, the world's population was increasing, while the lines of the poem implied stability. "I would therefore take the liberty of suggesting that in the next edition of your excellent poem the erroneous calculation to which I refer be corrected as follows":

> Every moment dies a man,
> And one and one sixteenth is born.

Baggage went on to note that even this figure was a concession to meter, since the actual ratio was 1:167, and perhaps Tennyson could find a way to incorporate the more precise figure, Baggage, himself, not being a poet. Tennyson attempted to be accommodating by changing "minute" to "moment," but this hardly satisfied Baggage's criteria of accuracy and precision (Sutherland, 1975: 228).

The practical principles of data analysis that follow attempt to achieve a balance between Tennysonian and Babbagian perspectives in an effort to enhance utility, while safeguarding accuracy.

SIMPLICITY AS A VIRTUE

Unless one is a genius, it is best to aim at being intelligible.

Anthony Hope

William of Occam with his razor would have made an excellent analyst of evaluation data. Look first for the simplest presentation that will handle the facts. Evaluators may need and use sophisticated and complex statistical techniques to uncover the nuances of evaluation data, but simple and straight-forward statistical presentations are needed to give decision makers access to evaluation findings.

The social sciences go through fads where certain kinds of data analysis are particularly favored when one wants to have an article published in a major journal. For awhile multiple regression techniques are all the rage; some journals are particularly enamored of path analysis; still others seem to have a fascination with factor analysis, or log-linear techniques, or a propensity for examining different interactions under varying assumptions and building mathematical models of social processes. These complex and sophisticated techniques have allowed major advances in the analysis of social and behavioral science data. The problem is that very few decision makers understand such techniques; these sophisticated procedures are easily abused and misrepresented when the assumptions on which they rest are violated; and sophisticated statistical presentations are intimidating to non-statisticians.

When I first joined the evaluation training program at Minnesota the primary emphasis was on increasing the sophistication of evaluation measurement and data analysis techniques. In attending professional meetings in sociology, psychology, political science, and evaluation during my postdoctoral years of study, there were regular and predictable calls for the implementation of ever more elaborate research designs and the use of increasingly sophisticated analysis techniques in evaluation research. At the same time I began working on evaluations with decision makers at the federal, state, and local levels. Almost universally I encountered people who were fairly intimidated by percentages, unsure of correlation coefficients, and wary of what they considered to be statistical gobbledy-gook.

I remember sitting in on a committee hearing in Congress where a prominent researcher was presenting the findings of an elaborate research project related to social policy. The findings were presented through a series of regression equations. As the researcher built up steam and got into the heavier parts of his presentation, there was considerable head nodding (of the "yes I understand" variety). As I watched what was happening, however, it became clear to me that there was an inverse relationship between the amount of enthusiastic head nodding and the extent to which these legislators understood what was being said. I later talked to a committee staff member I knew who confirmed this hypothesis and told me that when the hearings had adjourned for the day, the members of Congress had great fun quoting statistical expressions to each other and making it clear that they didn't put much faith in the researcher's magical incantations.

I am not implying that sophisticated techniques, where appropriate and helpful, should not be used. I am suggesting that it is the height of folly to center one's public presentations and decision making discussions around complex statistical findings. I have been told by some of my colleagues that they make such presentations because they consider it part of their responsibility to educate public officials about statistics. From my observations I would suggest that what they are educating them about is not how to use such statistics but rather about the overall uselessness of social science research findings for decision making, and convincing them of the inability of social scientists to communicate in a simple and straight-forward manner to those responsible for public policy.

Evaluation research, if it is to be accessible to and understandable by critical decision makers, must depart from the trends of the various social science disciplines and return to simplicity as a virtue of data analysis and presentation. This does not mean that one cannot use sophisticated techniques. Rather, it means that having used those techniques to tease out the nuances in the data and to confirm the strength and meaningfulness of discovered relationships, the next step is to creatively think about how to translate those findings into simple, straightforward, and understandable statistics. This means, for example, that the results of a regression analysis might be reduced to nothing more complex than a chi-square table or a set of descriptive statistics (percentages and means). This need not distort the presentation. Quite the opposite, it will usually focus and highlight the most meaningful findings while allowing the investigators to explain in a footnote and/or an appendix that more sophisticated techniques have been used to confirm the simple statistics here presented.

Simplicity as a virtue means that we must reward evaluators for clarity, not complexity. Like the skilled acrobat who makes the most dazzling moves look easy, the audience being unaware of the long hours of practice and the sophisticated calculations involved in what appear to be quite simple movements, evaluators must find ways of so perfecting their public performances that those involved in working with them to make sense out of the data will believe that *even they* can understand and participate in the analysis, all the while being perhaps unaware of the long hours of arduous work involved in sifting through the data, organizing it, arranging it, testing out relationships, taking the data apart, and creatively putting it back together to arrive at that moment of public unveiling.

Simplicity as a virtue means that we are rewarded not for how much we confuse people, but for how much we enlighten them; it means that we emphasize building up others' feelings that they can master what is before them, rather than intimidating them with our own expertise, knowledge, and sophistication. Simplicity as a virtue means separating the complexity of analysis from the clarity of presentation and using the former to inform and guide the latter. Simplicity as a virtue is not simple. In the end it often involves considerably more work and creativity to simplify than simply to rest content with a presentation of the complex statistics as they originally emerged in the analysis. Simplicity as a virtue is not simple but it can be effective.

STRIVE FOR BALANCE

The counterpoint to my preceding sermon on simplicity is that evaluation findings are seldom really simple. In striving for simplicity, one must be careful to avoid simplemindedness. It is simpleminded to present only one point of view. This happens most often in evaluation when results are boiled down, in the name of simplicity, to some single number—a single percentage, a single cost/benefit ratio, or a single proportion of the variance explained. Striving for simplicity means making the data understandable, but balance and fairness need not be sacrificed in the name of simplicity. Balance means that the complexity and multiple perspectives of a situation can be represented through several different numbers, all of them presented in an understandable fashion. Advertising is based upon the deception of single representations of facts. Evaluation, to maintain credibility and integrity, requires multiple statistical representations for a full and balanced picture of the situation. Some examples may help clarify what I mean.

In the 1972 presidential campaign, Nixon made the claim that "under his Administration black incomes had risen faster than white incomes." In the same campaign McGovern made the claim that "after four years of Nixon, blacks were worse off than whites in terms of income." Both statements were true. The distortion comes in that both statements represent only part of the picture. To understand what was happening in the relationship between black and white income one needed more than any single statistic.

Consider the data given in Table 10.1 to illustrate this point. These data illustrate how it is possible for both political statements to be true: black incomes rose faster than white incomes but blacks were worse off than whites at the end of the four-year period under study. At a minimum, a balanced view required *both* the absolute changes and the percentage changes. When a report gives only one figure or the other, i.e., only absolute changes or only percentage changes, the reader has cause to suspect that the full picture has not been presented. A balanced viewpoint requires both kinds of numbers.

TABLE 10.1   Illustrative Data (Constructed)

	Beginning Level	Level Four Years Later	Absolute Amount of Change	Percentage Change
Median White Income	$10,000	$10,706	$606	6
Median Black Income	$ 5,500	$ 6,050	$550	10

A more relevant example for evaluation purposes comes from a study of Internal Revenue Service audits conducted by the U.S. General Accounting Office (GAO). The cover page of the report carried the sensational headline that the study had found that IRS audit procedures in five selected districts missed $1 million in errors in four months:

> These districts assessed incorrect tax estimated to total $1.0 million over a 4-month period because of technical errors, computation errors, or failure to make automatic adjustments.

The IRS response to the GAO report points out that the same audit cases containing the $1 million in errors had revealed over $26 million in errors that led to adjustments in tax. Thus the $1 million represented only about 4 percent of the total amount of money involved. Moreover, when one reads the details behind the headline it turns out that the $1 million resulted from different methods of calculation used by IRS and GAO because GAO included all differences while IRS ignored differences of $100 or less. In the data presented by GAO it is impossible to tell what proportion of the $1 million involves errors of under $100, which are routinely ignored by IRS. Finally, a detailed reading of the report also shows that the $1 million error involves cases of two types: instances in which additional tax would be due to IRS *and* instances in which a refund would be due the taxpayer from IRS. In point of fact, the $1 million error would result in virtually no additional revenue to the government had all the errors been detected and followed up.

The gross simplification of the evaluation findings and the headlining of the $1 million error represent considerable distortion of the full picture. Simplicity at the expense of accuracy is no virtue; complexity in the service of accuracy is no vice. The point is to make those complex matters accessible to and understandable by the relevant decision makers. The omitted information from the GAO report could not be justified on the basis of simplification. The omission represented distortions of the situation rather than simplification.

Striving for balance means thinking about all the information decision makers need to have for a full picture of the situation under study. It means generally including both numbers representing absolute changes and percentage changes; it means watching for situations in which it is appropriate to report a mean, median, and/or mode in order to fully represent the distribution of data; it means providing different estimates or indicators of an attitude or behavior under study; it means categorizing data in more than one way to see what differences those categorical distributions make; it means providing information about mean, range, and standard deviations (represented as straightforward and understandable confidence limits); and it means finding ways to say the same thing in more than one way to minimize misinterpretation and misunderstanding.

Striving for balance through the presentation of multiple statistics will save evaluators from the embarrassment of being caught making a report that sounds like the classic joke about the man who drowned crossing a stream with an average depth of six inches. We shall return to this issue in the next chapter when considering the processes of interpreting data in order to make recommendations. The next section describes an exercise that can be used to involve evaluation task force members or other decision makers and information users in the search for balance.

ADVOCACY-ADVERSARY ANALYSIS

The advocacy-adversary model of evaluation usually refers to using two teams to conduct the evaluation, one of which gathers evidence to support the proposition that the program is ineffective (the adversary team) and the other gathers information to support the proposition that the program is effective (the advocacy team). This approach emerged out of the concern that a single evaluation team could not maintain neutrality and objectivity throughout the evaluation process and give fair attention to both negative and positive findings. Thus drawing on the legal model of evidence presentation, the advocacy-adversary model was an attempt to make sure that both sides of the issue were given careful consideration (see Wolf, 1975; Kourilsky, 1974; Owens, 1973). For discussion of an actual application of the advocacy-adversary approach in an evaluation, see NWREL (1977), Popham and Carlson (1977), and Popham (1982).

Experience with the advocacy-adversary approach to evaluation suggests several problems and limitations. First, having two separate teams of evaluators can be quite expensive. Second, the approach works best in summative evaluations where the proposition to be debated concerns continuation or termination of the program. Third, the model is subject to the same abuses that have occurred in the criminal justice system, especially the relationship between the effectiveness of the presentation style of the advocate or adversary (how good your lawyer is) and inequalities in the competence and abilities of the two teams. Fourth, it requires that evaluation problems and questions be stated as dichotomies and opposites so that the debate can be clear and concise. Many evaluation issues and program decisions are too complex to be reduced to an either/or choice. The question may not be whether or not to continue the program, but which parts to increase, which parts to decrease, and by how much in each case.

An advocacy-adversary approach to data analysis, however, alleviates many of these concerns. Under this approach, a single evaluator or evaluation team works with stakeholders to conceptualize and conduct the evaluation, including data gathering and even initial organization and arrangement of the data for analysis and interpretation. At the analysis and interpretation stages, however, two, three, or more teams can be formed to represent different viewpoints about the evaluation. One team might be formed to focus on all the findings that appear to lead to negative conclusions about the program, e.g., the program was not properly or completely implemented, client needs were not met, goals were not attained, and so on. Another team is commissioned to investigate the data looking for positive conclusions about the program. Program strengths would be highlighted by this team, e.g., areas of particular effectiveness, client satisfaction, program uniquenesses. Yet a third team might be formed to take a balance perspective, sifting through the data looking for the most important findings that ought to be given special attention in an evaluation report.

This advocacy-adversary-balanced analysis increases the likelihood that the various nuances of the data will be brought to life. Moreover, by directly involving members of the evaluation task force, interested decision makers, information users, and stakeholders in the analysis, their understanding and commitment to evaluation findings will be increased. People are typically better able to manage the problem of analysis interpretation if they can take on the task with a specific purpose or focus in mind.

In considering the use of an advocacy-adversary approach to data analysis, it may be helpful to recall the origins of the term "devil's advocate." When the Catholic Church considers canonizing some person as a saint, it appoints a devil's advocate to present the case against canonization. Formalizing this antagonistic role makes it more likely that alternative evidence will be considered, and has been found in many organizations to be "a corrective to groupthink" (Anderson, 1980: 67, 90).

There is a danger in this process that positions will crystallize around the assignments being undertaken so that those persons exploring the negative findings will become highly committed to and focused on only the negative aspects of the program and not really open to the positive findings of the other team, and vice versa. In anticipation of this problem I have sometimes switched assignments after the initial presentation so that the group that presented negative findings is asked to take the positive findings of the other group and use those positive findings to make recommendations about the program; the group that focused on positive findings is asked to take the negative results and make recommendations based on those data.

In my experience, where participants are willing to take the time to get involved in the analysis and interpretation process, the advocacy-adversary approach can be not only enlightening and fair, but also fun. Moreover, in looking for negative findings team members will encounter the positive data and often attempt to anticipate positive conclusions and look for the data to counter those conclusions; likewise, the team looking for positive findings will attempt to anticipate negative results and counter those. Notice that by focusing on positive and negative aspects of the program, it is not necessary to limit debate to a single dichotomous proposition that the program is effective or ineffective. Thus it is possible to bring to the surface information about program improvement as well as summative information. The team with responsibility for providing a balanced perspective can counter some of the extremes that may emerge from a purely positive or negative orientation.

In the advocacy-adversary model of evaluation, where two teams are formed for the entire process, the composition of the two teams is usually determined randomly, assuming that any biases evaluators may have at the beginning of the process will be randomly distributed between the two groups. In conducting an advocacy-adversary analysis, random assignment can also be used. However, where decision makers and stakeholders have known predispositions favoring the program or attacking the program, it may be more enlightening and useful to assign those with negative predispositions to the positive findings team and those with positive predispositions to the negative findings team. This can force people to examine more carefully their predispositions and to give a fair hearing to data that may not support their initial views.

How elaborate the advocacy-adversary analysis process is will vary from situation to situation. For complex and large-scale evaluations the process may involve a few weeks of advocacy-adversary analysis. For more focused questions and smaller-scale, local evaluations I have conducted the entire analysis in a half-day or one-day workshop.

This technique can also be useful in evaluation and research workshops aimed at introducing people to data analysis in general. For this purpose I simulate a set of data that addresses some public issue. The data are purposely manipulated so that a variety of evidence, some of which is contradictory, is provided. For example, a few years ago the citizens of Minnesota were engaged in heated debate about whether or not to build a domed stadium. We simulated some data from a mock survey concerning citizens' positions on the domed stadium with variations in background characteristics of respondents, potential use patterns, citizen opinions, and sports behaviors. At the workshop, three teams were created; each was given the same set of data— no more than two or three pages of descriptive statistics and sometimes a few simple chi-squares. Each team was also given some newsprint and markers. Working in groups of four or five the participants drew graphs and presented data that supported various viewpoints on the issue at hand—in this case, the domed stadium. One group represented the Chamber of Commerce that supported the building of the stadium; another group represented the Citizens Opposed to a Domed Stadium; and a third group represented a neutral citizens' council. Each group was given 45 minutes to prepare its presentation. Following the actual presentations, participants critiqued what each group had done.

This is an effective way of teaching people how data can be manipulated while helping them see the necessity of sorting through contradictory findings in an attempt to get at a balanced perspective. They learn that findings are seldom clear cut and straightforward. Some data will indicate one interpretation while other data will indicate a quite different interpretation. By directly engaging in this process of biased and focused data analysis, participants learn through direct experience the problems of conducting data analysis. Such experiences can be considerably more powerful than a lecture making the same points.

When engaging in an adversary-advocacy analysis process, it is helpful to keep in mind the wisdom of Joseph Joubert:

The aim of argument, or of discussion, should not be victory, but progress.

The principles that follow relate to both simplicity and balance in an effort to enhance our ability as evaluators to communicate both clearly and accurately.

First Description, Then Inference

Most data analysis consists of both descriptive statistics and inferential statistics. This section concerns the balance between these two kinds of data. I regularly come across, and am sent, evaluation reports and research studies filled with interesting and important inferential statistics and measures of association that fail to provide the descriptive statistics that would give me information about the distributions and frequencies involved for the variables about which inferences are being made. I am always cautious about inferences being made when I don't have access to the descriptive statistics.

Descriptive statistics are the simple numbers indicating how many people responded in what way on each item being analyzed. The descriptive statistics consist of absolute frequencies, percentages, means, standard deviations, and similar statistics that basically *describe* the results obtained. Inferential statistics include statistics that permit generalization from samples to larger population units and measures of association that give information about the relationship between variables through correlation coefficients, regression coefficients, and the like.

The first problem with not being given the descriptive statistics is that it is often not possible to tell precisely what was measured without the actual descriptive frequencies. The labels given to variables can be quite misleading, a point we take up below. Second, the meaning and meaningfulness of measures of association depend quite a bit on what kinds of distributions were found for the variables being interrelated. The correlation coefficient expressing the relationship between two variables will mean something quite different to me if the range of responses for those two variables is heavily skewed toward only the upper end of the possible distributions than if the range of responses obtained is distributed throughout the possible range of measurement. Third, I find that the descriptive results are often the most revealing, the most useful, and the most convincing in terms of providing real insights about the nature of the evaluation results. The bulk of statistical training and statistical coursework involves inferential and predictive statistics. Having learned those techniques, evaluators seem compelled to highlight their knowledge in their evaluation reports. They seem to spend considerably less time in carefully examining the meaningfulness and implications of simple descriptive statistics than they do in looking at more complex interactions. This, or course, relates back to the sermonette on simplicity that began this chapter. Finally, descriptive statistics are the most accessible and understandable to the decision makers. Their examination of the descriptive results will often lead them to ask inferential kinds of questions. Soliciting those questions from participants in the analysis process can help create interest in and a willingness to examine inferential relationships. Beginning with inferential statistics risks confusion about what was actually measured and the distributions obtained.

Arranging Data for Ease of Interpretation: Focusing the Analysis

Providing descriptive statistics in a report does not mean simply reproducing the results in relatively raw form. Data need to be arranged, ordered, and presented in some reasonable format that permits decision makers to quickly detect patterns in the data. Consider the three presentations of data shown in Table 10.2 Each of these presents the same data, but the ordering and presentation of the data are different in each case.

The first presentation shows the data in the order in which they appeared on the questionnaire with the percentage responses for each category of response. It is very difficult to look at that table and detect patterns in the data. There are a great many numbers and a considerable amount of information to absorb. Working with a group of decision makers in an evaluation task force they would need several minutes to study this table in order to reasonably discuss the patterns in the data.

The second presentation shows a common way of simplifying the data, simply dividing the scale at the midpoint and reducing the four categories to two categories. There are times when such an analysis would be very revealing. In this case, such an analysis disguises the real patterns in the data. Decision makers would look at the second presentation in Table 10.2 and conclude that there was no way of using the survey data to establish priorities for programs.

The third presentation arranges the descriptive data in such a way that decision makers can immediately see the pattern in the results. It is important for decision makers to know that when the two highest categories of response are combined, they fail to distinguish among expressed needs. The data in the third table, however, make it clear that there is much more support for employment programs, for example, than for social programs to entertain the disabled and keep them socially busy. Failure to arrange the data as it is

TABLE 10.2   Three Presentations of the Same Data

Expressed Needs of 478 Physically Disabled People	Great Need For This	Much Need	Some Need	Little Need
Presentation 1: Raw results presented in the same order as items appeared in the questionnaire.				
Transportation	35%	36%	13%	16%
Housing	33	38	19	10
Educational opportunities	42	28	9	21
Medical care	26	45	25	4
Employment opportunities	58	13	6	23
Public understanding	47	22	15	16
Architectural changes in buildings	33	38	10	19
Direct financial assistance	40	31	12	17
Changes in insurance regulations	29	39	16	16
Social opportunities	11	58	17	14
Presentation 2: Results divided at the midpoint of the scale.				
Transportation	71%	29%		
Housing	71	29		
Educational opportunities	70	30		
Medical care	71	29		
Employment opportunities	71	29		
Public understanding	69	31		
Architectural changes in buildings	71	29		
Direct financial assistance	71	29		
Changes in insurance regulations	68	32		
Social opportunities	69	31		
Presentation 3: Results computed and arranged to highlight patterns in the data.				
Employment opportunities	58%			
Public understanding	47			
Educational opportunities	42			
Direct financial assistance	40			
Transportation	35			
Housing	33			
Architectural changes in buildings	33			
Changes in insurance regulations	29			
Medical care	26			
Social opportunities	11			

shown in the third table is a failure to focus the data analysis for decision makers.

Missing Data: When Absence Makes the Heart Fonder and the Data Murkier

One of the issues that must be dealt with in computing and presenting descriptive statistics is how to handle missing data. Some evaluators routinely delete missing data, subtracting the number of missing responses from the total, and computing percentages based on the actual number of respondents to an item. Other evaluators routinely include missing data as an additional column, and compute the percentages for all columns on the basis of the total number of questionnaires returned. The problem in both cases is with the *routine* nature of these operations. Sometimes it is appropriate to delete missing data; at other times it is appropriate to show the percentage of nonrespondents as a separate column. *The decision on how to handle missing data should be a conceptual one rather than a routine one.* That decision must be based upon the meaningfulness of the missing responses and the ways in which inclusion or deletion of missing data affects a decision maker's ability to make sense out of the data.

I was recently asked to examine and review a school evaluation that included a section on teacher ratings of pupil progress in a special compensatory education program. The teachers doing the ratings were the students' regular classroom teachers. They were rating the progress of their students in a number of areas following their participation in the compensatory program and their return to their regular studies. The report included the following statement:

> Teachers rated students in ten areas of progress: reading, math, spelling, social studies, science, self esteem, self-control, ability to follow instructions, completion of work, and overall improvement. In none of these areas did more than 40% of the teachers rate student progress as excellent or good. The highest rating was self-esteem, which received the 40% rating. Only 24% of the teachers rated progress in reading as excellent or good. Clearly, the teachers who are receiving students from this program do not rate student progress very high.

The appendix of the report contained the actual questionnaire with the raw data for each category of response. In examining that data, it turned out that, of the 40 responding teachers, fewer than half completed any single item on which students were being rated. I had no information about why the response rate on these items was so low because on many other items all of the teachers responded. It may have been that many of these teachers felt that they could not rate their students on the items identified in the questionnaire. Some of the teachers, I later learned, were special resource teachers who would not have had the students for some of the subjects listed in the questionnaire. At any rate, if one deleted the missing data in computing the descriptive statistics for these ratings, the picture changed drastically. Fully 92 percent of all the *responding teachers* rated progress in self-esteem as excellent or good. Only 8 percent rated progress as fair or poor. In reading, 75 percent of the responding teachers rated progress as excellent or good. Indeed, in not one of the ten subjects for which there were ratings had fewer than 50 percent of the responding teachers rated progress as excellent or good. These data, computed in this way, present a radically different view of teacher perceptions of the program than the view presented in the evaluation report.

The first thing to have done, of course, upon finding such a high nonresponse rate would have been to conduct follow-up interviews with a subsample of teachers to find out reasons for nonresponses on these items. It is difficult to intrepret the data without knowing more about the meaning of those nonresponses. Nevertheless, it is hardly fair to the program to compute the data in the way that makes the results look most negative, without at least presenting those computations that make the program look quite successful. In point of fact, the teachers who did complete these items reported that the program had had quite positive effects on their students.

While inclusion or deletion of missing data will seldom make for such dramatic shifts in the possible interpretations of the findings, it is not at all unusual for adjustments to the data of this kind to result in percentage changes of 10 percent or 15 percent. Because the missing data category is not directly comparable to the other categories in most questionnaire items, and because the number of nonrespondents on any particular item is usually relatively small, the best way to provide real comparability between questions is to delete missing responses in computing the missing percentages on each item. Leaving the missing data in the reported results of main tables focuses the comparison on the percentage of nonrespondents in each item rather than focusing the analysis on the substantive responses in each item. Nevertheless, the critical issue is what kind of presentation will make the results most meaningful and useful to decision makers. That decision cannot be made by following some rote or uniform analysis procedure. It requires careful consideration on a case-by-case, questionnaire-by-questionnaire, test-by-test basis.

Be Clear About Definitions

A frequent source of misunderstanding in evaluation is confusion about what was actually measured or studied. In workshops on data analysis I give the participants statistics on farmers, on families, and on recidivism. In small groups the participants are asked to discuss the meaning of the different sets of data. Almost invariably they jump right into making interpretations without asking how farmer was defined in the data collection, how family was defined, or what recidivism actually represents in the data at hand. A simple term like "farmer" turns out to be enormously variant in its use and definition. When does the weekend gardener become a farmer, and when does the large commercial farmer become an "agribusinessperson"? There is a whole division of the Census Bureau that wrestles with this problem.

Defining "family" is no less complex. There was a time, not so long ago, when our society may have shared a common definition of family. Now there is a real question about who has to be doing what to whom under what conditions before we call it a family. Before interpreting any statistics on families it would be critical to know how family was defined.

Recidivism is by no means unusual as a concept in evaluation research. But the term offers a variety of different definitions and measures. Recidivism may mean: (1) a new arrest, (2) a new appearance in court, (3) a new conviction, (4) a new sentence, (5) or actually committing a new crime regardless of whether the offender is apprehended. The statistics will vary considerably depending on which definition of recidivism is being used.

Earlier in this chapter I cited a "study" published by the National Federation of Decency concerning the decadent content of Phil Donahue television shows. One of the categories of analysis in the study included Donahue programs that encouraged "abnormal sex." The author of the report later acknowledged that it was probably a bit excessive of the federation to have included breast feeding in this category (Boulder Daily Camera, September 30, 1981: 2). But, then, definitions of abnormal sex do seem to vary somewhat. Any reader of a research report on the subject would be well advised to look with care at the definition used by the researcher. Of course, any savvy evaluator involved in such a study would certainly be careful to make sure that his or her own sexual practices, whatever they might be, were categorized as normal.

In the 1972 presidential campaign Nixon gained considerable press attention for making a major budget shift from defense spending to spending for social services. One had to listen quite attentively and read quite carefully to learn that all that had happened was moving the Veterans Administration expenditures from the defense side of the ledger to the social services side of the ledger. The statistical changes in proportion of expenditures for different purposes were entirely an artifact of the change in definition of those services.

Such examples are not meant to make people cynical about statistics. Many distortions of this kind are inadvertent, due to sloppiness of thinking, unexamined assumptions, hurrying to complete a final report, or basic incompetence. But those are reasons not excuses. A Sufi story illustrates the importance of being clear about definitions before drawing conclusions.

Mulla Nasrudin and a friend went to the circus together. Many of the performances were outstanding but the most dazzling of all was the tightrope walker. All the way home from the performance Mulla's friend kept raving about the performance of the tightrope walker. After a while the Mulla tired of this conversation but the companion resisted all attempts to change the subject. Finally, in frustration, Nasrudin said, "It was really not such a great feat as all that to walk a tightrope. I myself can do it."

The companion was angry at Nasrudin's brazen statement, so he challenged him to a substantial wager. He was determined to put an end to Mulla Nasrudin's vain boasting. They set a time for the attempt in the center of the marketplace so that all the village could be witness to who won the wager.

At the appointed hour Mulla Nasrudin appeared with the rope, laid the rope out on the ground, walked along it, and demanded his money.

The friend was incredulous. "But the tightrope must be in the air for you to win the wager!" exclaimed the companion.

"I wagered that I could walk a tightrope," replied Nasrudin. "As everyone can see I have, indeed, walked the tightrope."

The village judicial officer ruled in Nasrudin's favor. "Definitions," he explained to the assembled villagers, "are the things of which laws are made."

They are also the things of which evaluation research are made.

Make Comparisons Carefully and Appropriately

Virtually all data analysis in evaluation ends up in some way being comparative. Numbers in isolation, standing alone without a frame of reference or basis of comparison, seldom make much sense. A recidivism rate of 40 percent is a meaningless statistic. Is that high or low? Does that represent improvement or deterioration? An error of $1 million in IRS audits is a meaningless number. Some basis of comparison or standard of judgment is needed in order to interpret such statistics. The problem comes in selecting the appropriate basis of comparison. In the example of the IRS audit, the U.S. General Accounting Office believed that the appropriate comparison was an error of zero dollars, absolute perfection in auditing. The IRS considered such a basis of comparison completely unrealistic in either practice or theory, and they suggested a basis of comparison against the total amount of corrections made in all audits.

During the writing of this book, there has been considerable controversy about the profits of oil companies in the United States. The oil companies want to compare their profits to those of the television networks to show just how low their return on capital really is in comparison to an industry— television—in which profits are high. Those who are interested in showing oil profits to be exorbitant would prefer to choose as a basis of comparison the profits of the automobile industry, which is currently experiencing a depression. There are a variety of ways of computing the profits: return on sales, return on investment, profit in absolute dollars, percentage profit over a five-year period, profits this year compared to last year, actual profits compared to expected profits. All of these figures turn out to be quite different, the general result being that the public is confused and skeptical.

Similar skepticism can occur in evaluation analyses where the basis for the comparisons appears to be arbitrary and contrived. It is important to think carefully about what kind of comparisons are appropriate, preferably before data analysis, so that the evaluation question is carefully focused on information that will illuminate the situation and provide a clear basis for action and decision. This is no easy task for the available choices are quite varied.

The outcomes of a program can be compared to:

(1) the outcomes of "similar" programs;

(2) the outcomes of the same program the previous year;

(3) the outcomes of model programs in the field;

(4) the outcomes of programs known to be having difficulty;

(5) the stated goals of the program;

(6) external standards of desirability as developed by the profession;

(7) standards of minimum acceptability, e.g., basic licensing standards;

(8) ideals of program performance; or

(9) guesses made by staff or other decision makers about what the outcomes would be.

Consider the new jogger or running enthusiast. At the beginning runners are likely to use as a basis for comparison their previous sedentary lifestyle. By that standard, the initial half-mile or one-mile run appears to be pretty good. Then the runner discovers that there are a lot of other people running, many of them running three miles, four miles, five or ten miles a week. By that standard, they haven't done so well and so they push on. On days when they want to feel particularly good, they compare themselves to all the people who don't run at all. On days when they need some incentive to push harder, they compare themselves to people they know who run twice as much as they do. Some adopt the standards from medical people about the minimum amount of running needed for basic conditioning, something on the order of thirty minutes of sustained and intense exercise a least three times a week. Some measure their progress in miles, others in minutes and hours. Some compare themselves to friends; others get involved in official competitions and races.

In politics it is said that the conservatives compare the present to the past and see all the things that have been lost, while the liberals compare the present to what could be in the future and see all the things yet to be attained. None of these comparisons is right or wrong; they are simply different. Each basis of comparison provides a different perspective, a different way of looking at things, and different information. Evaluators must work carefully with decision makers to decide which comparisons are appropriate and relevant to give a full and balanced view of what is happening in the program.

One of the areas in which there is the greatest confusion when making comparisons is the use of norms. Darrell Huff, the ingenious author of *How To Lie With Statistics,* has commented on how easily people are beguiled by normative comparisons.

Let a parent read, as many have done in such places as Sunday rotogravure sections, that "a child" learns to sit erect at the age of so many months and he thinks at once of his own child. Let this child fail to sit by the specified age and the parent must conclude that this offspring is "retarded" or "subnormal" or something equally invidious. Since half the children are bound to fail to sit by the time mentioned, a good many parents are made unhappy. Of course, speaking mathematically, this unhappiness is balanced by the joy of the other fifty percent of parents in discovering that their children are "advanced." But harm can come of the efforts of unhappy parents to force their children to conform to the norms and thus be backward no longer.

Hardly anyone is normal in any way. . . . Confusing "normal" with "desirable" makes it all the worse [1954: 44-45].

Evaluators can work with decision makers and information users to help them avoid thinking that, for example, everyone should be above the norm. The norm is simply an average score, so for a general population norm, half of the population must, *by definition,* fall below the norm. Another way of helping the people with whom one is working become more sophisticated about comparisons is to be sure to include a discussion of potential sources of error in data analysis presentations.

Error

> *It ain't so much the things*
> *we don't know that get us in*
> *trouble. It's the things we*
> *know that ain't so.*
> Artemus Ward

Statistics are seductive in their apparent precision. To say, for example, that a student has scored at the 70th percentile on a standardized achievement test sounds terribly precise and scientific. It is easy to forget that the numbers are merely probabilistic indicators of real things; the numbers are not the thing. Eminent psychologist Ann Anastasi has commented on this kind of confusion with regard to IQ scores. "One still hears the term 'IQ' used as though it referred, not to a test score, but to a property of the organism" (Anastasi, 1973: xi). In other words, the numbers that come out of standardized tests or other evaluation instruments are not embedded in the genes or on the foreheads of students. They are only rough approximations of some characteristic at a specific point in the time under particular conditions. Test results are only one piece of information about a person or a group—a piece of information that must be interpreted in connection with other information we have about that person or group. Test scores then are neither good nor bad. They are pieces of information that are subject to considerable error—and that are more or less useful depending on how they are gathered, interpreted, applied, abused, and used.

All kinds of statistical information are subject to error. I've chosen to focus on standardized tests in this section on errors because nonscientists seem particularly subject to a belief in the absolute accuracy of such evaluation instruments. The importance of looking for sources of error in any analysis is, however, a principle that applies generally. For many reasons, all tests and other evaluation instruments are subject to some measurement error. Henry Dyer, a president of the highly respected Educational Testing Service (ETS), tells of trying to explain to a governmental official that test scores, even on the most reliable tests, have enough measurement error that they must be used extremely cautiously. The government official, who happened to be an enthusiastic proponent of performance contracting, responded that test makers should "get on the ball" and start producing tests that "are 100 percent reliable under all conditions."

Dyer's comments on this conversation are particularly relevant to an understanding of error in evaluation instruments. He asks:

> How does one get across the shocking truth that 100 percent reliability in a test is a fiction that, in the nature of the case, is unrealizable? How does one convey the notion that the test reliability problem is not one of reducing measurement error to absolute zero, but of minimizing it as far as practicable and doing one's best to estimate whatever amount of error remains, so that one may act cautiously and wisely in a world where all knowledge is approximate and not even death and taxes are any longer certain [Dyer, 1973: 87]?

Sources of error are many. For example, continuing with the problem of errors in test scores, there are myriad reasons why a particular student's score may be subject to error. The health of the child on the day the test is given can affect the score. Whether or not the pupil had breakfast can make a difference. Noise in the classroom, a sudden fire drill, whether or not the teacher or a stranger gives the test, a broken pencil, and any number of similar disturbances can change a test score. The mental state of the child—depression, boredom, elation, a conflict at home, a fight with another student, anxiety about the test, a low self-concept—all of these factors affect how well the student performs. Simple mechanical errors such as marking the wrong box on the test sheet by accident, accidentally skipping a question, or missing a word while reading are common problems for all of us. Students who have trouble reading will perform poorly on reading tests; but they are also likely to perform poorly on social studies, science, and arithmetic tests, because all of these tests require reading. Thus the test may considerably underestimate the real knowledge of the child.

Some children perform better on tests because they have been taught how to take written tests. Some children are simply better test takers than other children because of their background or personality or how seriously they treat the idea of the test. Some schools make children sit all day long taking test after test, sometimes for an entire week. Other schools give the tests for only a half day or two hours a day to minimize fatigue and boredom. Some children like to take tests; some do not. Some teachers help children with difficult words, or even read the tests along with the children; others do not.

Some schools devote their curriculum, or at least some school time, to teaching students what is in the tests. Other schools, notably alternative schools—open classrooms, free schools, street academies—place little emphasis on test-taking and paper-and-pencil skills, thus giving students less experience in the rigor and tricks of taking tests.

All these sources of error—and I have scarcely scratched the surface of such possibilities—can seriously affect an individual child's score. Moreover, they have virtually nothing to do with how "good" the test is, how carefully it was prepared, or how valid its content is for a given child or group. *Intrinsic to the nature of standardized testing, these errors are always present to some extent and are largely uncontrollable. They are the reason that statisticians can never develop a test that is 100 percent reliable.*

The errors are more or less serious depending on how a test is used. When looking at test scores for large groups, we can expect that because of such errors some students will perform above their true level and other students will perform below their true score. For most groups, statisticians believe that these errors cancel each other. The overly high scores of some students compensate for the overly low scores of others so that the group result is relatively accurate. The larger the group tested, the more likely this is to be true.

However, for a specific individual, no other scores are available to make up for the error in his or her score. The only hope is that the questions the student answered wrong because of error will be compensated for by the questions he or she got right either accidentally or by guessing. This type of error compensation is much less reliable in correcting for error than the situation described for large groups. The least reliable result is one individual's answer on a single quesiton. Nothing can compensate for error in this case. Thus *one must be extremely cautious about making too much of results for individuals particularly on single, specific test questions and short tests.*

Different evaluation instruments are subject to different kinds of errors. Measurement error can also result from the sampling procedures employed, the way instruments are administered, and other design problems. Whether the evaluation includes data from tests, questionnaires, management information systems, government statistics, or whatever—the analysis should include attention to potential sources of error. Statistical procedures are available for computing the relative size of various kinds of error.

The point is that evaluators do their clients a disservice when they treat lightly the problem of errors in evaluation data. Evaluators need not be defensive about errors. Decision makers and information users can be helpful in identifying potential sources of error. In my experience, their overall confidence in their ability to use evaluation data correctly and appropriately is increased when there has been a frank and full discussion of both the data's strengths and weaknesses. In this way, evaluators are helping to make evaluation clients more knowledgeable so they will understand what Dyer's government official did not:

The problem is not one of reducing measurement error to absolute zero, but of minimizing it as far as practicable and doing one's best to estimate whatever amount of error remains, so that one may act cautiously and wisely in a world where all knowledge is approximate and not even death and taxes are any longer certain.

INVOLVEMENT IN DATA ANALYSIS

Presentations of evaluation data can be deadly boring. Number follows number, table follows table, and participants at the data analysis presentation begin to nod off. They hear some results, but don't hear others. Some of it makes sense, but it is difficult to process a great deal of data and determine its relevance when more data are already on the way. How, then, can active involvement and interest in evaluation findings be increased?

The trick is to move people from passive reception—from audience status—to active involvement and participation. This requires a framework for interpreting specific statistics and results. One way of having participants establish such a framework is to provide them with tables that have all the categories specified but where the spaces for numbers are blank. Participants are then asked to do two things. First, they are asked to specify what they would consider to be a desirable result in the data. Then they are asked to specify what they would guess the actual result to be.

Consider, for example, a table that presents simple descriptive statistics on participant reactions to a program. The questions concern satisfaction level, how much they learned, and other typical questions aimed at getting participant feedback. In the data analysis session participants are given the questionnaire items with two columns. The first column asks them to specify what percentage response they would consider desirable, and the second column asks them to consider and specify what percentage response they believe was actually obtained in the evaluation.

Having specified a standard of desirability, and having taken a guess at actual results, participants now have a greater stake in and a framework for looking at the actual findings. The discussion can then focus on the implications of the data falling below, at, or above the desired response, and why the actual findings were different from or the same as what any given participant guessed the results would be. In my experience, such discussions are highly animated, and allow participants to become very actively involved in the data analysis and interpretation process.

The major limitation of such an approach is that the amount of data presented must be highly focused and limited so that participants are able to deal with the entire process. Carefully constructed tables and highly focused analysis can make such presentations lively, interesting, and quite valuable.

I find that, given the time and proper encouragement, workshop participants with virtually no methods or statistics training can readily identify the strengths and weaknesses in many statistical presentations. Another one of the exercises I use in data analysis workshops is aimed at giving participants experience in drawing on their own common sense to inspect statistical statements. I collect advertising statements from the popular media and give those statements to workshop participants, having them simply think about (1) what the statement actually tells them, (2) what information is missing from the statement that is needed to really understand the issue at hand, and (3) what design and measurement questions would one want to have answered before acting on the reported data. Participants rapidly warm to such an exercise, usually offering their own examples before the exercise has proceeded very far. They find that, with a little thought, they can be quite astute in their statistical thinking.

The point of both of these exercises is to involve actively participants and decision makers in data analysis in such a way that they feel empowered to understand and use statistical findings.

READING STATISTICAL REPORTS

How do you read reports and articles? Think about it for a moment. Analyze your own reading style. Do you open a book at the back and glance first at the final chapter looking for conclusions? Do you begin in the middle? Or with the table of contents? Do you read methodology sections? Do you like to read the conclusions, findings, and recommendations first?

Different people have different styles of reading reports. In exploring reading styles with hundreds of participants in workshops, one common pattern has emerged. Most people don't look carefully at statistical tables, charts, and graphs. They prefer to read what the author says about the data, and they commonly assume that what the author says will be substantiated by the tables presented—so why bother to try to make sense out of those tables on one's own?

I propose trying an alternative approach. Read the statistical tables, graphs, charts, and other data presentations *before* reading the author's narrative. Take the time to make sense out of tables. At first, this may require some effort for people who are used to avoiding the reading of tables. But with a little practice, tables can become quite easy to decipher. A little more practice, and it becomes much quicker when scanning an article to draw conclusions on the basis of a quick reading of tables than to plow more slowly through the narrative.

The first advantage of this alternative approach is that the reader is able to draw his or her own conclusions about the data without being influenced and biased by the author's conclusions. Second, the reader is forced to think seriously about the nature of the data presented in the report, and to become familiar with the measures used and the analysis undertaken. Third, having taken a look at the basic data, the reader can then approach the narrative with specific questions that emerge from that data. This makes the reading of the narrative more focused, more memorable, and often more interesting. Fourth, the reader is more likely to examine carefully the author's conclusions and interpretations having first arrived at conclusions and interpretations independent from those offered by the author. Finally, as noted above, this approach is often much quicker. The practiced reader can learn to grasp tables with speed and insight so that the essentials of the article are readily available through a rapid interpretation of the data presented in the report. Since most reports present only data on the main issues, this approach allows the central points to emerge quite rapidly.

Given limited time, and the difficulty of keeping up with the literature, it behooves us to find ways of increasing our ability to grasp the essence of evaluation reports and articles decisively and quickly. Given a choice of possible styles, the approach of looking first—and sometimes only—at the actual data can be a powerful and effective alternative to reading the narrative. At a minimum, readers need to develop the discipline of looking at the actual data on which evaluation conclusions are based. To assume that whatever the author says can be backed up by the data presented in the tables is a dangerous and misleading assumption. I find that, more often than not, a careful reading of the data opens up interpretations not included in the author's analysis.

This approach is also a good test of how well constructed one's own statistical tables are. A table should be readable without reference to the narrative. Statistical tables, charts, and graphs should stand on their own. This means that they must be fully labeled and explained. Test out the clarity and completeness of your tables by having someone relatively unfamiliar with the project look at the tables by themselves and attempt to understand and interpret them. A well-constructed table is equivalent to the picture that is better than a thousand words. Attempts to understand tables without reference to the narrative rapidly expose the inadaquacies of statistical presentations.

THE PURPOSE OF DATA ANALYSIS

The beginning of data analysis in an evaluation is an exciting time. After much time devoted to conceptualizing the evaluation and gathering the appropriate data, the results are about to emerge. The process of focusing and conceptualizing the evaluation is like planting a seed; the period of data collection is like the period of cultivation—watering and nourishing the plant, pulling out weeds, and watching the plant gradually grow to maturity; finally, the fruit appears, and data analysis is like the harvest time, a period of intense hard work with very visible payoffs. Of course, once the fruit is harvested, there is still the problem of carefully storing the fruit to avoid spoilage and pest infiltration, and there is the task of preparing the fruit for consumption, or marketing it for the consumption of others. In many agricultural societies over 50 percent of the harvest is lost to spoilage, waste, and pest infiltration. My sense is that a great deal of evaluation data is lost because of careless handling, improper preparation, and poor packaging and marketing.

Data collection is not simply a routine application of technical procedures. It is a creative and demanding process that is too often squeezed into the last few days before a report is due. The purpose of data analysis is to inform decision making. Too much analysis is done for its own sake, the evaluator getting caught up in the fascinating nuances of data dredging and loosing sight of the real focus of evaluation. When the evaluator looses sight of the real purpose of data analysis, a fine harvest of numbers and statistics may be accumulated, but without any use ever being made of those numbers, and no real consumption of those statistics taking place. A Sufi story illustrates what can happen when data collection and analysis procedes without clear purpose.

> Mulla Nasrudin was visiting the village of a relative when he noticed a man in the village going about counting things. Throughout the day the man could be seen going about the village with paper and pen in hand counting all sorts of things—houses, trees, birds, children, stones, etc. When Nasrudin inquired of people in the village he was told that the man was believed to have powerful connections in the capital city and that he was counting things for the ruler. This was an impressive explanation and the Mulla decided to talk further with this distinguished statistician.
>
> "I have noticed your work and, being a little interested in understanding the world myself, I would appreciate an opportunity to learn about the things you have discovered."
>
> The man looked about him on all sides and then asked Nasrudin: "I note that you are a stranger here. Can you be trusted with private information?"
>
> Nasrudin assured the man that he could count on Nasrudin's discretion and that he would treat whatever was told him with complete confidentiality.
>
> "What I have to tell you then is that I have nothing to tell you. All of my business in counting is merely for appearances. I have no other work to do and because the unemployed are quickly conscripted for military service I have adopted this subterfuge to give an impression of being greatly occupied with important dealings. You are the first person who has asked me what my counting means and I cannot tell you for I myself have discovered no purpose in it."

SUMMARY

This chapter has reviewed some fundamental principles of data analysis and statistical reasoning. These are not the only fundamentals that are important. Rather, they are indicative of the kinds of basic issues that undergird a practical approach to collaborative evaluation practice. Thus much of the emphasis has been on ways of introducing nonstatisticians to the culture of science in general and the subculture of statistics more specifically. The points made about management information systems in the last chapter are also generally applicable to program evaluations. In addition, this chapter has stressed the following principles of data analysis in program evaluation:

(1) Decision makers and information users are more likely to use data they have worked with, believe in, and understand.

(2) Users of evaluation are concerned with both the utility and accuracy of findings. The collaborative analysis process is, therefore, aimed at elucidating both the strengths and weaknesses of the data, thereby enhancing the potential for utilization while guarding against misutilization.

(3) Resistance to and cynicism about statistical analysis should be acknowledged and dealt with rather than ignored or belittled.

(4) Numbers must be interpreted to have meaning.

(5) Numbers in evaluation are usually indicators or estimates of program processes and outcomes. Just as a map is not the territory it describes, the statistical tables on a program are not the program.

(6) Analyzing evaluation data depends in part on adopting a probabilistic perspective. Accuracy and precision are relative statistical concepts, not absolute ones.

(7) Simplicity is a virtue in data analysis. Straightforward reporting is a valuable skill; some would say a gift.

(8) Data analysis should be balanced. This means considering multiple possible interpretations and analyzing various kinds of indicators. Single indicators are seldom adequate in the search for balance. Multiple indicators, multiple analytical approaches, and multiple perspectives are needed for balance. Adversary-advocacy analysis is one kind of group process that can contribute to balance.

(9) Descriptive statistics are needed to provide an interpretive context for inferential statistics. Inferential questions often emerge from decision makers in response to descriptive presentations. Balance involves both descriptive and inferential statistical analyses.

(10) Data need to be organized and arranged for easy and practical decision maker analysis and interpretation.

(11) Analysis must be focused. Decision makers and information users can only deal with a limited amount of data.

(12) Decisions about how to deal with missing data depend on the nature of the analysis and the kind of questions being asked of the data. This, and other analysis problems, should be handled as deliberately as a decision, not as a routine procedure.

(13) Clarity about definitions, and the content of analytical categories, is crucial.

(14) Comparisons should be made carefully and appropriately.

(15) Both strengths and weaknesses of the data should be discussed, and the nature and size of errors should be a part of the analysis.

(16) Users of evaluative data need to work actively at the analysis process rather than rely on the conclusions of others. In a collaborative, utilization-focused analysis process, it is part of the evaluator's job to facilitate decision maker involvement in data analysis and interpretation.

Purposeful data analysis is not the final step in the evaluation process but only preparation for that final step. Having inspected, arranged, and ordered the evaluation data, the final step is interpreting the data, making judgments about it, generating recommendations for action, and identifying options for decision. The next chapter discusses some ways of thinking about drawing conclusions from evaluative data.

CHAPTER 11   *Practical and Useful Recommendations*

Unapplied knowledge is knowledge shorn of its meaning.

A. N. Whitehead

This chapter is about what one does with evaluation data once the data are organized and analyzed. This is typically the point at which evaluators begin to worry about utilization. That is not the case when a collabortive, utilization-focused evaluation process has been used. In such a process, concern for utilization enters into the evaluation at the very first interaction between decision makers and evaluators. The process of generating recommendations, therefore, is simply a continuation of the utilization-focused process, not the beginning of a concern with how findings are to be applied.

Two of the most common complaints I hear from program staff, administrators, and funders are that recommendations in evaluation reports are impractical ("they can't be implemented") and that they don't seem to be derived from the data ("the recs just come out of nowhere"). Evaluation reports that are otherwise quite professionally done can fall apart at the recommendations section. Skill at statistical analysis and skill at drawing recommendations from data are two quite different things. Evaluators seem to get lots of training in the former, but not so much in the latter.

I've done workshops on how to generate recommendations with the evaluation staffs of several organizations that had been "burned" by the release of evaluation reports containing what subsequently turned out to be "off-the-wall," or erroneous, recommendations.

One state program director for a federal LEAA program told me:

We need a workshop—and we need it badly—on how to write evaluation reports. More specifically, we need to somehow, some way, get into the heads of our county and regional evaluators that they can't just write whatever comes to their minds by way of recommendations. The standard format we use for reporting has a section for recommendations. Our people do a careful job of reporting program goals, evaluation methods, data collection procedures, and empirical results, but when they get to the recommendations section it's like something goes off in their heads and they feel some great surge of power so they just start making up things. I've seen some incredible recommendations that had nothing to do with the subject of the evaluation. They don't seem to realize that what they write for recommendations can have serious and disastrous consequences for programs when county board members, or state legislators, or the newspapers see this stuff. If we can't get our people trained I'm simply going to have to rule that no evaluation reports will include any recommendations, just delete the whole damn thing.

In our study of the utilization of federal health evaluations (Patton et al., 1977) we asked twenty decision makers about the usefulness of the recommendations in specific evaluation reports they had received. The following reactions were typical:

I don't remember the specific recommendations.

The recommendations weren't very useful or anything we could do much with. It was the overall process that was useful, not the recommendations.

I remember reading them, that's about all.

The recommendations were the least useful part of the report. They looked like they'd been added as an afterthought.

RECOMMENDATIONS IN PERSPECTIVE

Before looking specifically at the processes of interpreting evaluation data and generating recommendations, it may be helpful to position recommendations within the overall evaluation process. In Chapter 3, the problem of defining utilization was discussed. That discussion suggested that evaluations are useful in ways that go beyond a narrow focus on implementing recommendations or making concrete, specific decisions about immediate courses of action. Participation in an evaluation process affects ways of thinking about a program; it can clarify goals, increase (or decrease) particular commitments, and reduce uncertainties; and the process can stimulate insights, the consequences of which may not be evident until some distant time in the future. Recommendations, then do not bear the full brunt of the hopes for utilization in an evaluation.

Nevertheless, recommendations are often the most visible part of an evaluation report. Well-written, carefully derived recommendations and conclusions can be the catalyst that brings all the other elements in an evaluation process together into a meaningful whole. When done poorly, recommendations can become the center of an attack on an evaluation process, discrediting what was otherwise a professional job, because of hurried and sloppy work on a last-minute recommendations section.

In considering recommendations, it is helpful to keep in mind the evaluator's training function that has been emphasized throughout this book. Involving decision makers and information users in the processes of interpreting data, making judgments, drawing conclusions, and generating recommendations is all part of the process of helping stakeholders become more sophisticated about data-based decision making. Herbert Kohl nicely summarized this perspective when he said, "An evaluation document should be a teaching document" (Far West Lab, 1976: 85).

Thinking about the evaluation process as a teaching and learning experience recalls the distinction in the first chapter between the evaluation process and the content of the evaluation. The content provides substance to the process, but is also derived from the process. The new standards of evaluation apply to both the process and the content. Generating recommendations is the process, while the actual recommendations generated are the content. In this regard, the new standards mandate that recommendations should manifest utility, feasibility, propriety, and accuracy. More specifically, the standards state:

> The conclusions reached in an evaluation should be explicitly justified, so that the audiences can assess them.
>
> The conclusions of an evaluation, which represent judgments and recommendations, must be defensible and defended. To be defensible, conclusions must be based on sound logic and appropriate information. To be sufficiently defended, they must be reported along with an account of the evaluation's procedures, information, and underlying assumptions, and with a discussion of possible alternative explanations of the findings and why they were rejected.
>
> This standard is important for at least two reasons. Unverified conclusions may be faulty, leading the audience to inappropriate actions. And, the conclusions may be disregarded, whatever their merits, if the audience does not receive sufficient information for determining whether they are warranted [Joint Committee, 1981: 135].

The remainder of this chapter discusses some practical ways of generating recommendations (the process) that meet these standards in terms of what is said and how it is said (the content).

SEPARATING FINDINGS, INTERPRETATIONS, JUDGMENTS, AND RECOMMENDATIONS

At the workshops I've done on report writing and generating recommendations, participants spend a fair amount of time working on the distinctions between findings, interpretations, judgments, and recommendations. Evaluators ignore these distinctions at their peril. A major source of problems in evaluation reports, or in working with task force participants, is the failure to make clear distinctions among these four quite different kinds of statements.

- *Findings:* the facts of the case; the basic presentation of the data from the evaluation; the empirical results.
- *Interpretations:* explanations offered about the findings; speculations about interrelationships, causes, reasons for the findings, and meanings given to the data.
- *Judgments:* values brought to bear on the data; specific criteria applied to the findings stating that they are "good" or "bad"; "positive" or "negative"; "in the desired direction" or "in an undesired direction"; "above expectations," "in line with expectations," or "below expectations."
- *Recommendations:* suggested courses of action; proposed changes in the program or things to be maintained as they are in the program; and advice to funders, program administrators, program staff, and others about how to improve the program based on findings, interpretations, and judgments.

During the workshops we play a game that is aimed at increasing participants' ability to make these critical distinctions. Sitting in a circle we begin with someone who is asked to look around the room and make an empirical observation about the room; the next person is asked to make an interpretation of that empirical observation; the next person adds a judgment; and the fourth person makes a recommendation based upon the preceding three statements.

- *Person 1* (empirical observation or finding): All but one of the women are wearing slacks.
- *Person 2* (interpretation): The women are trying to diminish the appearance of differences between women and men in professional settings.
- *Person 3* (judgment): It is good for women to wear slacks in professional settings and to diminish the dress differences between men and women.
- *Person 4* (recommendation): The sponsors of this workshop should include in future brochures a statement encouraging casual and comfortable dress at workshops.

The characteristics of findings, interpretations, judgments, and recommendations differ. Findings should be information about which people can agree. When a group of decision makers and information users examine the presentation of findings they should all be able to agree on the empirical nature of the results. The addition of a single word to a statement of findings, however, can change that statement from empirical statement to evaluative judgment. The addition of a clause can turn the finding into an interpretation. Consider the four sentences that follow:

Forty-two percent of the juveniles in the program had been arrested for new offenses within one year. (Finding)

Only forty-two percent of the juveniles in the program had been arrested again within one year. (Judgment)

Forty-two percent of the juveniles in the program had been arrested again within one year because they were easy targets for the police. (Interpretation)

Since only forty-two percent of the juveniles in the program were arrested again in one year the program should be continued for another year. (Recommendation)

In the latter three sentences, the statement of findings is confounded by being included with an interpretation, a judgment, or a recommendation. These are not minor differences of semantics. These different statements represent fundamentally different messages. At the beginning of workshops, I find that participants have great difficulty making these distinctions. It may be because so few evaluators realize when they have moved beyond the data that they later find themselves in trouble because of the statements they've made (an interpretive statement on my part). I believe this is an unfortunate situation (a judgment on my part). I therefore recommend that evaluators practice making these distinctions and keep these distinctions in the forefront of their consciousnesses as they write their reports (a recommendation).

The starting point, then, is a clear understanding of the findings of the evaluation unencumbered by interpretations, judgments, and preconceived recommendations. It is then possible to add interpretations and judgments in the process of moving toward recommendations. Because of the speculative nature of interpretations, disputes often arise among different analysts about the meaning of a particular data set. In discussing different interpretations it is important to return regularly to the empirical findings and to keep the interpretations grounded in those findings. As is the case in interpreting legal cases, one must continually return to the facts of the case and base interpretations on those facts. In many cases it will be impossible to resolve differing interpretations. When people say that there is basic disagreement about the findings of the evaluation I find that they more often mean that there is disagreement about the interpretations of the data rather than disagreement about the findings. In a carefully done piece of research it should be possible to agree on the findings even though interpretations of those findings may vary considerably (one of the interpretations being that the data are invalid or unreliable even though there is agreement on what the actual facts are as represented by those invalid and unreliable data).

The making of judgments requires some kind of criteria. When qualifying phrases like "only," "as much as," and "unusually high" are added to statements of findings, some hidden criterion has been applied to judge the meaning of the results obtained. It is incumbent upon evaluators to make these criteria explicit. They most often come from program goals and objectives or comparisions to either past performance or other programs. Again, different analysts may apply different judgments to the same set of findings. This creates no difficulty as long as the criteria being used by each set of judges are made explicit.

Finally, then, we come to recommendations. With clear statements of findings, interpretations, and judgments, the recommendations typically follow quite naturally. One way of checking on the reasonableness of a recommendation is to make sure that it is logically backed up by a set of findings, a reasonable interpretation of those findings, and a judgment applied to those findings. I prefer to always have recommendations placed in the context of the specific findings, interpretations, and judgments on which they are based. Therefore, I have workshop participants practice taking a set of data and writing a final section of a report in which they summarize the findings, interpretations, judgments, and subsequent recommendations all in one place. These connections are too easily lost in reports that are organized so that there is a findings section of the report, an interpretations section of the report, and an overall conclusions or judgments section of the report, and then a set of recommendations. The reader is left to make the connection between the recommendations and the earlier findings, interpretations, and judgments. Many of the difficulties decision makers have with evaluation reports is that they can't see those connections that seem so obvious to the evaluator. In writing a report it is the reponsibility of the evaluator to make those connections as explicit and clear as possible. The best way to do that is to put them all in one place.

THE NECESSITY OF THOUGHT

Once there was a scientist who was studying how far frogs could jump. He yelled at a frog, "jump!" and the frog jumped 10 feet.

Then he cut off one leg of the frog. He yelled "jump!" and the frog jumped 5 feet.

Then he cut off a second leg. He yelled "jump!" and the frog jumped one foot.

Then he cut off a third leg. He yelled "jump!" and the frog jumped 4 inches.

Then he cut off the fourth leg. He yelled "jump!" The frog did not move.

The scientist concluded: When you cut off four legs of a frog, the frog becomes deaf!

Keeping clear the distinctions among findings, interpretations, judgments, and recommendations can help avoid confusion, but there are few guidelines one can offer for how to come up with meaningful interpretations and recommendations. It's necessary to work at the process of thinking through alternative possibilities. In my opinion, one of the most common reasons evaluators get in trouble when writing recommendations is that they haven't allowed enough time to really think through the possibilities and discuss them with people who have a stake in the evaluation. After months of work on an evaluation, I've known many cases where the recommendations were generated hours before a final reporting session, under enormous time pressure.

Drawing conclusions and making recommendations can rapidly become not only intellectually challenging, but highly amusing, if one indulges in considering a full range of possibilities. John Hickey's (1977) struggle with the implications of statistics on automobile accidents illustrates this point. The National Safety Program found that 75 percent of car accidents occur within 40 miles of home. He suggests that there are several ways of reacting to this finding.

(1) People driving near home should be particularly vigilant.
(2) People driving near home should drive as fast as possible to get out of the 40-mile danger zone into the surrounding safe area.
(3) Since the farther one is from home, the smaller the chance of an accident, people should register their cars at a "home" 500 miles away and never go near there.
(4) Instead of registering their car at some randomly chosen "home" some 500 miles away, the safer thing to do would be to register it in a place much farther away which has a very low accident rate. The South Pole comes to mind.

Of course, these shrewd recommendations merely scratch the surface of the possibilities. Indeed, Hickey's example illustrates a related point about recommendations. Single-sentence findings based on one or two statistics are particularly useful for generating unusual recommendations, since one is not hampered by any information about the complexity of the situation. For example, if one added to the statistics on accidents the data that 90 percent of the driving occurs within 40 miles of home, but only 75 percent of the accidents, the area around home suddenly looks much safer, and the recommendations might be quite different.

At least Hickey considered a number of alternatives. One important way of reducing the risk of presenting absurd recommendations is to present and discuss options. That is the subject of the next section.

PRESENTING OPTIONS

One way of helping make sure that an evaluation report is not perceived as biased, overly value laden, or unbalanced in favor of only one viewpoint is to present recommendations as a series of options. Beginning with a basic set of findings but playing out varying interpretations of those findings and applying different values to those findings to arrive at contrasting judgments, it is possible to come up with a full range of recommendations covering many of the different possibilities open to decision makers. One way of building support for options is to work backwards. One begins with a slate of recommendations: terminate the program, reduce funding for the program, maintain program funding at its current level, increase program funding slightly, and increase program funding substantially. The evaluator then builds a case for each one of these recommendations showing which findings, assumptions, interpretations, and judgments combine to support each of the designated options.

The evaluator does not have to be neutral about which set of assumptions and which line of reasoning seem most powerful and which make the most sense. However, the evaluator should do as good a job building a case for those options judged by the evaluator to be less compelling as in building the case for the option favored by the evaluator.

My experience suggests that decision makers very much appreciate being provided with a set of carefully thought out alternatives, and that they rapidly see the strength and weaknesses in each argument. Moreover, I find that they are much more likely to accept my view of things if I have fairly presented the opposing arguments than they are if I have built a single, overwhelming presentation directed at a single conclusion. Experienced decision makers know that there are always alternatives and multiple points of view. If the evaluator doesn't include some discussion of optional approaches in the evaluation report the decision maker will have to spend some time thinking through those options before feeling comfortable in acting on the recommendations in the report. My experience suggests that in the long run balanced reports carry more weight than reports heavily loaded to present only one perspective.

One hindrance in attempting to identify and represent fairly options is that after months of studying a program the evaluator will often arrive at quite firmly held convictions about what needs to be done. It is difficult at that point in time to return to an earlier state of innocence when no such strongly held opinions had been formed. The evaluator may find that the needed course of action is so clear that it is difficult to build any kind of reasonable case for alternatives. Here again is where the evaluation task force can play a particularly important role. Members of the task force are often more aware than the evaluator of possible options and often better at spinning out alternative scenarios. Finding that you are having difficulty coming up with reasonable alternatives to the convictions you have formed is often a good sign that you've gotten too close to the situation and lost your perspective. I operate on the assumption that there are always reasonable options and alternatives. The trick is to identify them.

DIFFERENT KINDS OF RECOMMENDATIONS

Not all recommendations are created equal.

Many evaluation reports end with a section on "Recommendations" that consists of a long, undifferentiated list of proposed actions. In the same list, separated only by a different number in the listing, may be a recommendation to double the funding level of the program, a recommendation to involve clients more in program decision making, a recommendation to print the newsletter on colored paper, and a recommendation to replace the squeaky vent in the conference room. Including relatively insignificant recommendations in the same list with suggestions for major program changes diffuses and reduces the power of those major recommendations.

One clear point of separation is between those recommendations that deal directly with the central questions or issues in the evaluation and those recommendations that relate to secondary issues that emerged in the course of studying the central issues in the evaluation. In most cases, the data bearing on central evaluation questions will be of a substantially different quality than data bearing on issues that the evaluator became aware of after the basic conceptualization of the evaluation focus and methods. It is the secondary recommendations that often get evaluators into trouble because they are unexpected and decision makers don't know where they came from.

In most any evaluation that involves some direct contact between the evaluator and the program, the experienced and insightful evaluator will become attuned to things that are going on in the program that could be improved but were not included in the original focus of the evaluation. Essentially, these insights are derived from the informal fieldwork connected with carrying out the formal evaluation. Yet the evaluator has not gathered systematic data on these issues, and the focus of these insights was not planned in the original evaluation design, so the evaluator doesn't really have any place to put those insights in the report. As a result, recommendations that stem from the evaluator's personal insights from having direct contact with the program are often simply added on as additional items in the long list of recommendations. The data on which they are based are not discussed and they thus appear to be "off the wall" and "not related to the findings in the report."

Many of the insights that occur to evaluators as a result of their direct contact with the program are quite important; in some cases they will be the most important outcomes of the evaluation. Evaluators can help build a context for including such insights in the evaluation process by alerting decision makers and information users during the early conceptualization period of the evaluation to the possibility that such insights will emerge. As observations of the program lead the evaluator to think about suggestions for change it becomes important to document carefully the observations on which those suggestions are based. In point of fact, the evaluator is conducting fieldwork. All the rules of evidence that apply to qualitative methods should apply to such fieldwork (see Patton, 1980). If the evaluator keeps careful field notes of informal program observations it will be possible to more firmly support suggestions and recommendations that emerge from those observations.

From my point of view, if the evaluator is going to include recommendations derived from direct contact with the program in the final report (recommendations that go beyond the scope of the initial evaluation design), the evaluator is obligated to present the observations which those recommendations are based along with the relevant interpretations and judgments that support those recommendations. It is inappropriate to simply conclude the evaluation report by adding, "and in addition to the recommendations above we also think the program should . . ." and not provide the same kinds of evidence and support that undergirded the recommendations related to central evaluation issues.

There are other ways of organizing recommendations. Distinctions should be made between summative and formative recommendations. Recommendations can be grouped according to those that are related to management and day-to-day operations issues, those that concern basic program policies, those that concern program funding, those that concern program content, those that concern program processes, and those that concern program organization. In still other cases it may be helpful and important to distinguish between recommendations that can be implemented immediately, recommendations that can be implemented in the short term (within six months to a year), and recommendations aimed at the long-term development of the program. In still other cases it may be appropriate to orient recommendations toward certain groups of people: recommendations for funders, recommendations for program administrators, recommendations for program staff, and recommendations for clients or program participants.

Another way of differentiating between types of recommendations is to clearly specify which recommendations are strongly supported by the data and have the solid support of the evaluator and/or the evaluation task force versus those recommendations that are less directly supported by the data or about which there is dissension among members of the task force. In similar fashion, it is important to distinguish between recommendations that involve a firm belief that some action should be taken from recommendations that are meant merely to stimulate discussion or suggestions that might become part of an agenda for future consideration and action.

The basic point here is that long, indiscriminate lists of recommendations at the end of an evaluation report diffuse the focus and diminish the power of central recommendations. By making explicit the different amounts of emphasis that the evaluator intends to place on different recommendations, and by organizing recommendations so as to differentiate among different kinds of recommendations, the evaluator increases the usefulness of the recommendations as well as the likelihood of the implementation of at least some of them.

PRACTICAL AND THOUGHT-PROVOKING
RECOMMENDATIONS

In an important article on the utilization of research, Weiss and Bucavalas (1980) described two ways in which decision makers were likely to use research findings. The first element of utility concerned practical changes that could be implemented on their actual work; the second element of utility concerned things that challenged their existing beliefs and helped them to see things in a new way. The evidence from the research by Weiss and Bucavalas suggests that evaluators should pay particular attention to this distinction in writing recommendations. Which recommendations are likely to challenge existing ways of thinking about the program under study? And which recommendations are aimed at concrete program practices? Different kinds of utilization result from these different kinds of recommendations. Concrete and practical recommendations for immediate implementation can be judged by the extent to which they lead to direct action. However, recommendations that involve major shifts in thinking or challenge existing ways of conceptualizing the program are not likely to lead to immediate implementation. The latter kinds of recommendations, while quite important, lead to less direct utilization of findings. Anticipating the different reactions to these two different kinds of recommendations, the sensitive evaluator can write the recommendations in such a way that it is clear when matters of practice are being discussed. The implications of pursuing each kind of recommendation should then be spelled out in the report.

One way of thinking about the implications of recommendations is the distinction between Type I and Type II errors—often studied in statistics courses, but little utilized in evaluation reports. In research that involves hypothesis testing, two kinds of errors are possible. We can reject the null hypothesis when, in fact, it is true; that is, we may conclude that there is a difference between the two populations being studied when, in fact, there are no significant differences. This is the Type I error. On the other hand, we might accept the null hypothesis as tenable when, in fact, it is false; that is, we may decide that the two populations are basically similar when, in fact, they are significantly different. This is referred to as Type II error. The distinction between Type I and Type II errors clearly introduces matters of judgment into statistics. In most circumstances the two kinds of errors involve quite different costs—whether economic costs, political costs, social costs, or simply human energy costs. Since virtually all recommendations involve guesses and speculations about the outcomes that would come from taking a particular course of action, it would be helpful if evaluators clearly spelled out the implications of the actions that they are suggesting in terms of Type I and Type II errors.

I am not suggesting that one jargonize an evaluation report by introducing and explaining the statistical basis for and differentiation between Type I and

Type II errors. Rather, I am suggesting applying the *logic* of Type I and Type II errors to evaluation findings and recommendations. In the logic of hypothesis testing we are comparing samples from two populations to determine if they are same or different. The two types of errors involved are in thinking that populations are the same when in fact they are different, or thinking they are different when in fact they are the same. If, applying this logic to evaluation, we think of the two things to be compared as the existing program and the recommended program, then we are concerned with the error of thinking that the recommended program is better than the existing program when in fact there is no difference, or the error of thinking that the existing program is just as good as recommended changes when in fact the recommended changes would be superior. The purpose of identifying the two possible types of error is to assess the risks and costs in each.

Suppose that a school evaluation recommends a new method of teaching; the data suggest that the new method is superior to the existing method. However, the new method would involve extensive training of teachers, purchase of new curriculum materials, and parent/student concerns about curriculum discontinuities. Since the recommendations involve considerable expense, the school system should not make the changes unless there is considerable assurance that the new program would indeed be superior. In other words, it would be quite costly to make a Type I error and conclude that the new method is better when in fact it is not. On the other hand, if there were no major differences in cost—economic, political, or social—in adopting the new program, concern about a Type II error might lead to an unjustified barrier to implementing the suggested changes when in fact the changes would create a better program.

It is worth noting that evaluators have more than just Type I and Type II errors to worry about and to use in guiding their data interpretations. Deaton and Gephart (1980) have helpfully extracted several other error types from the evaluation literature, to wit:

- *Type III Error:* Giving the right answer to the wrong problem.
- *Type IV Error:* The incorrect interpretation of a correctly rejected hypothesis.
- *Type V Error:* Meaningless application of numbers to a question not prepared for quantitative analysis.

All of this is by way of reminding ourselves, yet again, of the importance of dealing with the *substantive significance* of data in making recommendations—not just looking at statistical significance. British statistican M. J. Maroney (1951: 218) has spoken eloquently to the point:

When we get a result which is very unlikely to have arisen by chance we say that the result is *statistically significant.* By this we mean simply that it would be rather fantastic to ascribe it to chance, and that the difference must, in all common sense, be accepted as a real difference.

What practical points arise out of all this? In the first place there can never be any question, in practice, of making a decision *purely* on the basis of a statistical significance test. Practical considerations must always be paramount. We must never lose sight of commonsense and all those other relevant factors which cannot possibly be taken care of statistically. An engineer doing a statistical test must remain an engineer, an economist must remain an economist, a pharmacologist must remain a pharmacologist. Practical statistics is only one tool among many.

COSTS AND BENEFITS OF PROPOSED PROGRAM CHANGES

From time to time it has been suggested that Congress, before passing new legislation, should carefully study, document, and make public the costs and benefits associated with that new legislation. In similar fashion I am suggesting that, when making recommendations, particularly major recommendations involving substantial changes in program operations or policies, evaluators should study, specify, and include in their reports some consideration of the benefits and costs of making the suggested changes, including the costs and risks of *not* making the suggested changes.

The importance of non-statistical considerations will be apparent if we consider a hypothetical case. Suppose I did a fancy bit of research and found that my new process gave results which were highly significant, $p = .001$, i.e., there was only one chance in a thousand of the result arising by chance. I am naturally very pleased. But there are a lot of matters to be considered before I should be justified in putting the new process forward to replace the standard process. Firstly, the high statistical significance relates only to the *reality* of the difference between my process and the standard. Now a very real difference may yet be very small. Atoms are no less real because they are invisible to the unaided eye. I should have to show not only that my process is statistically significant, but also that the difference is of practical importance in magnitude. How great the difference will have to be in this respect will depend on how costly and how disturbing a changeover in process will be.

There is a lot of bunk talked about large companies suppressing the practical use of new developments and inventions. It would be possible only in a lunatic asylum for every invention to be put straight into production just because it proved a little better than what was already being done. Economically we must wait until the standard process has had its run; that is, until newer methods are so superior that the changeover can be made without punishing the customer with a savage rise in price for an incommensurate improvement in what he buys.

Thus, the choice of significance levels involves taking into account not only our degree of certainty but also the question of economic and practical feasibility. Logically, we have first to establish the reality of the difference, and then to estimate its magnitude and practical importance [Maroney, 1951: 218-219].

One other thing evaluators can check out to help make sure that their recommendations are practical and truly useful is the extent to which the decision makers addressed in the evaluation report actually have some control over the changes recommended for adoption. A major source of frustration for many decision makers is that the recommendations in evaluation reports relate mainly to things over which they have no control. For example, a school desegregation study that focuses virtually all its recommendations on needed changes in housing patterns is not very useful to school officials even though they may agree that housing changes are needed. Is the implication of such a recommendation that the schools can do nothing? Was the implication that anything the school does will be limited to the extent that housing patterns remain unchanged? Or again, are there major changes a school could make to further the aims of desegregation but the evaluator got sidetracked on the issue of housing patterns and never got back to concrete recommendations for the school? Of course, the best way to end up with recommendations that focus on manipulable variables is to make sure that in the conceptualization of the evaluation the focus is on manipulable variables, and that the focus is maintained right on through to the writing of recommendations.

NEGOTIATING THE NATURE OF RECOMMENDATIONS IN ADVANCE

Another safeguard in the evaluation process as well as an additional way of preparing decision makers for the eventual utilization of evaluation information is to negotiate quite clearly and explicitly the contents of the evaluation report early in the evaluation process with particular emphasis on agreeing to the kinds of conclusions that will be made in the evaluation report. By negotiating I mean the active-reactive-adaptive process during which alternatives are considered, strengths and weaknesses of various approaches are assessed, values are clarified, and agreements are reached (including agreement on areas in which disagreement is recognized as appropriate).

An evaluator who is interested in providing recommendations to a program is in a more powerful position if the request for those recommendations comes from the decision makers rather than if the the evaluator has to try to convince the decision makers to allow the inclusion of recommendations in the report. Moreover, the earlier in the evaluation process that clarity can be attained about the nature of the final report, the earlier it is possible for the evaluator to begin focusing on the specific contents of the report and preparing for the actual writing of the report.

(1) In some cases decision makers simply contract for data gathering; the evaluator collects raw data and hands it over to the contracting agency for analysis,

interpretation, and judgment. The only thing being sought, in this case, by an external evaluation contract is the integrity of the data collection itself.

(2) Moving toward increased complexity, the next level is the report that provides a basic analysis of the data, i.e., a statement of evaluation findings without any interpretation, judgment, or recommendations. In this case the decision makers have contracted for data collection and data analysis, but reserve the right of interpretation and judgment to themselves.

(3) The next level of complexity involves a report that presents findings and either interpretations or judgments, or both. In this report the evaluator is asked to discuss the meaning of the findings and to apply some criteria that allow judgment, but the report stops short of making actual recommendations. The evaluator discusses what the data mean; the decision makers decide what actions follow from the data and/or what judgments to make.

(4) The highest level of complexity is the report that includes all of the previous elements plus recommendations. In this case the evaluator is asked to take the final step and apply his or her judgment, experience, insight, and knowledge in laying out possible paths of action.

These four options make it clear that the evaluator ought not automatically assume that every evaluation report includes a section on recommendations. Rather, by raising this issue with decision makers early in the process, the evaluator helps clarify the nature of the evaluator's role and the precise expectations of the decision makers. In almost every evaluation in which I have been involved the decision makers encouraged and welcomed recommendations. By raising the question, however, I was then able to begin my discussion of recommendations by pointing out that these recommendations were being written at the direct request of the participants in the evaluation task force, and that they had been involved in generating the recommendations. In those cases in which the decision makers decided they did not want recommendations in the final report they indicated that they wanted to talk with me privately about my insights but that the written report should focus only on evaluation findings. In each such case political factors made it necessary for the decision makers to proceed cautiously throughout the evaluation process.

SENSITIVE ISSUES

In negotiating with decision makers about how the evaluator is going to handle the information collected and analyzed in the study it can also be helpful to clarify procedures for handling particularly delicate or sensitive information to which the evaluator may become privy unexpectedly. In the process of talking with program staff, clients, funders, or community people, in examining program records, or in just observing the program in operation, information may surface that is well outside the scope of the evaluation focus but is of sufficiently important consequence that it cannot be ignored. Examples of such information from my own experience include evidence of program fraud, gross incompetence, illegal staff activities, illegal client activities, sexual harassment of clients by staff, institutional racism, and unethical political activities. In none of these cases were we looking for this kind of information. In each of these cases we were faced with a difficult dilemma about what to do with the information we had happened upon. Should we reveal the information immediately, and if so, to whom? Should we investigate further before talking to anyone? Should we wait and see what happened before we became involved? Should we go public with the information if the people to whom we reported decided not to do anything with it?

Since social scientists have no immunity from prosecution once they have become aware of information that has legal implications, these questions involve not only ethical issues but fundamental legal issues. There is no way of anticipating in advance exactly what kind of information may surface, but it is well to give some thought to a contingency plan so that when these kinds of problems do arise the evaluator is able to act fairly quickly and with integrity. These problems are mentioned here in the discussion of recommendations only because such information usually has direct and immediate consequences for the program and becomes one element in the overall feedback chain between evaluators and decision makers. Thus it is important not only to reach agreement about what information and judgments will be provided by the evaluator but also to reach agreement on what kind of information will *not* be divulged by the evaluator, what information will remain confidential, and what criteria are to be applied in making judgments about information to be revealed and information to be withheld. One's entire credibility and integrity may be at stake in these issues.

WALK A MILE IN MY SHOES

So far we have been talking entirely about the conceptual substance of recommendations. It is worth saying a few words about the actual language to use in writing recommendations. Important recommendations can be lost in vague and obtuse language. Powerful recommendations can be diluted by an overly meek style, while particularly sensitive recommendations may be dismissed by an overly assertive style. In trying to find the right tone and style for writing recommendations I suggest role playing along the lines of the song lyric "Walk a Mile in My Shoes." Ask yourself the questions, "If I were in their place with their responsibilities, their political liabilities, their personal perspectives, how would I react to this recommendation stated in this way? What arguments would I raise to counter the recommendations? What word would turn me off or turn me on? What words would tend to confuse me or distract me from the central message?"

In a collaborative evaluation process, one doesn't have to guess at these things. The nature of the evaluation report is the subject of direct negotiations with decision makers and information users. During the course of working with task force members, the evaluator has an opportunity to observe directly the language used by participants, their concerns, their interests, and their biases. It is on this empirical basis that the evaluator walks a mile in the shoes of information users.

The actual job of writing an evaluation report will usually fall to the evaluator. Here, again, it is important to stay focused on the needs of users. An article by Ken Jackson (1973) challenges the assumption that all evaluation reports should be carefully written, logically sequenced research monographs. Such reports follow the evaluator's training but may not communicate effectively with evaluation users. Jackson calls on evaluators to study the ways in which decision makers receive information. Does the client for the evaluation want an outline only? a full research monograph? an oral presentation? a visually oriented presentation? a lengthy report? a short report? a beautifully bound report? a looseleaf notebook report that connotes something to be added to and changed over time? Which of these alternatives are used can make a big difference in how a report is received, used, and disseminated.

Just as there is variation in how an overall report is prepared, there is variation in how recommendations are written. Formats should be meaningful to the people who will read and use the recommendations. There is no single right way of writing recommendations. Much of what I suggested about writing goals (see Chapter 4) I would also adhere to in writing recommendations. Each recommendation should be a singular statement so that it does not get confused unnecessarily with other recommendations and so that it can be accepted or rejected in its own right and not just in combination with another recommendation (although it is certainly appropriate to point out connections between recommendations). It should be possible to tell exactly what is being called for in the recommendation; some clear change should be specified in the content of the recommendation. The language should be as clear and straightforward as possible to communicate the idea effectively; jargon that would be known to only a few people should be avoided. The statement should reflect the amount of importance the evaluator attaches to it and the degree of confidence the evaluator has in the recommendation.

Lack of clarity about just what a recommendation means is a common complaint among evaluation report readers. Given the difficulties evaluators seem to have, in many cases, in coming up with meaningful recommendations, S. A. Goudsmit (1977) suggests that obscurity may be quite functional:

> But there is still another reason for writing an obscure paper. It is the common subconscious fear of exposing oneself to scrutiny. If a paper is too clear, it might be too easy for readers to see through it and discover its weaknesses. We observe this same behavior with the lecturer who writes a formula on the blackboard and erases it almost immediately. We see it with speakers who address the blackboard instead of the audience and who keep the room dark between slides. They themselves do not realize that they are subconsciously afraid of being clearly understood.

One important reason for involving decision makers and information users in face-to-face discussions of findings and recommendations is to make sure that there are shared understandings about what is meant. Clarity is essential. Obscurity may appear to protect the evaluator from political conflicts, but obscurity itself can become a political issue. Moreover, when an evaluator is less than crystal clear about what is being recommended, it is easy for recommendations to be distorted, abused, and misused.

The foundation on which all these specific ideas rests is that the writing of recommendations is a strategic undertaking. Recommendations are intended to bring about action. At the point at which one becomes involved in writing recommendations for action, one has become a change agent. This strategic role involves calculating how to bring about the desired changes. Sometimes a lot of background work is needed. Sometimes a flanking maneuver works best. Often diplomacy is essential. Sometimes you agree to delete certain sections in order to strengthen other sections.

Putting words on paper is a serious matter. This section concludes with a reminder of the responsibility one assumes in writing recommendations and an evaluation report.

> Writing is an audacious and insolent act. When we write, we call the other members of our tribe to order. We command their attention. We assert that what we have to say is valuable enough that they should give over their idle chitchat about the weather. It had better be [Mitchell, 1979: 43].

SURPRISE FINDINGS

On occasion the element of surprise can be effective. I used this tactic only once, but in this particular case the effect was superb. I was chairing an external team of three evaluators who were doing one of those quick, one-day site visits to a university program. The program was an innovative effort housed within a major, traditional department. It immediately became clear that the traditional faculty and the program staff in the innovative project were at each others' throats. They weren't speaking to each other; they expressed open disdain for each other; they steered students away from each other's programs; in short, they did everything in their power to tear down what the other was trying to build. Two of the members of the evaluation team worked diligently with the two factions to try to find some areas of compromise or to identify points at which communication could begin to be enhanced. Both were skilled group facilitators. Both said that they had never run into such a complete breakdown of communications and such absolute narrowmindedness about the issues involved. However, in interviews with key people throughout the day it became clear that what they expected from our team were some recommendations about how they could get these two groups together and foster communications between them.

When our evaluation team met at the end of the day, before providing feedback to the program staff and department members as well as to some key administrative figures, we could locate no points of leverage at which we felt meaningful communications could be established. We decided what they really needed was to be hit over the head with just how bad the situation really was. We needed somehow to get them to pay attention to just how far things had deteriorated. We decided on a strategy of surprise. Since we knew what they were expecting us to say and recommend, we decided to say and recommend just the opposite.

Late in the day when the program staff, department members, and administrative representatives assembled to hear our report, I began with a series of relatively minor and straighforward recommendations concerning program structure and content. None of these recommendations was particularly controversial and we had already discussed most of them with the key actors before the formal session. At the end of those recommendations, I paused and said the following,

> It has also come to our attention, being unusually astute evaluators, that there are some minor tones of disharmony in the department concerning the program. Indeed, in talking with you we have found generous portions of unprofessional conduct, petty bickering, backbiting, backstabbing, and other modest indicators of mutual disdain and disrespect. Having found that a considerable amount of our time has been taken up in dealing with this issue, we have deliberated on it quite carefully. We therefore recommend that for the next year the participants in the opposing factions have absolutely *no* contact with each other; that it be formally and publicly made clear that none of them are to discuss the others' programs; that administrative decision making processes will be immediately implemented such that no participant in one program will have any decision making power over the other program; and that no attempts be made to foster communications of any kind between the two groups. Rather, we recommend that each group pour all of its energies into strengthening its own program and ignore the existence of the competition.

The silence following that recommendation was of the proverbial deafening variety. This was followed by a most heated reaction from a usually quite cool senior university official who questioned the ethics of our making such a recommendation. The objects of the recommendations said nothing, but at the end of the session the leaders of the respective factions were seen to be having a friendly conversation, by all reports the first one they had had in some time, agreeing with each other about how interesting the evaluation had been. Subsequent reports indicated that by removing all the pressure for forced cooperation, members of the warring groups were able to find casual and appropriate times for interaction that began to build some bridges and establish some communication linkages.

I was reminded in this situation of the well-known Sufi story of Mulla Nasrudin trying to get his stubborn donkey to move along the road. A friend happened along and saw that the Mulla was hitting the donkey over the head with a thick board. The friend asked what was going on and Nasrudin explained that he was trying to get his donkey to move forward, but the stubborn creature had resisted all of his appeals. The friend asked why, if he wanted the donkey to move forward, he was hitting him over the head instead of hitting him in the rear. Nasrudin explained that it was his intention, feeling basically humane toward the lower creatures, to stand there in the road and have a perfectly reasonable and reasoned conversation with the donkey about their mutual interests in moving forward. First, however, he had to get the donkey's attention. That's why he was hitting him over the head.

Writing recommendations is a strategic and creative process. It is the culmination of the evaluation effort. The recommendations represent the most visible linkage between the data and subsequent utilization of the evaluation findings. As Halcolm put it:

> The purpose of evaluation research is not just truth and knowledge, but action and decision.

Recommendations are the mechanism for moving from knowledge and truth to action and decision.

INVOLVING DECISION MAKERS IN GENERATING RECOMMENDATIONS

One of the key principles of utilization-focused evaluation is that the evaluator should involve people who have primary responsibility for using evaluative information in the process of focusing evaluation questions, making methods decisions, and interpreting the data. These people should also play a major role in generating recommendations based on evaluation findings. There are two basic reasons for this strategy. First, involving key decision makers, information users, and stakeholders in moving from findings to recommendations is a way of safeguarding against the evaluator getting carried away or overly imposing personal values at the point of making concrete recommendations. Second, by involving the people who actually have to act on the recommendations, their commitment to following through on those recommendations is enhanced from the very beginning. It is a hollow victory, indeed, for an evaluator to write a sterling set of recommendations that is ignored by the people with the power to implement it. The psychological and human relations basis for this strategy is rather straightforward: People are more willing to believe in and act on ideas they come up with themselves than ideas handed to them or forced on them by others.

In working with an evaluation task force, the evaluator will often have to help participants get into the spirit of data interpretation and the process of generating recommendations. This will involve taking risks and stimulating participant creativity (Patton, 1981). Jerome Bruner described the process this way:

> The schrewd guess, the fertile hypothesis, the courageous leap to a tentative conclusion—these are the most valuable coin of the thinker at work. But in most schools guessing is heavily penalized and is associated somehow with laziness.

To facilitate meaningful participation in the data interpretation process, the evaluator must communicate a genuine openess to the ideas and insights of others. This is a manifestation of the evaluator's confidence and professionalism. A powerful illustration of this kind of professionalism is provided by Don Schula, coach of the Miami Dolphins football team. The following story was told by John Keasler, a writer for the Miami *News*.

Keasler was assigned to cover the 1973 Super Bowl between the Miami Dolphins and the Washington Redskins. He was not a sports writer. His assignment was to provide "color commentary," a view from a nonsportswriter, professional journalist. His most memorable recollection of that assignment came on the plane to California.

> We had just boarded the plane in Miami for the trip out.
>
> In the crowded aisle, I found myself crammed face-to-face with Shula, who was already talking to five people at once.
>
> At this point, Crittenden, the sports editor, never at a loss for a gag, elbowed his way to where we were standing and said solemnly to Shula: "Coach, I want you to meet a friend of mine—he's got some suggestions on how you can win the Super Bowl."
>
> My jaw dropped, even as Don Shula instantaneously stopped his other conversations, looked directly at me—a stranger obviously not of the football world—and with absolute sincerity asked me:
>
> "Yeah? What are your ideas?"
>
> My only answer, of course, was duhhhhhhhh. Shula grinned, when he saw it was a gag, and moved on . . . but for that second, by damn, he had meant it and I knew it.
>
> When you can be the very best at what you do and still be totally open to ideas from a stranger, *that's* being a pro. It is not something you forget [Keasler, 1982: 1C].

Being open to the ideas of evaluation task force participants does not mean that the evaluator has to be completely limited to what emerges from the group process. It is entirely appropriate for the evaluator to share insights and make suggestions that go beyond those that emerge from the evaluation task force. Sometimes such suggestions may be made formally; and other times these suggestions may appear as formal recommendations in written report. The point is not to limit the evaluator to those recommendations that emerge from the group process, but rather to make the group process the beginning point and the focal point for generating recommendations with the clear knowledge that the recommendations that emerge from that process have a higher probability of acceptance and implementation than those put forth by the evaluator alone.

HALCOLM'S RIDDLE OF THE SPHINX

A young man came to Halcolm to complete his studies. In his audience with the great sage he explained that he had mastered all the many methods of collecting evaluation data. He felt no further needs there. He also knew the many ways of arranging and analyzing the data he collected. His problem was in interpreting and drawing conclusions from evaluation data.

Halcolm called for a piece of paper and a pen. After writing for a few moments he handed the paper to the young man and said, "Return to me when you have completed this assignment."

The young man bowed respectfully and retreated outside, determined to work quickly on his assignment. He opened the paper and read:

Five things is wrong with this statement: how can you drew conclusions if you can't spot errers.

The young man immediately spotted three things that were wrong. The verb form in the first phrase should be "are;" the verb tense in the second phrase should be "draw;" and the final word should be spelled "errors." Correcting these mistakes he was at a loss to find the remaining two errors.

After a restless night's sleep he returned to his task. Just before noon he discovered the fourth error. The phrase following the colon is a question not a statement. The assignment now read:

Five things are wrong with this question: how can you draw conclusions if you can't spot errors?

A week passed with no further progress. The young man despaired of ever finding the fifth error. After another week he returned sheepishly to Halcolm. When he reported his failure the wise teacher again called for paper and pen.

"Because of your great learning in methods and analysis I may have assumed too much and given you too difficult a problem to solve. Try this more simple assignment."

After thanking Halcolm profusely for his great patience and kindness the young man hurried home to work on his new assignment.

There are two errers in this item. Find them both.

The young man quickly corrected the spelling of "errors," but beyond that he could find no second mistake in the item. After four tortured weeks he knew the situation was hopeless so he returned to Halcolm to announce his failure on even this simple exercise.

"You have not failed, my child. You have simply left part of the task undone. You have discovered that you have limitations. Is that not a worthy discovery? And is it not wise to seek assistance from others so that together you can move beyond your separate limitations?

"Your first limitation was a self-imposed assumption that you had to go off in solitude to work on the assignments I have given you. While there is a time for solitary study in drawing conclusions and making interpretations, there is also a time for working with others, particularly others who may know more about the situation than you do. Let us then work together on this assignment.

"How many errors did you find in the first assignment?"

"I found four."

"How many errors did you find in the second assignment?"

"I found only one."

"Why do you feel you have failed when you have discovered so many errors?"

"Because in each case one error remains unknown to me. The first assignment called for the discovery of five errors; the second assignment required discovery of two errors."

"And what is an error?"

"Verb forms that are incorrect; misspelled words; inaccurate information."

"And if you have corrected all the verb forms and spelled words as they should be spelled, then there remains only the matter of inaccurate information."

Suddenly the young man understood the final error in each case. The final error was the number of errors stated in the assignment. For example, in the last assignment the final error is the statement that there are two errors when there is only one. The young man's joy at his discovery was quickly tempered by a feeling of foolishness. "How could I have been so stupid?" he asked more to himself than to Halcolm. "I'll never be able to interpret data wisely if I can't solve simple riddles."

"You have discovered your second limitation—letting your assumptions get in the way of the data. You assumed a narrow definition of 'errors' that kept you from seeing what was really there. The obvious was hidden from you by your determination to make the problem fit *your* definition of the situation."

"Interpretations and conclusions are not things to be forced on data. Interpretations and conclusions reside in the data to be discovered and understood as you open yourself to what is before you. While much of what you discover will be as straightforward as simple spelling and grammatical errors; much more remains to be discovered when you put aside your assumptions and open yourself to what is there, allowing possibilities not yet considered to emerge into obviousness."

"Go now and open yourself to what the world has to teach. There is much to be understood. Know also that despite your most diligent efforts much will elude you. It is the way of the world that it reveals its secrets ever so slowly and in small pieces, so that the impatience of youth can turn in upon itself to emerge again as childlike contentment with the many small wonders opened to us if only we look."

PART IV   *Return to the Mandate*

- *Want to know about resistance to utilization of scientific knowledge? Interview evaluators who (a) smoke, (b) don't use seat belts, (c) overeat, (d) don't exercise regularly, (e) haven't learned how to really relax, and (f) . . .*

- *Evaluation koan: When is a flower also a weed—and vice versa? (Dangerous is the evaluator who hasn't struggled with this question.)*

- *A penny saved is a little bit more to see you through until the next proposal is funded.*

- *Evaluator's Creed: There's never been a perfect program, or an entirely bad evaluation.*

- Says he to she: *"Evaluators make better lovers because they know how to assess their performance to improve it."*
  Says she to he: *"Knowledge is as knowledge does. It's not the knowing, but the doing, that matters in the end."*

From Poor Halcolm's Almanac

CHAPTER 12 *Practical Evaluation*

We must live within the ambiguity of partial freedom,
partial power, and partial knowledge. All important
decisions must be made on the basis of insufficient
data. . . . What do you know . . . for sure . . . anyway?

Sheldon B. Kopp

A practical evaluation is doable and applicable. It is doable in that the design is feasible and can be implemented within the financial, time, and political constraints of a particular situation. It is applicable in that the evaluation findings can be used, i.e., appropriately and relevantly applied, by decision makers and information users. Concern for practicality centers on both evaluation content and evaluation processes. First, the way in which the evaluation is carried out, i.e., the process, should be feasible. Second, the findings, i.e., the content, should be usable and useful. These are simple and straightforward ideals, but as the previous chapters have demonstrated, achieving these ideals is not always so simple and straightforward. The starting point, at least, is a determination to work at conducting practical, utilization-focused evaluations.

This book has discussed a variety of practical evaluation issues from initial project conceptualization and task force formation to analyzing data and making recommendations. The topics discussed included models and methods, communications clarity and consultative collaboration, managing information systems and managing a task force, evaluations with and without goals, using qualitative and quantitative approaches, questionnaires and interviews, and practical creativity, or, if you prefer, creative practicality. While the topics and issues have ranged the spectrum of evaluation concerns, a few basic themes recur throughout the preceding chapters. Those themes, taken together, constitute much of the overarching framework of practical evaluation. This final chapter reviews briefly these themes: (1) taking the professional standards seriously, (2) being grounded in fundamentals, (3) situational responsiveness, (4) actively involving decision makers and information users in evaluation processes, (5) multiple evaluator roles and responsibilities, and (6) individual style.

TAKING THE PROFESSIONAL STANDARDS SERIOUSLY

An important sign of the coming of age of a profession is the development of professional standards of practice. Evaluation now has such a set of standards indicating what constitutes excellence and acceptable behavior. The first chapter discussed the nature, origin, and importance of the standards. Before about 1975, the premises and standards of evaluation research could scarcely be differentiated from those of basic researchers in the traditional social and behavioral sciences. Technical quality and methodological rigor were not only primary, but were about all that counted. The emergent standards of evaluation research broadened the responsibilities of social and behavioral scientists engaged in the professional practice of evaluation. The new standards focus on four criteria: utility, feasibility, propriety, and accuracy. These are our standards of excellence.

Taking the standards seriously means consciously and deliberately integrating attention to the standards into each evaluation one conducts. Taking the standards seriously means that, as an evaluator, one is part of a profession, and one is accountable to one's professional colleagues to uphold professional standards of excellence. The corollary to this professional accountability is that decision makers and information users have a right to expect evaluators with whom they contract to uphold professional standards in the conduct of their work. Taking the standards seriously means translating them from abstract values into concrete patterns of practice. The point here is that the standards have real, practical implications for how an evaluation is conducted.

The utility and feasibility criteria have received the most attention in this book, partly because they represent the greatest departure from traditional scientific standards, partly because the standards of propriety and accuracy have been dealt with to a greater extent in other evaluation texts, and partly because utility and feasibility are the highest priorities in utilization-focused evaluation specifically, and in the new standards generally. Dan Stufflebeam, chair of the Evaluation Standards Committee, has reported that in the committee's deliberations the standards were ranked in order of importance as follows: utility, feasibility, propriety, and accuracy.

> Their rationale is that an evaluation should not be done at all if there is no prospect for its being useful to some audience. Second, it should not be done if it is not feasible to conduct it in political terms, or practicality terms, or cost-effectiveness terms. Third, they do not think it should be done if we cannot demonstrate that it will be conducted fairly and ethically. Finally, if we can demonstrate that an evaluation will have utility, will be feasible and will be proper in its conduct then they said we could turn to the difficult matters of the technical adequacy of the evaluation [Stufflebeam, 1980: 90].

In line with the logic reported by Stufflebeam in this quotation, a basic premise throughout this book has been that evaluations should be first and foremost utilization focused, i.e., that the driving force in an evaluation should be a concern for how decision makers and information users will use evaluation findings and processes. But how can a concern for utility be ranked above a concern for accuracy? Can inaccurate data be useful?

A concern for utility includes concern about misutilization and data abuses. Decisions made with bad (inaccurate) data may be bad decisions. On the other hand, participants in an evaluation process can learn a tremendous amount just by having gone through an assessment process, and still end up with findings that, for a variety of reasons, are not as accurate as had been hoped. The utility criterion includes the possibility that an evaluation can be worth doing because it helps people conceptualize things in a new way; it helps them find out what they don't know; it lets them find out what is feasible in evaluation; it makes them more sophisticated about the complexities of program development and human service delivery; it helps them identify manipulable variables for future study; it encourages staff to look more carefully at what they're doing; it gets clients involved in program decision making; and on and on and on. There are a variety of ways in which an evaluation process can be useful quite apart from the nature, content, or accuracy of findings. The primacy of the utility criterion calls attention to the complexity of utilization, the multidimensionality of usefulness, and the obligation incumbent on evaluators to examine the full context within which an evaluation process occurs to find out how the process *and* the findings will be used.

This concern for the primacy of the utility criterion is reflected in every chapter of this book. In the second chapter of definitions, models, and types of evaluation, the emphasis was on being flexible and adaptive with regard to conceptual issues so as to be able to respond to decision makers' concerns and interests, thereby enhancing the likelihood that an evaluation would be relevant to and understandable by stakeholders, and thereby increasing the potential for and likelihood of utilization. The subsequent chapters on goals, questionnaires, interviewing, alternative methods, creative data collection approaches, data analysis, and recommendations point to the implications of making a concern for utilization the driving force in an evaluation.

The other standards—feasibility, propriety, and accuracy—take on added meaning and importance when viewed in terms of how they contribute to utilization. Feasible designs enhance utilization by being cost effective, politically viable, and capable of completion in accordance with stakeholder expectations. Attention to the criterion of propriety helps safeguard the integrity of an evaluation without which decision makers will stay at arm's length, lest they be tainted themselves by charges of impropriety, e.g., failure to respect the rights of program clients. The standards aimed at assuring accuracy speak to the importance of scientific rigor in guaranteeing that evaluation findings are worthy of use. Taken together, the standards express a commitment to fulfilling the promise of evaluation, namely, providing high-quality information for use in improving and making decisions about programs.

Taking the standards seriously means using them to guide practice, not just talking about them. Taking the standards seriously means being a truly professional evaluator—a "pro," someone who knows what needs doing and how to do it. Taking the standards seriously means being grounded in the fundamentals of evaluation practice, a second theme of practical evaluation.

BEING GROUNDED IN FUNDAMENTALS

This book grew out of my observation that the usefulness of many evaluations is undercut by weaknesses in fundamentals. Throughout this book I have commented on the importance of mastering and applying simple fundamentals in evaluation practice. At the risk of sounding harsh and arrogant, or of being perceived as overly critical and deprecatory of my colleagues, let me share some of the experiences that have given rise to my concern about evaluation fundamentals by way of illustrating what I mean by fundamentals, and thus recalling the reason this book has focused on the kind of material presented in previous chapters.

I have worked on evaluations with well-trained sociologists who were wizards at regression analysis and multivariate statistics but didn't know how to arrange frequency distributions from a questionnaire so that nonscientists, people with no more than a high school diploma, could understand and interpret the data. Communicating clearly with nonscientists is an evaluation fundamental. I've worked with psychologists who didn't know the difference between a clinical interview for counseling purposes and a qualitative interview for evaluation purposes. As a result, they tended to do in their evaluation work what they did in their counseling—lead respondents to insights perceived by the psychologist to be important rather than provide respondents with truly open-ended questions that would elicit the genuine insights of the people being interviewed. Genuinely open-ended interviewing is an evaluation fundamental. I've worked with economists who could decipher the composition and interrelationships among five different marginal utility estimates to make cost/benefit predictions under different assumptions, but who couldn't decipher the composition and interrelationships in a five-person evaluation task force to predict and handle utilization constraints and concerns. Being able to analyze group dynamics and facilitate group decision making are evaluation fundamentals. I've worked with educators who could talk at ease about recommendations they had for improving the nation's schools, but were unable to generate a single, meaningful recommendation from a specific school evaluation data set. Generating meaningful, data-based recommendations is an evaluation fundamental. I've worked with anthropologists who were skilled observers of program settings, but were completely intimidated by program documentation stored in management information systems. Making sense of management information systems is an evaluation fundamental.

The point of these observations is this: *The effective practice of evaluation requires fundamental skills that are different from those of any single social or behavioral science and broader than the basic scientific skills of academic scholarship. Just as the new standards of evaluation are different from the traditional standards of the academic disciplines, so too the professional skills needed by practicing evaluators (at least those who take the new standards seriously) are different from the scholarly skills of basic sciences.*

This book covers what I consider to be some of the fundamental skills required to conduct practical, utilization-focused evaluations. I've concentrated on simple, straightforward basics, the mastery of which will provide a foundation for competent professional practice and ongoing professional growth, particularly growth in confidence and flexibility so that one can develop and apply creative variations and adaptations of these fundamental approaches in response to the demands, needs, and constraints of new situations. Such situational responsiveness has been another major theme of this book.

SITUATIONAL RESPONSIVENESS

Judgments about the relative practicality of a particular evaluation process or evaluation finding can only be made with reference to a particular situation involving specific people, a specific program, and specific constraints. The standards of evaluation are not absolute behavioral guidelines. They require adaptation and interpretation in the context of specific circumstances and constraints.

The new standards recognize that there is no one best way to conduct evaluations routinely. Every evaluation situation is unique. A successful evaluation, i.e., one that is useful, practical, ethical, and accurate, emerges from the special characteristics and conditions of a particular situation—a mixture of people, politics, history, context, resources, constraints, values, needs, interest, and chance. This constitutes a major shift in perspective from evaluation judged by a single, standard, and universal set of criteria (methodological rigor as defined by the hypothetico-deductive paradigm) to situational evaluation in which judgment criteria are multiple, flexible, and diverse.

Finding useful and feasible solutions to complex and situation-specific problems is the epitome of the evaluation challenge. It's relatively easy to generate a great deal of information with sophisticated evaluations made possible by fairly ample resources. It's also relatively easy to design an extremely simple evaluation with very limited resources, one that generates a certain minimum amount of acceptable information. What is more difficult is to generate a great deal of information with relatively scarce resources. The latter challenge seems also to be the most typical, and the one requiring the most creative situational responsiveness. Far from being mundane, mechanical, and simple, the conceptualization and implementation of practical evaluations challenge the evaluator to produce useful information under typically severe constraints of limited time, limited finances, limited knowledge, and seemingly unlimited politics. The elegance of practical solutions often disguises the creative work, skilled diplomacy, and disciplined talent contained therein.

To decide what is "practical" in a particular situation, some hard judgments have to be made. To make these judgments you have to know your decision makers and information users, know yourself, and, where applicable, know your staff. Let's take each of these in turn.

To decide what is practical from the point of view of stakeholders some of the following kinds of questions are important: What do they want the evaluation to do, and what do they want to do with the evaluation? How much do they care? What are their motivations, vested interests, and power bases? What will frighten them? What will entice them? How much time will they devote to the evaluation process? How supportive, or resistant, will they be? How knowledgeable are they about evaluation? About the program being evaluated? About themselves? What risks are involved for them? What potential benefits? Answers to these kinds of questions help determine what is practical and useful from the point of view of decision makers and information users.

Then there are the questions one must ask oneself, as an evaluator: How much do I care about this evaluation? What do I want out of it? How hard am I willing to work on it? How do I want to be compensated? What personal and professional goals will be furthered by doing this evaluation? How do I feel about the people with whom I'll be working, the decision makers, program staff, colleagues? What roles do I want to take? What expectations do I have for myself? How much effort am I willing to put into this evaluation?

A similar assessment can be made of the evaluation staff on a project. How hard are they willing to work? What special incentives are there for staff? What are the risks for staff? What skills will they bring to the evaluation? What training will be needed? What are the opportunities for personal and professional growth?

Most of these questions involve some degree of psychological assessment concerning motivations, incentives, expectations, and benefits. These psychological assessments are made at the same time that one is thinking about such concrete and traditional constraints as time, money, methods, and contractual arrangements. The psychological context for the evaluation can be the most important factor in determining what is practical and useful in a particular situation. Napoleon is reported to have said, "In warfare, the psychological is to the material as three to one." I suspect the ratio is at least that high in evaluation. That's why there can be no absolute definition of what is practical. As Halcolm said at the end of the first chapter: *You can do what you can do.*

In deciding what can be done in a particular situation, some creative evaluation thinking can go a long way toward opening up new practical possibilities. Situational responsiveness is the challenge to which creative evaluation thinking is the response. Situational responsiveness is a challenge because the evidence from behavioral science is that in most areas of decision making and judgment, when faced with complex choices and multiple possibilities, we fall back on a set of deeply embedded rules and standard operating procedures that predetermine what we do, thereby effectively shortcircuiting situational adaptability. This may help explain why so many evaluators who have genuinely embraced the ideology of situational evaluation find that the approaches in which they are trained and with which they are most comfortable *just happen* to be particularly appropriate in each new evaluation they confront—time after time.

The first chapter referenced research findings from studies of human heuristics that support this claim that most of the time evaluators, and the decision makers with whom they work, are running—and thinking—according to preprogrammed tapes. It turns out that most of the time, in order to make even trivial decisions, we rely on routine heuristics, rules of thumb, standard operating procedures, tricks of the trade, and scientific paradigms with their prescriptions about how to proceed. The seventh chapter on thoughtful methods decisions focused specifically on the problem of being situationally responsive in the face of the limitations imposed by operating within the framework of a single paradigm.

A major difficulty posed by the human reliance on paradigms and heuristics for problem solving and decision making is not just their existence, but our general lack of awareness of their existence. Autonomic thinking systems and conditioned reflexes are barriers to creative evaluation thinking. It is difficult to be attuned and responsive to the uniqueness of each new situation when our programmed heuristics and paradigms are controlling the analytical process, screening unfamiliar data, anchoring the new situation within the narrow parameters of our past experiences, and making available to us primarily those definitions and approaches we've used most often in the past. Yet there is also evidence that, while it is neither easy nor usual, it is possible to become aware of our paradigms and heuristics and in that awareness take control of our decision processes, thereby releasing our creative potential and enhancing our ability to be truly situationally responsive and adaptive. This book has been aimed at increasing heuristic awareness and enhancing the potential for practical, utilization-focused, and situationally responsive evaluation by grounding evaluation practice in fundamentals, focusing attention on the practical implications of the new standards and actively involving decision makers and information users in the evaluation process.

ACTIVELY INVOLVING STAKEHOLDERS
IN THE EVALUATION PROCESS

The stakeholder assumption is the idea that key people who have a stake in an evaluation should be actively and meaningfully involved in shaping that evaluation so as to focus the evaluation on meaningful and appropriate issues, thereby enhancing the likelihood of utilization. The consultative evaluation approach described in Chapter 3 is based on the stakeholder assumption. The stakeholder assumption includes the expectation that stakeholders need to expend time and effort to figure out what is worth doing in an evaluation; they need help in focusing on worthwhile questions; and they need to experience the full evaluation process if that process, which is really a learning process, is to realize its potential, multilayered effects. The practical view of utilization-focused evaluation offered throughout these pages broadens the notion of evaluation impact to include use of the entire evaluation process as a stakeholder learning experience, not just use of the findings in a report. However, Chapter 3 also noted that the extent to which utilization is enhanced by a group process depends on (1) who participates in that process and (2) the questions dealt with by the group, i.e., the focus and quality of the process, thus the importance of group facilitation skills. In facilitating the work of an evaluation task force, the evaluator invites participants in the process to enter into the *culture of science,* and, in so doing, to adopt an *empirical* perspective with regard to the program(s) under study. One of the primary responsibilities of the evaluator in a task force is to keep the focus on the empirical nature of evaluation work. That empirical focus, in the context of the culture of science, is the key to the integrity of the group process—and the integrity of the evaluation. It is also important to keep in mind that it is not the amount of time working with people that makes for an effective consulting process, though some commitment of time is clearly necessary; it's the *quality* of time spent working together that matters the most.

A basic premise of this book has been that situationally responsive and active-reactive-adaptive evaluators will find opportunities in virtually any evaluation to train decision makers, funders, information users, staff, and stakeholders of all kinds in the basics of evaluation. Training is not something to be restricted to traditional classroom settings. When working with a group of people in an evaluation process the situation can be defined as partly a training exercise aimed at empowering participants to assert greater control over program implementation and outcomes through their increased knowledge about understanding of both program and evaluation processes. When a program evaluation is defined as a learning opportunity for participants—learning about program evaluation as well as learning about the program being evaluated—the evaluator is helping build an increasingly sophisticated group of consumers able to better use information for program improvement. My premise has been that all effective evaluators are trainers, and as trainers, all evaluators can enhance their professional practice by actively involving decision makers and information users in all stages of the evaluation process. Thus a recurring theme in every chapter from conceptual issues through data collection to data analysis and generating recommendations has been the importance of and ways to involve stakeholders, thereby increasing their understanding of the evaluation and their commitment to use evaluation findings. This perspective is nicely summarized and supported by recent research on the factors related to what messages people remember and act on:

> When the recipient [of a message] is required to participate in forming the message, even if it is only to fill in implicit premises, the chances of perceiving the message as important and the chances of remembering it would seem to be greatly improved [Knapp et al., 1981: 32].

Actively involving decision makers and information users in an evaluation process is a way of having them participate in forming the evaluation message so as to increase the chances that they will perceive the message of the evaluation as important—and remember the message as they go about their program-related activities.

MULTIPLE EVALUATOR ROLES AND RESPONSIBILITIES

Another theme that runs throughout this book is the diversity inherent in the role of the practical, utilization-focused evaluator. Evaluators are called on to be scientists, program consultants, group facilitators, keen observers, statisticians, project administrators, diplomats, politicians, writers, and trainers. In order to be truly situationally responsive, the evaluator needs to be able to draw on a large repertoire of techniques, approaches, models, and methods. The image of the professional evaluator that I hope has emerged in these pages is of a flexible, adaptable generalist. Since graduate schools are designed to produce subject matter and methods specialists, it is not easy to become a generalist—a person able to use a variety of methods and approaches. Kipling advised us to "love all men, but none too much." The evaluation corollary is to love all methods and models, but none too much.

A Sufi story tells of a musician who sat in the town plaza every day strumming over and over the same string on his lute. Whenever one of the townspeople would ask why he played only one string, he responded that he was a specialist, and he did not intend to take up the study of another string until he completely mastered his first specialty. I am reminded of this story when evaluators explain to me that they're satisfied doing only one type of evaluation in which they feel confident and well trained. Specialists are not renowned for their situational adaptability, except for their skill in adapting situations to fit their specialty. Practical evaluators who take seriously the charge to adapt themselves and their methods to the needs of specific situations and decision makers may find that they can make good use of specialists, thereby securing the depth that they may need in a particular instance, without becoming a specialist.

The new standards, it seems to me, imply the importance of being able to play multiple roles and take on multiple responsibilities. The traditional standards of "value-free" social science held that the scientist's only responsibility was to produce accurate information and new knowledge. How that information and knowledge might be used was not the scientist's concern. Nor does the history of science show much concern, until recently, for the rights of research subjects. In the search for truth, research subjects were objects of study, not objects of respect. Today, the evaluator is called on to take responsibility for how evaluative information is used, to take responsibility for the correct implementation of evaluation procedures, to be responsible for the protection of human subjects in evaluation research, as well as the traditional responsibility to produce accurate information.

The eminent humanistic psychologist Carl Rogers uses a metaphor with his students that dramatically captures this change in responsibilities. In the past scientists have been like ammunition wagons, loaded with powerful knowledge just waiting to be used, and available to either the good guys or the bad guys. Now, applied social scientists, particularly evaluators, are called on to target their knowledge and take responsibility for what they "hit." Rogers (1961) puts it quite forcefully:

Don't be a damn ammunition wagon. Be a rifle.

At the heart of the multiple roles the creative evaluator plays is the role of communications facilitator. Whether acting as an information broker, a data manager, a storyteller, an artist, a humorist, or a scientist, the evaluator is facilitating communications. Helping people communicate about their information needs, helping them interpret data, helping them translate data into decisions and program improvements, and helping them develop realistic goals for both programs and evaluation of programs—these are processes that involve skilled communications facilitation. Skillful communications and information brokering require a keen sensitivity to the needs and interests of those with whom one is working—and a keen awareness of self. The final piece needed to complete the picture of the practical evaluator is recognition that the evaluator, as a unique person, is part of that whole that is the evaluation situation. A wholistic approach to practical, utilization-focused evaluation includes attention to and awareness of the ways in which each evaluator's individual style contributes to the situational definition of what is useful and practical.

INDIVIDUAL STYLE

A major theme of *Creative Evaluation* (Patton, 1981) was that creative evaluation requires creative evaluators. Likewise, practical evaluation requires practical evaluators. Creativity and practicality both, in the end, have their locus in individuals. Practical, utilization-focused evaluations don't just happen. The process has to be facilitated by a practical, utilization-focused evaluator. That's where individual style comes in—and comes in with a vengeance. You'll find no discussion of evaluator-proof techniques in these pages.

Just as evaluation situations and program decision makers are unique, thus establishing the importance of situational responsiveness and user-focused evaluation, so too, are individual evaluators unique. Evaluators bring to evaluation situations their own styles, personal histories, and professional experiences. The notion of being active-reactive-adaptive explicitly recognizes the importance of the individual evaluator's contribution by placing the mandate to be "active" first in this consulting trinity: active-reactive-adaptive. Situational responsiveness does not mean rolling over and playing dead (or passive) in the face of decision maker interests or perceived needs. Just as the evaluator in utilization-focused evaluation does not unilaterally impose a focus and set of methods on a program, so too, the decision makers are not being set up to impose unilaterally their initial perceptions on the evaluation. It is a negotiated process that allows the individual style of the evaluator to intermingle with the host of other factors that affect an evaluation, thus giving uniqueness and relevance to the final design and product. All of the techniques and ideas presented in this book are subject to the skill, ability, understanding, and style of the individual using them. It cannot be otherwise. The standards can only provide guidelines and direction. Individual evaluators have the final responsibility for interpreting and implementing the standards. Practical, utilization-focused evaluation requires practical, utilization-focused evaluators.

THE FINAL WORD

This chapter has reviewed six major themes that constitute much of the overarching framework of practical evaluation. The premises presented in the first chapter, the techniques and approaches presented throughout the book, and the themes of this final chapter may not, as one reviewer of the manuscript pointed out, fit together into a cohesive whole. No single book, no single approach, and no one evaluator's limited perspective can aspire to capture the richness, diversity, and complexity of evaluation. The professional practice of evaluation is not a single, whole thing. The field of evaluation encompasses all the higher functions of the human mind: sensory experience, observation, analysis, categorization, comparison, synthesis, interpretation, judgment, problem solving, and decision making, to name but a few. Evaluation embodies our highest aspiration as a species: our desire to make sense of the world, to understand, and, perhaps, even to control it, or at least parts of it for short periods of time. Evaluation does this specifically in the hope of improving the quality of human existence by improving the programs, services, and organizations that so drastically affect the quality of life in modern society. Given these high hopes, the enormity of the challenge, and the complex diversity of actual evaluation practice, what closing thoughts can I leave with the reader who has labored through these pages? I leave the final word to Halcolm.

HALCOLM'S FINAL WORD

The day came, as it always comes, when it was time to leave the security of the retreat and go off into the world. On the appointed day, Halcolm's young apprentices assembled together before the Master's humble abode. They waited all morning, but Halcolm did not appear. At noon, Halcolm's assistant came to the expectant youths.

"Halcolm is not here today," he told them.

"Not here?" they replied in astounded unison. "But it's the day appointed for our departure," said one youth, the hurt obvious in his tone. "Surely the master has some final word of wisdom to focus our reflections during the journey ahead."

"It seems the Master anticipated your desire for some final instruction," replied the assistant. "But it comes in the form of example rather than a final word. The Master is today consulting with the staff of a new program on their statement of goals and evaluation plans. He is out in the world, practicing. He asked me to assure you that you know from him what you need to know. What you lack now is practice, miles and miles of practice, to build your professional practice."

The assistant paused to see if the faces of the students reflected an understanding of Halcolm's gesture. After a moment he continued.

"Soon a new group of apprentices will arrive. Before their arrival, the Master wanted to further hone his goals clarification skills. He commented, as he left, that he is still trying to understand the peculiar role of goals in human endeavors. I can see that many of you are disappointed that he is not here; some of you are hurt, or even angry. I think he felt that the best thing he could give you to take with you is his example . . . , the example of one who is still practicing, still learning, still studying, still growing."

"There is no final word. He cared enough not to be here to see you off, but rather to be where you are going, into the world, practicing your profession, your craft, your art, your science—practicing evaluation. Off with you now, to start your practice, for when you have stopped practicing, you have stopped practicing."

References

Alkin, Marvin C. Wider context goals and goals-based evaluators. *Evaluation Comment,* 1972, 3(4), 10-11.

Alkin, Marvin C., Richard Daillak, and Peter White. *Using evaluations: Does evaluation make a difference?* Beverly Hills, CA: Sage, 1979.

Alkin, Marvin C., and Fred S. Ellett. Evaluation models. *International Encyclopedia of Education: Research and Studies.* New York: Pergamon, forthcoming.

Allison, Graham T. *Essence of Decision.* Boston: Little, Brown, 1971.

Alwin, Duane F. *Survey design and analysis.* Beverly Hills, CA: Sage, 1978.

Anastasi, Anne. Preface. *Assessment in a pluralistic society.* Proceedings of the 1972 Invitational Conference on Testing. Princeton, NJ: Princeton University Press, 1973.

Anderson, Barry F. *The complete thinker.* Englewood Cliffs, NJ: Prentice-Hall, 1980.

Argyris, Chris. *Interpersonal competence and organizational effectiveness.* Homewood, IL: Irwin, 1972.

Argyris, Chris. *Theory in practice: Increasing professional effectiveness.* San Francisco: Jossey-Bass, 1974.

Argyris, Chris. *Increasing leadership effectiveness.* New York: John Wiley, 1976.

Asante, Molefi K., Eileen Newmark, and Cecil Blake (Eds.). *Handbook of intercultural communications.* Beverly Hills, CA: Sage, 1979.

Azumi, Koya, and Jerald Hage (Eds.). *Organizational systems.* Lexington, MA: D. C. Heath, 1972.

Barkdoll, Gerald L. Type III evaluations: Consultation and consensus. *Public Administration Review,* 1980, March/April, 174-179.

Bennis, Warren. *Changing organizations.* New York: McGraw-Hill, 1966.

Bennis, Warren, K. Berne, R. Chen, and K. Corey (Eds.). *The Planning of change.* New York: Holt, Rinehart & Winston, 1976.

Berdie, Doug, and John Anderson. *Questionnaires: Design and use.* Metuchen, NJ: Scarecrow, 1974.

Bernstein, Ilene, and Howard Freeman. *Academic and entrepreneurial research.* New York: Russell Sage, 1975.

Bertcher, Harvey J. *Group participation: Techniques for leaders and members.* Beverly Hills, CA: Sage, 1979.

Blumer, Herbert. *Symbolic interactionism.* Englewood Cliffs, NJ: Prentice-Hall, 1969.

Blundell, William E. The software kid inveighs against the witch doctors. *Wall Street Journal,* July 6, 1981: 12.

Boruch, Robert, and David Cordray. *An appraisal of educational program evaluations: Federal, state, and local agencies, report to the Congress.* Washington, DC: Office of the Assistant Secretary for Management, U.S. Department of Education, 1980.

Boruch, Robert, and David Cordray. *Reactions to the Holtzman report. Educational Researcher,* 1981, 10(10), 10-12.

Boruch, Robert, Cordray, D. S., Pion, G. and Leviton, L. A. A mandated appraisal of evaluation practices: Digest of recommendations to the Congress and the Department of Education. *Educational Researcher,* 1981, 10(4), 10-13, 31.

Braskamp, Larry, and R. D. Brown (Eds.). *Utilization of evaluative information.* San Francisco: Jossey-Bass, 1980.

Campbell, Donald T., and Julian Stanley. *Experimental and quasi-experimental designs for research.* Chicago: Rand McNally, 1963.

Caplan, Nathan. The two-communities theory and knowledge utilization. *American Behavioral Scientist,* 1979, 22(3), 459-470.

Caplan, Nathan, Andrea Morrison, and Russell Stambough. *The use of social science knowledge in policy decisions at the national level.* Ann Arbor: Center for Research on Utilization of Scientific Knowledge, Institute for Social Research, University of Michigan, 1975.

Cervantes Saavedra, Miguel de. *Don Quioxte.* New York: Signet Classics, 1964.

Clark, David. The configurational perspective and goal-free planning. Pp. 38-47 in Paul D. Hood (Ed.), *New perspectives on planning, management, and evaluation in school improvement.* San Francisco: Far West Laboratory for Educational Research and Development, 1979.

Cook, Thomas D., Judith Levinson-Rose, and William E. Pollard. The misutilization of evaluation research: Some pitfalls of definition. *Knowledge: Creation, Diffusion, Utilization,* 1980, 1(4), 477-498.

Cronbach, Lee J. Beyond the two disciplines of scientific psychology. *American Psychologist,* 1975, 30, 116-127.

Deaton, William L., and William J. Gephart. To err is probable, to type divine. *CEDR Quarterly,* 1980, 13(2), 7.

DeGroot, A. Perception and memory versus thought: Some old ideas and recent findings. Pp. 19-50 in B. Kleinmuntz (Ed.), *Problem Solving.* New York: John Wiley, 1966.

Delbecq, Andre, and Sandra Gill. Political decision making and program development. Pp. 23-44 in Robert Rich (Ed.), *Translating evaluation into policy.* Beverly Hills, CA: Sage, 1979.

Dickey, Barbara. Utilization of evaluations of small-scale educational projects. *Educational Evaluation and Policy Analysis,* 1981, 2(6), 65-77.

Dillman, D. A. *Mail and telephone surveys: The total design method.* New York: John Wiley, 1978.

Dreman, David N. *Psychology and the stock market.* New York: Warner, 1977.

Dreman, David N. *Contrarian investment strategy.* New York: Random House. 1979.

Dunn, William N. The two-communities metaphor and models of knowledge use. *Knowledge: Creation, Diffusion, Utilization,* 1980, 1(4), 515-536.

Dyer, Henry S. Recycling the problems in testing. *Assessment in a pluralistic society.* Proceedings of the 1972 Invitational Conference on Testing. Princeton, NJ: Princeton University Press, 1973

Eisner, E. W. *The perceptive eye: Toward the reformation of educational evaluation.* Stanford, CA: Stanford Evaluation Consortium, 1975.

Eisner, E. W. *The educational imagination.* New York: Macmillan, 1979.

Engel, Brenda S. Objecting to objectives. *Studies in Educational Evaluation,* 1981, 7, 151-160.

Evaluation Research Society. *Standards for evaluation* (draft). Washington, DC: ERS, 1980.

Evaluation Standards Committee. See Joint Committee on Standards for Educational Evaluation, 1981.

Fairweather, G. W., D. Sanders, and L. Tornatzky. *Creating change in mental health organizations.* New York: Pergamon, 1974.

Far West Laboratory for Educational Research and Development. *Proceedings: Educational evaluation and public policy, a conference.* San Francisco: Far West Lab, 1976.

Fienberg, S. E. The collection and analysis of ethnographic data in education research. *Anthropology and Education Quarterly,* 1977, 8, 50-57.

Fitz-Gibbon, Carol, and Lynn Morris. *How to design a program evaluation.* Beverly Hills, CA: Sage, 1978.

General Accounting Office. *Internal Revenue Service audits of individual taxpayers and its audit quality control system need to be better.* GGD 79-59. Washington, DC: Government Printing Office, 1979.

Gephart, William J. Watercolor painting. Pp. 247-272 in Nick L. Smith (Ed.), *Metaphors for evaluation.* Beverly Hills, CA: Sage, 1981.

Glaser, Barney G., and Anselm L. Strauss. *Discovery of grounded theory: Strategies for qualitative research.* Chicago: AVC, 1967.

Goudsmit, S. A. Obscurantism. In J. Ertel (Ed.), *Selected papers: The Journal of Irreproducible Results.* Chicago: Journal of Irreproducible Results, 1977.

Guba, Egon G. *Toward a methodology of naturalistic inquiry in educational evaluation.* Monograph Series No. 8. Los Angeles: UCLA Center for the Study of Evaluation. 1978

Guba, Egon G. Investigative reporting. Pp. 67-86 in Nick L. Smith (Ed.), *Metaphors for evaluation.* Beverly Hills, CA: Sage 1981.

Guba, Egon G., and Yvonna S. Lincoln. *Effective evaluation: Improving the usefulness of evaluation results through responsive and naturalistic approaches.* San Francisco: Jossey-Bass, 1981.

Hage, Jerald, and Michael Aiken. *Social change in complex organizations.* New York: Random House, 1970.

Havelock, Ronald G. *Planning for innovation through dissemination and utilization of knowledge.* Ann Arbor: Center for Research on Utilization of Scientific Knowledge, Institute for Social Research, University of Michigan, 1971.

Havelock, Ronald G. *The change agent's guide to innovation in education.* Englewood Cliffs, NJ: Educational Technology Publications, 1973.

Hawkins, David. How do you evaluate an eolith? *Proceedings: Educational evaluation and public policy, a conference.* San Francisco: Far West Lab, 1976.

Heilman, John G. Paradigmatic choices in evaluation methodology. *Evaluation Review,* 1980, 4(5), 693-712.

Henderson, Thomas H. The University of the West Indies and agricultural extension work in the Caribbean. *Agricultural Progress.* 1973, 48.

Henerson, Marlene, Lynn Morris, and Carol Fitz-Gibbon. *How to measure attitudes.* Beverly Hills, CA: Sage, 1978.

Hickey, John. Reducing automobile accidents. In J. Ertel (Ed.), *Selected papers: The Journal of Irreproducible Results.* Chicago: Journal of Irreproducible Results, 1977.

House, Ernest. *The logic of evaluative argument.* CSE Monograph Series in Evaluation No. 7. Los Angeles: UCLA Center for the Study of Evaluation, 1977.

House, Ernest. Assumptions underlying evaluation models. *Educational Researcher,* 1978, 7, 4-12.

House, Ernest. *Evaluating with validity.* Beverly Hills, CA: Sage, 1980.

Huff, Darrell. *How to lie with statistics.* New York: W. W. Norton, 1954.

Inbar, Michael. *Routine decision making.* Beverly Hills, CA: Sage, 1979.

Jackson, Ken. Your medium is not the message. *CEDR Quarterly,* 1973, 6(3).

Joint Committee on Standards for Educational Evaluation. *Standards for evaluations of educational programs, projects, and materials.* New York: McGraw-Hill, 1981.

Keasler, John. Super memories. Miami News, January 20, 1982: 1C.

Kiresuk, Thomas J., and S. H. Lund. Goal attainment scaling. In C. C. Attkisson, W. A. Hargreaves, M. J. Horowitz, and J. E. Sorenson (Eds.), *Evaluation of human service programs.* New York: Academic, 1978.

Knapp, Mark L., Cynthia Stohl, and Kathleen K. Reardon. Memorable messages. *Journal of Communication,* 1981, 31(4), 27-41.

Kourilsky, Marilyn. An adversary model for educational evaluation. *Evaluation Comment,* 1974, 4(2).

Kuhn, Thomas. *The structure of scientific revolutions.* Chicago: University of Chicago Press, 1970.

Larsen, Judith K. Knowledge utilization: What is it? *Knowledge: Creation, Diffusions, Utilization,* 1980, 1(3), 421-442.

Lenke, Hal. Cosmogony. *Two-Step.* Prescott, AZ: Lizard's Head Press, 1978.

Lincoln, Yvonna S. Personal communication, 1980.

Lindblom, Charles E. The science of muddling through. *Public Administration Review,* 1959, 19, 79-99.

Lofland, John. *Analyzing social settings.* Belmont, CA: Wadsworth, 1971.

Lynd, Robert S. *Knowledge for what?* Princeton, NJ: Princeton University Press, 1939.

Lynn, Laurence E. Crafting policy analysis for decision makers. Interview with Michael Kirst, *Educational Evaluation and Policy Analysis,* 1980, 2(3), 85-90.

Lynn, Laurence E. *Designing public policies: A casebook on the role of policy analysis.* Santa Monica, CA: Goodyear, 1980.

Lyson, Thomas. Non-academic employers surveyed. American Sociological Association Footnotes, 1981, 9(8).

Machlup, Fritz. *The production and distribution of knowledge in the United States.* Princeton, NJ: Princeton University Press, 1962.

Maroney, M. J. *Facts from figures.* Baltimore, MD: Viking, 1951.

Mitchell, Richard. *Less than words can say.* Boston: Little, Brown, 1979.

Nicolle, R. *Practicality: How to acquire it.* New York: Funk & Wagnalls, 1915.

Northwest Regional Educational Laboratory [NWREL]. *3-on-2 evaluation report,* 1976-1977. Portland, OR: NWREL, 1977.

Nunnally, James C., Jr. *Introduction to psychological measurement.* New York: McGraw-Hill, 1970.

Owens, Thomas. Educational evaluation by adversary proceeding. In Ernest House (Ed.), *School evaluation: The politics and the process.* Berkeley, CA: McCutchan, 1973.

Parkinson, C. H. *Parkinson's law and other studies in administration.* New York: Houghton Mifflin, 1957.

Parlett, Malcolm, and David Hamilton. Evaluation as illumination: A new approach to the study of innovatory programs. Pp. 140-157 in Gene Glass (Ed.), *Evaluation studies review annual* (Vol. 1). Beverly Hills, CA: Sage, 1976.

Patton, Michael Q. *Utilization-focused evaluation.* Beverly Hills, CA: Sage, 1978.

Patton, Michael Q. *Qualitative evaluation methods.* Beverly Hills, CA: Sage, 1980.

Patton, Michael Q. Making methods choices. *Evaluation and program planning,* 1980, 3, 219-228. (a)

Patton, Michael Q. *Creative evaluation.* Beverly Hills, CA: Sage, 1981.

Patton, Michael Q., Patricia S. Grimes, Kathy Guthrie, N. Brennan, B. French, and D. Blyth. In search of impact. Pp. 141-164 in Carol Weiss (Ed.), *Using social research in public policy making.* Lexington, MA: D. C. Heath, 1977.

Payne, Stanley L. *The art of asking questions.* Princeton, NJ: Princeton University Press, 1951.

Popham, James. Melvin Belli, beware! *Educational Researcher,* 1982, 11(1), 5, 11-15.

Popham, James W., and Dale Carlson. Deep dark deficits of the adversary evaluation model. *Educational researcher,* 1977, June, 3-6.

Price, D.D.S. *Big sciences, little sciences.* New York: Columbia University Press, 1963.

Provus, Malcolm. *Discrepancy evaluation for educational program improvement.* Berkeley, CA: McCutchan, 1971.

Raizen, S., and P. Rossi (Eds.). *Program evaluation in education: When? how? to what ends?* Washington, DC: National Academy of Sciences, 1981.

Reichardt, Charles S., and Thomas D. Cook. Beyond qualitative *versus* quantitative methods. In T. Cook and C. S. Reichardt (Eds.), *Qualitative and quantitative methods.* Beverly Hills, CA: Sage, 1979.

Reichardt, Charles S., and Thomas D. Cook. Paradigms lost: Some thoughts on choosing methods in evaluation research. *Evaluation and Program Planning,* 1980, 3, 229-339.

Reilly, Mary (Ed.). *Play as exploratory learning.* Beverly Hills, CA: Sage, 1974.

Rist, Ray C. On the relations among educational research paradigms: From disdain to detente. *Anthropology and Education,* 1977, 8, 42-49.

Rogers, Carl R. *On becoming a person.* Boston: Houghton-Mifflin, 1961.

Rogers, Everett, and F. Shoemaker. *Communication of innovations.* New York: Free Press, 1971.

Ross, John. Decision rules in program evaluation. *Evaluation Review,* 1980, 4(1), 59-74.

Rossi, Peter H., Howard E. Freeman, and Sonia R. Wright. *Evaluation: A systematic approach.* Beverly Hills, CA: Sage, 1979.

Rutman, Len (Ed.). *Evaluation research.* Beverly Hills, CA: Sage, 1977.

Rutman, Len. *Planning useful evaluations: Evaluability assessments.* Beverly Hills, CA: Sage, 1980.

Scriven, Michael. The methodology of evaluation. Pp. 39-83 in R. Tyler, R. Gagne, and M. Scriven (Eds.), *Perspectives on curriculum evaluation.* AERA Monograph Series on Curriculum Evaluation, No. 1. Chicago: Rand McNally, 1967.

Scriven, Michael. Objectivity and subjectivity in educational research. Pp. 94-142 in L. Thomas (Ed.), *Philosophical redirection of educational research.* Chicago: Rand McNally, 1972.

Scriven, Michael. Prose and cons of goal-free evaluation. *Evaluation comment,* 1972, 3(4), 1-7.

Scriven, Michael. Goal-free evaluation. In Paul D. Hood (Ed.), *New perspectives on planning, management, and evaluation in school improvement.* San Francisco: Far West Laboratory for Educational Research and Development, 1979. (a)

Scriven, Michael. "Snapshots by Scriven." *Evaluation Network Newsletter,* 1979, 11, 35-37.

Scriven, Michael, and Michael Q. Patton. *A perspective on evaluation.* Videotape interview. Minneapolis: Program Evaluation Resource Center, 1976.

Seuss, Dr. *Sneetches and other stories.* New York: Random House, 1961.

Shah, Idries. *Learning how to learn.* London: Octagon, 1978.

Smith, Nick L. Studying evaluation assumptions. *Evaluation Network Newsletter,* 1980, Winter, 39-40.

Smith, Nick L. (Ed.). *Metaphors for evaluation: Sources of new methods.* Beverly Hills, CA: Sage, 1981.

Stake, Robert. The countenance of educational evaluation. *Teachers College Record,* 1967, 68, 523-540.

Stake, Robert. *Evaluating the arts in education: A responsive approach.* Columbus, OH: Merrill, 1975.

Steele, Fritz. *Consulting for organizational change.* Amherst: University of Massachusetts Press, 1975.

Stevens, William F., and Louis G. Tornatsky. The dissemination of evaluation: An experiment. *Evaluation review,* 1980, 4(3), 339-354.

Stufflebeam, Daniel. An interview with Daniel L. Stufflebeam. *Educational evaluation and policy analysis,* 1980, 2(4).

Stufflebeam, D. L., W. J. Foley, W. J. Gephart, E. G. Guba, L. R. Hammond, H. O. Merriman, and M. M. Provus. *Educational evaluation and decision making in education.* Itasca, IL: Peacock, 1971.

Sutherland, James. *The Oxford book of literary anecdotes.* New York: Simon & Schuster. 1975.

Thompson, Mark. *Evaluation for decision in social programmes.* Lexington, MA: D. C. Heath, 1975.

Tikunoff, William (with Beatrice Ward). *Interactive research and development on teaching.* San Francisco: Far West Laboratory for Educational Research and Development, 1980.

Trend, M. G. On reconciliation of qualitative and quantitative analysis. *Human Organization,* 1978, 37, 345-354.

Tyler, Ralph W. *Basic principles of curriculum and instruction.* Chicago: University of Chicago Press, 1949.

Weiss, Carol H. (Ed.). *Using social research in public policy making.* Lexington, MA: D. C. Heath. 1977.

Weiss, Carol H. Knowledge creep and decision accretion. *Knowledge: Creation, Diffusion, Utilization,* 1980, 1(3), 381-404.

Weiss, Carol H., and Michael Bucuvalas. Truth test and utility test: Decision makers frames of reference for social science research. *American Sociological Review,* 1980, April, 302-313.

Wolf, Robert L. Trial by jury: A new evaluation method. *Phi Delta Kappan,* November 1975.

Worthen, Blaine R., and J. R. Sanders. *Educational evaluation: Theory and practice.* Worthington, OH: Charles A. Jones, 1973.

Wright, Sonia R. *Quantitative methods and statistics: A guide to social research.* Beverly Hills, CA: Sage, 1979.

Young, Carlotta J., and Joseph Comtois. Increasing Congressional utilization of evaluation. In Franklin M. Zweig (Ed.), *Evaluation in legislation.* Beverly Hills, CA: Sage, 1979.

Index

About the Author

Michael Quinn Patton is on the faculty of the University of Minnesota, where he has been Director of the Minnesota Center for Social Research (1975-1980) and where he was named outstanding teacher of the year in 1976 for his innovative evaluation teaching. His Ph.D. in Sociology is from the University of Wisconsin. He has worked on a broad range of evaluation projects spanning the human services spectrum, including evaluation of programs, in agricultural extension, education, criminal justice, health, energy conservation, community development, welfare, commercial banks, manpower planning, mental health, charitable services, youth development, wilderness experiences, and private businesses. He has done evaluations at local, county, state, national, and international levels, including a two-year project at the University of the West Indies (Trinidad) during which this book was completed. He is the author of numerous articles, reports, and conference papers on evaluation, as well as three previous books: *Utilization-Focused Evaluation* (1978); *Qualitative Evaluation Methods* (1980); and *Creative Evaluation* (1981).